Changing Society

Changing Society

Readings for the Engaged Writer

Jerome Schwab

Amy Love

San Francisco State University

Prentice Hall

Boston   Columbus   Indianapolis   New York   San Francisco
Upper Saddle River   Amsterdam   Cape Town   Dubai   London
Madrid   Milan   Munich   Paris   Montreal   Toronto   Delhi   Mexico City
Sao Paulo   Sydney   Hong Kong   Seoul   Singapore   Taipei   Tokyo

VP/Editorial Director: Joe Opiela
Senior Acquisitions Editor: Brad Potthoff
Assistant Editor: Jessica Kupetz
Editorial Assistant: Nancy C. Lee
Director of Marketing: Tim Stookesbury
Executive Marketing Manager: Megan Galvin-Fak
Senior Marketing Manager: Sandra McGuire
Marketing Assistant: Jean-Pierre Dufresne
Senior Managing Editor: Linda Behrens
Senior Operations Supervisor: Nick Sklitsis
Operations Specialist: Mary Ann Gloriande
Cover Art Director/Designer: Jayne Conte
Cover Art: Gisuke Hagiwara/Photonica/ Getty Images, Inc.

Manager, Rights and Permissions: Zina Arabia
Manager, Visual Research/Photo Researcher: Beth Brenzel
Manager, Cover Visual Research & Permissions: Karen Sanatar
Image Permission Coordinator: Frances Toepfer
Media Director: Paul Crockett
Full-Service Project Management: GGS Higher Education Resources
Composition: GGS Higher Education Resources
Printer/Binder: Edwards Brothers
Cover Printer: Lehigh-Phoenix Color Hagerstown
Text Font: Palatino-Roman 10/12

Credits and acknowledgments for material borrowed from other sources and reproduced, with permission, in this textbook appear on page 452.

Many of the designations by manufacturers and seller to distinguish their products are claimed as trademarks. Where those designations appear in this book, and the publisher was aware of a trademark claim, the designations have been printed in initial caps or all caps.

Library of Congress Cataloging-in-Publication Data

Changing society : readings for the engaged writer / [compiled] by Jerome
    Schwab and Amy Love.
        p. cm.
    Includes bibliographical references and index.
    ISBN-13: 978-0-13-237940-3 (alk. paper)
    ISBN-10: 0-13-237940-6 (alk. paper)
    1. Social change. 2. Computers and college students. 3. Technology—Social
aspects. I. Schwab, Jerome. II. Love, Amy.
    HM831.C437 2010
    303.48'4071173—dc22

                                               2009027139

10 9 8 7 6 5 4 3 2 1

Prentice Hall
is an imprint of

PEARSON

www.pearsonhighered.com

Student ISBN 10:   0-13-237940-6
        ISBN 13: 978-0-13-237940-3
Exam ISBN 10:   0-205-65094-5
        ISBN 13: 978-0-205-65094-1

Contents

Today's college students experience challenges their predecessors could hardly have imagined. College has become a prerequisite for a job with a living wage, yet the true cost of a degree has skyrocketed and the financial aid system has shifted, so students often face decades of debt. Technology can divide student attention, making it difficult for them to focus on their studies, and fundamentally alters student-faculty relationships.

The current generation has been described in terms ranging from materialistic and cynical to pragmatic and concerned, and, compared with previous generations, these young adults are indeed less interested in traditional politics. But this does not mean they are uninvolved: they promote social causes through other means and gravitate to volunteering. In fact, many of their most valuable experiences come when school and service are combined—the theoretical joined to the real. The heroes of the new millennium may not be politicians or warriors, but those who steadfastly work to right wrongs and preserve what they hold dear.

The producers of TV news, reality shows and advertising often
claim that they merely reflect society, showing people as they are,
offering what they ask for. But in America today, no one is immune
(and few are indifferent) to the transformative powers of media.
Overtly and covertly, the media influence everything from personal
appearance to political choice. Understanding how the media shape
opinion can produce a clearer picture of ourselves and our place in
our communities.

SECTION IV THE CHALLENGE OF CHANGE 347

Pollution, dwindling oil reserves, an exploding prison population
are just a few of the issues that confront the nation today. In the
face of such concerns, many feel powerless, unable to influence
what is happening. As inaction means accepting whatever comes
along, for many, conscious action makes more sense. Small movements have transformed even the habits of an entire culture; history teaches that individuals matter, whether defending tradition
or changing society.

PREFACE FOR INSTRUCTORS

Changing Society is an issues-based reader designed specifically for students in college and university writing classes. The title underscores a message reinforced throughout the book—although society is changing, often at a frenzied pace, students can play key roles in shaping the world. Successfully tested in undergraduate classes with diverse populations, it has generated animated discussions and passionate written responses, proving itself an effective resource in the fight against student apathy toward traditional essay assignments, reading and politics. The selections offer students opportunities to explore issues that affect them directly as well as broader concerns that shape our nation. As students write best when they are actively engaged, *Changing Society* encourages students to approach writing as more than simply the fulfillment of an academic requirement, but as a skill that has practical applications in the real world, an essential means of self-expression and an important tool for active citizens in a democratic society.

STRUCTURE

Changing Society consists of twelve chapters, each with six readings, mixing articles from major newspapers and periodicals with deeper, more reflective pieces. While each chapter is completely independent, giving teachers great flexibility, earlier chapters focus on more personal topics, gradually moving outward to broader social issues. Five types of prompts encourage careful reading and analysis and can be used in a number of ways:

- Pre-reading questions, at the beginning of each chapter and article, activate students' prior knowledge and promote engagement.
- **Reflection and Discussion** topics ask students to examine the readings and probe key ideas, and respond in journals or discuss with each other, in-class or online.
- **Writing Matters** assignments call for closer reading of the text, using critical thinking skills and sometimes directing them to research key ideas.

- **Making Connections** prompts, at the end of each chapter, synthesize the issues raised in the chapter, asking students to delve more deeply into the issues raised or address the most effective ways to cope with a problem or concern.
- **Taking Action** options give students the opportunity for real-world writing, addressing specific external audiences in forms common to political and social action.

Changing Society offers additional support with sections on the writing process, reading to write effectively, research papers and using sources, set apart from the topical chapters to allow instructors to use them as desired.

MYCOMPLAB

MyCompLab empowers student writers and facilitates writing instruction by uniquely integrating a composing space and assessment tools with market-leading instruction, multimedia tutorials, and exercises for writing, grammar and research.

Students can use MyCompLab on their own, benefiting from self-paced diagnostics and a personal study plan that recommends the instruction and practice each student needs to improve their writing skills. The composing space and its integrated resources, tools, and services (such as online tutoring) are also available to each student as they write.

MyCompLab is an eminently flexible application that instructors can use in ways that best complement their course and teaching style. They can recommend it to students for self-study, set up courses to track student progress, or leverage the power of administrative features to be more effective and save time. The assignment builder and commenting tools, developed specifically for writing instruction, bring instructors closer to their student writers, make managing assignments and evaluating papers more efficient, and put powerful assessment within reach. Students receive feedback within the context of their own writing, which encourages critical thinking and revision and helps them to develop skills based on their individual needs.

Learn more at www.mycomplab.com.

ACKNOWLEDGEMENTS

We want to first recognize our students, who inspired *Changing Society*. We thank the many members of the San Francisco State University academic community, too numerous to list, who have supported our professional lives, but especially those who have taught us to teach: Helen Gillotte-Tropp, Francis Gretton, Jo Keroes, Michael Krasny, Catharine Lucas, William S. Robinson, Eric Solomon, Deborah Swanson and Elise Wormuth. This book would not have been possible without our innovative editor, Brad Potthoff. We thank our reviewers, whose many suggestions have greatly improved our text: Neil Archer, Parkland College; Sydney Bartman, Mt. San Antonio College; Jason Chaffin, Cape Fear Community College; Alan Church, University of Texas at Brownsville/Texas Southmost College; Alette Corley, Bethune-Cookman College; Hannah J. Denbow, Ohio University; Anne Fernald, Fordham College at Lincoln Center; Ruth A. Gerik, University of Texas at Arlington; Janet P. Gerstner, San Juan College; Leonard Guida, Bethune-Cookman College; Barbara Hamm, Diablo Valley College; Jefferson Hancock, Cabrillo College; John Heinbockel, College of San Mateo; Marlene Hess, Davenport University; Reinold Hill, Ferris State University; Mary C. Hutchinson, Penn State Lehigh Valley; John T. Ikeda Franklin, Pittsburg State University; Patricia Jenkins, University of Alaska Anchorage; Richard Johnson, Kirkwood Community College; David Kellogg, Northeastern University; Beatrice Mendez Newman, University of Texas-Pan American; Jeffrey L. Mitchell, Los Medanos College; Lyle Morgan, Pittsburg State University; Andrea M. Penner, San Juan College; Lowell Pratt, Menlo College; Michael W. Raymond, Stetson University; Gordon Reynolds, Ferris State University; Jeff Rice, Wayne State University; Darlene Smith-Worthington, Pitt Community College; Derek Soles, Drexel University; Sharon Strand, Black Hills State University; Kevin Waltman, University of Alabama; Carmaletta M. Williams, Johnson County Community College; and Susan Yoes, De Anza College. And finally, we are grateful to our families, who encouraged and sustained us throughout this project: Chris and Zippy; Joe, Kris and Scudo.

Jerome Schwab
Amy Love

Introduction

Computerization, corporatization, globalization—society is changing, like it or not. Whether you want to preserve some value you cherish or fight for something new, you will have to keep informed and express yourself effectively in writing. *Changing Society* includes the kind of political, social and personal issues that ordinary citizens now wrestle with throughout their lives, with most articles taken from the newspapers and magazines that you will continue to read after college. The assignments give you practice in writing for the real world, not just in college, beginning with a review of what it means to read critically and write independently.

READING EFFECTIVELY

What Is Reading?

Many of you may be tempted to skip this section, considering yourselves to be expert readers. Most college students read everyday material on familiar subjects with familiar vocabulary so automatically that they don't think about reading at all. Like natural athletes who find it difficult to tell someone how to replicate their perfect golf swings or tennis serves, good readers can read, but may have a hard time describing what exactly they are doing. If anything, you may think back to preschool or kindergarten, when you triumphantly sounded out c = ca + a = ah + t to get "cat," and define reading as an exercise in decoding, mentally sounding out letters to get words that you recognize.

But think of the last time you had to spend time reading something difficult, perhaps a credit card contract or a loan agreement.

1

What made that text harder to read than the front page of the newspaper? When you look at a term like *annual percentage rate*, you may begin to see how reading is more than decoding, and at least some of the difficulty stems from something more than vocabulary. Although you know what each word of that phrase means, you may not understand what the three words mean together in the context of the contract. But woe to you if you sign that contract without knowing that *annual percentage rate* represents the actual yearly cost of borrowing money.

We might get a better definition of reading if we step back and consider all the different ways we use the word. We say, "I can read you like a book," "I can't read this diagram," and "When you read between the lines, you'll find another story." We read music and paintings, faces, maps and actions. In all of these cases, reading is an act of interpretation in which we use our prior knowledge and experience to make meaning. For college-level texts, we need to draw on everything we have learned—what we know about how the world and people work, our specific knowledge of subjects like music or physics, and our experience with language and different types of texts.

College courses require you to probe deeply into more difficult material, to go beyond first impressions to develop a critical understanding of the material. While you still need to identify and understand the author's main points, you must do much more, evaluating texts, looking for strengths and weaknesses, entering into a dialogue with the writer. To do that, you need to pick out the author's purpose for writing, identify the intended audience, consider the tone adopted and closely examine the evidence and analysis. You can't do all these things well with one reading of an article, no matter how carefully you try, but you will be surprised how easy it is if you break the reading into three phases.

Phase I: Before You Read

Not long ago, a friend told me about a great pizza place on a block I pass all the time. I tried to picture it, but could only think of the dry cleaner, liquor store and gas station on the corner. "Don't worry," he said. "You can't miss it." He was right. The next time I drove by the block, I saw the rather large pizza sign. Why hadn't I seen it before?

Quite often, we only see what we expect, which is why we may not notice a friend's new hair style or pick up the absurdity of a spoof in the newspaper on April Fool's Day. To get the most out of our reading, we have to know what we expect from a piece. "Reading is asking questions of printed text. And reading with comprehension becomes a matter of getting your questions answered," according to Frank Smith.

To ask good questions and get them answered, we need to know why we are reading and as much as we can about the text itself before we start to read it.

Sometimes you will approach a reading assignment with a clear purpose in mind, responding to a teacher's detailed assignment or looking for certain information. Often, though, teachers give less guidance, just listing the articles or pages to be read. In these cases, you must discover your own reason for reading. You'll find that relatively easy to do after previewing the text, which will let you know what the author and editor find significant. To preview, look at everything that stands out from the text: title, author, introductions, headings, graphics, words in italic or boldface, summaries. In this book, pay particular attention to the material before and after each article, including:

- where and when the article first appeared
- information about the author
- questions designed to connect your past experience with the subject before you read and others that guide your reflection and analysis after you've read.

If you think about it, you preview texts automatically in your casual reading, looking at the titles or headlines, checking out the star-rating before reading a restaurant or movie review. From this information, you usually can get a good idea of what the article is about and the type of article—a story, opinion piece or more objective reporting.

For a more complex article, you may find you also need to preread. For most texts, you can do this by reading the first sentence of every paragraph, which will give you most of the main points as well as the overall organization of the text. If the paragraphs are very short (most common with newspaper articles), you can get the same benefits by reading the first paragraph of each section and the conclusion.

To complete your preparation, consider your purpose and think of the questions you want to ask of the text.

Phase II: As You Read

The first time you read a text, resist the temptation to take notes and use the dictionary, because these activities will only bog you down, getting in the way of your understanding the article or section as a whole. Don't worry if you don't understand every word—most authors explain unusual words if they are important. Simply read along, checking your comprehension now and then to make sure you are getting the general concepts. If the piece is relatively long, read and record your notes a section at a time.

Phase III: After You Read

Once you've completed your first reading, you can solidify your learning in a number of ways, such as annotating the text, writing in a dialectical journal or creating a graphic organizer. Whichever approach you choose, you'll want to note:

- the author's main points, significant concepts, important words and phrases
- answers to the questions you asked before reading, noting any question unanswered
- your reactions—agreement, disagreement, confusion—in light of your purpose for reading.

Annotating the Text

When you annotate a text, you make your notes directly in the book, underlining or highlighting important points and concepts, writing questions and comments in the margins. Simple, but you've probably seen used textbooks with so much highlighting that the page is almost completely yellow, making it impossible for the reader to quickly pick out the important points. You'll find that previewing and reading before making notes will prevent most overannotation because you'll start making notes after you have a better sense of what's important for your purpose. See Figure I.1 for a sample annotation.

Dialectical Journal

While you may find it easy to annotate a text, you won't have a lot of room to record your own reactions and you'll still have to page through the whole article to find what you're looking for. The dialectical journal addresses both of those problems by separating your notes from the text. To create a dialogue journal entry, put the bibliographic information at the top of the page and divide the rest of your document into two columns, as in the sample shown in Figure I.2.

After your first reading, go through the text again, noting the author's main points on the left. Use direct quotations for particularly important wording, but otherwise try to paraphrase—the act of putting the idea in your own words reinforces your comprehension and memory. In either case, note the page numbers so that you can easily refer back to the text when you discuss the article in class or want to use a quotation when you are writing. On the right side, enter your feelings, questions and other notes, lining them up so that you can easily see their relationship to the author's points.

While you may be tempted to handwrite this journal, we encourage you to write it on the computer. Unless you have very small, neat

SKATEBOARDING SAFETY

By S.K. Andres

According to the Consumer Product Safety Commission, 26,000 skateboarders are treated in emergency rooms each year, with about 4% sustaining head injuries serious enough to require longer hospitalization, a small number even dying. Many of these injuries could be prevented with proper safety equipment.

When skateboarding was at its height, a number of entrepreneurs cashed in on the fad by opening up parks, but they were also saving lives. "They provided a safe environment for skaters, and required the use of helmets, kneepads and gloves," remembered Mike DeLucca, manager of Balboa Cyclery, a bike shop that also sells skateboard supplies. "But the parks closed…[and] skate punks can't be bothered with helmets, [and] think you're trying to rip them off if you recommend helmets."

Why no more parks?

DeLucca has more success with younger children. "Their parents come in to buy the boards, and will listen to our recommendations. When the parents have spent their money on safety equipment, they also make sure the equipment is used."

Just buying a helmet is not enough. DeLucca cautions against most skateboard helmets, which are merely plastic shells lined with foam, recommending helmets certified to meet the SNEL standards. Mike Johnson of Concrete Jungle thinks the better quality skateboard helmets are sufficient, even if they aren't certified, and are a lot cheaper than cycling helmets. "I always say, `A $10 helmet for a $10 head.' That goes for pads, too."

Ban nonstandard helmets?

FIGURE I.1 Note how easy it is to pick up the most important points when the annotations are focused.

Article Title: Skateboarding Safety	**Author:** S.K. Andres
Author's Main Points	**Reflections/Questions/ Comments/Vocabulary**
26,000 in emergency room each year; 4% need "longer hospitalization," some die (p. 1)	How many skateboard? Compared to bicycling?
no more skateboard parks which provided/required safety	Why did they disappear?
Parents make younger children use helmets	
Not all helmets meet SNEL safety standards	SNEL = standard set by nonprofit foundation established after Pete Snell died while racing without a helmet. Why are they allowed to make them?

FIGURE I.2 Sample Dialectical Journal Entry: The left column records the author's points; the right column, your own.

handwriting, you'll find it difficult to keep the author's points aligned with your ideas. Typing in the author's points will save you time and error when you want to use the information in an essay. Many writers, even professionals, find they introduce errors when they type from their handwritten notes.

Graphic Organizers

Both in-text annotations and dialectical journals look at articles one at a time, but as you discuss issues in class and prepare to write, you may look for a way to combine notes from several articles, grouping points so that you get a better understanding of your topic than you could get from any one article. Graphic organizers make this activity easy; while these examples show the notes from a single article, you can easily see how information from other articles can be added easily.

Graphic organizers have other advantages. You increase your comprehension when you make the information your own by moving it into another form. These charts and graphs also appeal to different learning styles. Visual learners may want to use a free-flowing form like a cluster diagram (Figure I.3) while text-based learners may prefer the order of a matrix (Figure I.4). There are many kinds of graphic

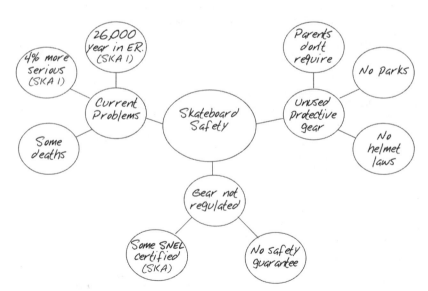

FIGURE I.3 Sample Cluster Diagram: The physical grouping of ideas helps visual learners, but doesn't have room for full quotations. Facts that may need to be quoted are referenced with the author's initials and the page number in parentheses.

Skateboard Safety Notes

Issue	Details
Current problems	26,000 in emergency room each year; 4% need "longer hospitalization," some die (Andres 1)
Use of protective gear	no more skateboard parks which provided/required safety (Andres 1) Parents make younger children use helmets, but not older children. No helmet laws
Regulation of protective gear	Not all helmets meet SNEL safety standards (Andres 1) No legal safety standard

FIGURE I.4 Sample Chart: The matrix allows full quotations with citation information.

organizers and no strict rules on how to create them, but keep two things in mind:

- Previewing all the articles will make it easier for you to plan out the space for your graphic organizer. If you enjoy this method of making notes, you may want to try one of the many software programs that make this type of brainstorming easier.
- Be sure to note the author and page number of information that may need to be cited. Nothing is more frustrating than having to reread a long chapter looking for a specific quotation. Since cluster diagrams don't have much space for your notes, try using the author's initials and page number.

THE WRITING PROCESS

What Are Your Writing Habits?

We all follow routines when we write, some of which we are consciously aware of and others that we perform automatically. These writing habits can change according to variables like why we are writing in the first place and who our readers are. If asked by a friend to describe what you do at work, you'd probably be able to explain it easily in writing. But you would normally have more trouble writing an essay of several pages on an unfamiliar topic assigned by your English teacher. The task might require research and careful organization; you might have to draft two or three versions before you are satisfied with what you wrote. Purpose, audience and task difficulty are just some of the factors influencing how we proceed when we write.

In order to get a clearer picture of what your current writing habits are, let's conduct an experiment. Imagine that your roommate has asked to make a video of you as you work on your written English assignments throughout the semester, each on a topic related to articles your class has read. Your classmates and your teacher will be your audience and you'll be graded on each assignment. What will the video reveal about how you wrote your essays?

You as a Writer—A Moving Picture

When the semester is over, the edited version of the video project will be complete. Try predicting the story it will tell. (Take some notes about why you answered as you did.)

1. When did you start writing your papers?
   - just after they were assigned while everything was fresh
   - usually after a day or two
   - a few days before the deadline
   - at the last minute
2. As you prepared to write, did the camera record you studying the essay prompts for clues about what to do and how to organize your essay?
   - always
   - often
   - sometimes
   - seldom
   - never
3. Did the video record you making an organizing plan for your papers?
   - always
   - often
   - sometimes
   - seldom
   - never
4. If you did plan your papers, which of these methods did you use and how well did they work?
   - made some quick notes
   - drew some kind of diagram
   - noted down main points
   - created detailed outlines with main and supporting points
   - other (describe)
5. How often was the first draft of your essay also your final draft?
   - always
   - often

- sometimes
- seldom
- never

6. When you got feedback from classmates about rough drafts, how did you react?
- I seldom wrote very much, so I didn't get much useful feedback.
- Often I ignored it.
- I'd take one or two suggestions and try to incorporate them.
- Usually any changes I made were cosmetic—a few small alterations.
- If I got good feedback, I'd change whole parts of my paper.

7. Throughout the experiment, how often did the camera catch you procrastinating?
- often
- sometimes
- seldom
- never

Judging from the feedback and grades you've gotten on past papers, how well are your writing habits working for you?

The Ticking of the Clock

Due dates are a fact of life. They can stimulate us to get started on a task or hang over our heads like a thundercloud. College students often talk about how deadlines provide the impetus to finally sit down and grapple with an assignment; in fact, the most popular reason students give for procrastinating on essays is that they "work better under pressure." For whatever reason—family, friends, work, other courses—essays for English class often get a student's attention just before they are due.

Although teachers systematically encourage their students to avoid procrastination, some writers seem to have a talent for keeping ideas in their heads, mulling them over and refining them until they are ready to be put down on the page. This is easier to do when writers have a clear idea of what they want to say and much more difficult when the task is new or complex. While many students have made careers out of procrastinating and still get decent grades, they often wish they could avoid the anxiety and turmoil of writing at the last minute.

Students who have learned to work on their papers well before the deadline have made comments like these:

When I allow myself more time to write, I often come up with new thoughts. Sometimes in the morning, I find my brain was working on my paper while I was asleep.

Extra time gives me a chance to work on my style.
When I'm away from my paper for a while, I can begin to see it
more objectively.
I like that I don't get so nervous.
Having extra time to go over my paper allows me to cut down on
my proofreading errors.

If any of these comments make sense to you, consider reevaluating your time management habits. Since postponing crucial decisions until the last minute yields poor results, try thinking of your essay due date in terms of mini-deadlines, establishing provisional dates for the different parts of your project. You could set one deadline for reading, note-taking and information gathering; another for planning and drafting the paper; and a third for revision and final proofreading. Rather than trying to get everything done in one enormous push, try attacking the task in stages. Then by comparing your feedback or grade with previous results, you can determine how well this method works for you. In any case, approaching the writing task from a different angle will help you learn about not only the kind of writer you are, but also what works and doesn't work for you.

Recursiveness and Writing

Think of the last time you were in the midst of drafting an essay on an assigned topic. If you are at all typical, you didn't write from beginning to end without stopping. After writing for a time, you paused and looked back at something you already wrote, then forged ahead until you hesitated, looked back at a previous line and moved forward again. This is how most writers proceed, in a recursive pattern, which corresponds with how our minds work. Looking back, we might feel the need to change a line or a whole section before we can move forward again. Sondra Perl talks about the momentum writers experience, involving not only the eyes and brain but the emotions. As we write, we seem to be listening to our words, testing out how they sound on the page, weighing how accurately they express how we feel.

Recursiveness has other implications. Because of the way ideas come to us, steps like brainstorming, free-writing, outlining, drafting and revising are not meant to be followed inflexibly in a rigid order. We don't always have to complete one to move on to the next. We often combine elements or skip around, depending on who the audience is, why we are writing or how much time we have. How we feel about the task and how complex it is also influence how we proceed.

When writers talk about their experiences writing, one element keeps reappearing—the hard work needed to get a satisfying finished product. So if you feel that writing is difficult, you are not alone. Still, some ways of writing yield better results than others, which is why we are talking about the writing process in the first place. Find out what works for you and you can make the hard work of writing less painful. What emerges from your efforts and what you learn along the way will be the rewards.

Starting with the Prompt

Keeping in mind that writing is never a strict sequential series of steps—first this and then that—writers eventually have to begin somewhere. Before attacking the drafting stage, they may brainstorm or freewrite, make a diagram or outline. In "Reading Effectively," you encountered notetaking methods that may start the writing process. Annotations, journal entries and graphic organizers help us organize what we have read and assist us in keeping a record of our responses.

Whatever point of departure you use, when writing on an assigned topic for a college essay, examine the essay prompt assigned by your teacher. Not only will the wording provide clues about how to get started, it will give you a clearer picture of whom you are writing to. Some prompts will suggest an audience of your teacher and peers; others will direct you toward a larger campus audience, members of your community or elected officials. In order to engage successfully with a writing prompt, you need to pay close attention to key words. For example, the term *discuss* asks that you examine several aspects of a particular issue or point while the word *argue* suggests that you take a clear position and defend it, taking into consideration the likely arguments of those who might oppose you. If the wording of a prompt confuses you or raises questions, you should ask for clarification from your teacher. Keep the prompt in front of you as you write, underlining or highlighting parts you consider important.

This may seem obvious, but a surprising number of students (and other writers, too) lose track of the task they have been assigned. We can be influenced by thoughts and emotions that tempt us in a number of directions, which is why understanding the prompt and returning to key words in it are so useful. You can write a powerful essay but if you haven't addressed the prompt or completed the assigned task, you risk confusing or alienating your audience. This is another reason to consider the practice of recursiveness. Key words or phrases from the prompt serve as points of reference for continued writing. We look back to them for inspiration and direction. If you are in the middle of a paragraph, for instance, words that came before will demand explanation, challenging you to be more specific, to provide examples or to confirm a point by making it concrete. Being aware of our own recursive habits and developing new ones can help us stay on track at the same time that we deliver to our readers what we have promised.

Planning

Let's assume you've done the required reading or research, have the essay prompt in front of you and feel ready to write. In what order will you present your points? Do you have an organizing plan?

Some writers visualize what their main points will be by clustering ideas on the page, connecting them with lines that resemble spokes on a wheel or the branches of a tree, like Figure I.3 in "Reading Effectively." New ideas can easily be added and previous ones eliminated. Other writers will start out with a simple sketch outline, noting major points that seem related to the topic and then listing subpoints. Another option is a more detailed outline made up of sentences which state more precisely the writer's main points and examples. (Those who use this method may have learned it in high school and found it effective.) Writers who use each of these techniques mention the benefits of time invested in the planning stage, finding it easier to identify inconsistencies before they have spent a lot of time writing. A carefully constructed outline allows them to make a provisional arrangement of ideas, quotes and explanations from their notes; it helps them see where their papers are headed.

Keep in mind that organizing plans differ according to the length of the task and its complexity. If you are unfamiliar with a topic, you may need to research it and then organize your findings in a careful, systematic fashion. However, a prompt asking for a brief response (like one of the items in the *Reflection and Discussion* parts of this book) may require little or no planning. Adapt your plan to the assignment and if you have doubts about what plan to apply, ask your teacher.

We should also remember that even the best plan is provisional since in the course of writing your paper you may find your ideas changing. A position or point in your plan may appear less tenable once you've had time to think about it. As you write, your attitude toward your topic—your opinion on the subject or even your choice of subject—may change, which is why you should not feel constrained by a plan. At some point, however, we have to adapt our original plan to include the new elements. In this way we can check that our paper still has a sense of order and that it relates directly to the prompt.

Drafting

As you work on a draft of your essay, consider the path of least resistance—start where you feel comfortable. Some students like to immediately get a thesis down on paper as a guide. Others feel constrained by having to commit to one. They prefer to begin by elaborating on ideas they feel strongly about, coming back later to formulate a thesis that reflects the points they developed.

As you write, avoid obstacles that stop your momentum. When you can't think of the precise word you want, choose the closest one possible and add a note to return to it later. Let your outline or organizing plan guide you, but if you find yourself going down a different path, explore it. Later you can decide whether you want to change your plan to fit your draft or vice versa. Take breaks when you feel tired, but try to crank out sections of your paper which are as complete as possible.

In many college composition classes, teachers require students to produce a minimum of two drafts of their papers—a rough and a final. Since the feedback you get on your rough draft will help you build a better final version, give it the time it deserves. However rough a draft is, it should contain the essential elements of your paper: your thesis, the main points which relate to your thesis and supporting sentences which explain and illustrate your main points. Without this essential information, classmates will have a difficult time evaluating your draft. Remember, too, that a good rough draft is not the same as a freewrite. The latter is a more open-ended exploration of the topic. A good rough draft is a disciplined attempt to address the prompt and explain yourself systematically.

The feedback you get on your rough draft will vary from classmate to classmate, so you may find yourself wondering what advice to take. (When in doubt, ask your teacher.) A rough draft is a way of testing out your ideas on your readers. Here you get to see whether or not they are following you or whether their ideas agree with yours. This is a test-run of your paper, and with practice, you will learn who in your class can be relied on to give you useful criticism.

When you think your rough draft is approaching completion, look at it critically, comparing it to your organizing plan. If you see differences from your plan, check to make sure your departures were intentional and that in doing so you have improved your paper. At key points in your rough draft, refer back to topic sentences to make sure that you are staying on track. Also, look back to the prompt to ensure that you haven't strayed off topic.

The more comfortable you get writing rough drafts and showing them to classmates, the better you will be at seeing your paper as your readers do. Because they will be looking for a clear thesis and main points, you will find yourself being more conscious of these elements, too. As they give you feedback about how logical and convincing your paper is, you will learn to be more careful and consistent in what you write. And as your writing gets clearer and stronger, so will your skills as a constructive critic of your classmates' work.

When you review other students' work, you will benefit from the variety of responses. You will encounter opinions and points that you may disagree with or that you may never have considered. As you work on your own drafts, remain open to the thought that not everyone will agree with you. By acknowledging ideas opposed to yours, you let your readers know that you appreciate the complexity of the issue. Few topics are simply black and white (and those that are may not be very interesting). So don't be afraid to consider the other side as you write, even if you do it with just a nod. This can help give your paper balance and show your readers that you appreciate the nuances of your topic.

Revising

When students get feedback on their rough drafts, they are sometimes satisfied with changing a word here or a punctuation mark there. They may feel reluctant to abandon the result of hours of work. Revising, however, involves a readiness to make more significant changes. It means being willing to rethink the organization, development and logic of the paper, as well as improve the proofreading. It might mean altering the thesis of the paper, substituting a more appropriate or more powerful main point to the body of the paper or revamping the way some of the sentences are structured or worded. Revision is an act of boldness, an attempt at making your paper significantly better rather than just fine-tuning it.

When revising, consider some of these suggestions:

- Be sure your introduction orients your reader.
- Check that the thesis and topic sentences are clear and related to the prompt.
- Confirm that your conclusion logically follows the rest of your essay, giving your readers something to think about or evaluating the importance of your main points.
- Make sure that the sentences in each paragraph follow one another logically.
- Add more support, detail and discussion to paragraphs that look thin.

- Check that you have properly identified your quotations and other references and that you are not overly dependent on other writers' language.
- Eliminate redundant words, points and ideas.
- Find choppy sentences and join them.
- Examine word choices and practice being concrete.
- Examine the paper carefully for your most frequent proofreading errors.

Don't give up or get discouraged. The rewards of discovering something important about yourself are worth all the effort involved.

Section

I

A New Millennium on Campus

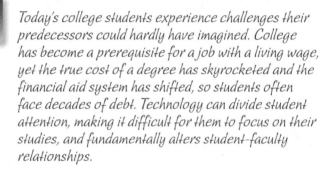

Today's college students experience challenges their predecessors could hardly have imagined. College has become a prerequisite for a job with a living wage, yet the true cost of a degree has skyrocketed and the financial aid system has shifted, so students often face decades of debt. Technology can divide student attention, making it difficult for them to focus on their studies, and fundamentally alters student-faculty relationships.

1

Student Debt

In the past, financial counselors often recommended against going into debt for anything other than a home loan, but today many, if not most, students face a dilemma not covered by that advice. They know that they'll never find a well-paying job without a college degree, but they can't afford the degree without going deeply into debt, even if they choose a school with relatively low tuition. Recognizing this problem as a business opportunity, financial institutions have jumped in, sometimes forming unethical partnerships with schools to capture the market for educational loans and credit cards. Loans and credit cards give students the financial freedom to pursue their education comfortably, but also present irresistible temptations. Indeed, this freedom comes at a high cost, for many are unable to make the minimum payments while attending school fulltime, so they must reduce their academic loads, delaying both graduation and the higher-paying job it might bring. Caught in a vicious cycle, many drop out of school, while others declare bankruptcy. How can students pay for college without incurring a lifetime of debt?

BEFORE YOU READ

Have your experiences charging purchases been mainly positive or negative? What lessons have you learned? Is your credit limit appropriate to meet your needs? Do you have outstanding balances and, if so, are they manageable?

Think about how you obtained your credit cards and loans. Were you informed about all the important details? If you don't

FIGURE 1.1 How tempting is the credit card trap?

have a credit card or a loan, ask friends or family and find out what they know about payment schedules, annual percentage rates, credit limits and penalties.

Econ 101: College Is the Time to Budget

Kim Clark, *US News & World Report,* December 12, 2005

Kim Clark is a senior writer for US News & World Report.

Before college, what kind of experience did you have budgeting and being responsible for your own expenses?

New college students may know how to ace the SATs, but many are 1 flunking the most important math test of all—real-life budgeting and economizing. Some 79 percent say they've never even talked with their parents about a budget. Little wonder, then, that parents often have unrealistically Spartan, and students unrealistically extravagant, expectations for the expenses of campus life. The ugly reality can lead to financial troubles that can have lifelong repercussions, such as debt loads that force students to drop out or declare bankruptcy.

"I don't think you can underestimate the potential for problems" 2 caused by students' poor preparation for Dorm Economics 101, says Robert D. Manning, a Rochester Institute of Technology finance professor and author of *Credit Card Nation.* "For some of them, it can be a nasty, nasty situation."

3   Creating a realistic budget for discretionary items isn't hard, but it does require a little research. Parents often forget they attended college back in the days before laptops, cell phones and $100 textbooks. What's more, some colleges—at times in an effort to lure students by making their cost of attendance look low—tell families to plan on spending as little as $1,200 a year on books and extras. In fact, nationwide surveys show the average student now pays about $900 a year for textbooks alone, triple the cost of the mid-1980s. Depending on factors like a school's location or whether the students eat in the cafeteria or keep a car, students also typically spend anywhere from $140 to $750 a month on nonacademic extras.

4   Parents and students who want an accurate estimate of the cost of campus living would do better to get the skinny from the folks who really know: upperclassmen and, if possible, their parents. Parents have to apply their own common sense as well, says June Walbert, a planner for the financial services firm USAA. Cars, although one of the most desirable extras on campus, are also the biggest budget busters, she says. Next are the spring-break adventures and ski and football weekends that many students hope to make part of their college life. "Driving the parents into deeper debt to satisfy those classic college experiences doesn't make sense," Walbert says.

5   Party on. Students who celebrate their new freedom from parental oversight by going on a spree can quickly get into real trouble. And many students arrive on campus primed to splurge. Banks hoping to snag lifetime customers early now send so many credit card solicitations out to high school students that an estimated 25 percent of college freshmen arrive with plastic in their wallets. Most of the rest get their cards on campus, where salespeople often set up booths offering free T-shirts or sandwiches to anyone who applies for a card.

6   One reason the demand for credit is great is that many students have big spending plans. A recent survey by USAA found that more than one fifth of students plan to lay out over $1,000 furnishing their dorm rooms. Students often try to buy social acceptance or the notice of the opposite sex, says Ty Kucera, an Arizona State University sophomore and peer financial counselor. He recalls one student who spent $400 on a big beanbag chair, mistakenly thinking it would draw the girls. And [the research organization] Student Monitor reports that nearly half of all female undergraduates have bought something in a Victoria's Secret store in the past month.

7   The best way to rein in the urge to splurge is to make students responsible for earning their discretionary spending money, says Lewis

Mandell, a finance professor at the University at Buffalo-SUNY. Studies show students who work up to 15 hours a week during the school year actually do better academically than students who don't work. Mandell recommends that some students, especially freshmen, be limited to no more than 10 hours of work a week to ensure plenty of time for study and to limit the amount of spare cash they have to spend. Even at minimum wage, that should put about $200 a month in the student's pocket, plenty for a cell phone, laundry, pizzas, and maybe even textbooks.

Sometimes, that actually works. Karl Sandberg, who runs a consumer credit counseling office near Dallas, insisted that both his daughters earn their own spending money at college. His oldest daughter, Rebecca, 23, took her budget to heart when she enrolled at Baylor University in Waco, Texas. "My friends would want to go out constantly, and I'm like: 'Let's go eat in the cafeteria and rent a movie.'"

But some students, such as Sandberg's younger daughter, Jennifer, 21, don't maintain that discipline. Within months of enrolling at Baylor, Jennifer signed up for a credit card and started "paying for other people's partying, picking up the bills, trying to impress people," says her father. It was only after the bills started piling up that Jennifer finally realized what her father had been trying to tell her about the dangers of splurging on credit. "It came as quite a shock that you actually have to pay for it," she says. And she's still adjusting. Now a senior, Jennifer recently called to ask her dad for $700 to cover bills, many of which were caused by several nights of celebrating her 21st birthday.

Sandberg decided to bail her out one last time to keep her focused on coursework that would allow her to graduate this winter, a semester early, cutting his tuition bill by almost $10,000. Sandberg is right to worry about graduation. Finances are the most common reason college students give for dropping out.

Though painful, bailouts can serve as important teachable moments for students. Manning, for example, recommends that parents dangle incentives in front of students, such as offering to pay off portions of debts for students who stay within an agreed-upon budget and get good grades.

However they do it, students should learn to live within a budget by the time they graduate, finance experts say, since overspending can hurt credit ratings, which employers are increasingly using in making hiring decisions. Those who learn too late discover that students who live like professionals while in college are often doomed to live like students when they are professionals.

Reflection and Discussion

1. Clark says that some colleges understate the cost of books and other expenses to make the total cost of college look low. Do you think that families believe these costs? How did you and your family budget and plan for your college expenses? How might these incorrect estimates affect budgeting and financial aid? Do you think that the colleges are acting ethically?
2. Banks compete to sign up students for credit cards, in part because they are looking for long-term customers. What do you think of this competition? What else does competition say about students as credit card customers? Why might so many people stick with the first credit card they get?

Writing Matters

1. Clark brings up several issues that influence a student's decision to work during the school year. What is your experience balancing work and school? How does working help your studies? How does it hurt? Discuss the factors students should consider when choosing a part-time job and make your own recommendation as to how much they should work during the school year, if at all.
2. Cars are called "one of the most desirable extras" but "also the biggest budget busters." How much do cars really cost, considering all the factors—insurance, maintenance, repairs, gas—as well as the purchase price? Are there reasonable alternatives to owning a car on your campus? For example, if you need a car to go to work, how much does the job pay over the cost of the car? If you need a car to go to school, are there living arrangements close to campus that would eliminate your need for a car? Consider all these factors and give some practical advice to new students, explaining whether a car is truly necessary, supporting your proposal with good financial analysis and examples.

Students as Credit Card Customers

- Twenty-one percent of students pay off their credit card balance every month; another 44 percent make at least the minimum payment, but 11 percent pay less than the minimum.
- More than half of undergraduates carry outstanding balances under $1,000, but the average balance is over $2,100.
- Ninety-one percent of seniors have credit cards, and 56 percent of them have four or more cards.
- Almost 70 percent of students work 20 or fewer hours a week. Those who work more carry the highest credit card balances and are most anxious about paying their credit card bills.

Source: Nellie Mae, *Undergraduate Students and Credit Cards in 2004*

FIGURE 1.2 When this antique coin bank was made, most Americans saved their pennies. Now we lead the world in personal debt.

From University Class President to Bank Robber

Matt Assad, *Morning Call,* Allentown, PA, August 17, 2006

Matt Assad is a reporter for the Bethlehem office of the Morning Call. *This article won first place in the feature story category of the 2007 Keystone Press Awards, given by the Pennsylvania Newspaper Association to recognize "journalism that consistently provides relevance, integrity and initiative in serving readers, and furthers First Amendment values."*

Do you know someone who has fallen deep into debt? If you got into this kind of trouble, whom would you turn to for help?

Lehigh University sophomore Greg Hogan Jr. stood in line at a Wachovia   1
Bank in Allentown on a December day in 2005, listening to two voices in his head as he scribbled out a note. One voice told him, "Do it. Do it. It's your only way out. You're already here, just do it." The other countered, "Why are you here? This won't solve anything. This doesn't make sense."

2   By the time he walked into the Union Boulevard branch on that bright winter day, the genteel son of a Baptist minister was a frazzled, sleep-deprived mess—the result of a nearly two-week spree of online gambling and binge drinking. He wasn't trying to hide anything. He didn't even wear a mask. He had on a red baseball cap and the green fleece jacket his parents gave him for his birthday. He listened to the voices and then made his decision. He handed the stunned teller his note and demanded money.

3   Today Greg Hogan will be sentenced for a crime that, on the surface, makes no sense. Sophomore class presidents who play cello in the university orchestra simply don't rob banks. But a closer look reveals how a private school graduate and classical musician from a close-knit, protective and deeply religious Ohio family could have arrived at that moment in the bank.

4   He, his family and the people who know him best describe the 20-year-old as a high-energy student with an infectious personality and an insatiable thirst for success who was overwhelmed by an addiction that grew quickly from the moment he experienced the freedom of college life. In a little more than a year, this clean-cut, conservative kid who saw himself as a future financial mogul lost nearly $8,000 to his gambling addiction, culminating in a decision that will haunt him and his family for the rest of their lives.

5   "At that moment, I had the devil on one shoulder and an angel on the other," Hogan said. "Since then, I've come to realize that I have been wired to become a compulsive gambler since birth."

6   The kid who once worked tirelessly to please those who held so much hope in him has come to terms with the gambling addiction that made him steal from the family safe and even lie to his grandmother. As he talks about his addiction and how low it caused him to sink, the same confident smile that convinced his friends and family that he was a winner tops off his 5-foot-8-inch frame. His words ring with conviction and his determination appears unwavering. But his efforts now are focused, not on taking Lehigh University by storm or conquering Wall Street, but on beating back the urge to gamble.

7   The one difference: Greg Hogan now understands that he is not invincible.

An Early Performer

8   Maybe it was being a minister's son, or growing up with a talented older sister. Maybe Greg Hogan simply had a gene that drove him to excel. Whatever the reason, Hogan learned to perform at an early age. He began playing piano at 4, in part because his 6-year-old sister,

Nancy, already was accomplished. His parents realized quickly that he had a special talent. While Nancy toiled over the keys, using hard work and dedication to wring every ounce of potential out of her technically flawless music, Greg seemed to absorb the notes like a sponge. His blondish red hair cropped short, his little legs dangling from the piano bench, he instinctively played with flair and emotion, quickly surpassing his sister's expertise. Like most things, music came easy to Greg.

Still, that didn't keep him from striving to get better. When he 9 outgrew his nurturing first teacher, he began learning from a hard-driving instructor who believed talent could only flourish with long hours of practice and unwavering dedication. Hogan's mother, Karen, didn't like her. The teacher was too demanding, too tough. Such a small boy shouldn't be pushed so hard, Karen Hogan told her husband, Greg Sr. But the boy loved her. "Bring it on," he remembers thinking, relishing the idea of meeting near-impossible demands. Before a competition, he'd sit perched at his piano, sometimes practicing as much as five hours a day. "If I loved something," Greg said, "I dove into it head first."

He carried that attitude into most everything he did. Away from 10 school, if he wasn't playing music for nursing home residents or organizing food drives for the local homeless shelter, he was cultivating a growing appetite for politics. Even as a boy, he knew his opinions were conservative and decidedly Republican, from his belief in Reaganomics to his business-first attitude. When his father decided to run for a city council seat, Greg gathered his friends and canvassed the area in a door-to-door campaign. And Greg had a lot of friends. While most kids had a tight circle of confidants, he strived to be close friends with half the class.

By the time he was 14, he had twice performed at Carnegie Hall, 11 and his musical talent had earned him a scholarship to the exclusive University School in Hunting Valley, Ohio. The campus of the all-boys school was a 23-mile drive from his family's two-story Colonial home on the end of a cul-de-sac in Hudson, a comfortable suburb of Cleveland and Akron. But Greg's mother, who had homeschooled her son for seven years, was willing to make the 46-mile round trip twice a day because the opportunity for her son was too good to pass up.

With its rolling hills, its own fish hatchery and giant maple trees, 12 the day school campus appears almost collegiate. Students arrive each day for 8:05 AM assembly in blue blazers and ties, and administrators boast that 100 percent of their graduates move on to college. Unlike the families of most students at the $19,000-a-year private school, Greg's family was not affluent. His 51-year-old father, with his round face and easy smile that emits a sense of patience, has been a preacher for three decades. He speaks with the emphatic inflection and calm tone that keeps the attention of the nearly 200 people who come to services at his First Baptist Church of Barberton. But he always knew being a minister would not make him rich. So for years he had a second job as a school bus driver to help pay for his son's $50-an-hour music lessons. When he saved enough money, he moved his family to Hudson, where many of the 23,000 residents commute or work at the local Jo Ann Fabrics national headquarters.

13   Greg thrived at University. He was an outfielder on the baseball team and one of 10 leaders in the school's British-style system of houses. If a school event was being held, Greg was probably planning it. He couldn't just be a member of the Cadmean Society social service club, he had to be one of the students who consistently logged the most volunteer hours. He had good grades, but his parents believed that if Greg hadn't put his social priorities ahead of school work, he would have had a perfect 4.0, even at an elite institution such as University School.

14   School officials considered him exactly the type of student who would carry the school's reputation to one of the nation's top colleges. "He was a talented musician and . . . one of our brightest," said Whitney Lloyd, University's director of college guidance.

15   Greg was the only student to play two instruments—cello and piano—in the school orchestra. By then, he'd added the cello to his repertoire, not because he thought he had an aptitude for it, but because if Greg Hogan was going to do something, it had to be grand. "It sounds silly," he admits, "but I chose cello because it was the biggest. No other reason. It was just the biggest."

16   By the start of his senior year, in September 2003, Greg had become a member of the local Young Republicans club and had worked on political campaigns for now-federal Judge Christopher A. Boyko and Ohio state Sen. Robert F. Spada. Greg's youthful smile and easy conversation were almost irresistible as he worked local parades and knocked on hundreds of doors for Spada.

17   Like most everyone who met the young man, Spada was impressed. "He was so polite that it doesn't surprise me that he waited in line at that [Allentown] bank," Spada said. "Just a really good kid. He worked hard for us." Spada figured that Greg would someday be famous. He had no idea how soon fame would come or in what form.

18   For his senior yearbook page, Hogan chose a Winston Churchill quote to carry him into his future. It read, "History will be kind to me, for I intend to write it."

His First Poker Game

When Greg arrived in late summer 2004 at Lehigh University's campus 19 at the foot of South Mountain in Bethlehem, he again found himself at a school his parents couldn't afford. Yet, again, his musical talent and his academic prowess paved the way. After a sheltered childhood of learning at home and attending private school with some of Ohio's brightest young minds, Greg found himself 400 miles from home, awash in freedom. As the summer faded, the ambitious freshman decided he would guzzle freely from the cup of his newfound independence. "I can do just about anything I want," Greg thought to himself, "and I think I will. I'm going to do it all."

He decided on his first day on campus that he would run for class 20 president. By evening he was sitting at a table with 11 other students, joining a hot trend on campus by playing in his first poker game. The stakes were small—just a $5 buy-in—but Greg was already enjoying life at Lehigh. He placed fourth, one seat out of the money. As he thinks back to that night, he remembers no switch clicking, no urge blossoming. It was just an evening with new friends.

"I only played a couple more times that first two months," Greg 21 said of live poker.

That would change when a friend of his roommate introduced 22 Greg to online poker. He could do it right from his dorm computer, and all he needed was a bank account and a debit card. As the friend helped Greg get started, he joked, "You know, Greg, gamblers die broke." Greg just chuckled. For two weeks, he practiced without spending a dime. Almost instantly, the former chess club member fell in love with the strategy and challenge of Texas Hold'em, the exploding poker game in which each player is dealt two pocket cards, while five community cards are dealt on the table. He used play money on a practice site and parlayed $1,000 in imaginary chips into $20,000. To Greg, poker was beginning to feel like everything else he threw himself into—easy. "I practiced by playing, but I really didn't do my homework. I didn't read books on how to play," Greg said matter-of-factly. "I was going to develop my own style, play my own way. I was arrogant."

Meanwhile, he encountered "Phys," an online gambler whose 23 online account boasted winnings of more than $120,000. Greg began to think big. What he didn't realize was that practice sites are filled with inexperienced players. Nor did he know that the people trolling the real money sites include professionals and players with computer programs designed to find gambling sites with inexperienced players. So he used his debit card to deposit $75 into an account with PokerStars.com, which, Greg thought, graciously gave him a $25 bonus for joining. His screen name, geelehigh, displayed the kind of school spirit that sent him to Lehigh football games shirtless with his body painted Mountain Hawk brown and white. He had officially become part of the estimated 1.7 million college students gambling online, according to researchers at the University of Connecticut Health Center.

24   According to the American Gaming Association, Internet gambling is a blossoming epidemic. What was a $3-billion-a-year business in 2001 had revenues of $12 billion last year, and that is projected to increase to nearly $25 billion by 2010. And unlike casino gambling, where the patrons are predominantly people older than 60, online gamblers are predominantly men in their 20s.

25   That fall semester of 2004, he treaded water, winning some but losing more. The winning was just enough to keep him hooked. "We call that the lure of intermittent reinforcement," said Dr. Rina Gupta, director of the International Centre for Youth Gambling at McGill University in Montreal. "A famous study showed that if one lab rat has a lever that gives him food every time, the rat will only hit it a few times a day when he's hungry. But give him a lever that only gives him food sporadically and unpredictably, and the rat becomes obsessed with hitting the lever."

26   Greg remembers the hand that first sent him over the edge. It was November 2004 and he'd drawn a king-high flush. He quickly bet his entire online account of $300. His opponent called his bet and showed an ace-high flush. Rage swept through him. He cursed the screen, turned off his computer and vowed never to play again.

27   But within a few days, he was beginning to feel like that rat that hadn't eaten. When Greg went home to Ohio for Christmas break, his dad noticed a change in his son. It was his first inkling that his super-achiever son was in trouble. Rather than spend time with friends he hadn't seen in months, Greg Jr. watched television poker for hours at home. When he wasn't doing that, he was playing poker on the family computer in his father's basement office.

28   Greg got a rush from online poker he didn't get from sitting at a poker table. In live games like the one he joined that first night at Lehigh, he could play maybe 30 hands an hour. But online, he could play up to 75 hands an hour. Hands were dealt in seconds. The card flips were instantaneous, and his opponents were scattered around the world, sitting at their own computers. There was no between-hands chit-chat, no distractions to slow the game. Rock music from Green Day, Incubus and 311 blared from the stereo as Greg played for hours. The hands ran together in a blur. It was fast and exciting.

29   When Greg Sr. asked his son how he could waste his Christmas vacation playing online poker, his son didn't even look away from the

screen. He simply replied, "Don't worry, Dad, it's just play money." "That's when the lying started. When you are a compulsive gambler, you also become a compulsive liar," he said, reciting some of what he has learned in treatment.

Trying to Avoid Catastrophe

If there was a silver lining that Christmas, it was that Greg stopped 30 gambling when he had burned through most of the money he had saved for the next semester. With just $200 to carry him through nearly five months at Lehigh, he refocused his efforts on his classes, his social life and his work-study job in the university chaplain's office. By then, Hogan had decided online poker was rigged.

He did well in class, organized charity events as class president 31 and pledged the Sigma Phi Epsilon fraternity. He was only playing live poker with friends two or three nights a week. He was trying to pull himself away from catastrophe. In a stroke of good luck, he landed a summer job with a finance company back home near Cleveland. It paid him nearly $5,000 for less than three months' work, enough money to carry him through his sophomore year. But the job also gave Greg money to gamble. What hooked him again was an online ad on a college website offering a $50 bonus for a deposit of $50. Geelehigh was back in action.

As the summer of 2005 passed, Greg was losing. The conservative 32 who used to balance his bank account to the penny was logging frequent overdrafts in his account. Greg Sr. did not like what he was seeing in his son's behavior. In his role as a minister, he was experienced in spotting people in crisis. He watched with alarm as his son would creep out of bed and sneak into the basement to play poker, sometimes until dawn. And he knew about the mounting overdrafts.

Realizing how serious the situation had become, Greg Sr. and his 33 wife took drastic measures. They demanded that their son join Gamblers Anonymous. They also started attending support group meetings for families affected by gamblers. When the rest of the family left for vacation later that month, Greg Sr. gathered every computer in the house—even those used by his other children—carted them to his church and locked them in his office. "It sounds harsh, but by then we had decided we were not going to be enablers for his problem," said Greg Sr., a hint of his Georgia roots still evident in his voice. "We knew Greg was not able to control himself."

It seemed to work. But what Greg's parents didn't know was that 34 their son had won $2,500 gambling over the July Fourth holiday, money that was sitting in an account in Bethlehem. Once he was back at Lehigh, he was binge gambling again, six to eight hours a day for three- or four-day periods every few weeks.

35 As he watched television accounts of the devastation from Hurricane Katrina, Greg thought to himself, "I should be helping in Louisiana." The thought was fleeting. He turned up the stereo and flipped on his computer to play again. The winnings from July quickly evaporated. While he once played online at quarter and half-dollar tables with pots of $20 or $30, he was now playing at $3 and $6 tables with pots as high as $1,200. "I was fully on tilt," Greg said, using a gambler's term for an out-of-control player chasing losses by betting with emotion and desperation. "I was trying to win too much too fast. I couldn't accept that I was failing. I kept thinking, if I keep trying, I'll beat this." As his debts grew, Greg began using alcohol to forget them. In October 2005, campus police cited him for underage drinking, adding a $400 fine to his mounting debt.

36 Greg's past might well have set him up for a fall, said Gupta, the McGill University gambling expert. "A kid who has success all his life learns if you put in the effort, it will pay off," Gupta said. "That doesn't apply to gambling. It's hard for an ultra-successful kid to understand that."

37 The bank overdrafts started coming so frequently that Greg Sr. drove nearly seven hours from Ohio to Bethlehem to install a program blocking his son from accessing gambling sites on his fraternity room computer. Greg Jr. wanted to obey his father, but by then he was captive to his addiction. He turned to the computers in Lehigh's library. For hours he played there, often with the whisping sound of flipping poker cards coming from computers where students were playing a few tables away.

38 Back in Ohio, when the overdrafts still kept coming, Greg Sr. called Lehigh officials and begged them to go into the library and remove his son. "They told me that unless Greg was a danger to himself or others, there was nothing they could do," Greg Sr. said. "I felt helpless."

39 Greg Jr. attended classes but stopped doing homework and withdrew from his usually booked social calendar. In a blink, he was back in Ohio for Thanksgiving, financially and emotionally bankrupt. His money was gone, his fraternity brothers were asking him to pay back more than $600 he had borrowed from them, and 45 bank overdrafts left him more than $1,000 in debt to his bank. "Mom, I don't want to go back," Greg said to his mother in the laundry room of their home.

40 "Finish these two weeks, get through finals week, and then maybe you can take a break," his mother answered.

41 He could stay out of school after finishing the semester and enter a treatment program, Greg thought. Instead, he sneaked into the family

safe and took $1,200 in bonds that had been saved for him since birth. He knew he shouldn't have taken them, but he thought he would use the money to pay back his friends and at least make a dent in the overdraft debt. "When I got back to school, I started thinking I could double it," Hogan recalls, wondering how he could have missed the signs that now seem so clear to him. "My thinking was so twisted at that point."

He went on a four-day gambling binge. One minute he was up 42 $700, the next down $500. The measured, analytical style he once used to play was now a risky, rage-fueled approach. In the late afternoon of November 30, his bond money mostly gone, he sat with pocket kings and $300 in his account. He bet it all. His opponent, holding ace-queen, pulled an ace "on the river"—the fifth and final community card turned in Texas Hold'em—and won the hand with a pair of aces. Greg lapsed into a desperate 10-day fog, spending much of his time drinking beer and worrying how he'd pay his friends. His perfect façade was crumbling, but he had become an expert at hiding the cracks.

Sally Schray, the secretary to the Rev. Lloyd Steffen, university 43 chaplain, supervised Greg for two years in his work-study job in the chaplain's office. She spent hours talking with him, marveling at how easily he engaged everyone from the cleaning staff to then-college President Gregory Farrington. "Even when he was apparently sinking, I couldn't tell. He still held things together," Schray said. "He has this unique ability of being able to talk with anyone. I truly believe he'd be comfortable talking to President Bush. I would have been proud to have him as a son."

His best friend and class vice president, Matt Montgomery, also had 44 no idea of the torment that was dogging Greg. "Honestly, I couldn't tell. None of us could," Matt said. "To us, he seemed like the same, loyal, funny friend we all knew. He never told us how much he was hurting."

For the first time in his life, Greg felt he was letting people down. "These were good friends. They would have understood, if I had only told them," he said. "I didn't want them to know I had a problem. I always wanted people to think they could depend on me. I was blinded by my obsession."

He knew he could not call his parents for money, so he tried to bor- 45 row from other family members, including his youngest sibling, James. He even lied to his grandmother, asking her for $1,000 he said was for the orchestra's upcoming trip to South Africa. His parents found out and stopped her from agreeing. "I still can't believe I did that," Greg said. "I told myself I'd pay my friends back, but looking back, I probably would have gambled it away."

Out of options, he was on his way to see the movie *Chronicles of* 46 *Narnia* with Lehigh Senate President Kip Wallen and Matt Montgomery on December 9 when he asked Kip to stop his black Ford Explorer at the Wachovia in Allentown so he could cash a check. Kip and Matt remained in the car, oblivious to Greg's plan. Inside the bank, Greg waited his turn and handed the teller a note stating, "I want $10,000 in cash. I have a gun! Be quiet and quick, or I will shoot. No bait."

47 No bait meant no marked bills or exploding ink.

48 Seeing his polite demeanor and schoolboy looks, teller Hiyam Chatih gave him a look that seemed to say, "Is this real?"

49 "Yes," he nodded nervously, "this is real."

50 He walked out onto the bank's freshly shoveled walkway with $2,871, went to the movie, ate pizza with friends later and sat silently when a call came to one of his fraternity brothers at the table informing him that police had just raided the Sigma Phi Epsilon house. Greg Hogan was arrested less than an hour later when he arrived for orchestra practice. In that instant, as police handcuffed him outside Zoellner Arts Center, everything he'd worked for was gone. His chair in the Lehigh Philharmonic, his seat as class president, his place in the fraternity and his otherwise spotless reputation.

51 Back in Ohio, Karen Hogan was driving with her husband when her cell phone rang. When she heard what her son was telling her, she was so shaken that she pulled off the road, unable to safely navigate traffic.

52 "Mom, I'm in bad shape," her son said from a cell phone he had borrowed from an Allentown police detective. "I've done something really stupid. I'm under arrest."

53 Not only had her son robbed a bank, but he'd signed a confession, even before making his first phone call to his parents.

54 "At that moment, time stopped," said Greg Hogan Sr., recalling how he felt as he sat in that idling car. "At that moment, all of the plans we had for Greg were canceled."

55 Greg Jr. was about to spend his first night in jail.

"This Was a Cry for Help"

56 How many more nights, if any, Greg will spend in jail will be determined today when he is sentenced by Lehigh County President Judge William H. Platt. Greg proudly says it has been more than eight months since he's gambled and now that he's pleaded guilty, he wants to say something that's been pent up in him since the robbery.

57 "I really want to apologize," Greg said. "First to the bank and the teller—I can't imagine the fear I made her feel. Then to my friends, my family and finally the university. Lehigh's been good to me and it didn't need this kind of attention. I'm sorry I put everyone through this."

Since the robbery, Greg has gone through a 36-day treatment pro- 58
gram in Louisiana that cost his family $5,600, and he attends regular
Gamblers Anonymous meetings. He's had to accept that he's fallen off
the ladder he spent years climbing. His dream of working as a finance
company executive on Wall Street is gone. He can never hold large
amounts of cash, a credit card or even a debit card, he says. For the
foreseeable future, his parents will be in charge of his bank accounts.

For now, the kid whose future once seemed limitless chooses not to 59
look much beyond the next turn. He hopes to get a job and maybe go
back to college—probably an Ohio school close to home—next year.
That is, of course, if he's not in jail. . . .

Psychologists hired by his Allentown attorney, John Waldron, say 60
there's a reason Greg went into that bank unmasked and unarmed,
just as there's a reason he so quickly confessed to his crime. "This was
a cry for help," Waldron said. "Deep down, he wanted so badly to quit
gambling that it was actually a relief when he was arrested. That's
why he was so anxious to confess and so anxious to apologize for
what he'd done."

What Greg says he really wants now is to warn others. He says his 61
story should be told at universities around the nation to show students
that addiction can darken even the brightest star. "I will accept my sentence, whatever it is," Greg said. "But I feel I can do more good if I'm
not in prison. This is an epidemic that can hit any family. I want to tell
them that this is a problem you can't tackle alone. Parents, don't be
afraid to intrude on your children's privacy, and students, don't be
afraid to ask for help."

Reflection and Discussion

1. How does Assad feel about Greg Hogan Jr.? Point to specific aspects of the
   article that support your interpretation.
2. Hogan wants to tell his story as a warning to other students, but while
   many people lose money on Internet gambling, few become bank robbers.
   How effective are warning messages that focus on extreme cases?

Writing Matters

1. As a self-identified gambling addict, Greg Hogan Jr. has turned over control of his finances to his parents for now and says he will have problems
   with money for the rest of his life. Those addicted to chemical substances
   often have similar problems with money, fearing that having money available will lead them back to drugs or alcohol. Others consider compulsive
   spending itself to be a form of addiction; psychiatrists even prescribe

drugs for it, and programs like Debtors Anonymous have formed to treat out-of-control spenders using techniques developed for alcoholics and drug addicts. What are the main causes of overspending in people your age? Support your position with examples from what you've read and your own experience.

2. When Greg Hogan Sr. asked university officials to stop his son from gambling on library computers, they said they couldn't do anything unless he was a danger to himself or others. But many universities have stringent guidelines for acceptable use of their computer systems and some block access to certain sites. Should universities block access to Internet gambling sites through their computers? Weigh the cost of gambling to the student and the school against the loss of access for students without a gambling problem.

Fury over Student Loan Kickback Allegation

Jon Marcus, *The Times Higher Education Supplement,* London, May 11, 2007

Jon Marcus is an American journalist who serves as the US education correspondent for The Times of London. *He has been published in the* Los Angeles Times, Boston Globe, Washington Post *and other major newspapers, and has written several travel books about New England.*

How much have you relied on your school's recommendations of loan and credit card companies?

1   When cash-strapped students entering Johns Hopkins University this year needed private loans to help them pay their tuition fees, the university's financial aid office steered them to a short list of recommended lenders, including one called Student Loan Xpress. Along with its rivals in the lucrative US student loan industry, Student Loan Xpress reaps the profits from a fast-growing, $17 billion-a-year business that charges relatively high interest to finance spiraling education costs not covered by disappearing direct grants and lower-interest government-backed loans. Although they are not required to, 90 percent of students choose the loan companies recommended as "preferred" by their university financial aid offices. But these recommendations have become part of a scandal that is rocking US higher education.

2   Johns Hopkins student financial services director Ellen Frishberg was being paid consulting fees and travel reimbursements by Student Loan Xpress. Nor did Ms. Frishberg have to worry about how to pay

her own tuition fees when she attended a doctoral program at the University of Pennsylvania because Student Loan Xpress picked up the tab. In all, between 2002 and 2005, Ms. Frishberg received $63,000 from the private lender, a widening investigation has alleged—all without the knowledge of those she recommended Student Loan Xpress loans to.

At least six university financial aid directors accepted payments 3 from, and even held stock in, Student Loan Xpress, investigators now say. All, including Ms. Frishberg, have been suspended from their jobs. But the scandal is not limited to half a dozen universities or one lender. Financial aid officials nationwide are now known to have accepted cash, gifts, trips to exotic destinations and sponsorships of things such as awards dinners and association conferences from lenders they recommended to their students. Some of these lenders charge interest as much as four times as high as the rates on government-subsidized loans. Some lenders simply made cash payments to the universities themselves.

Investigators call these payments kickbacks, pure and simple. 4 Congressman George Miller, chairman of the House Education and Labor Committee, described them as "corruption and cronyism." "Students should be steered towards lenders that will give them the best terms, not towards companies that send college employees on an all-expenses-paid Caribbean vacation," Mr. Miller said.

One lender, EduCap, invited financial aid officers to an all- 5 expenses-paid weekend at a Four Seasons resort in Nevis in the Caribbean. And members of the National Association of Student Financial Aid Administrators at their annual conference were given portable DVD players and iPods by companies soliciting their loan business.

"At a time when more and more students and families are relying 6 on loans and incurring greater amounts of debt to pay for a college education, it is beyond shameful that some private lenders are courting colleges with gifts and incentives that often do not help students or parents," Mr. Miller said.

Universities largely shrugged off the simmering criticism of their 7 relationship with lenders until the attorney general of New York State, Andrew Cuomo, propelled it onto the front pages by demanding information from 400 universities that are in, or enroll students from, New York. Some of the universities were alarmed to receive subpoenas, and Mr. Cuomo announced that he would file suit against one, Drexel University in Philadelphia, which received $124,000 from a company called Education Finance Partners in exchange for making it the sole preferred source for private loans to Drexel students. "A preferred lender ought to mean that the lender is preferred by students for its low rates, not by schools for its kickbacks," said Mr. Cuomo, son of former New York Governor Mario Cuomo.

8   After first attacking the investigation as political grandstanding, universities have been quick to change their position in response to growing public anger. At least 35, including the University of Pennsylvania and New York University, have accepted Mr. Cuomo's demand that they abide by a code of conduct he devised and pay restitution to students equal to the amount of money they received from lenders. UPenn will distribute $1.6 million to students, and NYU $1.4 million. The American Association of Universities has drafted its own "statement of principles" for relationships between universities and student-loan providers "to help guide campus leaders as they review these relationships in the wake of recent developments," president Robert Berdahl said.

9   Still, university officials are privately stewing at the word "kickback."

10   "Kickback means to me that someone took a bribe or received some sort of benefit for personal gain," Dallas Martin, president of the financial aid administrators association, said. "If schools have negotiated agreements and they're getting some money back that is not at the expense of the borrower, and those funds are going into their student aid program, then I think that is an acceptable use of the proceeds of such agreements."

11   In fact, several top university financial aid officers received considerable personal benefits. David Charlow, senior associate dean of student affairs at Columbia University, Catherine Thomas, financial aid director at the University of Southern California, and Lawrence Burt, associate vice-president for student affairs at the University of Texas at Austin, each owned at least 1,500 shares of the parent company of Student Loan Xpress, which they listed as a preferred lender. Walter Cathie, dean of financial aid at Widener University, was allegedly paid $80,000 by the company. Capella University financial aid director Timothy Lehmann allegedly got $13,000. Mr. Cuomo said he was considering filing criminal charges against some financial aid officers.

12   And while universities say it would be impossible to prove that their deals with lenders forced students to pay more in interest, at least one school that accepted money in exchange for listing a lender as "preferred" found that the resulting loans carried interest rates of more than twice the rate the federal government collects. It cancelled the arrangement. Other private companies charge nearly four times the government rate.

13   The national government makes available about $70 billion a year in subsidized loans to university students, who are allowed to borrow

up to $4,000 annually at 5 percent interest from the primary loan program. Private US universities charge as much as $45,000 a year in tuition fees, and for room and board.

The amount of money distributed through private loans increased 14 by more than 1,000 percent in the past ten years as the cost of US higher education skyrocketed. Some private lenders charge as much as 19 percent interest. Yet, thanks in part to special arrangements with the universities, private lenders have faced little competition. On each of 300 American campuses, a single lender controls 99 percent of all the private student loans.

Mr. Martin and other higher education officials have tried to 15 deflect attention back onto the federal government, which they say should make more of its own loans available, reducing student dependence on private lenders. "This leads to families having no choice but to use private loans, which have higher interest rates and fewer borrower benefits," Mr. Martin said.

Mr. Cuomo, a Democrat, also wants to put the focus on the national 16 government. He said that the Republican Bush Administration had done little to protect students against lenders despite its promise to form a committee to study the issue. "The Department of Education has been asleep at the switch," Mr. Cuomo said. The education department, he said, had been "remarkably weak" in its oversight of the industry.

And, as if more proof were needed, the chief federal government 17 official responsible for regulating student loans, Matteo Fontana, has been suspended from his job. The reason? It was disclosed that he held at least $100,000 in stock in Student Loan Xpress.

At a Glance: US Student Loan System

- Grants are available to help cover the cost of tuition fees and come directly from universities or from the federal government.
- The federal government also offers so-called Perkins student loans of up to $4,000 per year for each student, up to a maximum of $20,000, at 5 percent interest. Smaller federal loan programs also exist.
- The government earmarks a total of $70 billion for student loans each year.
- Private lenders offer loans to students who need additional money to cover the cost of tuition fees and other higher education costs and are allowed to charge interest up to a maximum of 19 percent.
- The private market has grown by an average of 27 percent per year since 2001 and is now worth $17.3 billion, 12 times as much as a decade ago.

- Most university financial aid offices offer lists of "preferred lenders" from which students are encouraged to choose.
- Nine out of ten students pick from preferred lender lists.

Reflection and Discussion

1. How do you feel about school administrators accepting the kind of kickbacks described here? How does this affect your general feelings about school?
2. What responsibility, if any, do schools have to research and recommend lenders?

Writing Matters

1. Andrew Cuomo identifies "preferred lenders" by their low interest rates. What other factors should be considered when putting together a list of lenders to recommend to students? What factors should disqualify a lender? Write an essay arguing for your definition of "preferred lender."
2. What's a kickback? What's OK? Lenders have offered schools and individuals everything from ball point pens to cash to the luxurious trips mentioned by Marcus. Colleges have required potential lenders to provide financial responsibility seminars and to aggressively recruit students for credit cards benefitting the school. Does it make a difference if money going to the school is used to provide scholarships for needy students? Write an essay defining what goods and services would be ethical for individuals and colleges to accept from educational lenders.

Generation Debt: The Dirty Business of Deregulated Credit

Tamara Draut, excerpted from *Strapped: Why America's 20- and 30-Somethings Can't Get Ahead,* 2006

Tamara Draut is Director of the Economic Opportunity Program at the New York think-tank Demos.

How closely do you read the fine print on financial contracts when signing up for a credit card, loan or lease?

1   Although debt-for-diploma is preferable to no diploma at all, heavy doses of student loans are causing more grads to report serious side effects. In 2002, 14 percent of young adults reported that student loans caused them to delay marriage, up from 7 percent in 1991. One in five said their debt has caused them to delay having children, up from 12 percent in 1991. Forty percent reported they delayed buying a home

because of their loans, compared to just one quarter in 1991. And 17 percent, significantly, changed careers as a result of their student debt, about the same as in 1991.[1] Young adults from low-income families are much more likely to report these side effects.

But student loan debt is only part of the Generation Debt story. Over the last ten years, young adults have racked up record levels of credit card debt. When they lose a job or the car breaks down, that credit line quickly becomes a lifeline. And the reliance on credit cards starts early, just the way the credit card companies intended.

Prior to the early 1980s, credit card debt was virtually nonexistent. Credit cards weren't yet widely available, and they certainly weren't marketed to college students. According to data from the Federal Reserve, in 1983, the median consumer debt for 25-to-34-year-olds was $3,989 (in 2001 dollars).[2] By 2001, the median consumer debt for households under 35 had tripled to $12,000.[3] Consumer debt lumps together all debt other than mortgages, so it includes things like student loans, car loans, and credit card debt.

By the end of the 1980s, credit cards had sprung up like weeds and could be found in the wallets of most Americans. The story of how we became so indebted is in part a tale about deregulation, and in part a tale of economic change. As wages dropped or stagnated during the 1980s and 1990s, more and more people turned to credit cards to stay afloat. The new demand for credit cards was easily met by a hungry credit card industry, newly unbound from the chains of regulation. Since the early 1990s, the credit card companies have unleashed a tidal wave of direct-mail solicitations, television ads, and campus marketing. . . .

In addition to ramping up their marketing efforts during the 1990s, the credit card industry has also gotten much more aggressive about raising interest rates and levying high fees for quite minor infractions. Cloaked by deregulation and protected by a powerful Washington lobby, credit card companies are making record profits. And fleecing young adults.

During the 1980s, entire industries, including banking, were deregulated under the rationale that intense competitive pressures would compel corporations to police themselves. The paladins of laissez-faire ideology also propagated the myth that deregulated markets would empower individual citizens with more choices and cheaper products. In addition, freeing corporations from pesky regulations would enhance our democracy, as consumers took more control of their lives.[4] But like other sectors that were deregulated (energy being a good example of bad deregulation), the deregulation of the banking industry has proved especially bad for individual investors and borrowers—and fantastically good for CEOs and shareholders.

7   The story of deregulation of the credit card industry begins back in 1978 with a Supreme Court decision. In Marquette National Bank of Minneapolis v. First Omaha Service Corp. the Court interpreted a dusty old statute, section 85 of the National Banking Act of 1864, as allowing a national bank to charge its credit card customers the highest interest rate permitted in the bank's home state—as opposed to the rate in the state where the customer resides.[5] As a result, regional and national banks moved their operations to more lender-friendly states, such as South Dakota and Delaware, where there were no laws limiting the amount of interest that banks could charge for credit card loans. In domino-like fashion, states began loosening their own usury laws, limiting the chances for consumers to get a lower rate from a local or state bank.[6] Today, twenty-nine states have no limit on credit card interest rates.[7]

8   Look at the next bill or credit card solicitation that comes in your mailbox. Chances are it came from South Dakota or Delaware. Why? These states have no usury laws limiting the amount of interest on credit cards, so the credit card companies can charge any interest they want. Thanks to another decision by the Supreme Court in 1996, the same rules that apply to interest rates apply to fees as well. Prior to both of these cases, states set the maximum amount of interest and fees that lenders could charge. Most states outlawed interest rates above 20 percent and limited fees to $10 or $15. High rates and fees that were once considered usurious are now just considered profit for the credit card companies. The average late fee is now $32, which in 2004 provided a cool $10 billion in revenue for the card companies.[8]

9   The Marquette ruling had tremendous impact on the growth of the credit card industry and its profitability. Before Marquette, complying with fifty different state laws represented a high cost burden for the credit card companies. Also, during the high-inflation years in the 1970s, interest rates bumped up against state usury laws. The Marquette decision allowed banks to nationalize credit card lending and take full advantage of the ease of centralized processing provided by the Visa and MasterCard system. Better technology combined with the removal of interest caps also allowed credit card companies to expand their business to less creditworthy households by offering higher rates and fees for customers deemed a higher credit risk. As a result, credit cards, which were once the province of the wealthy and elite business class, quickly became part of mainstream American culture.

10   The rise in credit card debt during the eighties and nineties reveals how quickly credit cards swept the nation: in the two decades between 1980 and 2000, credit card debt grew from $111 billion to nearly $600 billion (both in 1999 dollars).[9] Today, Americans have

$800 billion in credit card debt. And this debt doesn't come cheap, to say the least.

Although our mailboxes get stuffed with offers for low rates like 11 5.9 percent for one year, the credit card companies have gotten very creative in finding ways to raise that "teaser" rate once you've gotten the card. Thanks to new "gotcha" tactics such as tripling the interest rate for a late payment, credit card companies are routinely charging interest rates of 29 to 34 percent—a rate of return that the old neighborhood loan sharks wouldn't dare charge. And "late" means being merely one minute past 1 PM or 2 PM on the specified due date. If a payment arrives a minute late, the credit card company will also charge a late fee.

But it's not just late payments that can land you in the penalty 12 zone. Credit card companies now routinely scan their cardholders' credit scores and if they see a credit problem elsewhere will raise the interest rate on your card—even if you've never been late or missed a payment. The industry rationalizes this preemptive strike by saying they are adjusting to a change in risk. But the logic doesn't hold. If the credit card companies were really concerned about risk, they would lower the customer's credit line to stop further indebtedness—not jack up their rates to 29 percent or more. . . .

The credit card industry gets away with something most other 13 lenders can't do. Next time you get a credit card solicitation, look at the fine print below the boxes that state how much the interest rate is on the card. On a BankOne solicitation I got in the mail recently, it said, "We reserve the right to change the terms (including APRs) at any time for any reason, in addition to APR increases which may occur for failure to comply with the terms of your account." There are plenty of rules for cardholders to follow, including getting their payment in by the minute, but absolutely none for the credit card companies. They can do what they want, when they want, for whatever reason.

But there's more to the capriciousness of these credit card contracts. 14 When a credit card company increases the rate on the card, the new APR is applied retroactively to the entire balance. Now, it'd be one thing for the company to raise your rate on any future purchases, but to apply the new rate to everything you've purchased with the card is essentially raising the price of everything ever bought on the card that hasn't been paid for. Let's say you buy a new computer on your Citibank card at the normal interest rate of 12.99 percent. One month your payment arrives a day late. As a result of this tardy payment, Citibank raises your rate to 27.99 percent. That computer just got a lot more expensive.

15   The sheer audacity of these practices led me to wonder just how in the world an industry can get away with such tactics. It wasn't too hard to find the answer.

16   After all, behind every deregulation story (energy, pharmaceuticals) is a tale of political contributions and powerful lobbies. And the banking industry is no slouch when it comes to fighting for its way in the nation's capital. . . . Although the Republicans' portion of the pot has been climbing steadily, Democrats do receive a substantial amount of money from the industry. Which might explain why majorities in both parties supported the bankruptcy "reform" legislation of April 2005, which the credit card industry had fought for since the mid-1990s.[10] The bankruptcy legislation President Bush signed into law will make it harder for people to erase their credit card debts and force any disposable income to be paid to the card companies.

17   The main argument for deregulating any industry is to provide a more competitive market, which in turn should lead to lower prices and more choices for consumers. Like so much of economics, what is supposed to happen in theory is often the opposite of what happens in practice. Since deregulation of the credit card industry in the early 1980s, debtors now actually have less choice and are paying more in interest and fees. The wave of major mergers among national banks facilitated by deregulation means that today fewer companies control the credit card market than ever before. In the year before Marquette, the top fifty issuers of cards controlled about half of the market. By 1990, the top ten issuers controlled 56.6 percent of the market. The latest bank mergers, between J. P. Morgan and Bank One, and Bank of America and Fleet, mean that now the top ten card issuers control nearly 90 percent of the market.[11]

18   So what has been the effect of all this on prices? Credit card interest rates began to soar in the high-inflation post-Marquette environment, reaching averages of 18 percent, and have remained relatively high in comparison to drops in the federal funds rate, the amount of interest banks pay to borrow money overnight from the Federal Reserve.[12] Several economists have remarked on the reasons why consumers continue to pay, and card companies continue to charge, exceptionally high interest rates. Some point to the high consumer transaction costs involved in switching accounts, and others point to a lack of competition in the credit card marketplace.[13] Whatever the reason, credit card companies did not lower their rates when inflation slowed and national interest rates came down. As a result, the card companies' "spread," the amount charged above what it costs them to lend funds, has remained consistently high—at or above 10 percentage points over the last fifteen years.

19   This trend persisted in the past decade, even as the federal funds rate and the prime rate (the rate banks offer their best customers)

dropped to historic lows. For example, in 2001 the Federal Reserve lowered rates eleven times, from 6.24 percent to 3.88 percent.[14] But these savings didn't get passed on to cardholders: during the same period, credit card rates declined only slightly, from 15.71 percent to 14.89 percent, and penalty rates shot through the roof.[15] Deregulation has been very bad for consumers and very good for the industry. The credit card industry rakes in $2.5 billion in profits each month.[16] No one would argue that the credit card industry shouldn't be profitable, but those profits should be made fairly and through good and transparent business practices. Neither of these characterizes the modern-day American credit card market. . . .

For now, young adults are stuck paying high rates, getting slapped with exorbitant fees, and having their welcome wagon at college sport MBNA, BankOne and Citibank logos. Young adults are borrowing their way into adulthood, and it's costing them greatly. Each payment to a credit card or student loan company is one less opportunity to save for the future. The average 25-to-34-year-old now spends about one out of every five dollars on debt payments. That's less money for the piggy bank or a house down payment or a 401(k) account.

References

1. Sandy Baum and Marie O'Malley, "College on Credit: How Borrowers Perceive Their Education Debt. Results of the 2002 National Student Loan Survey," Nellie Mae Corporation, February 6, 2003.

2. Robert B. Avery, Gregory E. Elliehausen, and Glenn B. Canner, "Survey of Consumer Finances, 1983: A Second Report," *Federal Reserve Bulletin,* December 1984, available at http://www.federalreserve.gov/oss/oss2/83/bulletin1284.pdf.

3. Ana M. Aizcorbe, Arthur B. Kennickell, and Kevin B. Moore, "Recent Changes in US Family Finances: Evidence for the 1998 and 2001 Survey of Consumer Finances," *Federal Reserve Bulletin,* January 2003, available at http://www.federalreserve.gov/oss/oss2/2001/bulletin0103.pdf.

4. For a good review of the free-market ideology and its promise to enhance democracy, see Thomas Frank, *One Market Under God: Extreme Capitalism, Market Populism, and the End of Economic Democracy* (New York: Knopf, 2001).

5. Vincent D. Rougeau, "Rediscovering Usury: An Argument for Legal Controls on Credit Card Interest Rates," *University of Colorado Law Review,* Winter, 1996.

6. Ibid.

7. Lucy Lazarony, "States with Credit Card Caps," Bankrate.com, March 20, 2002, http://www.bankrate.com/brm/news/cc/20020320b.asp.

8. "Card Fees 2003," Cardweb.com, http://www.cardweb.com/cardtrak/news/2003/july/18a.html.

9. Robert Manning, *Credit Card Nation: The Consequences of America's Addiction to Credit* (New York: Basic Books, 2000), pp. 12–13. Figures adjusted to 1999 dollars.

10. In 2005, the House voted 302–126 to pass the bankruptcy "reform" legislation and the Senate passed it 74–25. The bill was signed into law by President Bush in April 2005.

11. Manning, *Credit Card Nation,* and *Frontline:* "The Secret History of the Credit Card," *Frontline,* broadcast on PBS, March 17, 2005; see also the graph at http://www.pbs.org/wghb/pages/frontline/shows/credit/more/marketshare.html.

12. See Federal Deposit Insurance Corporation (FDIC), "Bank Trends—The Effect on Consumer Interest Rate Deregulation on Credit Card Volumes, Charge-Offs, and the Personal Bankruptcy Rate," May 1998, available at http://www.fdic.gov/bank/analytical/bank/bt_9805.html; see also David A. Moss and Johnson A. Gibbs, "The Rise of Consumer Bankruptcy: Evolution, Revolution or Both?" *National Conference of Bankruptcy Judges,* 1999, p. 13.

13. See Rougeau, "Rediscovering Usury."

14. Federal Reserve, "Federal Funds Rate, Historical Data," released April 28, 2003, available at http://www.federalreserve.gov/releases/h15/data.htm.

15. US Census Bureau, *Statistical Abstract of the United States: 2002* (Washington, DC: US Census Bureau, 2003), p. 728.

16. Patrick McGeehan, "Soaring Interest Compounds Credit Card Pain for Millions," *New York Times,* November 21, 2004.

Reflection and Discussion

1. Draut notes that credit card companies get away with many things that other lenders can't do. Review the powers that deregulation gave them. Which do you think are reasonable? Which are not? Why?

2. Draut concludes that young adults are stuck with the high cost of credit cards. Are young people really as powerless as she suggests? What alternatives can you think of?

Writing Matters

1. As Draut recounts the evolution of the credit card industry, she carefully chooses words and phrases to communicate her opinions. Reread the article, making a list of value-laden language. Analyze the effect of her language choices on the reader, comparing it to a straightforward persuasive argument in which the author stakes out her stance in a prominent early thesis.

2. Whom does Draut intend to address? Whom does she ignore? To see how intended audience affects the way we write, draft a letter to the head of a credit card company, suggesting a change in one of the practices you believe is unreasonable, backing up your request with information Draut has provided.

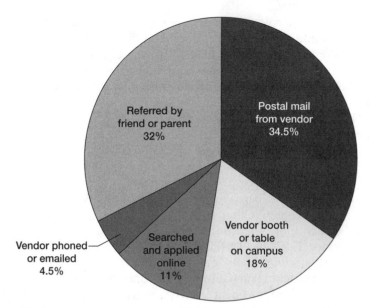

FIGURE 1.3 Where Students Got Their First Credit Cards, Nellie Mae's 2004 Survey

---

Debt Education: Bad for the Young, Bad for America

Jeffrey J. Williams, *Dissent,* Summer 2006

Jeffrey J. Williams teaches English literature and cultural studies at Carnegie Mellon University. He has edited the Minnesota Review *and the book* Critics at Work: Interviews, 1993–2003.

What is the highest level of education attained by your parents? If they went to college, how did they pay for it? If not, why did they stop their education when they did?

Student loans, for more than half those attending college, are the new 1 paradigm of college funding. Consequently, student debt is, or will soon be, the new paradigm of early to middle adult life. Gone are the days when the state university was as cheap as a laptop and was considered a right, like secondary education. Now higher education is, like most social services, a largely privatized venture, and loans are the chief way that a majority of individuals pay for it.

Over the past decade, there has been an avalanche of criticism of 2 the "corporatization" of the university. Most of it focuses on the impact of corporate protocols on research, the reconfiguration of the relative power of administration and faculty, and the transformation of academic into casual labor, but little of it has addressed student debt. Because more than half the students attending university receive, along with their bachelor's degree, a sizable loan payment book, we need to deal with student debt.

3   The average undergraduate student loan debt in 2002 was $18,900. It more than doubled from 1992, when it was $9,200. Added to this is charge card debt, which averaged $3,000 in 2002, boosting the average total debt to about $22,000. One can reasonably expect, given still accelerating costs, that it is over $30,000 now. Bear in mind that this does not include other private loans or the debt that parents take on to send their children to college. (Neither does it account for "post-baccalaureate loans," which more than doubled in seven years, from $18,572 in 1992–1993 to $38,428 in 1999–2000, and have likely doubled again.)

4   Federal student loans are a relatively new invention. The Guaranteed Student Loan (GSL) program only began in 1965, a branch of Lyndon B. Johnson's Great Society programs intended to provide supplemental aid to students who otherwise could not attend college or would have to work excessively while in school. In its first dozen years, the amounts borrowed were relatively small, in large part because a college education was comparatively inexpensive, especially at public universities. From 1965 to 1978, the program was a modest one, issuing about $12 billion in total, or less than $1 billion a year. By the early 1990s, the program grew immodestly, jumping to $15 billion to $20 billion a year, and now it is over $50 billion a year, accounting for 59 percent of higher educational aid that the federal government provides, surpassing all grants and scholarships.

5   The reason that debt has increased so much and so quickly is that tuition and fees have increased, at roughly three times the rate of inflation. Tuition and fees have gone up from an average of $924 in 1976, when I first went to college, to $6,067 in 2002. The average encompasses all institutions, from community colleges to Ivies. At private universities, the average jumped from $3,051 to $22,686. In 1976, the tuition and fees at Ivies were about $4,000; now they are near $33,000. The more salient figure of tuition, fees, room, and board (though not including other expenses, such as books or travel to and from home) has gone up from an average of $2,275 in 1976, $3,101 in 1980, and $6,562 in 1990, to $12,111 in 2002. At the same rate, gasoline would now be about $6 a gallon and movies $30.

6   This increase has put a disproportionate burden on students and their families—hence loans. The median household income for a family of four was about $24,300 in 1980, $41,400 in 1990, and $54,200 in 2000.

In addition to the debt that students take on, there are few statistics on how much parents pay and how they pay it. It has become common for parents to finance college through home equity loans and home refinancing. Although it is difficult to measure these costs separately, paying for college no doubt forms part of the accelerating indebtedness of average American families.

Students used to say, "I'm working my way through college." Now   7
it would be impossible to do that unless you have superhuman powers. According to one set of statistics, during the 1960s, a student could work fifteen hours a week at minimum wage during the school term and forty in the summer and pay his or her public university education; at an Ivy or similar private school, the figure would have been about twenty hours a week during term. Now, one would have to work fifty-two hours a week all year long; at an Ivy League college, you would have to work 136 hours a week all year. Thus the need for loans as a supplement, even if a student is working and parents have saved.

The reason tuition has increased so precipitously is more compli-   8
cated. Sometimes politicians blame it on the inefficiency of academe, but most universities, especially state universities, have undergone retrenchment if not austerity measures for the past twenty years. Tuition has increased in large part because there is significantly less federal funding to states for education, and the states fund a far smaller percentage of tuition costs. In 1980, states funded nearly half of tuition costs; by 2000, they contributed only 32 percent. Universities have turned to a number of alternative sources to replace the lost funds, such as "technology transfers" and other "partnerships" with business and seemingly endless campaigns for donations; but the steadiest way, one replenished each fall like the harvest, is through tuition.

Although state legislators might flatter themselves on their belt-   9
tightening, this is a shell game that slides the cost elsewhere—from the public tax roll to individual students and their parents. This represents a shift in the idea of higher education from a public entitlement to a private service. The post–World War II idea, forged by people like James Bryant Conant, the president of Harvard and a major policy maker, held that the university should be a meritocratic institution, not just to provide opportunity to its students but to take advantage of the best and the brightest to build America. To that end, the designers of the postwar university kept tuitions low, opening the gates to record numbers of students, particularly from classes previously excluded. I have called this "the welfare state university" because it instantiated the policies and ethos of the postwar, liberal welfare state.

Now the paradigm for university funding is no longer a public enti-   10
tlement primarily offset by the state but a privatized service: citizens

have to pay a substantial portion of their own way. I call this the "post-welfare state university," because it carries out the policies and ethos of the neoconservative dismantling of the welfare state, from the "Reagan Revolution" through the Clinton "reform" up to the present draining of social services. The principle is that citizens should pay more directly for public services, and public services should be administered less through the state and more through private enterprise. The state's role is not to provide an alternative realm apart from the market but to grease the wheels of the market, subsidizing citizens to participate in it and businesses to provide social services. Loans carry out the logic of the post-welfare state because they reconfigure college funding not as an entitlement or grant but as self-payment (as with welfare, fostering "personal responsibility"), and not as a state service but a privatized service, administered by megabanks such as Citibank, as well as Sallie Mae and Nellie Mae, the original federal nonprofit lenders, although they have recently become independent for-profits. The state encourages participation in the market of higher education by subsidizing interest, like a startup business loan, but eschews dependence, as it leaves the principal to each citizen. You have to pull yourself up by your own bootstraps.

11   This also represents a shift in the idea of higher education from a social to an individual good. In the postwar years, higher education was conceived as a massive national mobilization, in part as a carry-over from the war ethos, in part as a legacy of the New Deal, and in part as a response to the cold war. It adopted a modified socialism, like a vaccine assimilating a weaker strain of communism in order to immunize against it. Although there was a liberal belief in the sanctity of the individual, the unifying aim was the social good: to produce the engineers, scientists, and even humanists who would strengthen the country. Now higher education is conceived almost entirely as a good for individuals: to get a better job and higher lifetime earnings. Those who attend university are construed as atomized individuals making a personal choice in the marketplace of education to maximize their economic potential. This is presumably a good for the social whole, all the atoms adding up to a more prosperous economy, but it is based on the conception of society as a market driven by individual competition rather than social cooperation, and it defines the social good as that which fosters a profitable market. Loans are a personal investment in one's market potential rather than a public investment in one's social potential. Like a business, each individual is a store of human capital, and higher education provides value-added.

12   This represents another shift in the idea of higher education, from youthful exemption to market conscription, which is also a shift in our

vision of the future and particularly in the hopes we share for our young. The traditional idea of education is based on social hope, providing an exemption from work and expense for the younger members of society so that they can explore their interests, develop their talents, and receive useful training, as well as become versed in citizenship—all this in the belief that society will benefit in the future. Society pays it forward. This obviously applies to elementary and secondary education (although given the voucher movement, it is no longer assured there, either), and it was extended to the university, particularly in the industrial era. The reasoning melds citizenship ideals and utilitarian purpose. The classical idea of the American university propounded by Thomas Jefferson holds that democratic participation requires education in democratic principles, so it is an obligation of a democracy to provide that education. (The argument relates to the concept of franchise: just as you should not have to pay a poll tax to vote, you should not have to pay to become a properly educated citizen capable of participating in democracy.) The utilitarian idea, propounded by Charles Eliot Norton in the late nineteenth century and James Conant in the mid-twentieth, holds that society should provide the advanced training necessary in an industrially and technologically sophisticated world. The welfare state university promulgated both ideal and utilitarian goals, providing inexpensive tuition and generous aid while undergoing a massive expansion of physical campuses. It offered its exemption not to abet the leisure of a new aristocracy (Conant's aim was to dislodge the entrenched aristocracy of Harvard); it presupposed the long-term social benefit of such an exemption, and indeed the GI Bill earned a return of seven to one for every dollar invested, a rate that would make any stockbroker turn green. It also aimed to create a strong civic culture. The new funding paradigm, by contrast, views the young not as a special group to be exempted or protected from the market but as fair game in the market. It extracts more work—like workfare instead of welfare—from students, both in the hours they clock while in school as well as in the deferred work entailed by their loans. Debt puts a sizable tariff on social hope.

Loans to provide emergency or supplemental aid are not necessar- 13 ily a bad arrangement. But as a major and mandatory source of current funding (most colleges, in their financial aid calculations, stipulate a sizable portion in loans), they are excessive if not draconian. Moreover, as currently instituted, they are more an entitlement for bankers than for students. The way they work for students is that the federal government pays the interest while the student is enrolled in college and for a short grace period after graduation, providing a modest "start-up" subsidy, as with a business loan, but no aid toward the actual principal or "investment." For lenders, the federal government insures the loans. In other words, banks bear no risk; federal loan programs provide a safety net for banks, not for students. Even by the standards of the most doctrinaire market believer, this is bad capitalism. The premise of money lending and investment, say for a home mortgage, is that interest is assessed and earned in proportion to risk. As a result of these policies, the banks have profited stunningly. Sallie Mae, the largest lender, returned the phenomenal profit rate of 37 percent in 2004. Something is wrong with this picture.

14   There is no similar safety net for students. Even if a person is in bankruptcy and absolved of all credit card and other loans, the one debt that cannot be forgone is student loans. This has created what the journalists David Lipsky and Alexander Abrams have called a generation of "indentured students." We will not know the full effects of this system for at least twenty years, although one can reasonably predict it will not have the salutary effects that the GI Bill had. Or, simply, students from less privileged classes will not go to college. According to current statistics, the bottom quarter of the wealthiest class of students is more likely to go to college than the top quarter of the least wealthy students. Opportunity for higher education is not equal.

15   Debt is not just a mode of financing but a mode of pedagogy. We tend to think of it as a necessary evil attached to higher education but extraneous to the aims of higher education. What if we were to see it as central to people's actual experience of college? What do we teach students when we usher them into the post-welfare state university?

16   There are a host of standard, if sometimes contradictory, rationales for higher education. On the more idealistic end of the spectrum, the traditional rationale is that we give students a broad grounding in humanistic knowledge in the Arnoldian credo, "the best that has been known and thought." A corollary is that they explore liberally across the band of disciplines (hence "liberal education" in a nonpolitical sense). A related rationale is that the university is a place where students can conduct self-exploration; although this sometimes seems to abet the "me culture" or "culture of narcissism" as opposed to the more stern idea of accumulating knowledge, it actually has its roots in Socrates's dictum to know oneself, and in many ways it was Cardinal John Henry Newman's primary aim in *The Idea of a University*. These rationales hold the university apart from the normal transactions of the world.

17   In the middle of the spectrum, another traditional rationale holds that higher education promotes a national culture; we teach the profundity of American or, more generally, Western, culture. A more progressive rationale might reject the nationalism of that aim and posit instead that higher education should teach a more expansive and inclusive

world culture but still maintain the principle of liberal learning. Both rationales maintain an idealistic strain educating citizens—but see the university as attached to the world rather than as a refuge from it. At the most worldly end of the spectrum, a common rationale holds that higher education provides professional skills and training. Although this utilitarian purpose opposes Newman's classic idea, it shares the fundamental premise that higher education exists to provide students with an exemption from the world of work and a head start before entering adult life. Almost every college and university in the United States announces these goals in its mission statement, stitching together idealistic, civic, and utilitarian purposes in a sometimes clashing but conjoined quilt.

The lessons of debt diverge from these traditional rationales. First, 18 debt teaches that higher education is a consumer service. It is a pay-as-you-go transaction, like any other consumer enterprise, subject to the business franchises attached to education. All the entities making up the present university multiplex reinforce this lesson, from the Starbucks kiosk in the library and the Burger King counter in the dining hall, to the Barnes & Noble bookstore and the pseudo-Golds Gym rec center as well as the banking kiosk (with the easy access Web page) so that they can pay for it all. We might tell students that the foremost purpose of higher education is self-searching or liberal learning, but their experience tells them differently.

Second, debt teaches career choices. It teaches that it would be a 19 poor choice to wait on tables while writing a novel or become an elementary school teacher at $24,000 or join the Peace Corps. It rules out culture industries such as publishing or theater or art galleries that pay notoriously little or nonprofits like community radio or a women's shelter. The more rational choice is to work for a big corporation or go to law school. Nellie Mae, one of the major lenders, discounted the effect of loans on such choices, reporting that "Only 17 percent of borrowers said student loans had a significant impact on their career plans." It concluded, "The effect of student loans on career plans remains small." This is a dubious conclusion, as 17 percent on any statistical survey is not negligible. The survey is flawed because it assessed students' responses at graduation, before they actually had to get jobs and pay the loans, or simply when they saw things optimistically. Finally, it is fundamentally skewed because it assumes that students decide on career plans tabula rasa. Most likely, many students have already recognized the situation they face and adapted their career plans accordingly. The best evidence for this is the warp in majors toward business. Many bemoan the fact that the liberal arts have faded as undergraduate majors, while business majors have nearly tripled, from about 8 percent before the Second World War to 22 percent now. This is not because students no longer care about poetry or philosophy. Rather, they have learned the lesson of the world in front of them and chosen according to its, and their, constraints.

20   Third, debt teaches a worldview. Following up on the way that advertising indoctrinates children into the market, as Juliet Schor shows in *Born to Buy,* student loans directly conscript college students. Debt teaches that the primary ordering principle of the world is the capitalist market, and that the market is natural, inevitable, and implacable. There is no realm of human life anterior to the market; ideas, knowledge, and even sex (which is a significant part of the social education of college students) simply form sub-markets. Debt teaches that democracy is a market; freedom is the ability to make choices from all the shelves. And the market is a good: it promotes better products through competition rather than aimless leisure; and it is fair because, like a casino, the rules are clear, and anyone—black, green, or white—can lay down chips. It is unfortunate if you don't have many chips to lay down, but the house will spot you some, and having chips is a matter of the luck of the social draw. There is a certain impermeability to the idea of the market: you can fault social arrangements, but whom do you fault for luck?

21   Fourth, debt teaches civic lessons. It teaches that the state's role is to augment commerce, abetting consuming, which spurs producing; its role is not to interfere with the market, except to catalyze it. Debt teaches that the social contract is an obligation to the institutions of capital, which in turn give you all of the products on the shelves. It also teaches the relation of public and private. Each citizen is a private subscriber to public services and should pay his or her own way; social entitlements such as welfare promote laziness rather than the proper competitive spirit. Debt is the civic version of tough love.

22   Fifth, debt teaches the worth of a person. Worth is measured not according to a humanistic conception of character, cultivation of intellect and taste, or knowledge of the liberal arts, but according to one's financial potential. Education provides value-added to the individual so serviced, in a simple equation: you are how much you can make, minus how much you owe. Debt teaches that the disparities of wealth are an issue of the individual, rather than society; debt is your free choice.

23   Last, debt teaches a specific sensibility. It inculcates what Barbara Ehrenreich calls "the fear of falling," which she defines as the quintessential attitude of members of the professional middle class who attain their standing through educational credentials rather than wealth. It inducts students into the realm of stress, worry, and pressure, reinforced with each monthly payment for the next fifteen years.

If you believe in the social hope of the young, the present system of student debt is wrong. And if you look at the productivity statistics of the college-educated World War II generation, it is counterproductive. We should therefore advocate the abolition of student debt. Despite Nellie Mae's bruiting the high rate of satisfaction, a number of universities, including Princeton and UNC-Chapel Hill, have recognized the untenable prospect of student debt and now stipulate aid without loans. This is a step in the right direction. It should be the official policy of every university to forgo loans, except on an emergency basis. And it should be the policy of the federal government to convert all loan funds more than $50 billion to direct aid, such as Pell Grants.

Even if this can only be enacted in the long term, a short-term solution should be to retain the basic structure of student loans but to shift to direct lending administered from the federal government to colleges (which university administrators preferred, but bank lobbies overrode several years ago) or to regulate and reduce the interest rates. If banks still process loans, the loans are funded by the federal government, and the banks take no risk, then they should only receive a 1 percent or 2 percent administrative surcharge, such as charge card companies extract from businesses when processing a payment. If Sallie Mae makes a 37 percent profit on a public service, then it is no better than war profiteers who drain money from public coffers for a necessary service, and it should pay it back. Or there should be a national, nonprofit education foundation that operates at margin and administers the loans without profit.

A more far-ranging solution is free tuition. Adolph Reed, as part of a campaign of the Labor Party for "Free Higher Ed," has made the seemingly Utopian but actually practical proposal of free tuition for all qualified college students. If education is a social good, he reasons, then we should support it; it produced great benefits, financial as well as civic, under the GI Bill (see his "A GI Bill for Everyone," *Dissent*, Fall 2001); and, given current spending on loan programs, it is not out of reach. He estimates that free tuition at public institutions would cost $30 billion to $50 billion a year, only a small portion of the military budget. In fact, it would save money by cutting out the middle stratum of banking. The brilliance of this proposal is that it applies to anyone, rich or poor, so that it realizes the principle of equal opportunity but avoids "class warfare."

Another idea that I have proposed is for programs oriented toward loan abatements or forgiveness. These would help those in Generations X or Y who are already under the weight of debt. My proposal takes a few pages from European models of national service, programs such as AmeriCorps (but expanded and better funded), and throwbacks such as the Works Progress Administration. Such a proposal would also require federal funding, though it could be administered on the state or federal level. It would call for a set term of, say, two or three years of service in exchange for a fair if modest salary and forgiveness of a significant portion of education loans per year in service.

28   Several existing programs could be expanded. One is a very successful undergraduate program—the North Carolina Teaching Fellows Program—which carries a generous scholarship as well as other "enrichments" designed to recruit some of the better but usually less wealthy high school students into teaching. It requires that students teach in less privileged school districts, often rural or sometimes inner city, for a term of three or four years after graduation. On the postgraduate level, there are similar programs designed to bring doctors to rural or impoverished areas that lack them by subsidizing medical school training in exchange for a term of service. This program could extend to the Ph.D. level, helping to remedy graduate indebtedness as well as the academic job crisis in which there are too few decent jobs for graduates. A Ph.D. in literature or history, for instance, could be sent to community colleges or high schools to consult on programs and teach upgrade courses for veteran teachers on recent developments in scholarship or special courses to students. We should build a system of National Teaching Fellows who would teach and consult in areas where access to higher education has been limited.

29   Such a program would have obvious benefits for students, giving them a way to shed the draconian weight of debt, as well as giving them experience beyond school and, more intangibly, a sense of pride in public service. As a side effect, it would likely foster a sense of solidarity, as the national service of the World War II generation did for soldiers from varied walks of life, or as required national service does in some European countries. The program would put academic expertise to a wider public use, reaching those in remote or impoverished areas. As a side effect, it would foster a better image of academe, through face-to-face contact. Just as law-and-order political candidates promise more police on the streets, we should be pressuring political candidates for more teachers in our classrooms and thus smaller class sizes, from preschool to university.

30   These proposals might seem far-fetched, but a few short years before they were enacted, programs like the Works Progress Administration, Social Security, the GI Bill, or the Peace Corps, also seemed far-fetched. There is a maxim, attributed to Dostoyevsky, that you can judge the state of a civilization from its prisons. You can also judge the state of a civilization from its schools—or, more generally, from how it treats its young as they enter the full franchise of adult life.

Encumbering our young with mortgages on their futures augurs a return of debtors' prisons. Student debt impedes a full franchise in American life, so we must begin the debate about how to restore the democratic promise of education.

Reflection and Discussion

1. Look at the first eight paragraphs of this essay. What things has Williams done to orient you as a reader? What is his thesis?
2. Why are you in college? How does the cost of college affect your choice of courses and career?

Writing Matters

1. What have you learned from the pedagogy of debt? Review Williams' points and explain which have affected you, citing specific examples from your life. If you do not think that you yourself are affected, describe how this pedagogy affects people you know.
2. Consider Williams' suggestion of free tuition. In the past, some state colleges had free tuition, but the courses were so tough that more than half of freshmen dropped out after the first semester. Should the state provide unlimited free education for everyone, regardless of ability or commitment?

An Alert to the Dangers of Student Debt: The Student Debt Initiative

Michelle Singletary, *Washington Post,* November 17, 2005

Michelle Singletary specializes in personal finance, writing "The Color of Money" column and appearing weekly on the National Public Radio program "Day to Day."

How much do you expect to pay to complete your education? How much will you owe when you graduate?

In a recent report, the nonprofit College Board says we all need to keep 1
the rising cost of college in perspective. Yes, the cost of getting a higher education continues to escalate, the board says. But college still remains an "affordable choice for most families."

Oh, really. "Affordable?" Interesting perspective, because many 2
students have a different view. Take Jessa Coughlin, for example. She attends the University of Wyoming and expects to graduate in 2007 with a degree in elementary education. Coughlin wants to be a teacher.

But I wonder if she will ultimately choose to teach when faced with the $40,000 in student loans she has to pay back once she graduates. Nicole Lamarche is 26 and a graduate of the University of Arizona. She finished graduate school in May, earning a master of divinity at the Pacific School of Religion. Lamarche has a little more than $33,000 in student loans. "I suspect that it will end up meaning that I won't be able to think about buying a home anytime soon," she said. Then there is Thomas Dillon, a sophomore at the University of Connecticut. Dillon is studying to be a pharmacist. The price tag for his six-year program: more than $150,000. Certainly pharmacists make good money, but Dillon said he expects to spend the first 20 years of his working career paying down that debt.

3   All these students have an upfront view of what it costs to attend college. That's why they've chosen to become part of a new initiative in which students are encouraged to chronicle their experiences of paying for college on credit. The student Public Interest Research Groups and several state student associations have launched the Student Debt Alert Project, a virtual college yearbook where the questions aren't the typical ones about who is the class clown or the most popular student. It asks: "Why do you think students should not graduate with so much debt?" College students from around the country can sign on to the website www.studentdebtalert.org and share their debt stories. The Web-based yearbook already includes photos and personal stories from 500 students from 10 college campuses. "This campaign will enable students to be heard on the impact of their debt," said Christine Lindstrom, higher education program director for the student PIRGs, state-based groups that advocate for students.

4   Tuition costs loom over students and their decisions for years after they graduate, Lindstrom said. Clay Cunningham, a senior at the University of Wyoming who wants to be a counselor, wrote this: "When I graduate, I will have gone to school for six years in order to make $30,000 per year. I will not make enough money to buy a house and pay off my student debt." Nearly 39 percent of student borrowers graduate with unmanageable levels of federal student loan debt. The average student loan burden has increased by 60 percent in just seven years, Lindstrom said.

5   But keep this in perspective, the College Board says: About 60 percent of students attending four-year schools pay less than $6,000 a year for tuition and fees. That may be affordable for many. However, what if you have to borrow most of that $6,000 every year for four or five years? (And keep in mind that the $6,000 doesn't include housing.) The fact is, the number of students who graduate with more than $25,000 in loan debt has tripled since the early 1990s, Lindstrom notes. "There has

got to be a way to pay for college that doesn't plunge graduates into decades of debt," she said.

By collecting real stories from students and graduates in the online 6 yearbook, project organizers hope to begin a national dialogue on campuses across the country about the increasing use of loans to pay for college. "I'm angry and kind of stuck," said Casey Thomas, a junior majoring in social thought and political economics and history at the University of Massachusetts. Casey did what she could to reduce the amount of loans by opting to attend community college first. Still, Thomas, who wants to teach high school, said she will graduate with more than $20,000 in student loans.

This student debt initiative couldn't have come at a better time. 7 Congress is poised to make changes in the federal student loan program that will make it more costly for students and their parents to borrow for college. The single largest source of deficit-reducing savings in pending budget plans comes from higher interest rates, higher fees and other structural changes in the federal student loan program, according to a report by the New American Foundation, an independent public policy institute. "If we really want education to be accessible for everyone, our priority for funding should mirror that," Lamarche said.

I hope that every college student or graduate who has to pay for 8 their education with loans will log on to StudentDebtAlert.org and give their perspective of what it's like to face decades of debt. I also hope that those with the power to make a difference read the entries from the students. After all, it is really their perspective that counts.

Reflection and Discussion

1. How do you feel about the cost of college and the debt it is costing your generation? Have you considered taking action?
2. Singletary notes that almost two out of every five students graduate with "unmanageable levels of federal student loan debt." What does "unmanageable debt" mean to you?

Writing Matters

1. Nicole Lamarche, a divinity student, said, "If we really want education to be accessible for everyone, our priority for funding should mirror that." What are your thoughts on her assertion that we as a society should make education equally accessible to all? In what ways do student loans provide this accessibility? How do they fall short?
2. Go to the Student Debt Alert Project at www.studentdebtalert.org and read the entries from your school and neighboring schools. Write a similar

profile of your own, providing details of your current non-academic responsibilities, career plans and the effect student loans will have on you and your classmates in the future.

MAKING CONNECTIONS

1. Judging from the readings and other research you may do, are college students better off with or without credit cards? Evaluate the effect of credit cards on the individual students and the economy as whole for both the short and long term. How important is spending in keeping the American economy going? Does the growing national debt concern you?

2. Who is at fault when students fall into debt? The finance companies who offer students credit cards when they are too young, at high interest rates with complex terms? The lobbyists and politicians who deregulated the industry? The students themselves, who are legally adults but act irresponsibly? The current system of financial aid, which often leaves students deeply in debt before they start their careers? Or the schools themselves for inflating tuition and fees? To support your answer, you may wish to do additional research, for example, looking into how education is financed in other countries.

3. While many high schools offer instruction in personal finance, often students find that they still are not prepared for the economic challenges of college. Describe your own financial education, both formal and informal. What has helped you most in managing your money? What kind of training should high school students receive to prepare them for financial independence? Who should be responsible for this training?

4. Much student debt comes from discretionary spending. Students may choose more expensive schools, pricey spring break trips, clothing, and entertainment like their friends. Some schools put money into fancy recreation centers and amenities usually found only in better hotels. Look around your school and identify what could be eliminated or changed in order to make college more affordable.

5. Discuss the long-term implications of the current level of student debt, considering such factors as its effect on career choices, equal access to education, America's competitiveness in the world market. What does this say about us as a society?

TAKING ACTION

Research and analyze the way your school helps students become financially responsible. Are credit card marketers allowed on campus? If so, what restrictions are put on them? Are their tactics ethical? How much money, if any, does your school get from financial institutions, and how is that money used? Are there seminars or workshops promoting financial literacy? What do they cover and who organizes them? What suggestions would you make to regulate credit card marketers and promote financial literacy and responsibility?

Prepare a proposal to submit to your student government for action. Describe the strengths and weaknesses of what is currently offered and recommend improvements and additions. You should back up your plan with examples of programs that work and explain how any new programs will be paid for.

Digital Distractions

They're everywhere—cell phones, MP3 players, handheld games, laptops, PDAs, in-car navigation systems—electronic devices designed to keep us happy, informed, productive and connected. But a growing number of people are questioning the usefulness of these electronic companions, and some are giving up on them entirely, turning off their cells, replacing Palm organizers with index cards. What are the unintended effects of these technological aids on the individuals who use them, their family and friends and society as a whole? Which tools help students? Which get in the way? What rules, if any, do we need to adopt if we are to use them in a civil and effective manner?

BEFORE YOU READ

Which of the devices listed above do you have? Do you have others, not on the list? Which is your favorite? How has it changed your life? What devices, if any, have you abandoned? For what reasons?

FIGURE 2.1 Studying, but what?

The Multitasking Generation

Claudia Wallis, *Time,* March 27, 2006

Claudia Wallis is editor-at-large for Time, *specializing in health, science, education and issues affecting women and children. She has written and edited many cover stories for* Time, *winning national awards for her work on medical and educational topics.*

How do you differ from the rest of your family in the way you use technology?

It's 9:30 PM, and Stephen and Georgina Cox know exactly where their   1
children are. Well, their bodies, at least. Piers, 14, is holed up in his bedroom—eyes fixed on his computer screen—where he has been logged onto a MySpace chat room and AOL Instant Messenger (IM) for the past three hours. His twin sister Bronte is planted in the living room, having commandeered her dad's iMac—as usual. She, too, is busily IMing, while chatting on her cell phone and chipping away at homework.

By all standard space-time calculations, the four members of the   2
family occupy the same three-bedroom home in Van Nuys, CA, but psychologically each exists in his or her own little universe. Georgina, 51, who works for a display-cabinet maker, is tidying up the living room as Bronte works, not that her daughter notices. Stephen, 49, who juggles jobs as a squash coach, fitness trainer, event planner and head of a cancer charity he founded, has wolfed down his dinner alone in the kitchen, having missed supper with the kids. He, too, typically spends the evening on his cell phone and returning e-mails—when he can nudge Bronte off the computer. "One gets obsessed with one's gadgets," he concedes.

Zooming in on Piers' screen gives a pretty good indication of   3
what's on his hyperkinetic mind. OK, there's a Google Images window open, where he's chasing down pictures of Keira Knightley. Good ones get added to a snazzy Windows Media Player slide show that serves as his personal e-shrine to the actress. Several IM windows are also open, revealing such penetrating conversations as this one with a MySpace pal:

MySpacer: suuuuuup!!! (Translation: What's up?)
Piers: wat up dude

MySpacer:	nmu (Not much. You?)
Piers:	same

4   Naturally, iTunes is open, and Piers is blasting a mix of Queen, AC/DC, classic rock and hip-hop. Somewhere on the screen there's a Word file, in which Piers is writing an essay for English class. "I usually finish my homework at school," he explains to a visitor, "but if not, I pop a book open on my lap in my room, and while the computer is loading, I'll do a problem or write a sentence. Then, while mail is loading, I do more. I get it done a little bit at a time."

5   Bronte has the same strategy. "You just multitask," she explains. "My parents always tell me I can't do homework while listening to music, but they don't understand that it helps me concentrate." The twins also multitask when hanging with friends, which has its own etiquette. "When I talk to my best friend Eloy," says Piers, "he'll have one earpiece [of his iPod] in and one out." Says Bronte: "If a friend thinks she's not getting my full attention, I just make it very clear that she is, even though I'm also listening to music."

6   The Coxes are one of 32 families in the Los Angeles area participating in an intensive, four-year study of modern family life, led by anthropologist Elinor Ochs, director of UCLA's Center on Everyday Lives of Families. While the impact of multitasking gadgets was not her original focus, Ochs found it to be one of the most dramatic areas of change since she conducted a similar study 20 years ago. "I'm not certain how the children can monitor all those things at the same time, but I think it is pretty consequential for the structure of the family relationship," says Ochs, whose work on language, interaction and culture earned her a MacArthur "genius" grant.

7   One of the things Ochs' team of observers looks at is what happens at the end of the workday when parents and kids reunite—and what doesn't happen, as in the case of the Coxes. "We saw that when the working parent comes through the door, the other spouse and the kids are so absorbed by what they're doing that they don't give the arriving parent the time of day," says Ochs. The returning parent, generally the father, was greeted only about a third of the time, usually with a perfunctory "Hi." "About half the time the kids ignored him or didn't stop what they were doing, multitasking and monitoring their various electronic gadgets," she says. "We also saw how difficult it was for parents to penetrate the child's universe. We have so many videotapes of parents actually backing away, retreating from kids who are absorbed by whatever they're doing."

8   Human beings have always had a capacity to attend to several things at once. Mothers have done it since the hunter-gatherer

era—picking berries while suckling an infant, stirring the pot with one eye on the toddler. Nor is electronic multitasking entirely new: we've been driving while listening to car radios since they became popular in the 1930s. But there is no doubt that the phenomenon has reached a kind of warp speed in the era of Web-enabled computers, when it has become routine to conduct six IM conversations, watch *American Idol* on TV and Google the names of last season's finalists all at once.

That level of multiprocessing and interpersonal connectivity is 9 now so commonplace that it's easy to forget how quickly it came about. Fifteen years ago, most home computers weren't even linked to the Internet. In 1990 the majority of adolescents responding to a survey done by Donald Roberts, a professor of communication at Stanford, said the one medium they couldn't live without was a radio/CD player. How quaint. In a 2004 follow-up, the computer won hands down.

Today 82% of kids are online by the seventh grade, according to 10 the Pew Internet and American Life Project. And what they love about the computer, of course, is that it offers the radio/CD thing and so much more—games, movies, e-mail, IM, Google, MySpace. The big finding of a 2005 survey of Americans ages 8 to 18 by the Kaiser Family Foundation, co-authored by Roberts, is not that kids were spending a larger chunk of time using electronic media—that was holding steady at 6.5 hours a day (could it possibly get any bigger?)—but that they were packing more media exposure into that time: 8.5 hours' worth, thanks to "media multitasking"—listening to iTunes, watching a DVD and IMing friends all at the same time. Increasingly, the media-hungry members of Generation M, as Kaiser dubbed them, don't just sit down to watch a TV show with their friends or family. From a quarter to a third of them, according to the survey, say they simultaneously absorb some other medium "most of the time" while watching TV, listening to music, using the computer or even while reading.

Parents have watched this phenomenon unfold with a mixture of 11 awe and concern. The Coxes, for instance, are bowled over by their children's technical prowess. Piers repairs the family computers and DVD player. Bronte uses digital technology to compose elaborate photo collages and create a documentary of her father's ongoing treatment for cancer. And, says Georgina, "they both make these fancy PowerPoint presentations about what they want for Christmas." But both parents worry about the ways that kids' compulsive screen time is affecting their schoolwork and squeezing out family life. "We rarely have dinner together anymore," frets Stephen. "Everyone is in their own little world, and we don't get out together to have a social life."

12   Every generation of adults sees new technology—and the social changes it stirs—as a threat to the rightful order of things: Plato warned (correctly) that reading would be the downfall of oral tradition and memory. And every generation of teenagers embraces the freedoms and possibilities wrought by technology in ways that shock the elders: just think about what the automobile did for dating.

13   As for multitasking devices, social scientists and educators are just beginning to assess their impact, but the researchers already have some strong opinions. The mental habit of dividing one's attention into many small slices has significant implications for the way young people learn, reason, socialize, do creative work and understand the world. Although such habits may prepare kids for today's frenzied workplace, many cognitive scientists are positively alarmed by the trend. "Kids that are instant messaging while doing homework, playing games online and watching TV, I predict, aren't going to do well in the long run," says Jordan Grafman, chief of the cognitive neuroscience section at the National Institute of Neurological Disorders and Stroke (NINDS). Decades of research (not to mention common sense) indicate that the quality of one's output and depth of thought deteriorate as one attends to ever more tasks. Some are concerned about the disappearance of mental downtime to relax and reflect. Roberts notes Stanford students "can't go the few minutes between their 10 o'clock and 11 o'clock classes without talking on their cell phones. It seems to me that there's almost a discomfort with not being stimulated—a kind of 'I can't stand the silence.'"

14   Gen M's multitasking habits have social and psychological implications as well. If you're IMing four friends while watching *That '70s Show*, it's not the same as sitting on the couch with your buddies or your sisters and watching the show together. Or sharing a family meal across a table. Thousands of years of evolution created human physical communication—facial expressions, body language—that puts broadband to shame in its ability to convey meaning and create bonds. What happens, wonders UCLA's Ochs, as we replace side-by-side and eye-to-eye human connections with quick, disembodied e-exchanges? Those are critical issues not just for social scientists but for parents and teachers trying to understand—and do right by—Generation M.

Learning While Multitasking

Psychology professor Russell A. Poldrack of the University of California, Los Angeles, notes there are two different ways to learn:
- With **declarative learning,** we actively memorize information and can recall it as needed.
- When we are distracted, we learn by **habit** and may have more trouble accessing what we've learned.

If we learn a phone number by repeated use (habit learning), we may not be able to tell someone else the number without punching it out on a phone.

Source: "Multi-tasking Hinders Learning," *eSchool News*, 2006

Your Brain When It Multitasks

Although many aspects of the networked life remain scientifically 15 uncharted, there's substantial literature on how the brain handles multitasking. And basically, it doesn't. It may seem that a teenage girl is writing an instant message, burning a CD and telling her mother that she's doing homework—all at the same time—but what's really going on is a rapid toggling among tasks rather than simultaneous processing. "You're doing more than one thing, but you're ordering them and deciding which one to do at any one time," explains neuroscientist Grafman.

Then why can we so easily walk down the street while engrossed 16 in a deep conversation? Why can we chop onions while watching *Jeopardy*? "We, along with quite a few others, have been focused on exactly this question," says Hal Pashler, psychology professor at the University of California at San Diego. It turns out that very automatic actions or what researchers call "highly practiced skills," like walking or chopping an onion, can be easily done while thinking about other things, although the decision to add an extra onion to a recipe or change the direction in which you're walking is another matter. "It seems that action planning—figuring out what I want to say in response to a person's question or which way I want to steer the car—is usually, perhaps invariably, performed sequentially" or one task at a time, says Pashler. On the other hand, producing the actions you've decided on—moving your hand on the steering wheel, speaking the words you've formulated—can be performed "in parallel with planning some other action." Similarly, many aspects of perception—looking, listening, touching—can be performed in parallel with action planning and with movement.

17   The switching of attention from one task to another, the toggling action, occurs in a region right behind the forehead called Brodmann's Area 10 in the brain's anterior prefrontal cortex, according to a functional magnetic resonance imaging (fMRI) study by Grafman's team. Brodmann's Area 10 is part of the frontal lobes, which "are important for maintaining long-term goals and achieving them," Grafman explains. "The most anterior part allows you to leave something when it's incomplete and return to the same place and continue from there." This gives us a "form of multitasking," he says, though it's actually sequential processing. Because the prefrontal cortex is one of the last regions of the brain to mature and one of the first to decline with aging, young children do not multitask well, and neither do most adults over 60. New fMRI studies at Toronto's Rotman Research Institute suggest that as we get older, we have more trouble "turning down background thoughts when turning to a new task," says Rotman senior scientist and assistant director Cheryl Grady. "Younger adults are better at tuning out stuff when they want to," says Grady. "I'm in my 50s, and I know that I can't work and listen to music with lyrics; it was easier when I was younger."

18   But the ability to multiprocess has its limits, even among young adults. When people try to perform two or more related tasks either at the same time or alternating rapidly between them, errors go way up, and it takes far longer—often double the time or more—to get the jobs done than if they were done sequentially, says David E. Meyer, director of the Brain, Cognition and Action Laboratory at the University of Michigan: "The toll in terms of slowdown is extremely large—amazingly so." Meyer frequently tests Gen M students in his lab, and he sees no exception for them, despite their "mystique" as master multitaskers. "The bottom line is that you can't simultaneously be thinking about your tax return and reading an essay, just as you can't talk to yourself about two things at once," he says. "If a teenager is trying to have a conversation on an e-mail chat line while doing algebra, she'll suffer a decrease in efficiency, compared to if she just thought about algebra until she was done. People may think otherwise, but it's a myth. With such complicated tasks [you] will never, ever be able to overcome the inherent limitations in the brain for processing information during multitasking. It just can't be, any more than the best of all humans will ever be able to run a one-minute mile."

19   Other research shows the relationship between stimulation and performance forms a bell curve: a little stimulation—whether it's coffee or a blaring soundtrack—can boost performance, but too much is stressful and causes a fall-off. In addition, the brain needs rest and recovery time to consolidate thoughts and memories. Teenagers who

fill every quiet moment with a phone call or some kind of e-stimulation may not be getting that needed reprieve. Habitual multitasking may condition their brain to an overexcited state, making it difficult to focus even when they want to. "People lose the skill and the will to maintain concentration, and they get mental antsyness," says Meyer.

Is This Any Way To Learn?

Longtime professors at universities around the US have noticed that 20 Gen M kids arrive on campus with a different set of cognitive skills and habits than past generations. In lecture halls with wireless Internet access—now more than 40% of college classrooms, according to the Campus Computing Project—the compulsion to multitask can get out of hand. "People are going to lectures by some of the greatest minds, and they are doing their mail," says Sherry Turkle, professor of the social studies of science and technology at M.I.T. In her class, says Turkle, "I tell them this is not a place for e-mail, it's not a place to do online searches and not a place to set up IRC [Internet relay chat] channels in which to comment on the class. It's not going to help if there are parallel discussions about how boring it is. You've got to get people to participate in the world as it is."

Such concerns have, in fact, led a number of schools, including the 21 M.B.A. programs at UCLA and the University of Virginia, to look into blocking Internet access during lectures. "I tell my students not to treat me like TV," says University of Wisconsin professor Aaron Brower, who has been teaching social work for 20 years. "They have to think of me like a real person talking. I want to have them thinking about things we're talking about."

On the positive side, Gen M students tend to be extraordinarily 22 good at finding and manipulating information. And presumably because modern childhood tilts toward visual rather than print media, they are especially skilled at analyzing visual data and images, observes Claudia Koonz, professor of history at Duke University. A growing number of college professors are using film, audio clips and PowerPoint presentations to play to their students' strengths and capture their evanescent attention. It's a powerful way to teach history, says Koonz. "I love bringing media into the classroom, to be able to go to the website for Edward R. Murrow and hear his voice as he walked with the liberators of Buchenwald." Another adjustment to teaching Generation M: professors are assigning fewer full-length books and more excerpts and articles. (Koonz, however, was stunned when a student matter-of-factly informed her, "We don't read whole books anymore," after Koonz had assigned a 350-page volume. "And this is Duke!" she says.)

23   Many students make brilliant use of media in their work, embedding audio files and video clips in their presentations, but the habit of grazing among many data streams leaves telltale signs in their writing, according to some educators. "The breadth of their knowledge and their ability to find answers has just burgeoned," says Roberts of his students at Stanford, "but my impression is that their ability to write clear, focused and extended narratives has eroded somewhat." Says Koonz: "What I find is paragraphs that make sense internally, but don't necessarily follow a line of argument."

24   Koonz and Turkle believe that today's students are less tolerant of ambiguity than the students they taught in the past. "They demand clarity," says Koonz. They want identifiable good guys and bad guys, which she finds problematic in teaching complex topics like Hutu-Tutsi history in Rwanda. She also thinks there are political implications: "Their belief in the simple answer, put together in a visual way, is, I think, dangerous." Koonz thinks this aversion to complexity is directly related to multitasking: "It's as if they have too many windows open on their hard drive. In order to have a taste for sifting through different layers of truth, you have to stay with a topic and pursue it deeply, rather than go across the surface with your toolbar." She tries to encourage her students to find a quiet spot on campus to just think, cell phone off, laptop packed away.

Got 2 Go. Txt Me L8er

25 But turning down the noise isn't easy. By the time many kids get to college, their devices have become extensions of themselves, indispensable social accessories. "The minute the bell rings at most big public high schools, the first thing most kids do is reach into their bag and pick up their cell phone," observes Denise Clark Pope, lecturer at the Stanford School of Education, "never mind that the person [they're contacting] could be right down the hall."

26   Parents are mystified by this obsession with e-communication—particularly among younger adolescents who often can't wait to share the most mundane details of life. Dominique Jones, 12, of Los Angeles, likes to IM her friends before school to find out what they plan to wear. "You'll get IMs back that say things like 'Oh, my God, I'm wearing the same shoes!' After school we talk about what happened that day, what outfits we want to wear the next day."

27   Turkle, author of the recently reissued *The Second Self: Computers and the Human Spirit*, has an explanation for this breathless exchange of inanities. "There's an extraordinary fit between the medium and the moment, a heady, giddy fit in terms of social needs." The online

environment, she points out, "is less risky if you are lonely and afraid of intimacy, which is almost a definition of adolescence. Things get too hot, you log off, while in real time and space, you have consequences." Teen venues like MySpace, Xanga and Facebook—and the ways kids can personalize their IM personas—meet another teen need: the desire to experiment with identity. By changing their picture, their "away" message, their icon or list of favorite bands, kids can cycle through different personalities. "Online life is like an identity workshop," says Turkle, "and that's the job of adolescents—to experiment with identity."

All that is probably healthy, provided that parents set limits on 28 where their kids can venture online, teach them to exercise caution and regulate how much time they can spend with electronics in general. The problem is that most parents don't. According to the Kaiser survey, only 23% of seventh- to 12th-graders say their family has rules about computer activity; just 17% say they have restrictions on video-game time.

In the absence of rules, it's all too easy for kids to wander into 29 unwholesome neighborhoods on the Net and get caught up in the compulsive behavior that psychiatrist Edward Hallowell dubs "screensucking" in his new book, *CrazyBusy*. Patricia Wallace, a techno-psychologist who directs the Johns Hopkins Center for Talented Youth program, believes part of the allure of e-mail—for adults as well as teens—is similar to that of a slot machine. "You have intermittent, variable reinforcement," she explains. "You are not sure you are going to get a reward every time or how often you will, so you keep pulling that handle. Why else do people get up in the middle of the night to check their e-mail?"

Getting Them to Log Off

Many educators and psychologists say parents need to actively ensure 30 that their teenagers break free of compulsive engagement with screens and spend time in the physical company of human beings—a growing challenge not just because technology offers such a handy alternative but because so many kids lead highly scheduled lives that leave little time for old-fashioned socializing and family meals. Indeed, many teenagers and college students say overcommitted schedules drive much of their multitasking.

Just as important is for parents and educators to teach kids, prefer- 31 ably by example, that it's valuable, even essential, to occasionally slow down, unplug and take time to think about something for a while. David Levy, a professor at the University of Washington Information School, has found, to his surprise, that his most technophilic undergraduates—those majoring in "informatics"—are genuinely concerned about getting lost in the multitasking blur. In an informal poll of 60 students last semester, he says, the majority expressed concerns about how plugged-in they were and "the way it takes them away from other activities, including exercise, meals and sleep." Levy's students talked about difficulties concentrating and their efforts to break away, get into the outdoors and inside their head. "Although it wasn't a scientific survey," he says, "it was the first evidence I had that people in this age group are reflecting on these questions."

32   For all the hand wringing about Generation M, technology is not really the problem. "The problem," says Hallowell, "is what you are not doing if the electronic moment grows too large"—too large for the teenager and too large for those parents who are equally tethered to their gadgets. In that case, says Hallowell, "you are not having family dinner, you are not having conversations, you are not debating whether to go out with a boy who wants to have sex on the first date, you are not going on a family ski trip or taking time just to veg. It's not so much that the video game is going to rot your brain, it's what you are not doing that's going to rot your life."

33   Generation M has a lot to teach parents and teachers about what new technology can do. But it's up to grownups to show them what it can't do, and that there's life beyond the screen.

Reflection and Discussion

1. How have your experiences using technology as a learning tool shaped the way you want to learn at school, in traditional classrooms as well as in online courses? At the college level, should teachers be expected to entertain their students the way an educational DVD does?

2. A Kaiser Family Foundation study found that "one third of young people say they either talk on the phone, instant message, watch TV, listen to music or surf the Web for fun most of the time they're doing homework." Which of these activities has the greatest potential to help you study? Which is most likely to detract from your studies?

Writing Matters

1. Try this experiment: For one hour, in your usual study environment, keep track of time spent actually studying and the nature, number and length of interruptions. Then study one subject or read a book for an hour in a quiet place with no interruptions. Write a report describing your study environment, your experience and how it compares to students in the article.

r

2. College has traditionally been a place where people form lifelong friendships, often based on hundreds of hours of deep discussion, pondering the meaning of life. But electronically-mediated conversation is often superficial, "quick, disembodied." How might the reliance on electronic communication change the nature of college friendships?

The Next Step in Brain Evolution

Richard Woods, *Sunday Times,* London, July 9, 2006

Richard Woods writes for The Times of London *on a variety of subjects.*

How old were you when you started using a computer? A cell phone? Walkman or iPod?

Emily Feld is a native of a new planet. While the 20-year-old university   1
student may appear to live in London, she actually spends much of her time in another galaxy—out there, in the digital universe of websites, e-mails, text messages and mobile phone calls. The behavior of Feld and her generation, say experts, is being shaped by digital technology as never before, taking her boldly where no generation has gone before. It may even be the next step in evolution, transforming brains and the way we think. . . .

Emily [is] a "digital native," one who has never known a world   2
without instant communication. Her mother, Christine, on the other hand, is a "digital immigrant," still coming to terms with a culture ruled by the ring of a mobile and the zip of e-mails. Though 55-year-old Christine happily shops online and e-mails friends, at heart she's still in the old world. "Children today are multitasking left, right and center—downloading tracks, uploading photos, sending e-mails. It's nonstop," she says with bemusement. "They find sitting down and reading, even watching TV, too slow and boring. I can't imagine many kids indulging in one particular hobby, such as birdwatching, like they used to."

This generational divide has been evident for a while, but only   3
now is its impact becoming clear. Last month, Lord Saatchi, doyen of the advertising world, virtually declared the death of traditional advertising because digital technology is changing the way people absorb information. The digital native's brain is physically different as a result of the digital input it has received growing up, he claims. "It has rewired itself. It responds faster. It sifts out. It recalls less." Recall

rates for traditional television advertisements have plummeted. Instead, says Saatchi, companies must now be able to sum up their brands in a single word if they are to grab the attention of restless digital natives.

4   To some, a world flooded with endless info bits and constant stimuli is scary; to others, it is full of possibility and fascinating questions. Are digital natives charting a new course for human intelligence? And if so, is it better, faster, smarter? You don't have to take Saatchi's word for it: this phenomenon is acquiring scientific legs. And it isn't necessarily a trend from a dystopian sci-fi scenario. Many parents still fear that children who spend hours glued to computer screens will end up nerdy zombies with the attention span of a gnat. Cyberspace is full of junk, they worry, and computer games are packed with mindless violence. But it need not be like that, say some experts, and increasingly it isn't, as users exert more control and discrimination.

5   To evangelists of the digital age such as Marc Prensky, an American consultant and author, modern interactive computer games are "deep, complex experiences" that challenge the intellect far more than, say, passively watching *Big Brother*. Socializing through chat rooms and online forums, he argues, both requires its own etiquette and overcomes old prejudices: it doesn't matter nearly so much what you look like. The author Steven Johnson pursues a similar argument in his book *Everything Bad Is Good for You*. Far from popular culture dumbing down, he says, much of it has become more challenging; he points to the intricate, multi-layered plots of modern TV series such as *The Sopranos* or *24*, compared with the linear plots of programs 30 years ago.

6   This complexity is having an effect, say academics. "A few people have demonstrated that computer games can improve some aspects of attention, such as the ability to quickly count objects at the periphery of your vision," says Dr. Anders Sandberg, who is researching "cognitive enhancement" at Oxford University. "Is this a different way of thinking? Well, a little bit. Being instantly able to itemize objects is probably a useful skill in this world. Anecdotal evidence suggests people are becoming more visual than verbal. Some people are claiming that once computers gain good language understanding and you can speak to them, then reading and writing are going to seem cumbersome."

7   The sheer mass of visual, auditory and verbal information in the modern world is forcing digital natives to make choices that those who grew up with only books and television did not. "Younger people sift more and filter more," says Helen Petrie, a professor of human-computer

interaction at the University of York. "We have more information to deal with, and we pay less attention to particular bits of information, so it may appear attention spans are shorter." She also notes that the brevity of text messaging is spreading to e-mails and other communication, rewriting English with simpler spelling in the process. Though this may appear rude to traditionalists, it's merely sensible to digital natives in a wired world of dizzying speed. "But I don't think attention spans are diminishing per se," Petrie says. "If we find something that is engaging, then our attention span is just as long as it has always been. I bet you during the England-Sweden World Cup game people's attention span wasn't any shorter than it might have been before."

8 Studies by Pam Briggs, professor of applied cognitive psychology at Northumbria University, have shown that people surfing the web for health information often spend less than two seconds on a website before moving on. But this seems to be more a sign of incisive analysis than limited concentration. "We found that the sites people rejected within this very short timescale were generally not the kind of sites that would prove useful in the long term," she says.

9 The question, then, is how do digital natives learn to discriminate, and what determines the things that interest them? Parents who hope skills and boundaries are instilled at school may be fighting a losing battle. According to Prensky, the reason why some children today do not pay attention in school is that they find traditional teaching methods dull compared with their digital experiences.

10 Instead, parameters are increasingly set by "wiki-thinking," peer groups exchanging ideas through digital networks. Just as the online encyclopedia Wikipedia has been built from the collective knowledge of thousands of contributors, so digital natives draw on the experience and advice of online communities to shape their interests and boundaries. A telling symptom is blogging. Where once schoolchildren and students confided only in their diaries, now they write blogs or entries on MySpace.com—where anyone can see and comment on them.

11 Where is it all leading? Only one thing seems clear: changes propelled by the digital world are just beginning. Indeed, one of the markers between the natives and the immigrants—it's not simply a question of age—is the intuitive acceptance of rapid digital change.

12 "My parents are as [comfortable with] the Internet as I am," says Nathan Midgley of the TheFishCanSing research consultancy, "but what they are not used to doing is upgrading. They got the Internet seven years ago, but they bought it in the way you might have bought a TV 25 years ago: buy it and stick with it. People of my generation are much more used to the turnover of gadgetry. Other generations are left

out of the loop in the way it is speeding up." Faster broadband speeds, easier interfaces, smaller hardware—innovation is happening at such a pace that what was science fiction a few years ago is looming as fact. In experiments, human brain cells, for example, have already been linked directly to computers.

13   Andy Clark, a former director of cognitive science at Indiana University, believes we should already regard ourselves as cyborgs. Our thinking no longer goes on purely inside our heads, he contends; it is intimately bound up with the tools we use. He illustrates this with the example of people using software to trawl the web for news, music, information and goods personalized to their tastes. Where do the "thinking" and analysis stop? As the interfaces between people and computers become more sophisticated, he believes, "It will soon be harder than ever to tell where the human user stops and the rest of the world begins."

14   Will this lead to greater intelligence? Some might argue that is already happening. In what is known as the Flynn Effect, underlying IQ scores—before adjustments to keep the average steady—have been rising for years. Nobody is sure why this is so, though few believe it is simply because we are smarter.

15   "Otherwise you would have to conclude that people 100 years ago were all morons by our standards," says Nick Bostrom, director of the Future of Humanity Institute at Oxford University. Instead, the type of thinking we do may have changed. "It may be that there are certain kinds of abstract thinking that we get much more exposure to now, and that might simply make us better at taking IQ tests."

16   In the same way, Bostrom has no doubt that digital technology is influencing our mental processes. "Something as massive as our—for many people—daily interaction with computers and video players is bound to have a significant effect." Anecdotally, it seems a lot of natives in this digital culture are apt at multitasking, doing several things in parallel. But nobody knows exactly what that effect will be. "In a sense it is a grand-scale experiment we are running. We are raising a whole generation in this totally new environment—without any firm evidence of what will happen to them."

Reflection and Discussion

1. The title of this article suggests that brain functioning may actually be changing. Review the evidence given for this, paying particular attention to the qualifications of the experts cited. To what extent is the title supported?

2. What experience have you had with blogging? How would you compare it to keeping a private journal?

Writing Matters

1. Research the history of English spelling and past attempts to simplify it. Based on what you discover, write an essay predicting to what extent spelling may be changing in response to text-messaging and e-mails.
2. How effective is "'wiki-thinking'" compared to the traditional reliance on small groups of experts? Under what circumstances would you prefer each type of information source? Why?

The Techno-Flux Effect

Gary Rudman, *Brandweek,* April 3, 2006

Gary Rudman, president of GTR Consulting in San Francisco, specializes in market research on children and young adults. This article was adapted from the gTrend Report, an analysis of the relationship among teens, technology and society based on interviews of over 100 trendsetting adolescents.

If market researchers interviewed you to find new trends, how honest would your answers be?

Modern technology is reprogramming today's teenagers, who grew up playing with integrated circuits alongside their Legos. The pace at which new must-have technologies are being introduced into popular culture demands that teens upgrade their personal operating systems at a breakneck pace. This constant state of flux has driven some major behavioral shifts and some curious contradictions between what teens think and what they actually do, and has created a suite of unique neuroses.

Life Caching

To say teens think differently than adults isn't just an old adage; modern technology has literally changed the way teens' brains are wired. Memory is a prime example, as the amount of free storage and simple organizational utilities offered by companies like Google, Hotmail, Rediff and Yahoo! permit teens to engage in digital Life Caching. There's no need to commit anything to memory: They live as cybernetic organisms whose diaries, contact lists, social calendars and to-do lists are stored online or in their gadgets rather than in their head. This generation is exposed to more information than any other, yet they don't have the time, need or capacity to remember it all.

3   The onslaught of data, both internal and external, causes the brain to trade off in-depth memory storage for memory indexing—that is, the memory is not of the experience or knowledge itself, but rather the image or location of it. When the brain is trained to sort, process and outsource data instead of retain it, you get a generation of people who don't really know all that much; they just know where the answers can be found.

Brain Blur

4   The demand placed on the brain by modern technology is considerable. Teens might talk on the phone while instant messaging, watching TV, playing a video game and doing homework. As a result, they are rarely able to commit their full attention to any one of these activities, and they have difficulty focusing on one task alone. We call this phenomenon Brain Blur. Each new medium requires teens to manage another input, increasing the fragmentation of brain bandwidth. There's already the computer, the push-to-talk cell phone, the Sidekick, the home phone, instant messaging, e-mails, pagers, online communities, blogs and message boards.

5   Managing so much media makes being up-to-the-minute extraordinarily difficult and stressful, because the communication never stops. Teens will often type away to all hours of the morning just to ensure they're accumulating as much social currency as possible. This heightened, persistent state of multitasking is a defining element of the teenage consciousness.

Dataddiction

6   Information has rivaled nicotine as teens' drug of choice. In fact, they've become so dependent on the Internet as a source of stimulation they have trouble living without it. You might say they suffer from Dataddiction.

7   Yahoo! and OMD's Internet Deprivation Study, which involved 12 US-based families going without any kind of online access for two weeks (backed up by a survey among 1,000 online users), found that "regardless of age, household income or ethnic background, all participants in the ethnographic research study experienced withdrawal and feelings of loss, frustration, and disconnectedness when cut off from the online world." Furthermore, participants described their time offline as "having to resist temptation," missing their "private escape time" during the day and "feeling left out of the loop."

Chill-Challenged

Given the persistent stream of stimulation and information available 8
to them, most teens have grown up perpetually on the go. Few
moments are reserved for just sitting and thinking: their time is
always occupied by a stream of different activities. At home, they are
often multitasking in a Brain Blur and, when out, they live as
Technomads, playing games on their phones or PSPs, listening to their
MP3s, talking on the phone or doing all at the same time. These teens
are rarely disconnected from their gadgets, and when they are, they're
literally Chill-Challenged.

Even environments that have traditionally forced teens to "chill" 9
have changed dramatically. In the car with their parents, for instance,
teens are now often literally "plugged in" and "tuned out"—listening
to their MP3 players and/or headrest DVD players.

Deprived of their usual accessories, these teens often look and feel 10
lost, and tend to complain of being incredibly bored. As Judith Kidd,
associate dean of student life and activities at Harvard told the
Washington Post, "They don't know what to do with downtime. They
come to campus with day planners."

Implications

Living a life of constant engagement means teens are also living a life of 11
constant distraction. Any communication that intends to cut through
the multiple inputs calling for a teen's attention will have to be tighter,
faster and delivered in a more compelling style. Marketers must also
realize that teenagers—and the population at large—are looking for
distraction and places to plug in. They cannot stand being idle, and
marketers can capitalize on this.

As teens get older and deal with more technology and more 12
responsibilities, Brain Blur will increase, so they will look for ways to
distance themselves from the tornado of stresses in their life. Marketers
can work to develop strategies to help teens out of this crushing stress,
whether by developing appropriate messages, products or experiences,
or a combination of all three.

Reflection and Discussion

1. Rudman is a market researcher, writing for advertisers and other marketers. Review the article, looking for ways he sets the tone and appeals to
   his specific audience. What is he trying to accomplish in this article? How
   would it be different if he were writing to teens directly?

2. When do you use personal electronic devices (MP3 players, games)? How do these affect your relationships with your family and friends? Do they increase or decrease your ability to relax?

Writing Matters

1. How important is it to know things rather than to know where to find the information? Discuss what is gained and what is lost by each way of knowing.
2. Look up the Internet Deprivation Study online and analyze its findings. How much do people depend on the Internet because there really is no other way to perform everyday functions? How much dependency would seem to be psychological? How might this dependency have grown since the study was done in 2004?

Meet the Life Hackers

Clive Thompson, *New York Times,* October 16, 2005

Clive Thompson writes on science, technology and culture for a number of publications, including the New York Times Magazine, Wired, Discover, New York *magazine and* Wired News. *He regularly posts self-described weird discoveries on his blog, www.collisiondetection.net.*

How effective are your methods for tracking appointments and things to do?

1   In 2000, Gloria Mark was hired as a professor at the University of California at Irvine. Until then, she was working as a researcher, living a life of comparative peace. She would spend her days in her lab, enjoying the sense of serene focus that comes from immersing yourself for hours at a time in a single project. But when her faculty job began, that all ended. Mark would arrive at her desk in the morning, full of energy and ready to tackle her to-do list—only to suffer an endless stream of interruptions. No sooner had she started one task than a colleague would e-mail her with an urgent request; when she went to work on that, the phone would ring. At the end of the day, she had been so constantly distracted that she would have accomplished only a fraction of what she set out to do. "Madness," she thought. "I'm trying to do 30 things at once."

2   Lots of people complain that office multitasking drives them nuts. But Mark is a scientist of "human-computer interactions" who studies how high-tech devices affect our behavior, so she was able to do more

than complain: she set out to measure precisely how nuts we've all become. Beginning in 2004, she persuaded two West Coast high-tech firms to let her study their cubicle dwellers as they surfed the chaos of modern office life. One of her grad students, Victor Gonzalez, sat looking over the shoulder of various employees all day long, for a total of more than 1,000 hours. He noted how many times the employees were interrupted and how long each employee was able to work on any individual task.

When Mark crunched the data, a picture of 21st-century office 3 work emerged that was, she says, "far worse than I could ever have imagined." Each employee spent only 11 minutes on any given project before being interrupted and whisked off to do something else. What's more, each 11-minute project was itself fragmented into even shorter three-minute tasks, like answering e-mail messages, reading a Web page or working on a spreadsheet. And each time a worker was distracted from a task, it would take, on average, 25 minutes to return to that task. To perform an office job today, it seems, your attention must skip like a stone across water all day long, touching down only periodically.

Yet while interruptions are annoying, Mark's study also revealed 4 their flip side: they are often crucial to office work. Sure, the high-tech workers grumbled and moaned about disruptions, and they all claimed that they preferred to work in long, luxurious stretches. But they grudgingly admitted that many of their daily distractions were essential to their jobs. When someone forwards you an urgent e-mail message, it's often something you really do need to see; if a cell phone call breaks through while you're desperately trying to solve a problem, it might be the call that saves your hide. In the language of computer sociology, our jobs today are "interrupt driven." Distractions are not just a plague on our work—sometimes they are our work. To be cut off from other workers is to be cut off from everything.

For a small cadre of computer engineers and academics, this 5 realization has begun to raise an enticing possibility: perhaps we can find an ideal middle ground. If high-tech work distractions are inevitable, then maybe we can re-engineer them so we receive all of their benefits but few of their downsides. Is there such a thing as a perfect interruption?

Mary Czerwinski first confronted this question while working, 6 oddly enough, in outer space. She is one of the world's leading experts in interruption science, and she was hired in 1989 by Lockheed to help NASA design the information systems for the International Space Station. NASA had a problem: how do you deliver an interruption to a busy astronaut? On the space station, astronauts must attend to dozens of experiments while also monitoring the station's warning systems for potentially fatal mechanical errors. NASA wanted to ensure that its warnings were perfectly tuned to the human attention span: if a warning was too distracting, it could throw off the astronauts and cause them to mess up million-dollar experiments. But if the warnings were too subtle and unobtrusive, they might go unnoticed, which would be even worse. The NASA engineers needed something that would split the difference.

7   Czerwinski noticed that all the information the astronauts received came to them as plain text and numbers. She began experimenting with different types of interruptions and found that it was the style of delivery that was crucial. Hit an astronaut with a textual interruption, and he was likely to ignore it, because it would simply fade into the text-filled screens he was already staring at. Blast a horn and he would definitely notice it—but at the cost of jangling his nerves. Czerwinski proposed a third way: a visual graphic, like a pentagram whose sides changed color based on the type of problem at hand, a solution different enough from the screens of text to break through the clutter.

8   The science of interruptions began more than 100 years ago, with the emergence of telegraph operators—the first high-stress, time-sensitive information-technology jobs. Psychologists discovered that if someone spoke to a telegraph operator while he was keying a message, the operator was more likely to make errors; his cognition was scrambled by mentally "switching channels." Later, psychologists determined that whenever workers needed to focus on a job that required the monitoring of data, presentation was all-important. Using this knowledge, cockpits for fighter pilots were meticulously planned so that each dial and meter could be read at a glance.

9   Still, such issues seemed remote from the lives of everyday workers—even information workers—simply because everyday work did not require parsing screenfuls of information. In the 90s, this began to change, and change quickly. As they became ubiquitous in the workplace, computers, which had until then been little more than glorified word-processors and calculators, began to experience a rapid increase in speed and power. "Multitasking" was born; instead of simply working on one program for hours at a time, a computer user could work on several different ones simultaneously. Corporations seized on this as a way to squeeze more productivity out of each worker, and technology companies like Microsoft obliged them by transforming the computer into a hub for every conceivable office task, and laying on the available information with a trowel. The Internet accelerated this trend even further, since it turned the computer from a sealed box into our primary tool for communication. As a result, office denizens now stare at

computer screens of mind-boggling complexity, as they juggle messages, text documents, PowerPoint presentations, spreadsheets and Web browsers all at once. In the modern office we are all fighter pilots.

Information is no longer a scarce resource—attention is. David 10 Rose, a Cambridge, MA–based expert on computer interfaces, likes to point out that 20 years ago, an office worker had only two types of communication technology: a phone, which required an instant answer, and postal mail, which took days. "Now we have dozens of possibilities between those poles," Rose says. How fast are you supposed to reply to an e-mail message? Or an instant message? Computer-based interruptions fall into a sort of Heisenbergian uncertainty trap: it is difficult to know whether an e-mail message is worth interrupting your work for unless you open and read it—at which point you have, of course, interrupted yourself. Our software tools were essentially designed to compete with one another for our attention, like needy toddlers.

The upshot is something that Linda Stone, a software executive 11 who has worked for both Apple and Microsoft, calls "continuous partial attention": we are so busy keeping tabs on everything that we never focus on anything. This can actually be a positive feeling, inasmuch as the constant pinging makes us feel needed and desired. The reason many interruptions seem impossible to ignore is that they are about relationships—someone, or something, is calling out to us. It is why we have such complex emotions about the chaos of the modern office, feeling alternately drained by its demands and exhilarated when we successfully surf the flood.

"It makes us feel alive," Stone says. "It's what makes us feel impor- 12 tant. We just want to connect, connect, connect. But what happens when you take that to the extreme? You get overconnected." Sanity lies on the path down the center—if only there was some way to find it.

It is this middle path that Czerwinski and her generation of com- 13 puter scientists are now trying to divine. When I first met her in the corridors of Microsoft, she struck me as a strange person to be studying the art of focusing, because she seemed almost attention-deficit disordered herself: a 44-year-old with a pageboy haircut and the electric body language of a teenager. "I'm such a spaz," she said, as we went bounding down the hallways to the cafeteria for a "bio-break." When she ushered me into her office, it was a perfect Exhibit A of the go-go computer-driven life: she had not one but three enormous computer screens, festooned with perhaps 30 open windows—a bunch of e-mail messages, several instant messages and dozens of Web pages. Czerwinski says she regards 20 solid minutes of uninterrupted work as a major triumph; often she'll stay in her office for hours after work, crunching data, since that's the only time her outside distractions wane.

14   In 1997, Microsoft recruited Czerwinski to join Microsoft Research Labs, a special division of the firm where she and other eggheads would be allowed to conduct basic research into how computers affect human behavior. Czerwinski discovered that the computer industry was still strangely ignorant of how people really used their computers. Microsoft had sold tens of millions of copies of its software but had never closely studied its users' rhythms of work and interruption. How long did they linger on a single document? What interrupted them while they were working, and why?

15   To figure this out, she took a handful of volunteers and installed software on their computers that would virtually shadow them all day long, recording every mouse click. She discovered that computer users were as restless as hummingbirds. On average, they juggled eight different windows at the same time—a few e-mail messages, maybe a Web page or two and a PowerPoint document. More astonishing, they would spend barely 20 seconds looking at one window before flipping to another.

16   Why the constant shifting? In part it was because of the basic way that today's computers are laid out. A computer screen offers very little visual real estate. It is like working at a desk so small that you can look at only a single sheet of paper at a time. A Microsoft Word document can cover almost an entire screen. Once you begin multitasking, a computer desktop very quickly becomes buried in detritus.

17   This is part of the reason that, when someone is interrupted, it takes 25 minutes to cycle back to the original task. Once their work becomes buried beneath a screenful of interruptions, office workers appear to literally forget what task they were originally pursuing. We do not like to think we are this flighty: we might expect that if we are, say, busily filling out some forms and are suddenly distracted by a phone call, we would quickly return to finish the job. But we don't. Researchers find that 40 percent of the time, workers wander off in a new direction when an interruption ends, distracted by the technological equivalent of shiny objects. The central danger of interruptions, Czerwinski realized, is not really the interruption at all. It is the havoc they wreak with our short-term memory: What the heck was I just doing?

18   When Gloria Mark and Mary Czerwinski, working separately, looked at the desks of the people they were studying, they each noticed the same thing: Post-it notes. Workers would scrawl hieroglyphic reminders of the tasks they were supposed to be working on ("Test PB patch DAN's PC—Waiting for AL," was one that Mark found). Then

they would place them directly in their fields of vision, often in a halo around the edge of their computer screens. The Post-it notes were, in essence, a jury-rigged memory device, intended to rescue users from those moments of mental wandering.

For Mark and Czerwinski, these piecemeal efforts at coping 19 pointed to ways that our high-tech tools could be engineered to be less distracting. When Czerwinski walked around the Microsoft campus, she noticed that many people had attached two or three monitors to their computers. They placed their applications on different screens— the e-mail far off on the right side, a Web browser on the left and their main work project right in the middle—so that each application was "glanceable." When the ding on their e-mail program went off, they could quickly peek over at their in-boxes to see what had arrived.

The workers swore that this arrangement made them feel calmer. 20 But did more screen area actually help with cognition? To find out, Czerwinski's team conducted another experiment. The researchers took 15 volunteers, sat each one in front of a regular-size 15-inch monitor and had them complete a variety of tasks designed to challenge their powers of concentration—like a Web search, some cutting and pasting and memorizing a seven-digit phone number. Then the volunteers repeated these same tasks, this time using a computer with a massive 42-inch screen, as big as a plasma TV.

The results? On the bigger screen, people completed the tasks at 21 least 10 percent more quickly—and some as much as 44 percent more quickly. They were also more likely to remember the seven-digit number, which showed that the multitasking was clearly less taxing on their brains. Some of the volunteers were so enthralled with the huge screen that they begged to take it home. In two decades of research, Czerwinski had never seen a single tweak to a computer system so significantly improve a user's productivity. The clearer your screen, she found, the calmer your mind. So her group began devising tools that maximized screen space by grouping documents and programs together—making it possible to easily spy them out of the corner of your eye, ensuring that you would never forget them in the fog of your interruptions. Another experiment created a tiny round window that floats on one side of the screen; moving dots represent information you need to monitor, like the size of your in-box or an approaching meeting. It looks precisely like the radar screen in a military cockpit.

In late 2003, the technology writer Danny O'Brien decided he was 22 fed up with not getting enough done at work. So he sat down and made a list of 70 of the most "sickeningly overprolific" people he knew, most of whom were software engineers of one kind or another. O'Brien wrote a questionnaire asking them to explain how, precisely, they managed such awesome output. Over the next few weeks they e-mailed their replies, and one night O'Brien sat down at his dining-room table to look for clues. He was hoping that the self-described geeks all shared some common tricks.

23   He was correct. But their suggestions were surprisingly low-tech. None of them used complex technology to manage their to-do lists: no Palm Pilots, no day-planner software. Instead, they all preferred to find one extremely simple application and shove their entire lives into it. Some of O'Brien's correspondents said they opened up a single document in a word-processing program and used it as an extra brain, dumping in everything they needed to remember—addresses, to-do lists, birthdays—and then just searched through that file when they needed a piece of information. Others used e-mail—mailing themselves a reminder of every task, reasoning that their in-boxes were the one thing they were certain to look at all day long.

24   In essence, the geeks were approaching their frazzled high-tech lives as engineering problems—and they were not waiting for solutions to emerge from on high, from Microsoft or computer firms. Instead they ginned up a multitude of small-bore fixes to reduce the complexities of life, one at a time, in a rather Martha Stewart-esque fashion.

25   Many of O'Brien's correspondents, it turned out, were also devotees of "Getting Things Done," a system developed by David Allen, a personal-productivity guru who consults with Fortune 500 corporations and whose seminars fill Silicon Valley auditoriums with anxious worker bees. At the core of Allen's system is the very concept of memory that Mark and Czerwinski hit upon: unless the task you're doing is visible right in front of you, you will half-forget about it when you get distracted, and it will nag at you from your subconscious. Thus, as soon as you are interrupted, Allen says, you need either to quickly deal with the interruption or—if it's going to take longer than two minutes—to faithfully add the new task to your constantly updated to-do list. Once the interruption is over, you immediately check your to-do list and go back to whatever is at the top.

26   "David Allen essentially offers a program that you can run like software in your head and follow automatically," O'Brien explains. "If this happens, then do this. You behave like a robot, which of course really appeals to geeks."

27   O'Brien summed up his research in a speech called "Life Hacks," which he delivered in February 2004 at the O'Reilly Emerging Technology Conference. Five hundred conference-goers tried to cram into his session, desperate for tips on managing info chaos. When O'Brien repeated the talk the next year, it was mobbed again. By the

summer of 2005, the "life hacks" meme had turned into a full-fledged grass-roots movement. Dozens of "life hacking" websites now exist, where followers of the movement trade suggestions on how to reduce chaos. The ideas are often quite clever: O'Brien wrote for himself a program that, whenever he's surfing the Web, pops up a message every 10 minutes demanding to know whether he's procrastinating. It turns out that a certain amount of life-hacking is simply cultivating a monk-like ability to say no.

"In fairness, I think we bring some of this on ourselves," says Merlin 28 Mann, the founder of the popular life-hacking site 43folders.com. "We'd rather die than be bored for a few minutes, so we just surround ourselves with distractions. We've got 20,000 digital photos instead of 10 we treasure. We have more TV Tivo'd than we'll ever see." In the last year, Mann has embarked on a 12-step-like triage: he canceled his Netflix account, trimmed his instant-messaging "buddy list" so only close friends can contact him and set his e-mail program to bother him only once an hour. ("Unless you're working in a Korean missile silo, you don't need to check e-mail every two minutes," he argues.)

Mann's most famous hack emerged when he decided to ditch his 29 Palm Pilot and embrace a much simpler organizing style. He bought a deck of 3-by-5-inch index cards, clipped them together with a binder clip and dubbed it "The Hipster P.D.A."—an ultra-low-fi organizer, running on the oldest memory technology around: paper.

In the 1920s, the Russian scientist Bluma Zeigarnik performed an 30 experiment that illustrated an intriguing aspect of interruptions. She had several test subjects work on jigsaw puzzles, then interrupted them at various points. She found that the ones least likely to complete the task were those who had been disrupted at the beginning. Because they hadn't had time to become mentally invested in the task, they had trouble recovering from the distraction. In contrast, those who were interrupted toward the end of the task were more likely to stay on track.

Gloria Mark compares this to the way that people work when they 31 are "co-located"—sitting next to each other in cubicles—versus how they work when they are "distributed," each working from different locations and interacting online. She discovered that people in open-cubicle offices suffer more interruptions than those who work remotely. But they have better interruptions, because their co-workers have a social sense of what they are doing. When you work next to other people, they can sense whether you're deeply immersed, panicking or relatively free and ready to talk—and they interrupt you accordingly.

32   So why don't computers work this way? Instead of pinging us with e-mail and instant messages the second they arrive, our machines could store them up—to be delivered only at an optimum moment, when our brains are mostly relaxed.

33   One afternoon I drove across the Microsoft campus to visit a man who is trying to achieve precisely that: a computer that can read your mind. His name is Eric Horvitz, and he is one of Czerwinski's closest colleagues in the lab. For the last eight years, he has been building networks equipped with artificial intelligence (A.I.) that carefully observes a computer user's behavior and then tries to predict that sweet spot—the moment when the user will be mentally free and ready to be interrupted.

34   Horvitz booted the system up to show me how it works. He pointed to a series of bubbles on his screen, each representing one way the machine observes Horvitz's behavior. For example, it measures how long he's been typing or reading e-mail messages; it notices how long he spends in one program before shifting to another. Even more creepily, Horvitz told me, the A.I. program will—a little like HAL from *2001: A Space Odyssey*—eavesdrop on him with a microphone and spy on him using a Webcam, to try and determine how busy he is, and whether he has company in his office. Sure enough, at one point I peeked into the corner of Horvitz's computer screen and there was a little red indicator glowing.

35   "It's listening to us," Horvitz said with a grin. "The microphone's on."

36   It is no simple matter for a computer to recognize a user's "busy state," as it turns out, because everyone is busy in his own way. One programmer who works for Horvitz is busiest when he's silent and typing for extended periods, since that means he's furiously coding. But for a manager or executive, sitting quietly might actually be an indication of time being wasted; managers are more likely to be busy when they are talking or if PowerPoint is running.

37   In the early days of training Horvitz's A.I., you must clarify when you're most and least interruptible, so the machine can begin to pick up your personal patterns. But after a few days, the fun begins—because the machine takes over and, using what you've taught it, tries to predict your future behavior. Horvitz clicked an onscreen icon for "Paul," an employee working on a laptop in a meeting room down the hall. A little chart popped up. Paul, the A.I. program reported, was currently in between tasks—but it predicted that he would begin checking his e-mail within five minutes. Thus, Horvitz explained, right now would be a great time to e-mail him; you'd be likely to get a quick reply. If you wanted to pay him a visit, the program also predicted that—based on his previous patterns—Paul would be back in his office in 30 minutes.

With these sorts of artificial smarts, computer designers could re- 38
engineer our e-mail programs, our messaging and even our phones so
that each tool would work like a personal butler—tiptoeing around us
when things are hectic and barging in only when our crises have
passed. Horvitz's early prototypes offer an impressive glimpse of
what's possible. An e-mail program he produced seven years ago,
code-named Priorities, analyzes the content of your incoming e-mail
messages and ranks them based on the urgency of the message and
your relationship with the sender, then weighs that against how busy
you are. Super urgent mail is delivered right away; everything else
waits in a queue until you're no longer busy. When Czerwinski first
tried the program, it gave her as much as three hours of solid work
time before nagging her with a message. The software also determined,
to the surprise of at least one Microsoft employee, that e-mail missives
from Bill Gates were not necessarily urgent, since Gates tends to write
long, discursive notes for employees to meditate on.

This raises a possibility both amusing and disturbing: perhaps if 39
we gave artificial brains more control over our schedules, interruptions
would actually decline—because A.I. doesn't panic. We humans are
Pavlovian; even though we know we're just pumping ourselves full of
stress, we can't help frantically checking our e-mail the instant the bell
goes ding. But a machine can resist that temptation, because it thinks in
statistics. It knows that only an extremely rare message is so important
that we must read it right now.

So will Microsoft bring these calming technologies to our real- 40
world computers? "Could Microsoft do it?" asks David Gelernter, a
Yale professor and longtime critic of today's computers. "Yeah. But I
don't know if they're motivated by the lust for simplicity that you'd
need. They're more interested in piling more and more toys on you." . . .

Now that multitasking is driving us crazy, we treasure technolo- 41
gies that protect us. We love Google not because it brings us the entire
Web but because it filters it out, bringing us the one page we really
need. In our new age of overload, the winner is the technology that can
hold the world at bay. Yet the truth is that even Apple might not be up
to the task of building the ultimately serene computer. After all, even
the geekiest life hackers find they need to trick out their Apples with
duct-tape-like solutions; and even that sometimes isn't enough. Some
experts argue that the basic design of the computer needs to change: so
long as computers deliver information primarily through a monitor,
they have an inherent bottleneck—forcing us to squeeze the ocean of
our lives through a thin straw. David Rose, the Cambridge designer,
suspects that computers need to break away from the screen, delivering
information through glanceable sources in the world around us, the

way wall clocks tell us the time in an instant. For computers to become truly less interruptive, they might have to cease looking like computers. Until then, those Post-it notes on our monitors are probably here to stay.

Reflection and Discussion

1. Thompson is reporting research on office workers. How well does this information translate to your experience as a student? Which parts sound most familiar? Which seem alien?

2. Would you be willing to work in an environment where your work was being monitored by an artificial intelligence program? How might such a program help you be more productive? What might the downside be?

Writing Matters

1. Thompson includes a number of techniques for making workers more productive and calmer. Pick one of them—or one you find on a life hacking

FIGURE 2.2 Sometimes it's hard to keep your perspective when you're really involved in a call.

Source: © Guy & Rodd/Dist. by United Feature Syndicate, Inc.

website—and try it for a while and report on your experience. How well did it work for you? How difficult was it to stick with? Do you plan on continuing to use this technique?

2. Linda Stone says the constant interruptions "make us feel alive . . . important"; Merlin Mann believes, "We'd rather die than be bored." How much is technology to blame for our inability to focus? How serious is the problem, and what, if anything, can individuals do to get their focus back?

Just Too Much: Young Folks Burn Out on Online Sharing

Ellen Lee, *San Francisco Chronicle,* November 2, 2006

Ellen Lee writes about digital entertainment and technology culture for the San Francisco Chronicle. *For the sake of research, she listens to podcasts, watches homemade music videos online, plays Bejeweled on her cell phone, contributes to wikis and visits the occasional file-sharing sites. She is also the co-president of the Asian American Journalists Association's San Francisco Bay Area Chapter.*

How do you use social networking sites?

Aarica Caro is sick of sharing. That is, sharing online.   1

She has shared the lives of her cats. She has shared a list of her   2
favorite television shows and movies (*Grey's Anatomy,* chick flicks). She
has shared her reviews of Bay Area haunts (two stars for the Old
Spaghetti Factory in San Jose, five stars for the Starbucks in Morgan
Hill). And she has been invited to share some more.

If you believe the buzz, the latest incarnation of the Web is all about   3
sharing, connecting and community. Social networking sites such as
MySpace and Palo Alto's Facebook have exploded in popularity, drawing new users into the fold each day. Users create profiles about themselves, link to their friends and post photos, messages and updates about their daily lives. Like instant messaging and chat rooms before it, social networking has become a powerful way for people to communicate via the Web and another place for people to spend their time online.

But even as the phenomenon continues to swell, the effort to main-   4
tain an active social life on the Web is taking its toll. Some have grown
tired of what once was novel. Some feel bombarded by unsolicited
messages, friend requests and advertisements. And some are cutting
back. This suggests that as much as people want to connect through the
Internet, the practice also can have the opposite effect: social networking fatigue. "You join a lot, but you don't keep up," said Dave Taylor, a

44-year-old Internet marketing consultant who complained about having social networking fatigue on his blog after joining about 15 sites.

5   Social networking sites have steadily attracted more people this year, according to Nielsen/NetRatings. But between August and September, traffic to almost all popular social networking sites fell: MySpace's audience dropped from 49.2 million to 47.2 million; Facebook from 8.9 million to 7.8 million; Microsoft's Windows Live Spaces from 8.2 million to 7.8 million. Although those losses could be attributed to students returning to school, the decline also comes as an increasing number of sites compete for attention and the newness has begun to fade.

6   Last year, Caro, a 28-year-old escrow officer who lives in Morgan Hill, stopped writing about the adventures of her three cats on Catster. She didn't have the time. Though she has been invited to join other online communities such as Yahoo 360, she hasn't bothered to sign up. She said her MySpace page is enough. "It's getting pretty old," Caro said. "It makes no sense to have a million of those pages. I have one." Caro kept an online cat diary for six months and hooked up her cats with about 50 friends each. "At that point, I thought, 'Who cares?'" she said. "Who cares if my cats have friends?"

7   Her feelings highlight the challenge facing the social networking trend. Once someone has put together an elaborate profile online, connected with enough friends, found the love of her life, located old classmates and landed a job, what's next?

8   That depends. Teenagers and those in their 20s and 30s have been the early adopters, not just because they're Web-savvy but because they're at a time in their lives when they need to establish new ties, such as starting college, said Fred Stutzman, an Internet entrepreneur and graduate student at the University of North Carolina at Chapel Hill. "Social networking websites are relevant to people at different times in their lives," Stutzman said. "The more structure you have in your life, the less you need it as a crutch to understand the world around you. You already know what your friends are like. It's fun to look up their profile once in a while and check up on people, but it's not something you need every day." Yet even as one group outgrows it, another comes on board. "There's a whole generation, a younger subset, coming in," Stutzman said. "There is an exodus that goes on, but there are a ton of people just a couple of years younger who have those same needs."

9   Michigan State University Professor Nicole Ellison and her colleagues, who are studying how college students use Facebook, found that, without much effort, Facebook users could keep in touch with a wider network of casual acquaintances than those who didn't use it.

"Checking Facebook is routine," she said. "When they first get on the computer, they check their e-mail. They log on to instant messaging. They check their Facebook." Building a profile page also taps into the desire for self-expression. "They want to go out there and state their case and talk about their lives," said Roni Ruddell, a teen-marketing consultant.

Social networking took off in 2002 with Friendster. MySpace, 10 which has since reached critical mass and was acquired by News Corp. last year for $580 million, and Facebook, born out of a Harvard dorm room, followed. And in the past year, the space has turned into a packed, wall-to-wall party: SnowboardGang for snowboarders, Pearl Harbor Stories for survivors and their friends and family, Zebo for people who like to list what they own, even Hamsterster for hamster owners. Val Landi, co-founder of WiredBerries, a new site for women interested in health, predicts the next step will be networks splintering off by people's interests. "We're in the first-generation phase of social media," he said. "My sense is you're going to find more niche sites rather than these broad, general, catch-all platforms."

But success depends on whether members feel like their friends 11 and the people they want to meet use the same site. If not, they can move to a new one. When Friendster began experiencing technical problems and enforcing certain rules a few years ago, many members migrated to MySpace. In September, Facebook faced backlash after it introduced features that raised privacy concerns; the company responded and appeared to quell the uproar.

One in four who sign up for Catster, and its companion site 12 Dogster, become long-term members, said founder Ted Rheingold. But fostering an online community is more difficult than many entrepreneurs think, he said. "You can bring a person to a website, but you can't make them click" and interact, he said.

MySpace isn't immune, either. In recent months, Stephanie 13 Chow, a 15-year-old junior at Menlo School who used to spend hours on MySpace, has started to cut back. "It was fun doing it at the beginning," said Chow, who now prefers Facebook over MySpace. "But it started getting time consuming. I was changing my layout instead of doing my homework." She still maintains her MySpace page because not all her friends use Facebook. But the blinking advertisements on MySpace have become a turnoff, Chow said. Her complaint is echoed by those who fear that, as large corporations such as News Corp. and Google take over independent sites, they will strip away what made them attractive. "I just feel like it's becoming another way for companies to advertise their products," Chow said. "I just feel like I'm being used."

14   Her older sister, Tiffany Chow, a senior at Vassar who interned this summer at San Francisco's Six Apart, which runs the blogging site LiveJournal, also has curbed her use of MySpace and other sites. She has been a member, at one time or another, of MySpace, Facebook, Flickr, Vox, LiveJournal, deviantART, Mojizu, XuQa and Friendster. But she has canceled her account on Friendster and XuQa, and doesn't bother much with deviantART, Mojizu or MySpace. "Weird people started messaging me," Tiffany Chow said about MySpace. The messages came from people she didn't know, asking to be friends and making comments about her looks. "That's when I made a decision. For me the best way to use these social networking engines is to keep track of my friends and people I know."

15   That's not to say members are abandoning MySpace. On a weekly basis between September and October, comScore Media Metrix, an independent source for tracking Internet traffic, showed its audience going back up. "MySpace is an integral part of our members' lives," MySpace said in an e-mail response to questions. "There will always be anecdotes of people that love MySpace and people that don't, but we always like to rely on the numbers—both internal and third party—to show our continued, extraordinary growth. We are still experiencing enormous expansion domestically and abroad at an average rate of 320,000 worldwide new profiles added daily." MySpace is also evolving beyond social networking by offering song downloads, movie trailers and television shows such as *Prison Break.* "It's already so big that even if people start abandoning it, it's still attracting new people," said David Card, senior analyst at Jupiter Research.

16   So where to next? Six Apart is betting that as the MySpace generation grows up, they will want to be more discerning; MySpace profiles are public unless users designate them as private. On Vox, which Six Apart launched last week, users determine what their friends and family see. "I'm not sure MySpace is going to satisfy the needs of the next wave of your life," said Andrew Anker, executive vice president of Six Apart. "I'm not sure MySpace is the place where you want to post a picture of your kid."

17   The general expectation is that consumers ultimately will settle down with one or two social networks and that they will become a feature incorporated in more and more sites. YouTube, the popular online video-sharing site, and Flickr, an online photo-sharing site, for instance, include social networking. "I think it's been both overhyped and underestimated," Dogster's Rheingold said. Although some lofty expectations about how big of a business it could become won't pan out, "in the end it is going to be so much bigger than what people are seeing now."

Reflection and Discussion

1. How does Lee feel about social networking sites herself? Point to places in the article where she suggests her feelings.
2. In what ways do these sites change the meaning of the word *friendship*?

Writing Matters

1. Write a review of the profile a friend has posted on a social networking site. Examine it carefully with a fresh and objective eye, looking at both design and content. What kind of face is your friend putting out to the world? What are the values communicated? Who seems to be the intended audience? What impression does this profile give to potential employers? How might it affect your friend's job opportunities?
2. In addition to paid advertisements, some commercial enterprises set up false profiles as a means of viral marketing. How ethical is this? Do such commercial transactions represent the true nature of these sites; that is, are they designed for real communication among friends or are they a means to promote oneself as a product?

Hooked on the Web: Help Is on the Way

Sarah Kershaw, *New York Times,* December 1, 2005

Sarah Kershaw reports on a wide range of subjects for the New York Times.

What experiences have you had with people who have been addicted to drugs or alcohol?

The waiting room for Hilarie Cash's practice has the look and feel of 1 many a therapist's office, with soothing classical music, paintings of gentle swans and colorful flowers and on the bookshelves stacks of brochures on how to get help. But along with her patients, Dr. Cash, who runs Internet/Computer Addiction Services here in the city that is home to Microsoft, is a pioneer in a growing niche in mental health care and addiction recovery. The patients, including Mike, 34, are what Dr. Cash and other mental health professionals call onlineaholics. They even have a diagnosis: Internet addiction disorder.

These specialists estimate that 6 percent to 10 percent of the 2 approximately 189 million Internet users in this country have a dependency that can be as destructive as alcoholism and drug addiction, and they are rushing to treat it. Yet some in the field remain skeptical that heavy use of the Internet qualifies as a legitimate addiction, and one academic expert called it a fad illness.

3   Skeptics argue that even obsessive Internet use does not exact the same toll on health or family life as conventionally recognized addictions. But, mental health professionals who support the diagnosis of Internet addiction say, a majority of obsessive users are online to further addictions to gambling or pornography or have become much more dependent on those vices because of their prevalence on the Internet. But other users have a broader dependency and spend hours online each day, surfing the Web, trading stocks, instant messaging or blogging, and a fast-rising number are becoming addicted to Internet video games. Dr. Cash and other professionals say that people who abuse the Internet are typically struggling with other problems, like depression and anxiety. But, they say, the Internet's omnipresent offer of escape from reality, affordability, accessibility and opportunity for anonymity can also lure otherwise healthy people into an addiction.

4   Dr. Cash's patient Mike, who was granted anonymity to protect his privacy, was at high risk for an Internet addiction, having battled alcohol and drug abuse and depression. On a list of 15 symptoms of Internet addiction used for diagnosis by Internet/Computer Addiction Services, Mike, who is unemployed and living with his mother, checked off 13, including intense cravings for the computer, lying about how much time he spends online, withdrawing from hobbies and social interactions, back pain and weight gain.

5   A growing number of therapists and inpatient rehabilitation centers are often treating Web addicts with the same approaches, including 12-step programs, used to treat chemical addictions. Because the condition is not recognized in psychiatry as a disorder, insurance companies do not reimburse for treatment. So patients either pay out of pocket, or therapists and treatment centers bill for other afflictions, including the nonspecific impulse control disorder. There is at least one inpatient program, at Proctor Hospital in Peoria, Ill., which admits patients to recover from obsessive computer use. Experts there said they see similar signs of withdrawal in those patients as in alcoholics or drug addicts, including profuse sweating, severe anxiety and paranoid symptoms.

6   And the prevalence of other technologies—like BlackBerry wireless e-mail devices, sometimes called CrackBerries because they are considered so addictive; the Treo cell phone-organizer; and text messaging—has created a more generalized technology addiction, said Rick Zehr, the vice president of addiction and behavioral services at Proctor Hospital. The hospital's treatment program places all its clients together for group therapy and other recovery work, whether the

addiction is to cocaine or the computer, Mr. Zehr said. "I can't imagine it's going to go away," he said of technology and Internet addiction. "I can only imagine it's going to continue to become more and more prevalent."

There are family therapy programs for Internet addicts, and inter- 7 ventionists who specialize in confronting computer addicts. Among the programs offered by the Center for Online Addiction in Bradford, PA, founded in 1994 by Dr. Kimberly S. Young, a leading researcher in Internet addiction, are cyberwidow support groups for the spouses of those having online affairs, treatment for addiction to eBay and intense behavioral counseling—in person, by telephone and online—to help clients get Web sober.

Another leading expert in the field is Dr. Maressa Hecht Orzack, 8 the director of the Computer Addiction Study Center at McLean Hospital in Belmont, MA, and an assistant professor at Harvard Medical School. She opened a clinic for Internet addicts at the hospital in 1996, when, she said, "everybody thought I was crazy." Dr. Orzack said she got the idea after she discovered she had become addicted to computer solitaire, procrastinating and losing sleep and time with her family. When she started the clinic, she saw two patients a week at most. Now she sees dozens and receives five or six calls daily from those seeking treatment elsewhere in the country. More and more of those calls, she said, are coming from people concerned about family members addicted to Internet video games like EverQuest, Doom 3 and World of Warcraft.

Still, there is little hard science available on Internet addiction. 9 "I think using the Internet in certain ways can be quite absorbing, but I don't know that it's any different from an addiction to playing the violin and bowling," said Sara Kiesler, professor of computer science and human-computer interaction at Carnegie Mellon University. "There is absolutely no evidence that spending time online, exchanging e-mail with family and friends, is the least bit harmful. We know that people who are depressed or anxious are likely to go online for escape and that doing so helps them."

It was Professor Kiesler who called Internet addiction a fad illness. 10 In her view, she said, television addiction is worse. She added that she was completing a study of heavy Internet users, which showed the majority had sharply reduced their time on the computer over the course of a year, indicating that even problematic use was self-corrective. She said calling it an addiction "demeans really serious illnesses, which are things like addiction to gambling, where you steal your family's money to pay for your gambling debts, drug addictions, cigarette addictions." She added, "These are physiological addictions."

11   But Dr. Cash, who began treating Internet addicts 10 years ago, said that Internet addiction was a potentially serious illness. She said she had treated suicidal patients who had lost jobs and whose marriages had been destroyed because of their addictions. She said she was seeing more patients like Mike, who acknowledges struggling with an addiction to online pornography but who also said he was obsessed with logging on to the Internet for other reasons. He said that he became obsessed with using the Internet during the 2000 presidential election and that now he feels anxious if he does not check several websites, mostly news and sports sites, daily.

12   "I'm still wrestling with the idea that it's a problem because I like it so much," Mike said. Three hours straight on the Internet, he said, is a minor dose. The Internet seemed to satisfy "whatever urge crosses my head."

13   Several counselors and other experts said time spent on the computer was not important in diagnosing an addiction to the Internet. The question, they say, is whether Internet use is causing serious problems, including the loss of a job, marital difficulties, depression, isolation and anxiety, and still the user cannot stop. "The line is drawn with Internet addiction," said Mr. Zehr of Proctor Hospital, "when I'm no longer controlling my Internet use. It's controlling me." Dr. Cash and other therapists say they are seeing a growing number of teenagers and young adults as patients, who grew up spending hours on the computer, playing games and sending instant messages. These patients appear to have significant developmental problems, including attention deficit disorder and a lack of social skills.

14   A report released during the summer by the Pew Internet and American Life Project found that teenagers did spend an increasing amount of time online: 51 percent of teenage Internet users are online daily, up from 42 percent in 2000. But the report did not find a withering of social skills. Most teenagers "maintain robust networks of friends," it noted.

15   Some therapists and Internet addiction treatment centers offer online counseling, including at least one 12-step program for video game addicts, which is controversial. Critics say that although it may be a way to catch the attention of someone who needs face-to-face treatment, it is akin to treating an alcoholic in a brewery, mostly because Internet addicts need to break the cycle of living in cyberspace.

16   A crucial difference between treating alcoholics and drug addicts, however, is that total abstinence is usually recommended for recovery from substance abuse, whereas moderate and manageable use is the goal for behavioral addictions. Sierra Tucson in Arizona, a psychiatric hospital and behavioral health center, which treats substance and behavioral addictions, has begun admitting a rising number of Internet

addicts, said Gina Ewing, its intake manager. Ms. Ewing said that when such a client left treatment, the center's counselors helped plan ways to reduce time on the computer or asked those who did not need to use the Web for work to step away from the computer entirely.

Ms. Ewing said the Tucson center encouraged its Internet-addicted 17 clients when they left treatment to attend open meetings of Alcoholics Anonymous or Narcotics Anonymous, which are not restricted to alcoholics and drug addicts, and simply to listen. Or perhaps, if they find others struggling with the same problem, and if those at the meeting are amenable, they might be able to participate. "It's breaking new ground," Ms. Ewing said. "But an addiction is an addiction."

Danger Signs for Too Much of a Good Thing

Fifteen signs of an addiction to using the Internet and computers, accord- 18 ing to Internet/Computer Addiction Services in Redmond, WA, follow:

- Inability to predict the amount of time spent on computer
- Failed attempts to control personal use for an extended period of time
- Having a sense of euphoria while on the computer
- Craving more computer time
- Neglecting family and friends
- Feeling restless, irritable and discontent when not on the computer
- Lying to employers and family about computer activity
- Problems with school or job performance as a result of time spent on the computer
- Feelings of guilt, shame, anxiety or depression as a result of time spent on the computer
- Changes in sleep patterns
- Health problems like carpal tunnel syndrome, eye strain, weight changes, backaches and chronic sleep deprivation
- Denying, rationalizing and minimizing adverse consequences stemming from computer use
- Withdrawal from real-life hobbies and social interactions
- Obsessing about sexual acting out through the use of the Internet
- Creation of enhanced personae to find cyberlove or cybersex

Reflection and Discussion

1. Have you ever felt that you were addicted to the Internet, an electronic device or game, or anything else? What did you do about it?

2. More and more schoolwork requires students to spend considerable time on computers, much of it on the Internet. To what extent might this trend contribute to Internet addiction? How might students (addicted or not) do their homework without getting lost in cyberspace?

Writing Matters

1. What is the effect of calling something an addiction? Review the article, supplementing it with research. Write an essay arguing for or against officially recognizing Internet addiction as a psychiatric disorder.
2. Cash and therapists like her say they are finding that young patients addicted to the Internet lack social skills and have attention deficit disorder. To what extent does Internet use cause these problems? To what extent might the Internet be a crutch for troubled individuals?

MAKING CONNECTIONS

1. Since the invention of the Walkman in 1979, people have moved from experiencing shared environments to taking their private environment with them wherever they go. But the Walkman and later tools also reflect another trend—the addiction to busyness, the reluctance to tolerate even minutes of inactivity or seconds of silence, the fear of being out of touch with family, friends and co-workers for any length of time. During that same quarter century, America has seen growing interest in religion, meditation and other contemplative practices which require individuals to be silent, separate and still for substantial periods of time. What relationship is there, if any, between these two trends? What will happen in the future? Will society move toward greater use of tools that privilege the user and remote contacts over those physically present? Will it return to pre-Walkman, pre-cell phone relationships or strike some sort of balance? As you discuss your prediction, be sure to analyze the values that reflect and result from the adoption or rejection of technology.
2. In the past, students might pass handwritten notes during a class, but now they use cell phones, laptops and PDAs to exchange comments and test answers. Even when they don't communicate with each other, some spend class time surfing the Web, e-mailing and working on other projects. Some instructors have responded by completely forbidding the use of these devices in class and imposing penalties for students who violate this rule. Discuss the appropriate use of these wireless devices in class and what penalties, if any, should be imposed on those who stray from these norms. Support your answers considering the effect of these devices on everyone in the classroom: classmates with similar equipment, students who may not be able to afford the equipment, and the instructor, who may feel students engaged in these other activities are really "absent."

3. Customers delay check-out lines (or even medical treatments) by taking cell phone calls. Some people play their music so loudly that it leaks through the headphones, disturbing their neighbors. These and other digital devices seem to often be associated with behavior that would traditionally be considered rude. Is this a new social norm? If not, how should we restore civility? Are sufferers required to speak up or should electronic etiquette classes be required? Discuss the effectiveness of this approach based on your own experiences. Why should we place the burden of politeness on the people being imposed on?

4. The framers of the United States Constitution designed a representative democracy in part because they believed that governing was too important to be left to the masses, yet advances in technology have ignited interest in direct governance, with every voter able to vote on every issue. Discuss the feasibility and wisdom of such a change. For what types of issues would it be appropriate?

5. The advent of inexpensive personal digital devices has given rise to the technology-mediated life—the people who record and/or narrate almost every aspect of their day. The tourist who calls home as he ascends the Eiffel Tower, raising the cell phone to capture and transmit a photo of the view. The woman who takes movies of every aspect of her child's life, staging them so that the video is perfect. What is lost and what is gained? Why do these tools seem so compelling?

TAKING ACTION

The articles in this chapter have highlighted some of the ways popular digital devices interfere with students' concentration. Create a pamphlet or website with advice on how your fellow students can study more effectively by changing the way they use technology. While you will need to back up your advice with support, remember to focus on practical tips presented in a way that will persuade your audience.

Chapter 3

Cyber U.—Education Online

Technology has changed all of our lives, but particularly our work in school. Rather than going to the library, we research almost everything online, with many of us going to hard-copy books as the last resort. We can check our spelling automatically, look up a word or a fact in an instant, e-mail or post a question to a professor or a peer, not worrying about matching up schedules for a face-to-face meeting. Students expect course materials to be online and may enroll in online courses and even degree programs that never meet in person. While enjoying the ease and freedom that computers offer, we need to explore how they change the relationship between student and teacher and challenge our definition of scholarship.

BEFORE YOU READ

Make a list of all the ways you use computers as you work toward your degree, including all your dealings with your school as well as your coursework. Imagine accomplishing these tasks without a computer. In what cases do computers make the work simpler, friendlier, surer? Which would be better to do without technology? When do you learn more doing things the hard way?

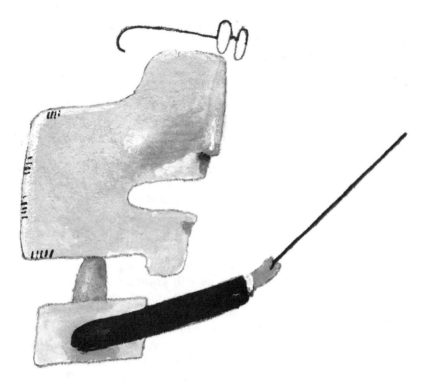

FIGURE 3.1 Who is the teacher for online classes?

School Away From School

Emily White, *New York Times Magazine,* December 7, 2003

Emily White is the author of the nonfiction book Fast Girls: Teenage Tribes and the Myth of the Slut.

What has been your worst time in school? Your best? What made them different?

Andy Markishtum's hair reaches past his shoulders, thick and shining. 1
He speaks in a low monotone, a rocker growl, and his favorite band is
Cradle of Filth. As a student at McKay High School in Salem, OR, Andy
was part of the stoner crowd—a self-described slacker with a backpack
full of half-finished assignments. "I'd get too distracted," he says.
"There would be kids sitting right next to me talking or something, and

instead of paying attention to the teacher, I would drift off. Someone would drop a book, and I'd have to look." Attention-deficit disorder was diagnosed; for a while, Andy took Ritalin, but it gave him migraines. His mom decided he needed to get out of McKay and leave behind his old scene, his old messed-up self. Andy enrolled in Salem-Keizer Online high school, and he says, "Now I can really concentrate."

2   Salem-Keizer Online, or S.K.O., is one in a growing number of public, private and charter schools available to kids who are looking for an alternative to a traditional education. Commonly called "virtual school," it's a way of attending school at home without the hovering claustrophobia of home-schooling. S.K.O. has 131 students enrolled in the Salem area. Nationwide, there were about 50,000 students in virtual courses last year. As a business, virtual school is booming. Jim Cramer, co-host of CNBC's *Kudlow & Cramer*, calls online-school-software companies a hot commodity.

3   Andy Markishtum says that without virtual school, he "probably would have dropped out." Now he will graduate almost on time. The biggest problem was that "too many people were too dumb." The teachers bored him, the homework flummoxed him, he hated the mandatory pep assemblies "that were really prep assemblies."

4   Walking through his old school, Andy points out the cafeteria table he and his friends used to sit at. "People would shun us, even though we had never done anything to them," he says. A sign reads "Drug and Gang Free: McKay Togetherness." The bell rings, and the hall floods with bodies. A few clean-cut kids grimace at Andy's flowing hair. It's not so hard to understand why Andy would want to get out of here, why he would rather enroll in a school he can log into anywhere—the public library or his mother's house. Now instead of walking through the dreaded double doors past a suspicious security officer, Andy enters a website where a plain white screen welcomes him: "Sign in!" He checks his e-mail and clicks on the day's assignments, blasting music from his stereo, free of the tyranny of class periods.

5   Virtual school seems like an ideal choice for kids who don't fit in or can't cope. "I'm a nervous, strung-out sort of person," says Erin Bryan, who attends the online Oregon-based CoolSchool. Erin used to attend public school in Hood River, OR, but "I didn't like the environment," she says. "I am afraid of public speaking, and I would get really freaked out in the mornings."

6   Kyle Drew, 16, a junior at S.K.O., says: "I couldn't get it together. I was skipping more and more classes, until I was afraid to go to school." Leavitt Wells, 13, from Las Vegas, was an ostracized girl with revenge on her mind. "The other kids didn't want anything to do with me," she says. "I'd put exploded gel pens in their drawers." Now she

attends the Las Vegas Odyssey Charter School online during the day, and when her adrenaline starts pumping, she charges out into the backyard and jumps on the trampoline.

On S.K.O.'s website, students can enter a classroom without being 7 noticed by their classmates by clicking the "make yourself invisible" icon—a good description of what these kids are actually doing. Before the Internet, they would have had little choice but to muddle through. Now they have disappeared from the school building altogether, a new breed of outsider, loners for the wired age.

Douglas Koch is only 12, but he is already a high-school sopho- 8 more. He says that he hopes to graduate by the time he's 15. Today he sits at his computer in his Phoenix living room—high ceilings and white walls, a sudden hard rain stirring up a desire to look out the shuttered windows. Douglas's 10-year-old brother, Gregory, is stationed across the room from him—he is also a grade-jumper. The Koch brothers have been students at the private Christa McAuliffe Academy, an online school, for more than a year now. While S.K.O. is a public school, C.M.A. is private, charging $250 a month and reaching kids from all over the country. From Yakima, WA, it serves 325 students, most of whom attend classes year-round, and employs 27 teachers and other staff members.

Douglas looks at his monitor, searching for evidence of his Spanish 9 teacher. "Oh, she's already there," he says, checking a box at the corner of the screen. He puts on a headset and greets her through the attached microphone. Her live voice comes through the computer speakers, tinny and distant. The lesson today is about El Salvador: its population and geography, with a brief mention of "la guerra." Before he speaks, he always presses "Talk." There's a moment of confusion when the teacher tries to chat about hurricanes; she can't remember the word in English. As she casts around for it, the speaker is silent, and it's hard to tell if she is still there. At one point, Douglas clicks the corner of the screen, and the lesson disappears. "Whoops!" he says, before he retrieves the page and the vanished teacher with it.

Across the room, Gregory answers multiple-choice math questions 10 about inverse numbers. He aces his answers, and the screen flashes "Good," "Excellent," "Well done." Gregory isn't in contact with a human teacher right now; he will turn in a test later and wait for an e-mail message telling him how he did. Both brothers have seen pictures of their teachers on the school website. When they graduate, they will travel to Washington State and meet them in the flesh.

At lunchtime they get up from their computers and go to the 11 kitchen together. They take a little time out to pacify the dog with biscuits. For the end of the school day there are stacks of games: ski racing, backyard baseball, chess masters, Lego racers. Their mother, Katie Craven, says that at first she wondered if keeping the kids home was the right thing. "It was only supposed to be temporary," she says, "but the kids really liked it."

12 The Koch brothers have an aura of success. The sons of a computer-programmer father, they are little versions of Bill Gates hatching in the incubator of their living room. Yet some of their talk sounds lonely.

13 "There used to be a guy in my brother's class," Douglas says. "He was from Guam. But then he graduated."

14 Sometimes, before class, they chitchat with other online kids about the weather: "It is snowing here." "It is 104 degrees here." Names light up on the screen to reveal who is speaking, what remote computer the voice is coming from. Then the class begins, and the chitchat stops. No notes passed, no spit wads thrown, no stories concocted about what the teacher does when she goes home, no eye contact.

15 Do virtual-school kids miss the volatile human combustion of the classroom? Douglas and Gregory don't seem to. They seem happy to be able to stay at home and never put their shoes on. Andy admits to missing it sometimes. "Every once in a while I think it would be cool to go back to high school because there are tons of people there," he says. "But at the same time, there are too many problems for me."

16 Andy lost contact with most of his friends when he left McKay. He doesn't know where they are anymore. While virtual school doesn't require that you leave your peers behind, it makes it harder to feel as if you're part of a crowd. Erin Bryan, from CoolSchool, still keeps in touch with her two closest friends, but sometimes, she says, she feels as if she lives in a separate world. "I'll look at photo albums at their houses, and I'll feel left out," she says. "There are pictures of parties I didn't go to."

17 Just as video games provide cartoon versions of real landscapes, the virtual school imitates the spaces of a real school. Kids take tests in virtual gymnasiums, they click into virtual classrooms and hand in papers to icons made to look like teacher mailboxes. Some virtual schools have student stores where kids can buy pens, notebooks or T-shirts imprinted with the school name to make them feel as if they're part of a real institution.

18 S.K.O.'s administrators say they believe that they have found a cure for many educational ills. Since the kids are gone, they can't act up in school. "There tends to be less behavior problems that we see," says the program coordinator, Jim Saffeels. "We never do behavior referrals." Kids are never sent to the principal's office. Only when a kid has not been heard from over e-mail for a week or so do the adults start to worry, sending out messages: Are you there? Are you working?

I'm talking to Saffeels in the offices that S.K.O. shares with the dis- 19
trict's teen parent program. Pregnant girls drift in and out, some carrying babies on their hips—another school population that is encouraged
to make itself invisible. Phones ring incessantly. It's the first day of
school, and there's a glitch: many S.K.O. students never received their
passwords. They can't get through the virtual-school doors. (The computer problems are numerous. Later, I'll go to a boy's house and see
this message on his screen: "Cannot resolve educator cookie.")

The principal, Mary Jean Sandall, rushes in wearing a crisp 20
pantsuit; she seems exhilarated, running in high gear. When she talks
about the transition into a new Web-based program (which one teacher
calls "a scramble"), it is clear that Sandall isn't a tech geek. She has an
amusing computer language all her own: content is "chunked into" an
electronic frame; the system doesn't require students to download files
that "suck up lots of stuff." Sandall explains the origins of S.K.O.: eight
years ago, word came down from the school board to "pursue distance
options," and the Salem-Keizer school district began offering online
courses. Demand was so great that the virtual model eventually
received public financing.

Sandall sees online kids as vessels of the future. "This is a 21st- 21
century model of learning," she says. "If you're a total face-to-face
learner, you may not get that. But as industry goes to a model of learning online, and professional advancement means you have to do things
online, I think these kids have an advantage."

Burt Kanner, a math teacher, appears in the doorway, and Sandall 22
waves at him excitedly. Kanner, a gray-haired, soft-spoken man, nods
back at her. He seems skeptical about all this virtual-school hype. For
most of his 45 years as a teacher, Kanner has dealt with kids face to
face. Now he spends a good deal of the time trying to figure out how to
navigate the new website, sending e-mail messages to faceless kids,
messages that sound like the comments the computer generated for
Gregory Koch: "Good job," "Well done," "Keep going."

"It doesn't really feel like teaching," he tells me as we leave the 23
office and his bosses. "I miss the performance aspect of teaching, where
you own the knowledge and have some control. Now I am mainly a
troubleshooter." I ask him if he resisted becoming a virtual teacher. He
says that it's just one more change in the rules of the game. "My whole
career is about changes," Kanner says. "I take it all one step at a time."

Lacey Calvo, 16, was assigned Kanner for online algebra last year. 24
She describes him as "really helpful." She enjoys having invisible
teachers, because "most of the time teachers get on my nerves," she
says. "They treat us like children, and you can't really be independent."
Lacey enrolled at S.K.O. a year and a half ago, after she and her mom

decided that South Salem High School was a nest of trouble. "All the girls came to school half-dressed," she says. "Students would be disruptive, and you can't concentrate at all. And you actually spend more time socializing than anything else."

25   Lacey wore makeup, although she makes it clear that "I never had black fingernails or anything." She took part in the gossipy world, she says, but it started to pull her in and fill up her thoughts, and she would skip classes and hang out with "trampy" girls. "I didn't care about anything or anybody. I did whatever I wanted to do. Now I help my mom pay the bills and take my brother to school."

26   Lacey doesn't worry about makeup anymore. She doesn't have to go shopping for back-to-school clothes or worry that some random girl is going to hate her outfit. She goes to school at a desk in the living room, surrounded by video games, unwashed dishes, her brother's toy car collections. She copies down lesson goals in a neat looping script in multicolored notebooks. Inside each of them she has written her name and address and her list of classes. She is taking more classes than most kids because she wants to finish soon and be released from high-school limbo. For P.E. credit, Lacey takes long walks around the neighborhood, a run-down area where the streets are named after birds: Finch, Song Sparrow. It seems remarkable that this is actually P.E.—an evening stroll instead of the horror of chin-ups and rope climbs, the locker room where girls calculate who wears the biggest bra.

27   Lacey has rejected the wild life she led at South Salem, but there are traces of her restlessness in certain stories she tells me. "I like to get out and go downtown and look at the cute guys," she says. "A couple of weeks ago, I went to the river and jumped off a bridge." Like Andy, Lacey does not quite trust the self that emerged in the halls of high school, and she says that if she had stayed, she would have entangled herself in a bad fate.

28   When talking to virtual-school kids, this is a common thread: the sense that they have escaped something dangerous by getting out of high school. "I saw the way the social system was set up, and I wanted to get away from that," says Kristen Dearing, a student at Basehor-Linwood charter school in Kansas.

29   MacKenzie Winslow, 14, who attends the Laurel Springs school in Ojai, CA, from her home in Colorado, says: "I didn't want a bad experience. I had a lot of friends who'd gone to high school, and they said the kids were pretty nasty. I didn't want to deal with that."

30   Efforts are made to socialize virtual-school kids; dances are held, game nights and bowling nights. At Odyssey Charter School in Las

Vegas, the students occasionally get together for trips to the Nevada History Museum or to the shark-reef exhibit at the Mandalay Bay hotel. At Electronic Charter School in Kansas, there are nights at a "fun center." Jennifer Vandiver is the prom coordinator at Christa McAuliffe Academy. In a dreamy voice, she describes the prom, which takes place in a "room full of mirrors" with a cardboard Eiffel Tower. Kids fly in from far-flung locations; there's a get-acquainted picnic the day before. Faces are put to screen names. The kids are like tourists thrown together to see the sights. They are exotic to one another.

These efforts at cheery socialization are exactly what Andy 31 Markishtum is grateful to escape. Walking through his old school, he laughs when we are confronted with banners promoting school spirit days: Sleepy Seniorzzz (pajama day) and Juniors of the Caribbean (pirate day). For Andy, it's good riddance to all that fake togetherness. "Hat day was the only day I liked," he says. "Then they took it away." Now he can turn in his assignments at midnight if he wants to.

Because the phenomenon of full-time online education is relatively 32 new, there is little research into its lasting effects—whether its practitioners become introverts and computer zombies or whether, as MacKenzie Winslow's mother puts it, the kids "have gathered their energy so they can go out into the world and be more effective."

Before Columbine, the social Darwinism of the hallway was seen 33 as character-building. Now we effortlessly imagine those "characters" hiding guns in trench coats, or dead. Promoters of virtual school promise that their websites are safe from online predators, and traditional school is portrayed as a haven for bullies, a brutal, corrupted environment in which violent confrontations are bound to occur.

Yet it is also true that there is a beauty in high school: those long, 34 exhausting hours full of other kids, everyone trying to interpret one another. It's a beauty that Gus Van Sant evokes in his new Columbine-inspired film, "Elephant"—kids break dancing and taking pictures and making out, even as the school day is headed for darkness.

For Lacey Calvo, virtual school has meant a taming and organizing 35 of her restlessness. "I have grown up, and I have a grip on reality," she says. Now she can help her overworked single mom around the house. "My mom knows I am here for her and always will be," she says. When the buzzer rings on the washer, she can get up from her earth science class to shift the load over to the dryer, and no teacher says, "Sit down, young lady." She can take breaks in the garage and watch her neighbor's new lawn being delivered. She doesn't have to sit in a classroom, wondering if she can trust herself or the kids around her, wondering what she forgot at home.

Reflection and Discussion

1. What do students who attend virtual high schools miss out on? How are the other students affected when loners and nonconformists are no longer part of the regular campus?
2. Considering all factors, not just academics, what is the purpose of a high school education? How well do virtual schools like S.K.O. serve this objective? What changes would you recommend?

Writing Matters

1. White includes only the stories of students and educators who prefer online learning. Research the relative success of virtual high schools compared with traditional schools. You may interview current and former students and teachers from a cyber academy or look for statistics like graduation and drop-out rates. What characteristics of the school and the student determine the success of this form of online learning?
2. Principal Mary Jean Sandall believes that businesses will require employees to take courses online, giving S.K.O. students an advantage, yet businesses have consistently placed great value on interpersonal relationships and teamwork. Evaluate the relative difficulty of learning to learn online and acquiring these personal skills, and then argue whether S.K.O. students will be helped or hurt by their decision to learn online.

To: Professor@University.edu
Subject: Why It's All About Me

Jonathan D. Glater, *New York Times,* February 21, 2006

Jonathan D. Glater writes on education, technology and the law for the New York Times.

How much do you adjust the style of your e-mails to fit the person you are writing to? Do you address your grandmother the same way as you do a friend?

1 One student skipped class and then sent the professor an e-mail message asking for copies of her teaching notes. Another did not like her grade and wrote a petulant message to the professor. Another explained that she was late for a Monday class because she was recovering from drinking too much at a wild weekend party.

2 Jennifer Schultens, an associate professor of mathematics at the University of California, Davis, received this e-mail message last

September from a student in her calculus course: "Should I buy a binder or a subject notebook? Since I'm a freshman, I'm not sure how to shop for school supplies. Would you let me know your recommendations? Thank you!"

At colleges and universities nationwide, e-mail has made profes- 3 sors much more approachable. But many say it has made them too accessible, erasing boundaries that traditionally kept students at a healthy distance. These days, they say, students seem to view them as available around the clock, sending a steady stream of e-mail messages—from 10 a week to 10 after every class—that are too informal or downright inappropriate.

"The tone that they would take in e-mail was pretty astounding," 4 said Michael J. Kessler, an assistant dean and a lecturer in theology at Georgetown University. "'I need to know this and you need to tell me right now,' with a familiarity that can sometimes border on imperative." He added: "It's a real fine balance to accommodate what they need and at the same time maintain a level of legitimacy as an instructor and someone who is institutionally authorized to make demands on them, and not the other way round."

While once professors may have expected deference, their expert- 5 ise seems to have become just another service that students, as consumers, are buying. So students may have no fear of giving offense, imposing on the professor's time or even of asking a question that may reflect badly on their own judgment. For junior faculty members, the barrage of e-mail has brought new tension into their work lives, some say, as they struggle with how to respond. Their tenure prospects, they realize, may rest in part on student evaluations of their accessibility.

The stakes are different for professors today than they were even a 6 decade ago, said Patricia Ewick, chairwoman of the sociology department at Clark University in Massachusetts, explaining that "students are constantly asked to fill out evaluations of individual faculty." Students also frequently post their own evaluations on websites like rateyourprofessor.com and describe their impressions of their professors on blogs.

Last fall, undergraduate students at Syracuse University set up a 7 group in Facebook.com, an online network for students, and dedicated it to maligning one particular instructor. The students were reprimanded.

Professor Ewick said 10 students in one class e-mailed her drafts of 8 their papers days before they were due, seeking comments. "It's all different levels of presumption," she said. "One is that I'll be able to drop everything and read 250 pages two days before I'm going to get 50 of these." Kathleen E. Jenkins, a sociology professor at the College of

William and Mary in Virginia, said she had even received e-mail requests from students who missed class and wanted copies of her teaching notes. Alexandra Lahav, an associate professor of law at the University of Connecticut, said she felt pressured by the e-mail messages. "I feel sort of responsible, as if I ought to be on call all the time," she said.

9   Many professors said they were often uncertain how to react. Professor Schultens, who was asked about buying the notebook, said she debated whether to tell the student that this was not a query that should be directed to her, but worried that "such a message could be pretty scary." "I decided not to respond at all," she said.

10   Christopher J. Dede, a professor at the Harvard Graduate School of Education who has studied technology in education, said these e-mail messages showed how students no longer deferred to their professors, perhaps because they realized that professors' expertise could rapidly become outdated. "The deference was probably driven more by the notion that professors were infallible sources of deep knowledge," Professor Dede said, and that notion has weakened.

11   Meanwhile, students seem unaware that what they write in e-mail could adversely affect them, Professor Lahav said. She recalled an e-mail message from a student saying that he planned to miss class so he could play with his son. Professor Lahav did not respond. "It's graduate school, he's an adult human being, he's obviously a parent, and it's not my place to tell him how to run his life," she said. But such e-mail messages can have consequences, she added. "Students don't understand that what they say in e-mail can make them seem very unprofessional and could result in a bad recommendation."

12   Still, every professor interviewed emphasized that instant feedback could be invaluable. A question about a lecture or discussion "is for me an indication of a blind spot, that the student didn't get it," said Austin D. Sarat, a professor of political science at Amherst College.

13   College students say that e-mail makes it easier to ask questions and helps them to learn. "If the only way I could communicate with my professors was by going to their office or calling them, there would be some sort of ranking or prioritization taking place," said Cory Merrill, 19, a sophomore at Amherst. "Is this question worth going over to the office?"

14   But student e-mail can go too far, said Robert B. Ahdieh, an associate professor at Emory Law School in Atlanta. He paraphrased some of the comments he had received: "I think you're covering the material too fast, or I don't think we're using the reading as much as we could in class, or I think it would be helpful if you would summarize what we've covered at the end of class in case we missed anything."

Students also use e-mail to criticize one another, Professor Ahdieh 15 said. He paraphrased this comment: "You're spending too much time with my moron classmates and you ought to be focusing on those of us who are getting the material."

Michael Greenstone, an economics professor at the Massachusetts 16 Institute of Technology, said he once received an e-mail message late one evening from a student who had recently come to the realization that he was gay and was struggling to cope. Professor Greenstone said he eventually helped the student get an appointment with a counselor. "I don't think we would have had the opportunity to discuss his realization and accompanying feelings without e-mail as an icebreaker," he said.

A few professors said they had rules for e-mail and told their stu- 17 dents how quickly they would respond, how messages should be drafted and what types of messages they would answer. Meg Worley, an assistant professor of English at Pomona College in California, said she told students that they must say thank you after receiving a professor's response to an e-mail message. "One of the rules that I teach my students is, the less powerful person always has to write back," Professor Worley said.

Reflection and Discussion

1. When did you first start using e-mail? What rules, if any, have you been taught about how to e-mail various types of people? How do you feel about the rules that seem to be implied in this article?

2. Look through the student e-mails in the article and identify the writers' underlying assumptions about the relationship between student and professor, the relative importance of school in general and class attendance in particular. What is gained or lost by communicating these feelings to the professor?

Writing Matters

1. Professor Patricia Ewick questions students' presumptions about her ability and willingness to provide quick feedback on long papers; student Cory Merrill says she would have to prioritize if asking the question would require her to go to the professor's office. Survey your friends and classmates about their e-mail experiences with teachers. What kind of help are they asking for? What do they and you feel when a teacher takes more than a few days to respond to questions? How does this influence their and your opinion of the quality of the professor's teaching?

2. Write a short guideline for incoming freshmen explaining how to communicate politely and effectively with their teachers. Illustrate your point with both good and bad examples, translating the underlying assumptions of each, particularly in light of the power relationship.

Internet Creates New Opportunities for Cheating, but Also Learning

Stephanie Dunnewind, *Seattle Times,* August 27, 2005

Stephanie Dunnewind, a Seattle Times *staff reporter, writes frequently on education and Northwest living.*

Be honest with yourself. When have you cheated on a paper? Have you downloaded a whole essay or a bit here or there? Used a cell phone photo to get the questions in advance?

1   Teachers can fight plagiarism: A simple Google search can catch wannabe cheaters. What's harder to combat, educators say, is the attitude that the quickest route is the best—even if it subverts learning.

2   When students use the Internet for research or homework aid, who decides which shortcuts are too short? Homework websites, for example, offer quick, comprehensive information, translating foreign languages, figuring out math problems and providing chapter-by-chapter plot summaries.

3   In a Pew Internet & American Life Project survey released this month, nearly four out of 10 teens say they believe "too many" of their peers use the Internet to cheat. Just one out of four parents say the same thing. "Even if students are not plagiarizing, there is so much information available now," said Chip Kimball, assistant superintendent and chief information officer for the Lake Washington School District. "The question is, How do students synthesize a large body of information and make something meaningful out of it? Do students really understand how all the parts connect to each other? That's one of our challenges [as educators]."

4   Some experts see the growing use of Internet shortcuts as a symptom of larger societal pressures emphasizing grades over actual learning. Others say the Internet is not only changing the face of cheating, it's altering the very nature of learning and teaching—in some ways for the better. Nationally, half of high-school students report they cut and pasted information off the Internet without attribution, according to compiled surveys of 18,000 students over the past five years by Don McCabe, a professor at Rutgers Business School in New Jersey. Even as more teachers—down to the middle- and junior-high school level—use such high-tech weapons as Google and the professional anti-plagiarism site Turnitin to catch plagiarism, McCabe says the amount of cheating continues to increase.

That's because it's not just the Internet to blame, some experts say. "What's changed so dramatically over the last 15 or 20 years is the scope and volume of cheating," said Timothy Dodd, executive director of The Center for Academic Integrity at Duke University in North Carolina. "But ascribing that increase solely to new means of cheating misses one of the critical reasons—an 'achieve at any cost' mentality."

In McCabe's high-school surveys, nearly half of students (45 percent) weren't sure or didn't consider copying a sentence without citation as cheating. "Students say, 'I got it off the Internet so it's public information,'" said McCabe, a national expert on cheating and plagiarism. "They don't consider it to be a big deal." While the ease does encourage a few more students to cross the line, "the primary thing technology has done is lead to more cheating by those who are already cheating," McCabe said. "It's another weapon in their arsenal that is so fast and so easy."

More than three-quarters of public-school students admitted cheating on an exam in the past year, either by copying, using crib notes or helping another student, he said. Some students justify dishonesty as a fairness issue, he said. "Everyone wants to go to the Ivy League school, so when they find out others are cheating and getting away with it, they feel like they have no choice," he said. That's especially true when kids feel pressured to excel by parents. "Students respond by any means available," he said.

Dodd blames schools and parents for emphasizing quantity—both in the amount of homework and number of after-school activities—over quality. "There are students who are scrambling from assignment to assignment just trying to keep their heads above water," he said. "When schools are giving planners to sixth-graders and parents are signing up eighth-graders for extracurriculars six days a week until 9 PM, should we be surprised that these students are resorting to shortcuts to 'manage' their time?" Dodd asked. "For too many students and their families, getting into the best schools seems to be valued more than the education received."

Teachers now watch for Internet shortcuts as well as in-class text messaging (cell phones and personal digital assistants), answers downloaded on MP3 players and cheat-sheets printed on water-bottle labels. Students often ignore school rules prohibiting phones and gadgets in class.

10   McCabe sees cheating most by very good students worried about maintaining their grades at any cost and by poor students who don't care and just want their diploma. Average students content with a B or C+ are less likely to feel the need to take the risk, he said.

11   Washington Middle School math teacher Taigen Riggs says for him, the most important thing is for kids to "get it." Even if students flunk a test, they can go back and improve their score once they really understand the concept. "I don't like to penalize kids for the process," he said. "The cheating part falls by the wayside if kids know they're not going to be beat up for trying."

Are Kids Learning?

12   Seven out of 10 online teens said they used the Internet as the major source for their most recent major school project or report, according to a 2001 report by the Pew Internet & American Life Project. A more recent Pew survey, conducted last fall, found the number of teens using the Internet at school grew 45 percent since 2000.

13   "Students literally go on a scavenger hunt for information on the Internet, which they throw against a Word document file," Dodd said. "Suddenly they think they have a paper. But what has the student internalized of the subject matter? Kids are skimming over their work and forgetting it as soon as they're done because they have seven other things they have to do."

14   Kimball argues that, done right, figuring out which sources are legit and combining diverse resources are actually more difficult—and relevant—skills than the simple regurgitation of facts required of previous generations. "It is a different kind of learning," he contends, "but they're not learning less. If you look at the kind of work kids do, the learning may be more challenging."

15   At Redmond Junior High School, Dave Sudmeier's history classes often do research on the Internet. What he wants to see is how students then evaluate and synthesize the data. "That's where the teaching begins," he said. "Does the information help them generate new questions or new ideas?" He might, for example, ask students to gather climate averages for a particular area, then plan a crop rotation, or look up occupations for US presidents and suggest political strategies based on trends in leaders' backgrounds.

Good teachers will adapt but others won't, McCabe said. At the 16
college level, his surveys of professors suggest the threat of cheating
can encourage educators' creativity or lead them to rely primarily on
in-class tests in place of research papers.

"Colleges are already concerned about students coming in with 17
poor writing skills," he said. If high-school teachers figure it's not
worth assigning papers because kids just cheat, "it will exacerbate the
problem even more."

In her English classes at Lake Washington High School, Lis 18
Christiansen requires regular working drafts and annotated bibliographies in which students analyze and summarize each source. She also
comes up with creative writing topics. That can be challenging when
students read classics—How many different angles are there for
Huckleberry Finn?—but she tries to relate questions to specific classroom discussions so that no generic paper will work.

"It is more time-consuming and more work, but it's worth it in the 19
end when you don't have so many kids cheating," she says, "because
they can't."

Reflection and Discussion

1. How much pressure do you feel to succeed in college? What coping mechanisms work best for you? What options do you think you have if you're short on time and overwhelmed by work?
2. Timothy Dodd suggests that students aren't learning much when they piece together an essay from a number of Internet sources, yet Chip Kimball claims that such assignments are both more difficult and more meaningful when done correctly. Do you try to learn as much as possible from each assignment or do you find yourself just trying to keep up? What could teachers do to encourage students to learn actively and not just complete the assignment?

Writing Matters

1. Why do students cheat? How much does technology contribute to this problem? Review the causes Dunnewind identifies and any other factors you may think of and explain which factors seem most important for students like yourself.
2. Look at your school's policies on academic integrity. How effectively are these policies enforced? How completely are they integrated into the syllabi of your classes? Research the policies of other schools and recommend any changes needed to update them and their enforcement.

Don't Discredit My Online Degree

Karen Glover, *Library Journal,* October 15, 2005

Karen Glover, a librarian at Georgia Institute of Technology, earned her masters degree from Florida State University's online program.

How much would you respect a professional whose only degrees were from an online university?

1   When I graduated with an MLIS from an online program, it never occurred to me that I would have a hard time finding a job. Unfortunately, I am finding that many employers view my online degree as worth less than a traditional degree.

2   According to a survey conducted by Vault.com, out of 239 human resource professionals, 37 percent of those surveyed believe that an online graduate school degree is as credible as a traditional degree, while 54 percent said that it was not as credible but acceptable. But these are the interesting numbers: roughly 40 percent of employers said they believed my degree is credible. That means 60 percent of employers view my degree as second class, which makes finding a job that much harder for me than someone with a traditional degree.

Some Common Misconceptions

3   This bias is quite perplexing. I was under the impression that employers wanted mature self-starters with independence and motivation—the very skills needed to be successful in an online program. So why is there a bias against the validity of online programs? Vault.com also asked employers to describe what they see as the drawbacks of online programs. The top three reasons: "students don't socially interact with peers," "too new to gauge effectiveness," and "loss of real-time pedagogical exchange."

4   These are common misconceptions. As far as social interaction goes, I found my online program to be better than my traditional undergraduate program. In fact, many professors in online programs require participation and foster group projects. Because of the virtual nature of the program, my classmates and I were able to contact each other at all hours of the day and night, not bound by location. We communicated via chat, discussion boards, and email. Often, our communication was even graded—and even if it wasn't graded, it was still necessary for our success. OK, so we didn't go to the movies together.

We did, however, often speak socially, beyond the assignment, offering encouragement and constructive criticism.

Too New?

If the idea of online degrees is too new to "gauge effectiveness," then 5 why are so many traditional institutions increasingly offering online classes both to traditional students as well as distance students? Apparently, online courses are valuable to the traditional student, yet the traditional student avoids the stigma of the online degree even though students in the online program take the same exact courses.

As for the pedagogical exchange from my online program, it was 6 just as effective and real as any exchange in a traditional classroom. In fact, there were added benefits to online exchanges. Not only could we contact our instructor any time, the chat program we used logged all of our discussions. That gave us the benefit of being able to miss a discussion and still read later what was discussed. What traditional student is able to go back and find out exactly what an instructor said, word for word? We also participated in discussion boards that facilitated instructor feedback and questions in a one-on-one manner, and these discussion boards were usually mandatory. How many traditional instructors demand that you come to their office once a week and ask a question or propose an idea?

More Value

Those of us who choose to take online courses, or earn an online 7 degree, do so because we often have jobs, families, and lives that cannot just stop for school. We may be nontraditional, but that does not make us less valuable. In fact, it may even make us more valuable. We multitask and organize. Our time management skills are impressive, and our commitment to our education is unmatched. Until employers know more about what it takes to succeed in an online program, however, the stigma will remain.

At one point, I was instructed just not to mention that my degree 8 was an online degree. That's a terrible idea. Potential employers would realize my degree was earned online as soon as they read my résumé. After all, I maintained full-time employment in a different state while receiving my degree. Employers tend to notice that type of discrepancy, and many might think I was being deceitful by not explicitly stating mine is an online credential.

9   Here's a better idea. If questions about your online degree come up in an interview, be honest and state all of the reasons why your online degree is more valuable than a traditional one. Not only will this improve your immediate chances for getting the job, it is the only way we can change employers' lingering misperceptions of online education.

Reflection and Discussion

1. Glover answers employers' concerns by describing her own experience. In what ways is this a valid approach? What information would make her argument stronger?

2. Glover says she believes in being completely honest on résumés and in interviews, but she had little choice because her résumé showed a discrepancy that needed to be explained. Suppose Glover's degree was from a local school, so that there was no discrepancy. Do you think she would have been so forthcoming? Should she have been? Why?

Writing Matters

1. Write a response to Glover. Evaluate the advantages of online courses that she mentions. What, if anything, has she overlooked? What weaknesses has she ignored?

2. Glover says that successful students in online programs must be "mature self-starters with independence and motivation." Why would she think those qualities are mandatory? If you agree with her, identify what additional prerequisites should be required for enrollment in online courses, or, if you disagree, describe what should happen to students who don't keep up.

Learning, Virtually

Kristin Bagnato, *Community College Week,* May 10, 2004

Kristin Bagnato is a senior writer at Community College Week *and former editor-in-chief of* Cooking Smart Magazine.

Which has been harder for you: getting the classes you want, when you want them, or keeping up with the workload?

1   The jury is still out on distance education, but everyone agrees on one point: It's here to stay. As much as colleges struggle with the growing pains of the distance-learning boom, most are committing ever more time and resources to it.

Variety seems to be the only constant in any discussion about 2 online education. "For us it's worked great, but no one should be forced to do it," said Bob Isaacson at Allan Hancock College in Santa Maria, CA, who found that his English courses translated easily to an online format, but added that the shift wasn't so simple for other departments. Even when the coursework makes the move without a hitch, the instructor still has to learn a completely new way to teach the course.

Virtually Complex

But some question whether the details are being considered to the 3 detriment of the greater goal of quality education. Becky Cox, a research associate at the Community College Research Center at Columbia University's Teachers College, said in their group's study of more than 700 faculty and students at 15 community college distance-learning programs they found that often it seemed the focus was on the logistics of distance learning rather than the quality of the education. "If you talk to administrators [they say] everything is fine; if you talk to teachers, there are problems," Cox said. But she adds that attitudes are changing so quickly that it's difficult to keep track.

That shifting opinion is what makes qualifying the state of distance 4 learning . . . such a challenge. "Part of it is the newness. It's difficult to do something in-depth enough to know what's going on. It's a point in time versus what's happening now, because it changes so fast," Cox said. "How do you get a fix on something that's virtual to begin with?"

Across the board, educators, from researchers to administrators, lament the dearth of hard information about distance learning. "We're still sorting through everything," said Scott Langhorst, associate vice president of distributive teaching, learning and services at Tidewater Community College in Norfolk, VA.

There are studies, but online learning is so new that three or four 5 years of data barely cover the learning curve from no one knowing what an online course was, to now, when a majority of community colleges offer some form of distance education—more than 90 percent of public institutions (including four-year schools) offer at least one online course, according to a 2003 study by the Sloan Consortium.

While distance learning in some form or another has been going on 6 since the days of the correspondence course, this recent boom can be traced to the advent of personal computers in the home and affordable Internet access. The technology itself is an obstacle that, with time, seems to be molehill-sized instead of the mountain it was a couple of years ago. At one time faculty agonized over the time they'd need to devote to online courses. Now that the technology of [course support programs] is more familiar, the amount of time needed has decreased. "Blackboard is surprisingly easy to use," Isaacson said. But he acknowledges that "initially I found it confusing and difficult." . . .

Paying the Piper

7 Despite budgets cuts, online education is undoubtedly thriving. But worries about where the money is coming from—never far away for community colleges—don't stop when the online student logs on. With no need for a bricks-and-mortar classroom, online learning was originally seen as a way to save money. But the reality is that the software and maintenance of the information technology is a costly process.

8   "Some years ago, there was a proposal floating at the state level to reduce classroom construction costs by increasing distance-learning offerings. I'm dreading the day someone remembers and resurrects it. To be frank, in California, construction funding has never kept pace with growth in students and demand for classroom space," said Lil Clary, dean of learning resources at Allan Hancock. "No amount of distance-learning is going to make up for the long-term neglect of community-college physical resources and overall lack of classrooms. And besides, distance learning isn't cheap! When you figure the cost of support, maintenance of a course management system, training and off-site testing arrangements, we aren't talking pennies." . . .

9   Program development costs are the biggest barrier to increased offerings, according to a study by the US Department of Education's National Center for Education Statistics. In schools that do have distance-education programs, 22 percent of them reported that expansion costs kept them from adding more. Concerns aside from cost, such as quality issues and lack of need, were not issues for schools that already offered distance learning, the study found.

A Giant Leap for Faculty?

10 When distance education first came on the scene, it seemed there were endless hours spent adapting or designing courses for the online student, and there was little or no extra compensation for the faculty willing to take the technological leap. A study published in the *Online Journal of Distance Learning Administration* found that schools were willing to pay faculty more to develop a course, but were much less likely

to increase compensation for those willing to teach an online course, even though faculty reported that the time required was greater than that of a traditional face-to-face course.

The authors of the study suggest that as faculty become more com- 11 fortable with the medium—and therefore spend less time with a course—they will be less likely to expect additional compensation. The study also suggests that instructors may spend even less time on an online course than a traditional course, as they learn how to best use the features of programs such as WebCT and Blackboard. "We think less and less in terms of this being different, as this being just another option," Tidewater's Langhorst said, adding that instructors are rounding the learning curve with online courses, and now it's becoming just another way of teaching a course.

As instructors grow familiar with the technology and the necessary 12 technical steps to get a course up and running, their time frees up. For example, in the beginning of online education, instructors found themselves answering the same questions over and over as each student asked them. Often—even if the instructor posted the question and answer—students would miss the posting and the instructor had to write yet another e-mail pointing the student in the right direction. Now that FAQs are an understood part of just about every online endeavor, students are in the habit of checking there before querying the instructor. "We're just getting better at what we do," Allan Hancock's Isaacson said. "And our students are getting better at the online experience."

But some find that even with skill in the medium, it just takes more 13 time. "I would say that there is more of a time commitment necessary to teach an online course," said Sonya Lizasuain, a psychology instructor and five-year veteran of online teaching at Tidewater. "There is more one-on-one interaction . . . and teachers are in a position to deal with individual concerns rather than group concerns, and that takes more time."

No More Experiments

When online instruction was new, everyone was feeling their way. But 14 now, as it becomes nearly as commonplace as traditional education, it seems the learning curve is ending—as are the misconceptions that an online class is one a student can breeze through. It seems that the "early years" of online learning were all an experiment for what's becoming a standard form of education. Even the perception that online learning was somehow easier or less rigorous academically than traditional coursework is changing. The method by which the information is imparted is different, certainly, but that method is no less valid, according to a Sloan study. While the study reported that faculty remain unconvinced that the quality of online education is up to the same standard as face-to-face learning, it also found that administrators believe that in a few years, the quality of online learning will meet or surpass that of traditional classes.

15   This divide between administrators and educators isn't new, and Cox of the Community College Research Center said it's one of the problems with online courses. "I think there's a way to make any configuration of students work, but it involves the time and energy of the instructor," she said, and depending on the school's philosophy toward distance education, that time and energy may or may not be there.

16   While some say it's easy for a student to disappear into the background in an online course, that may be changing as instructors learn to manage the technology and class sizes are limited. "It seems we are able to recognize where students are having trouble with online classes earlier, and that helps with the student success rate," Lizasuain said.

17   As online classes settle in, schools emphasize the efforts they make to maintain the academic integrity of online courses. At Tidewater, students may take many courses completely online, with the small caveat of two proctored activities, which may take the form of an exam, a class meeting or other face-to-face event, in an attempt to ensure that the person who's name is on the course is the person actually completing the work.

18   At Allan Hancock, 30 percent of the grade for English composition comes from participation—an activity easy to track, thanks to a Blackboard function that allows faculty to see how often and how long a student takes part in a discussion, for example. Lizasuain finds that her online students work harder than the students in her traditional classes: "There is more independence in an online class. Students must take initiative to clarify their confusion. In a face-to-face course, they are more likely to rely on each other and the teacher to succeed." . . .

Tech-Savvy Teaching

19 Just because it's distance doesn't mean it's all text in a file, either. Many schools are offering what Dallas County Community College District calls "telecourses"—where there is a video element that plays on your computer. This streaming video is a portable version of the courses sometimes seen on PBS stations or local cable channels. An upgraded version ("Telecourse PLUS") allows an element of interactivity meant

to help the student become even more invested in the course. Some courses are a blend of on-campus instruction and Web-based learning. These so-called hybrid courses are popular with some, less so with others. The Sloan study found that hybrid classes were a school's way of testing the water with online learning, but some instructors say it's twice the work for one course.

Convenience Is Key

As online education evolves, one element has remained the same: [20] Convenience is paramount. The student wants a class to "attend" after work, at work or when the baby has fallen asleep—or even on campus when the other sections of the class are full or conflict with the student's schedule. Meeting a requirement becomes much easier when it's a matter of choosing among several courses that can be accessed at any time versus one that meets for an hour three times per week.

Isaacson said that online offerings saved many of the classes in his [21] department. Classes with spotty interest suddenly picked up students when offered online. Convenience can't be underestimated, according to Cox. "Students that I talked to said, 'This is working for me, because I couldn't get into'" the face-to-face section of the course, Cox said.

Laurie White of Tidewater, as well as Ann Hatch of the Dallas [22] County Community College District and Isaacson all mentioned that online classes are a boon for students in the military. A student can be called away for duty or training, and still keep up with coursework. "We have students on submarines," Isaacson said.

While there's no consensus on how to do it, whether it's an effec- [23] tive learning method or where it's going, one thing is for sure: Distance learning is here, and as long as there are sailors on submarines, moms up in the middle of the night and students with schedule conflicts, it's here to stay.

Reflection and Discussion

1. This article was originally written for a weekly publication for community college faculty and administration. Identify the ways that Bagnato tailors it to her audience, looking at such aspects as vocabulary, point of view, interviewees. How do these choices affect you as someone who is not part of that audience?

2. A number of experts point out ways for technology to make teaching easier. For example, professors might have the computer calculate class participation grades based only on the length and frequency of posts. What are the advantages and disadvantages of such technical shortcuts?

Writing Matters

1. Is it all about money? Research the economic issues raised in the article. Should students be charged more for the convenience of online classes? Should teachers be paid more for the individualized attention?
2. Why would some instructors feel that online students work harder than those in traditional courses? What factors might make online courses themselves more motivating? In what ways are online students different?

A Congressman Questions the Quality and Rigor of Online Education

Andrea L. Foster, *Chronicle of Higher Education,* March 31, 2006

Andrea L. Foster writes frequently on educational technology.

What might tempt you to get one of the online degrees advertised in popular magazines? How would you know which were legitimate?

1   Rep. Vernon J. Ehlers, a soft-spoken Republican who has represented Michigan's third district since 1994, has become a thorn in the side of distance-education institutions. A former physics professor at Calvin College, in Grand Rapids, and a member of the US House of Representatives Committee on Education and the Workforce, Mr. Ehlers is skeptical about the value of distance education over the Internet. He persuaded the former chairman of the education committee to support a government-funded study into whether distance learning is as effective as face-to-face college instruction and hopes the new chairman, Howard P. (Buck) McKeon, a California Republican, will also support such a study.

2   [In 2005] Mr. Ehlers introduced an amendment to the College Access and Opportunity Act, HR 609, to require accrediting agencies to check whether a distance-education institution that experiences "significant growth has the capacity to serve its students effectively." . . . He offered another amendment that would have permitted only accrediting agencies that evaluate residential institutions to evaluate distance-education institutions. The measure, which failed, would have effectively shut down the Accrediting Commission of the Distance Education and Training Council, which accredits only distance-education institutions.

3   And he fought against the removal of the 50-percent rule, a regulation that required colleges to teach at least half of their courses using traditional classroom methods in order to qualify for federal student-aid

programs. Mr. Ehlers and other opponents of the rule argued that it was an important check against low-quality online colleges, but the rule was eliminated earlier this year.

The *Chronicle* sat down with Mr. Ehlers to discuss his views about online education. 4

Q: I understand you don't like distance education. 5

A: It's not true. But it's easy for people to get that perception because I've been urging caution on this whole issue. 6

Let me back up. First of all, I was a traditional professor. . . . So I try to bend over backward and not to say, "Well, it's wrong because it's not the way I did it." So I'm trying to be very open about it. Second thing, it's very hard for me to argue that an individual can't learn on their own because that's what I did the first 18 years of my life. I had severe chronic asthma, and so I couldn't go to school, and so for K-12, I was home schooled before there was such a thing as home schooling. . . . 7

It would be silly for me to be against distance education. . . . This proposal to drop the 50-percent requirement concerned me because one of the bases for that was that the Department of Education had done a study and determined that the results were just as good for distance education as not. So we looked at the study, and it was ridiculous. In fact, it had been dismissed by some academic groups as meaningless. . . . It just was not a good study. And there's no basis on which you could conclude from that study that distance education was equally as good as the normal education in the higher-education arena. 8

And so I simply said, "Look, if that's supposed to be the basis of our decision, we shouldn't make that decision because the basis isn't there." But the other members of the committee just wanted to go ahead. And I said, "Well, OK, but let's add an amendment to ask the National Academy of Sciences or some other reputable group to do an accurate, statistically and scientifically valid study of the efficacy of distance education as compared to residential education, so we really know what we're talking about." 9

Q: Do you think distance education can be as valid as face-to-face, traditional education? 10

A: It can be, but it depends on a number of things. One is the maturity of the student. And I know that from personal experience. It would have been very easy for me to coast through a lot of stuff all the way through eighth grade and through high school just by looking at the answers in the book and taking a test and stuff like that. I knew that if I did that, I'd graduate, sure, but what would I have learned, and would I be able to go to college and so forth? There are ways, I think, to subvert the learning process. 11

12   Q: How?

13   A: In taking tests, for example. Every test could be an open-book test, particularly when you get into math and science. There are different issues there. How one learns and how one does it. There are other issues with distance learning—and again my experience [is] in the sciences—I am convinced most students learn more from their fellow students than they learn from their professors because they work together on problems. And these are difficult problems.

14   The sciences are known for requiring students to think things through. And they benefit tremendously from working together. If you're taking a distance-learning course, and you're all by yourself, you're missing out on that interaction. So I just would like to see concrete evidence that they're equivalent. And if they're not, then what can we do to modify distance education to make certain that the learning is there?

15   In some ways, distance learning may be better. In some ways, it may be worse. But I have not seen any evidence—that doesn't mean it hasn't been done—that the people involved in distance learning have really studied the pedagogical issues, the educational attitude, the educational psychological issues that are different when you're in a classroom compared to when you're at a computer. . . .

16   I don't know if you're aware of the work we did, two years ago, on diploma mills. And it's downright shocking to see what's out there. We found a substantial number of federal employees who were getting much higher salaries than they deserved because they bought a degree online for anywhere from $1,000 to $5,000 without their doing any work. And these organizations are still out there.

17   Well, the opportunities are rife within distance education to do the same thing, to lessen the standards and give people degrees, which are meaningless, and make a lot of money doing it. . . .

18   [Proponents of distance education] think I'm an old curmudgeon who can't adapt to the times. They think I'm opposed to distance learning. I'm not. I've been through it, but I also know how easy it is to scam the system if you want to.

19   "It's very hard for me to argue that an individual can't learn on their own because that's what I did the first 18 years of my life."

Reflection and Discussion

1. Evaluate Ehlers' reason for retaining the 50 percent requirement. What other ways might there be to meet his objectives?
2. This piece is presented as a dialogue between the author and Ehlers rather than as an article. Why would Foster have taken this approach? What is gained and lost by this choice of form?

Writing Matters

1. How does distance learning serve disabled students? What other populations could benefit? Argue whether state university systems should be required to offer online degrees to meet the needs of people who cannot attend regular schools.

2. Ehlers is most concerned with higher (university) education, though he compares it with his own home schooling experience for primary and secondary school. How does home schooling compare to distance learning? Why might it be more important to regulate completely online university degrees?

MAKING CONNECTIONS

1. Federal law protects an author's intellectual property rights, the ability to benefit from one's writing and ideas, yet Internet users are constantly challenging rights by downloading pirated music, copying in text without attribution, pasting in graphics without the artist's name. Evaluate how this general challenge to intellectual property rights is affecting the way students respond to written assignments. What happens when we don't credit authorship? When we don't pay? Has the time come to change the rules? If so, what would we gain or lose as a society and as individuals?

2. Research the history of distance education. Where did it begin and how did it develop? Who were the earliest students and how did they differ from distance learners today? What are the most dramatic changes in distance learning over time? How do you expect these differences to affect the overall success or failure of online learning?

3. Research online diploma mills. Discuss how bogus online institutions create an attitude of distrust about distance education. Why would these shady online schools pose a greater problem than traditional degree mills?

4. Congressman Ehlers has tried to control online institutions more stringently than traditional schools. Examine his rationale and identify what special scrutiny, if any, is justified. To what extent is traditional learning already better regulated and less in need of government control?

5. Some find online learning attractive because they can work alone at their convenience. What, if anything, are they missing? Others argue that peer interaction is essential to learning, but are online chats, message boards and e-mail as good or better than face-to-face exchanges? How does e-mail help or hurt student-faculty relationships? Discuss these or other ways technology affects the relationships between students and their classmates, other students and teachers.

TAKING ACTION

Congressman Ehlers firmly believes that the government should fund a study to determine whether online distance education is as effective as traditional college learning, but such studies take time and cost money. Research the studies that have already been done, including the related issues the congressman raises, and the consequences of not having the type of comprehensive study Ehlers proposes. Decide whether such a study is indeed necessary, and, if it is needed, what should be done about online degrees until the study is completed. Write a letter to your congressional representative arguing for or against such a study, sending a copy to Congressman Ehlers.

Section

Agents of Change

The current generation has been described in terms ranging from materialistic and cynical to pragmatic and concerned, and, compared with previous generations, these young adults are indeed less interested in traditional politics. But this does not mean they are uninvolved: they promote social causes through other means and gravitate to volunteering. In fact, many of their most valuable experiences come when school and service are combined—the theoretical joined to the real. The heroes of the new millennium may not be politicians or warriors, but those who steadfastly work to right wrongs and preserve what they hold dear.

Chapter 4

Getting Involved

Trying to characterize an entire generation is no easy task, but this has rarely stopped people from trying. Many of today's students are the offspring of social and political activists who fought for civil rights, protested war or volunteered in the first Peace Corps. For not following a similar path, the current generation of students has been labeled self-centered, even narcissistic—especially for its perceived indifference to traditional politics and voting. Yet young people now are volunteering more than any generation in American history, suggesting a concern for community and the welfare of others. A close examination of college students of the new millennium reveals an intriguing picture, one filled with unique and complex features.

BEFORE YOU READ

How would you describe the mood on your campus? What are students interested in? What attitudes seem dominant—altruism, egoism, a mix of both? When students do get involved, how does this involvement manifest itself? How engaged are students politically? As volunteers? How competitive do they seem?

FIGURE 4.1 Too many choices? None that really matter?

My Freshman Year: What a Professor Learned by Becoming a Student

Cathy Small writing as Rebekah Nathan, excerpted from
*My Freshman Year: What a Professor Learned by Becoming
a Student,* 2005

Professor of Anthropology Cathy Small is a cultural anthropologist who wrote Voyages:
From Tongan Villages to American Suburbs. *To gather information for her book* My
Freshman Year: What a Professor Learned by Becoming a Student, *she took a
year's sabbatical, lived in a residence hall as a freshman and took classes at an institution
she called AnyU. In fact, it was really where she teaches, Northern Arizona University.*

**What people and groups do you feel most connected to on your
campus?**

One would be hard-pressed to find words more widespread in univer-   1
sity rhetoric than "community" and "diversity." As a student, one is
immediately enlisted to join the group, to get involved, to realize that
one has become a part of the AnyU "community."

2   It starts during Previews and Welcome Week. We sing the AnyU alma mater with leaders; we learn the AnyU cheer. At the convocation that commences our freshman year, we are welcomed to AnyU with some statistics about our class, and then an entertaining PowerPoint presentation with voice-over begins: "In the year that you were born . . . "—it goes back eighteen years and shows a baby—"Ronald Reagan was president, AnyU was building its South Campus, and the movie that won the Academy Award was *Out of Africa.*" We see graphics of all this, and AnyU history, at least for the past eighteen years, is interspersed with the shared "history" of the audience, which consists primarily of movies, TV shows, and dramatic historical events. "In 1986," the story continues, "the Emmy goes to *L.A. Law,* and the explosion of the *Challenger* saddens the American public." The presentation takes us briefly through all eighteen years of the baby-who-is-us.

3   By 1991 we have torn down the Berlin Wall, constructed the new AnyU library, and arrived at the same year that *Seinfeld* begins. There is silence, clapping, or booing as the event being described moves us. Our history continues, year by year, to mention, among other things, the end of the TV series *Cheers* in 1993, the Monica Lewinsky scandal in 1998, the beginning of *Friends* in 1994 (to thunderous applause), and the September 11, 2001, attack. By 2002 we are eighteen and ready to go to college, and—the lights come on—here we are, part of the AnyU family.

4   The presentation works; it is relatively short, and students leave mildly entertained and energized, having experienced a compressed version of our joint heritage and our shared place at the starting line of something new. It is clear what the common heritage has been constructed to be. What holds students together, really, is age, pop culture, a handful of (recent) historical events, and getting a degree. No one ever remembers the institutional history or the never-sung alma mater.

How Community Works at AnyU

5   Youth, pop culture, and getting a degree are pretty accurately the ties that bind together a public state university "community." Unless it offers a big-time (and winning) sports team that draws large attendance and loyalty, there is little in the way of shared first-year experiences that three thousand or so freshmen will have in common. AnyU did have a Freshman Colloquium course that was mandatory for all first-year students. It was designed to be just such a community builder, one that required students to complete a summer reading assignment—usually a provocative contemporary novel chosen

collectively by the participating faculty—that would be discussed in small seminars before classes formally began.

The faculty had an ambitious, and what they thought exciting, intellectual agenda in mind. Students would read the same book, and then their academic career would start with a stimulating seminar-style discussion with only twenty or so participants. The entire freshman class would be engaged in the same reading, and thus have a common basis for debate and dialogue. Freshmen would then meet the book's author, who had been invited at great expense to give a talk following their small-group discussions. This experience would jump-start the colloquium that would follow: a small, seminar-based freshman course centered on readings about community and citizenship, diversity, environment, and technology, designed to help them explore their journeys as "thinking persons," including the purpose of the liberal education they had begun. For the administration, the course was also a way to build a sense of loyalty and community, and thus, according to official belief, to retain freshmen as paying students.

I was in one of the last freshman classes to take the course. It was nullified as a requirement because the university faculty and administration concluded that it wasn't working. For one thing, only about a third of the students actually did the summer reading. My own pre-course seminar was led by an impressive instructor who practically pulled teeth trying to get a response to questions raised by our reading: "Does a common enemy help to make people a community? What is a typical American or an ideal citizen? Can anyone think of places within America that seem like a different country? Does technology bring you closer to or farther away from other people—does it separate or connect?" She ended up letting us go a half-hour early because, I surmised, of our silence. Very few in my seminar had read the book, at least "all the way through," as one student qualified it.

According to student surveys, many disliked the course that followed, in particular the idea that they "had no choice and that they *had* to take it," but also because it was abstract and impractical, and they didn't learn anything "related to their interests." The requirement, designed as the only common academic experience the freshmen would have, was accordingly wiped from the books, leaving an elective course, chosen separately by each student, in its place.

One can learn from the fate of the freshman seminar. It is a good example of what happens nowadays when efforts at building community compete with the demand for choice. The freshman course had been designed and initiated at AnyU as part of a nationwide agenda, begun in the early 1990s, to engage students in their freshman year and quickly establish a "learning community." It was one local response to what educational policy analysts identified as a crisis in community that left the university to be experienced in "momentary and marginal ways." "Not only has cultural coherence faded," reads the thoughtful and influential 1990 report from the Carnegie Foundation for the Advancement of Teaching, "but the very notion of commonalities seems strikingly inapplicable to the vigorous diversity of contemporary life." Titled *Campus Life: In Search of Community*, the report called for a renewal of community in higher learning. Its authors wrote:

> It is of special significance, we believe, that higher learning institutions, even the big, complex ones, continue to use the familiar rhetoric of "community" to describe campus life and even use the metaphor of "family." Especially significant, 97 percent of the college and university presidents we surveyed said they "strongly believe in the importance of community." Almost all the presidents agreed that "community is appropriate for my campus" and also support the proposition that "administrators should make a greater effort to strengthen common purposes and shared experiences."[1]

10   It is a cry that has been taken up in earnest by university presidents around the country. Because *requiring* common experiences is vastly unpopular, and efforts often meet the fate of the freshman seminar, AnyU, like many universities today, encourages community through elective participation. "If you don't see what you like," said one Welcome Week booster, "start your own club." The 158 registered student organizations on campus don't tell the full story of the options that confront a student in a single week, from salsa dancing night at a downtown club, to the regular pickup game of coed volleyball, to the Overeaters Anonymous meeting, to the self-defense lesson in the dorm, to the plethora of academic events that are part of lecture and film series.

11   Every week the hall bulletin boards are plastered with notices about new events to attend, new music groups in town, or organizations offering enthusiastic invitations to their open house. The proliferation of event choices, together with the consistent message to "get involved," and the ever available option of dropping out, creates a self-contradictory system. Students are confronted with an endless slate of activities vying for their time. Every decision not to join but to keep one's time for oneself is interpreted as "student apathy" or "program irrelevance," and ever more activities are designed to remedy them. Each decision to join something new pulls at another commitment, fragmenting the whole even further. Not only people but also community are spread thin.

In my life as a student this process of community building 12
through elective involvement was repeated numerous times and in
numerous places within the university. On my dorm floor alone,
where we had not done much together as a group during my first
semester, the process worked like this. To begin our second semester
and usher in a renewed spirit of community, our enthusiastic RA
devised an "interest survey," which she administered at the first
mandatory hall meeting of that period. (Since it was second semester,
the turnout was decidedly sparse: only six people attended.) "Let's do
more things together," the RA suggested, and we agreed. It would be
desirable, the collective thinking seemed to be, to have more "community" in the dorm.

"What would we like to do this semester?" she asked us. To find 13
out, she distributed the survey with a written checklist that would
assist her in launching new dorm programs that fit our interests and
schedules. There were sixty-four activities suggested on the checklist in
ten categories (community living, health/wellness, social awareness,
employment skills, academic programs, relationship issues . . .), which
ranged from presentation and panels, to group games and activities, to
participatory workshops. We could write in activities if the ones presented did not suit. There was also an availability section of the form,
where we were asked to check our preferred times—which evenings,
which hours—for the activities. Because the showing at the meeting
was so meager, our RA placed questionnaires under each of the doors
on the wing, to be returned to her by a specified date. I asked whether I
could see the final tallies.

A total of 304 selections were made by all hall mates, with eight- 14
een of the sixty-four listed activities chosen by approximately half of
all respondents. The most popular choice was not an activity at all but
an expressed interest in buying floor T-shirts or boxer shorts. Among
activities, several—including swing or salsa dancing and playing
board games—were high on the list, but the RA decided to start her
local "community" program with the biggest vote-getter, "Movie
Night," endorsed by about three-quarters of the voting residents on
the floor.

Movie Night was an activity whereby once every other week we 15
would come to our RA's room, as in Welcome Week, to watch a movie
on video while sharing popcorn and other snacks provided by the RA
or anted up by the residents. The preferred time, according to the questionnaires, was 8 PM on Tuesday. And so Movie Night was instituted
twice a month on Tuesday nights, and slips of paper appeared under
our doors to announce the first movie. On the first Tuesday, two people
showed, besides the RA. The second time nobody showed. The RA

moved the night to Sunday. Still nobody showed. The program was canceled, leaving the RA wondering what she could do to "really involve" her corridor. . . .

The American Way: The Individualism in Community

16 To university administrators my story of Movie Night would be yet one more example of failing involvement and community on the contemporary college campus. By 1990 it was already becoming clear that few students participate in campus events; 76 percent of college and university presidents called nonparticipation a moderate to major problem on campuses.[2] An RA might count Movie Night as a personal failure, and become dispirited by the apathy of residents, or perhaps hear a call to invent more and better activities.

17 Students, I imagine, would see it a little differently. The activities chosen were not the "wrong" ones, nor were their RAs remiss. Nor had students been insincere in their desire for more community life in the dorm. If you had asked most students what happened with Movie Night, they would have answered, "I wanted to go, but when the time came, I didn't," or "I forgot." They genuinely want to have a close community, while at the same time they resist the claims that community makes on their schedule and resources in the name of individualism, spontaneity, freedom, and choice.

18 This is exactly how many students talk about sororities and fraternities. Fewer than 10 percent of AnyU residents are members of either. When I asked students whether they'd considered "rushing," instead of mentioning the "elitism" or "conservative politics" that dominated Greek critique in my day, students complained about "conformity" and "control of my life." Judy explained that she had almost rushed but then changed her mind because "you become lost. It's hard to know all ninety girls in a sorority. You become the same rather than an individual in a group. It can get, you know, almost cult-like, and you spend all your time there. You can't live in other dorms, or meet new people."

19 I found that students' greatest objections to the Greek system were its steep demands—that it required so much time ("I can't give up that many nights a week to one organization") and so many resources ("Why should I pay all that money to a fraternity to have friends when I can make friends for free?"), all of them mandatory ("I don't want people telling me what to do and where I have to be all the time"; "I'm an individual, not a group person"). Yet, the one AnyU student in ten who did join a fraternity or sorority was, according to 2003 surveys

conducted by the Office of Student Life, much less likely to drop out of school and much more likely to report the highest level of satisfaction with campus life.

There is a familiar dilemma here. "The very organizations that give security to students," concluded national policy analysts in 1990, "can also create isolation and even generate friction on the campus."[3] More than half of university presidents were reported to view Greek life as a problem, largely because it creates "little loyalties" that isolate students, removing them from the mainstream life of the university. It is not just Greek groups that operate this way. They are only illustrative of what one university president saw as "a great deal of 'orbital energy' among the many subgroups, a magnetism that tugs at these groups, pulling them away from any common agenda."[4]

Struggling with community in this way is, as observers of American life have pointed out, the American way.[5] The same things that make us feel connected and protected are the things that make us feel obligated and trapped as individuals and/or cut off from other groups with different agendas. For most students, as for most Americans in general, the "big community" has a dual connotation that includes both a warm and fuzzy side, all about "oneness" or "togetherness" or "common purpose," and a negative side that tends to surface with reference to government regulations, Big Brother images, and fears of conformity. When students talk about their educational community, these contradictory ideas of community are reproduced, bouncing between an entity that provides love and a sense of belonging and one that limits freedom and imposes new obligations.

References

1. Carnegie Foundation for the Advancement of Teaching. 1990. Campus Life: In Search of Community. Princeton: Carnegie Foundation for the Advancement of Teaching, 63–64.
2. Ibid., 48.
3. Ibid., 49.
4. Ibid., 50.
5. Varenne, Hervé. 1977. Americans Together: Structured Diversity in a Midwestern Town. New York: Teachers College Press.

Reflection and Discussion

1. Many of Small's conclusions were drawn from personally observing what took place among the students on her campus. Which of her observations ring true to you? Which ones don't fit with your experiences?

2. Small describes a struggle between the opportunities and obligations of being part of a community. Describe an experience you had joining a group. What time commitments did it require? What did you have to sacrifice in order to participate? What benefits did you gain and what, if anything, would you have done differently?

Writing Matters

1. Describe a community-building experience on your campus—one which a group or individual, perhaps a teacher, initiated to promote social cohesion among students. What did you get out of it? How did other students respond? Evaluate the overall effectiveness of the activity and recommend changes to improve it. How would you respond to a complaint that students are offered too many choices on campus and that these choices promote individualism at the expense of shared experiences?

2. Research projects, especially those undertaken by professional anthropologists, often involve a delicate balance between confidentiality and openness. Imagine the kinds of decisions Small had to make about revealing her true identity. In order to obtain the best possible results, how would you have gone about what she did? Who, if anyone, would you have been completely open with? Under what circumstances? What did she owe to the people she interviewed? What kinds of permissions would you expect her to need before publishing her research? Record your ideas. Then locate a copy of her book and refer to the section "Ethics and Ethnography." How accurate were your speculations and what did the activity teach you?

Gen Y's Ego Trip

Larry Gordon and Louis Sahagun, *Los Angeles Times,* February 27, 2007

Larry Gordon and Louis Sahagun are staff writers for the Los Angeles Times. *They have written numerous articles on higher education, politics, culture and a variety of other topics relevant to Southern Californians.*

What signs of self-centeredness, or "self-promotion," do you see in yourself? What about in the college students you come in contact with?

1 No wonder YouTube is so popular. All the effort to boost children's self-esteem may have backfired and produced a generation of college students who are more narcissistic than their Gen X predecessors, according to a new study led by a San Diego State University psychologist. And the Internet, with all its MySpace and YouTube braggadocio, is letting that self-regard blossom even more, said the analysis, titled

"Egos Inflating Over Time." In the study being released today, researchers warn that a rising ego rush could cause personal and social problems for the Millennial Generation, also called Gen Y. People with an inflated sense of self tend to have less interest in emotionally intimate bonds and can lash out when rejected or insulted.

"That makes me very, very worried," said Jean Twenge, a San 2 Diego State associate professor and lead author of the report. "I'm concerned we are heading to a society where people are going to treat each other badly, either on the street or in relationships." She and four other researchers from the University of Michigan, University of Georgia and University of South Alabama looked at the results of psychological surveys taken by more than 16,000 college students across the country over more than 25 years. The Narcissistic Personality Inventory asks students to react to such statements as: "If I ruled the world, it would be a better place," "I think I am a special person" and "I like to be the center of attention." The study found that almost two-thirds of recent college students had narcissism scores that were above the average 1982 score. Thirty percent more college students showed elevated narcissism in 2006 than in 1982.

Twenge said she and her coauthors are not suggesting that more 3 students today have a pathological narcissistic personality disorder that needs psychiatric treatment. Still, traits of narcissism have increased by moderate but significant amounts, said Twenge, who last year published a book titled *Generation Me: Why Today's Young Americans Are More Confident, Assertive, Entitled—and More Miserable Than Ever Before.* The narcissism report is under review for publication in a scholarly journal, which would give it the stamp of academic recognition it now lacks. It was released, Twenge said, in connection with the upcoming paperback edition of her book and with a student affairs workshop today at the University of San Diego at which she and another speaker will discuss how today's college students approach education.

Some of the increase in narcissistic attitudes was probably caused 4 by the self-esteem programs that many elementary schools adopted 20 years ago, the study suggests. It notes that nursery schools began to have children sing songs that proclaim: "I am special, I am special. Look at me." Those youngsters are now adolescents obsessed with websites, such as MySpace and YouTube, that "permit self-promotion far beyond that allowed by traditional media," the report says.

Other trends in American culture, including permissive parenting, 5 increased materialism and the fascination with celebrities and reality TV shows, may also heighten self-regard, said study coauthor W. Keith Campbell, psychology professor at the University of Georgia. "It's part of a whole cultural system," he said. The researchers seek to counter theories that current college students are more civic-minded and involved in volunteer activities than their predecessors. Because many high schools require community work, increases in volunteering "may not indicate a return to civic orientation but may instead be the means toward the more self-focused goal of educational attainment," the report says.

6   An annual survey of US college freshmen by the Higher Education Research Institute at UCLA has found growing interest in public service and social responsibility, presumably in response to Hurricane Katrina and other disasters around the world. But that survey also showed that current freshmen are much more interested in financial success and less in "a meaningful philosophy of life" than students were in the 1970s.

7   At Cal State Long Beach on Monday, an informal survey produced divided opinions about Gen Y personality traits. Students and teachers said they often see examples of inflated egos on campus: students who converse in the computer center while others are trying to concentrate, preen in front of the reflecting windows of the economics building or expect good grades simply for showing up at class. Laura Rantala, 26, a sociology major, said the phenomenon got in the way of a survey she conducted last semester on the attitudes of men and women about jury duty. "It took about three minutes to complete the survey," she recalled. "But many students were so self-absorbed they didn't want to participate. "I think it's because we all have our own cell phone and iPod with which we're doing our own thing in our own little world," she mused.

8   Some students seeking degrees in finance and management said, however, that they had good reason to stress confidence and esteem. James Coari, a lecturer in the College of Business Administration, agreed, to a point. In an interview in his office, Coari said, people looking for jobs "have to be concerned about image because competition is fierce." Marc Flacks, an assistant professor of sociology, said that he believed that narcissism was too harsh a description for current students and that it was more important to discuss why "we have a society in which narcissistic behavior is a good quality to have. This is a bottom-line society, so students are smart to seek the most direct route to the bottom line," he added. "If you don't have a me-first attitude, you won't succeed." Flacks summed up the attitudes he often encounters in students, who expect a tangible payoff from their education: "The old model was a collegial one in which students and professors alike sought knowledge for knowledge's sake. The new model is 'I paid my money, give me my grade and degree.' It makes me want to ask [students], 'Want fries with that order?'"

Reflection and Discussion

1. Discuss the differences between confidence based on accomplishment and confidence acquired by other means. What distinctions do you see between confidence and narcissism?
2. W. Keith Campbell said that the combination of indulgent parents, materialistic attitudes and celebrity culture can increase self-regard. Rank these from most to least significant and explain your choices. Where would you place the influence of schools and teachers?

Writing Matters

1. Should the practice of enhancing the self-esteem of young, impressionable students be continued, adapted or eliminated? Explain your position and defend it with a clearly reasoned and well-supported argument. When appropriate, use statistics, examples and specifics to make your case. To what extent do you agree with Laura Rantala's assessment of those on her campus? What about the opinions of the faculty members?
2. How is a campus a microcosm, reflecting the values of American society as a whole? In what ways are college campuses places where special rules and attitudes prevail? How much of college should be devoted to preparing students for a "tangible payoff" after graduation, in other words, career training? How much time should be devoted to personal growth, value formation and service to society? Explain yourself and back up your points with support from this article, your own experience and other sources.

Shaped by 9/11, Millennials Are Socially Conscious

Sharon Jayson, *USA Today*, October 26, 2006

Sharon Jayson has written numerous articles on social and cultural issues for publications like the Chicago Sun Times *and* USA Today.

When you think of making the world a better place, what kinds of efforts come to mind?

Alex Wells switched shampoos over animal testing. She won't buy   1
clothes produced by child labor. She yells at those who don't recycle. She spent a month in India this summer teaching English to preschoolers. Last year in high school, she helped organize a protest over genocide in the Sudan that raised $13,000 for Darfur relief. Wells, 18, of Los Gatos, CA, may be pretty typical of her generation. A growing body of academic and market research suggests millennials—who are in their

mid-20s and younger—are civic-minded and socially conscious as individuals, consumers and employees. This generation, also known as Generation Y and Echo Boomers, has been pressed for its vote, sought for its purchasing power and watched closely by sociologists and historians for insight into the way its members will shape the future.

2   They may be less radical than baby boom activists in the 1960s and 1970s, whose demonstrations for civil rights, women's equality and protecting the environment and protests against the Vietnam War became flashpoints for their times. But thanks in large part to the Internet, this generation is much more aware of the world. And because national tragedies such as the 9/11 terrorist attacks and Hurricane Katrina have scarred their youth and adolescence, experts see signs these young people are creating their own brand of social consciousness.

Among the Indicators:

- Sixty-one percent of 13- to 25-year-olds feel personally responsible for making a difference in the world, suggests a survey of 1,800 young people to be released today. It says 81% have volunteered in the past year; 69% consider a company's social and environmental commitment when deciding where to shop; and 83% will trust a company more if it is socially and environmentally responsible. The online study—by two Boston-based companies, Cone Inc. and AMP Insights—suggests millennials are "the most socially conscious consumers to date."

- Young people want to help their country by working for the government, suggests another study, also to be released today by the international consulting firm Universum Communications. Based on responses of 10,847 undergraduates at 115 US colleges and universities, it found that among ethnic groups in particular, federal jobs hold great allure. Among Hispanics, the CIA, the State Department and the FBI rank only below Walt Disney (the No. 1 choice) as an ideal employer. Among blacks, the FBI ranked second, the State Department fourth. The CIA rounded out the top 10.

- Two-thirds of college freshmen (66%) believe it's essential or very important to help others in difficulty, suggests a survey of 263,710 students at 385 US colleges and universities. The 2005 report, by the Higher Education Research Institute at the University of California at Los Angeles, found feelings of social and civic responsibility among entering freshmen at the highest level in 25 years.

- Volunteerism by college students increased by 20% from 2002 to 2005, says a study released last week by the federal Corporation for National and Community Service.

Some note, though, that many high schools require volunteering, and it has become a must-do for the college résumé. "Most research on volunteering doesn't translate to political involvement," says Curtis Gans of American University's Center for the Study of the American Electorate. Many of their parents don't vote or are "civically illiterate," he says. He adds that measurable declines in civic education, newspaper reading and knowledge of current events are other signs of a devaluing of civic involvement.

Harvard public policy professor Robert Putnam, whose 2000 book *Bowling Alone* is about the decline of civic engagement and social connection, says volunteering is class-driven. "This whole recent spurt is largely concentrated among kids of the upper middle class. . . . The have-nots are actually more detached than before. I am hopeful that we may be on the cusp of a new more civically engaged America, but if that is all defined very sharply in terms of social class, then the news is not so good."

A report in September by the National Conference on Citizenship, and based on nationally representative data from 1975 to 2004, echoes Putnam's concerns. It suggests a "large and growing civic divide between those with a college education and those without one."

Voting is another concern. A survey of 650 young people ages 18–30 released last month by the non-partisan Young Voter Strategies, a nonprofit project at George Washington University in Washington, DC, found that 69% said they were likely to vote in November, and 80% said they were registered to vote. But another survey of 1,804 adults released last week by the Pew Research Center for the People & the Press, in collaboration with the Associated Press, found that 40% of 18- to 29-year-olds are not registered to vote. That's double the percentage of 30- to 49-year-olds who aren't registered, and nearly three times greater than those 50 or older. Also, only 22% of young voters are regular voters compared with 42% of older voters and 35% of those 30 to 49.

Still, Putnam believes the terrorist attacks appear to have had a much more lasting effect on this generation's attitudes toward service. Though the surge in community-mindedness quickly evaporated for others, "for kids caught in their impressionable years by the events of 9/11, it has not yet gone away. They seem to have been permanently influenced."

Such students are those who come to Washington, DC, for a semester at American University—dubbed the most politically active school in the *Princeton Review*'s 2006 student survey. Senior Kirsten Reed, 20, a political science major at the University of Oregon in Eugene, wants to work for the federal government in national security. "I want to do something for the defense of the country," says Reed, of Pleasanton, CA. Brant Garda, a senior majoring in political science at Allegheny College in Meadville, PA, wants to work with his state's struggling steel mining towns. "I want to be around to rejuvenate the area politically, economically or whatever," says Garda, 21, of Washington, PA.

9   But not everyone in this generation shares such feelings, says a report released this month by the Center for Information & Research on Civic Learning & Engagement, based at the University of Maryland's School of Public Policy. The study of 1,658 young people, ages 15–25, measured their participation in 19 activities considered civic or political, such as being an active member of at least one group; raising money for charity; signing a paper petition or boycotting.

10   The study found that 58% of young people were considered "disengaged" because they participated in two or fewer of those 19 activities; 17% did none. Elise Cochrane, 20, a junior majoring in psychology at the University of Northern Iowa in Cedar Falls, says she voted in the presidential election, but she is conflicted about voting in November. "The advertisements have been bashing each other so bad, none of the candidates seem to fit for me," she says. "I kind of wish I was more interested so I would know more of what was going on, but I'm not seriously interested in being a Republican or Democrat."

11   Because many millennials say they're not interested in politics, efforts are under way to encourage civic and political involvement. A 2-year-old group called GenerationEngage is a non-partisan, youth civic engagement initiative aimed at college-age people who aren't students. It organizes events so that hundreds of young people can meet face-to-face and online with leaders and politicians, such as Al Gore and Newt Gingrich. Those who aren't in school "don't suffer from a lack of interest; they suffer from a lack of access," says co-founder Adrian Talbot, 26. A voter registration drive for 18- to 30-year-olds just wrapped up, and more than 400,000 young people registered.

12   The Cone study also found that young people are extending their social consciousness to the workplace. Of the 28% of ages 13 to 25 who are employed full time, 79% said they want to work for a company that cares about how it affects or contributes to society. "If they're going to work many, many hours, they need to work in a place where they're doing some good," adds Claudia Tattanelli, CEO of Universum, which helps companies attract workers.

13   Although Wells is just a freshman, she is thinking ahead to her career. She hasn't yet selected a major, but she knows she wants her work to be meaningful. "I want to major in something in international

or humanitarian aid or in the environmental sciences," she says. "I want to do something that helps in a positive way."

Reflection and Discussion

1. How do you explain the apparent conflict between a high interest in volunteering or helping others and a low interest in voting?
2. Jayson credits the Internet for making this generation of young people "much more aware of the world." In what ways does the Internet increase world awareness? How does this translate into being better informed? Where do traditional media sources like print, radio and television fit in?

Writing Matters

1. Who would be most interested in reading an article like this? Imagine the audience Jayson had in mind and identify parts of the article that seem particularly suited to those people. If you were to adapt Jayson's article as an essay for an English composition class, what would you change? How much do you consider your audience as you write for your college courses?
2. How convincing is Jayson's case that today's students are socially conscious? What do you think of her "academic and market research"? Which parts of her article helped personalize the topic? Examine carefully the beginning, middle and end of her article and comment on how well they work together.

Political Engagement and Service Learning, a Gandhian Perspective

Dilafruz Williams, *ENCOUNTER: Education for Meaning and Social Justice,* Summer 2002

Dilafruz Williams teaches service learning courses at Portland State University where she is a professor of education. Her publications include articles and books on civic engagement and environmental education.

How do you react when people describe college students of today as politically apathetic?

The purpose of life is . . . to know oneself.

—Mahatma Gandhi

"Let me be the change for the world." This is a profound political dictum practiced by none other than Gandhi, ordained "Mahatma and   1 saint" for his extraordinarily creative and sophisticated teachings of nonviolence or *satyagraha*. Yet, Gandhi considers himself to be an ordinary man connected to and working with ordinary people from "below," i.e., at the grassroots. For him, democracy is not about giving control to elected representatives to handle societal and local issues but rather it is about people taking responsibility for every act of the government, for he believes that government has no power or even existence independent of the people. Since democracy is about being free, it entails making informed choices that impact all individuals. It also entails making informed choices about whom we elect and consequently the policies that will likely affect the citizenry. While to participate in voting is a "must"—an inalienable right—democracy requires ongoing involvement in the political process, according to Gandhi.

2   Gandhi is increasingly relevant to the new millennium and the civilizational dilemmas brought about by the fateful events of September 11, 2001. In this article, I will highlight what the service-learning movement can learn and gain from Gandhian "political" philosophy. I hesitate to say "political" because, in essence, his is an all-encompassing philosophy of life. He views the individual, society, education, economics, spirituality, service, politics, and nonviolence as being connected and interrelated. What I argue is that Gandhi would have no difficulty connecting political involvement with service learning. In fact, he would never have approved of any service learning that did not have an active political and societal transformational element. How then does Gandhi link politics with service? He believes that service of the people is impossible without taking part in politics. I will elaborate on what I call the 3S's that are interconnected in Gandhi's perspective on service and political engagement: *spirituality, selflessness through sacrifice,* and *social justice.*

3   My interest on Gandhi as an impetus for service learning arises from the concerns that have been raised by many prominent leaders and researchers about the decline of political participation in the United States, especially by young people between the ages of 18 and 24. Moreover, I have personally used the pedagogy of service learning first as a faculty member and then as an administrator of faculty development at Portland State University (PSU). These experiences have made me acutely aware of the need to expand the discourse of service learning to include political engagement and civic responsibility. This is particularly pertinent because our commitment to democracy always renews the "so what" sort of questions.

4   How can we promote political participation and civic engagement particularly in universities? I derive my insights from my work to promote university–community partnerships at PSU and the study I carried

out on Gandhian schools in India under a Spencer Foundation grant. I was interested in Gandhi's holistic view of nonviolence that went beyond his world-renowned political strategy of *satyagraha*. What emerged from his writing and my study was that Gandhian nonviolence is a way of learning and living. In other words, education plays a significant role in advancing nonviolent living. Unfortunately, this is the least explored part of his legacy. Gandhi had proposed and implemented a program called *Nai Talim* (New Education) that has completely been ignored or marginalized by the professional canon of education. In my study (Williams 1993) I was able to see *Nai Talim* being put into practice. While I cannot go into the details of his entire program, I will highlight the importance of *service*, which is one of the components of his educational philosophy both in higher education and K–12 schools.

This article is divided into three sections. First, I will discuss the 5 recent concerns over political disengagement in the United States. Next, I will explore the Gandhian notion of service and political engagement. Finally, I will present an outline of the principles of practicing political engagement through service learning, pointing out the challenges we face and the opportunities we have.

Political Disengagement: Cause for Concern?

In a study of freshman college students' participation in civic responsi- 6 bility, Linda Sax (2000, 3–18) identifies two alarming trends. While involvement of students in volunteerism and community service is on the rise, their interest in politics is declining. In 1998, a record high 74% of college freshmen performed volunteer work during their last year in high school; this volunteerism has been on the rise over the past decade. Sax links the rise in volunteerism to: (1) a number of service programs offered by academic institutions and supported by federal and state governments, (2) increasing numbers of K–12 schools that offer service-learning opportunities, and (3) increasingly, high schools that require community service as a graduation requirement (p. 5). Despite this, however, students' interest in politics has declined drastically. This disengagement in politics, according to her, ranges from a serious decrease in voting to a lack of interest in political affairs.[1]

How can we take democracy for granted? Dewey (1914) had 7 warned that democracy is always in the making, which means that the people *are* what democracy is about. Even then, he decried the "eclipse of the public" (Dewey 1927) and would be appalled at the cynicism and sense of despair that sometimes permeates the lives not only of our youth but also the general public.

8   But why is there political apathy among youth? Some scholars and leaders link this to students' "negative perceptions of politics and politicians and a sense of skepticism," largely due to media coverage of political scandals, government gridlock, etc. There is a general sense of hopelessness about change through political approaches. Moreover, "college students feel a sense of disconnection or alienation from the political issues themselves" (Sax 2000, 7). Paradoxically, then, why is there a growing orientation toward service while there a declining interest in politics? Why do the habits of volunteerism and service fostered in high school and in college not translate into political activity?[2] . . .

9   I believe that the problem of political disengagement has to be confronted at two levels. One has to do with *pedagogy*, i.e., the realm of teaching and learning. The other has to do with *developing a sensibility of what a democratic polity entails;* in other words, recognizing what the "public" domain is about and how individuals *qua* individuals are implicated in the politics of democracy. I think the important point here is for students to understand that politics is not simply what politicians do in a place distant from the local community; rather it is something that citizens practice daily. Nor is it right to ignore voting because those we elect have much to do with the politics of our daily practice of democracy.

10   Having said that, I recognize that among the crucial challenges we face is the fact that no longer do people stay stable in a place. Traditional forms of living and "staying put" in one community are no longer possible. I do not wish to romanticize traditional communities, as not all of those forms were necessarily healthy. Nevertheless, as Wendell Berry (1987) points out, for the United States mobility, in particular, is one of the greatest problems we confront today in our search for commitment to community and place. Sustained deliberation and political discourse are also hampered due to lack of such stable communities and inhabitants.

11   Perhaps Gandhi provides a perspective that is fresh and comprehensive to underscore the dilemma we are facing. Let me now turn to Gandhi.

Gandhian Notions of Service and Political Engagement

12   In Gandhi's writings, true to his lived experience, we find the concept of service woven into his deep understanding of life: "The purpose of life is . . . to know oneself. We cannot do so unless we learn to identify ourselves with all that lives. The instrument of this knowledge is boundless, selfless service" (Gandhi 1960, 3). . . .

Gandhi has a holistic view of the political that is derived from the 13 concept of *advaita* (nondualism) or unity of life. We cannot divide "social, economic, political, and purely religious work into watertight compartments," he says. Nor can we be doing right in one facet of our life while doing wrong in another. The breadth and scope of life are one "indivisible whole" for him (Roy, 1985, 124).

If we accept Gandhi's notion that all life activities must be geared 14 toward and influenced by the central purpose of life, how then do our lived experiences of politics, economic affairs, social interactions, education, religion, and so on, help with that process? Gandhi says that these are the means for self-transformation; hence our conduct in these life activities must reflect a commitment to life beyond the "self." Further, because our contemporary era is the era of politics *par excellence,* we must confront the empirical reality that there will likely be conflicts over the choices that we make in the public realm. Almost all aspects of individual and social life are directly or indirectly organized and administered by the state and all human relationships are mediated politically. In a politically dominated age Gandhi considers it impossible for us to serve our fellow humans and eliminate social and economic ills without active political involvement, writes Bhikhu Parikh (1989, 98–106).

For Gandhi, then, the landscape of politics is central to all action in 15 contemporary times. But why is it our duty to become politically involved? Gandhi's answer, according to Parikh (1989, 101), would be that political engagement regenerates the country because it consists in revitalizing society, culture, and character. Working in communities or villages, helping people acquire courage and self-respect, fighting against local injustices, dealing with choices and consequently with conflicts, are examples of activities linked with politics. Politics is not solely connected with nor exhausted in the state. The state seems to have become the major and sometimes sole arena for political activity only because modern humans have surrendered their moral and social powers to it (Parikh 1989, 101–102). . . .

Because for Gandhi the state does not exist independent of its citi- 16 zens, politics should not mean the delegation of life to government. Since the "self" is a political being, Gandhi believes that the only way we can get citizens to participate more actively is for them to see that they are *responsible* for the actions of the state. The elected officials have no power or even existence independent of the people, according to Gandhi. Every citizen therefore renders herself or himself responsible for every act of the government. In other words, we are implicated in all acts of the state. For instance, I care deeply about the environment and feel responsible when the President of the United States downplays the Kyoto agreement.

17   How does Gandhi link politics with service then? Gandhi believes that service of the people is impossible without taking part in politics. With a broad stroke of a brush let us look at a variety of concepts such as spirituality, selflessness through sacrifice, and social justice—what I call the 3S's—that are interconnected in Gandhi's perspective on service and political engagement.

Spirituality

18 Gandhi gives political life a spiritual foundation because politics is a spiritual activity for him. While spirituality through personal introspection is important, spirituality is to be attained through engagement with others, not simply through contemplation in temples and on mountains as the yogis did in India. The *Bhagavat Gita* explains that the universe is one vast *yajna*—a system of uncoerced and interrelated offerings. Every part of it offers its services and contributes to the maintenance of the whole. "*Yajna* is an act directed to the welfare of others done without desiring anything in return for it—whether temporal or spiritual," writes Gandhi (1960, 11). Contrary to common understanding, by "act" Gandhi means thought, word, and action. Further, for him welfare of "others" means welfare of all life—not just that of humans. This practice of *yajna* frees us from bondage. Thus, self-realization, according to Gandhi, is impossible without being involved in the world. This may seem like a contradiction, but it is not. Because we are born debtors, we take collective responsibility for our inheritance and the legacies we leave behind for the future. Gandhi explains that if political life could be spiritualized, it would have a profoundly transformative effect on the rest of society. Confronted by entrenched colonial relations in India, he considers political action as the only available path to *moksha* or salvation.

Selflessness Through Sacrifice

> The path of service can hardly be trodden by one who is not prepared to renounce self-interest. . . . Consciously or unconsciously, every one of us does render some service or other; hence, we need to cultivate the habit of selfless service.
> (Gandhi in Easwaran 1978, 20)

19 Deriving much of his understanding from the *Gita*, Gandhi believes that to attain *moksha*—to become one with or dissolve oneself into the cosmic spirit—there has to be an interplay of attachment and

detachment. Selfless service is about this interplay and is its own reward (Gandhi, n.d.).

Social Justice

> I cannot imagine anything nobler than that for, say, an hour a
> day we should do the labor the poor must do, and thus iden-
> tify ourselves with them, and through them, with all
> mankind. (Gandhi 1960, 5)

This is one way to understand suffering. Gandhi uses the metaphor of 20 *bread labor* or manual work to symbolize our connection with the poorest in our society. As is well known, for Gandhi the daily use of the charkha or spinning wheel to make thread from cotton is a symbolic act. Instead of using only our minds, we should use our hands to connect with the poor. By engaging in work that has historically denigrated a certain group of people, we dissolve the caste and class link. Through productive bread labor, we also get on a path of self-sufficiency whereby we break the cycle of economic dependence and colonization, since menial labor in India was done by the *shudras* who were members of the lowest caste. Humble, unselfish work is important in addressing social injustices. It should be noted here that Gandhi acknowledges that deeply entrenched social and economic inequalities cannot be removed by moral persuasion alone. Trusteeship does not simply arise through the "enlightenment" of those who are powerful, wealthy, or both. Politics and law must also be called upon to address inequities. However, his appeal was that the conflicts that undergird the distribution of public goods must be dealt with in nonviolent ways.

In Gandhian terms, education serves as an important means to 21 develop the sensibilities discussed above. A key component to participation in democracy is service. Thus, service learning for Gandhi would be a mode of action and a method of inquiry. Service learning necessarily engages us in the method of political inquiry. It necessarily engages us in the politics of democracy, and by extension, life. In his program of *Nai Talim*, for instance, at one of the institutions of higher education that I visited students are not charged any tuition. Instead, they are required to do a total of 350 to 400 hours of socially useful productive service in the surrounding villages by connecting their work with the academic content of rural regeneration. Moreover, adhering to Gandhi's concern for social justice and welfare of the least well-off members of society, students are expected to participate for 20 days in *adivasi* camps in tribal areas. Through service learning, not only do we develop the virtues of humility, but by working with others to address communal issues, we expand the notion of "self" and gain deeper political understanding of our links with others who are not necessarily similar to us. . . .

Capacity Building for Political Engagement

22 Gandhian philosophy requires that we develop capacity for political engagement by immersing ourselves in the work of politics. To do so, I believe, we must meet the following three criteria:

> *Teach students how to deliberate in public.* As Alasdair MacIntyre writes, "We have lost forums of genuine, extended public debate. Ask yourself when last the US Senate assembled with senators ready to have their opinions formed through debate, rather than bringing intransigent opinions to the debate." (Briand 1999, 3). I know that reflection is a critical component of service learning. Drawing upon Gandhi, I suggest that we should also teach our students contemplation, introspection, mindfulness, and imagination as they become grounded in the community's politics. Skills of deliberation force us to go beyond our personal opinions.
>
> *Balance passionate advocacy with dispassionate listening.* As educators we must strive to balance being advocates who are passionately committed to political issues with the need to provide space for different points of views, beliefs, and values. There is tremendous stimulation of intellectual engagement when passions abound; however, Gandhian *ahimsa* requires dispassionate listening. That is, we learn to be compassionate and more understanding of others' perspectives if we are willing to let go of our judgments when we engage others.
>
> *Practice nonviolent conflict resolution.* Gandhi clearly states that nonviolence *(ahimsa)* is more than just the absence of violence. It is a positive force, a lifestyle that stresses action based on refusal to do harm. His holistic approach requires that we address nonviolence comprehensively through our thoughts, words, and actions. Nonviolence must pervade the whole being and not be applied to isolated acts (Gandhi 1936). Acknowledging that conflicts are inevitable especially in participatory democratic life, Gandhi's nonviolence is a way of life, a way to address choices for public goods as much as a way to create community. Service-learning experiences, in particular,

provide innumerable opportunities for students, faculty, and community partners to practice nonviolence, broadly defined. . . .

Doing away with dualisms of theory and practice, of learning and living, as Gandhi urges, is going to be tough. In order to establish the holistic connection between learning and living, we would need simultaneous commitment to community and place by the citizenry. Furthermore, I think we would need to highlight those pockets of work where people are successfully engaging the "politics of place" even as they are learning. Our educational work would need to be grounded in a deep mind shift that we are not *consumers* of democracy. We are *makers* of democracy. We are growers of democracy. We are democracy!

References

Berry, Wendell. 1987. Does community have a value? *Home economics.* San Francisco: North Point Press.

Briand, Michael. 1999. *Practical politics: Five principles of a community that works.* Urbana: University of Illinois Press.

Campus Compact. 1999, July. *Fourth of July declaration on the civic responsibility of higher education.* Campus Compact.

Dewey, John. 1914. *Democracy and education.* New York: Free Press.

Dewey, John. 1927. *The public and its problems.* New York: Henry Holt.

Easwaran, Eknath. 1978. *Gandhi the man.* Petaluma, California: Nilgiri Press.

Ehrlich, Thomas, ed. 2000. *Civic responsibility and higher education.* Phoenix: American Council on Education and The Oryx Press.

Gandhi, Mohandas K. n.d. *The collected works of Mahatma Gandhi.* New Delhi: Government of India publications.

Gandhi, Mohandas K. 1936, September 5. *Harijan.*

Gandhi, Mohandas K. 1960. *Bread labor: The gospel of work.* Ahmedabad, India: Navjivan Press.

Gandhi, Mohandas K. 1980. *Nai Talim: Towards new education.* Ahmedabad, India: Navjivan Press.

Palmer, Parker. 1998. *The courage to teach: Exploring the inner landscape of a teacher's life.* San Francisco: Jossey-Bass.

Parajuli, Pramod. 2001. Learning from ecological ethnicities: Towards a plural political ecology of knowledge. In *Indigenous traditions and ecology,* edited by John Grim. pp. 559–589. Cambridge: Harvard University Press.

Parajuli, Pramod and Smitu Kothari. 1998. Struggling for autonomy: The lessons from local governance. *Development: Seeds of Change* 41(3): 18–29.

Parikh, Bhikhu. 1989. *Gandhi's political philosophy: A critical examination.* Notre Dame, IN: University of Notre Dame Press.

Rilke, Rainer M. 1993. *Letters to a young poet.* Translated by S. Mitchell. Boston: Shambhala.

Roy, Ramashray. 1985. *Self and society: A study in Gandhian thought.* New Delhi: Sage.

Sax, Linda J. 2000. Citizenship development and the American college student. In *Civic responsibility and higher education,* edited by Thomas Ehrich. Phoenix: American Council on Education and Oryx Press. pp. 3–18.

Walker, Tobi. 2000. The service/politics split: Rethinking service to teach political engagement. *PS: Political Science and Politics* 33(4): 647–649.

Williams, Dilafruz. 1993, August. The unity of learning and living for ecological sustainability: Gandhi's educational philosophy in practice. *Holistic Education Review* 6(3): 1823.

Williams, Dilafruz. 2000, Fall. Participants in, not spectators of, democracy: The discourse of civic responsibility in higher education. *Michigan Journal of Community Service Learning* 7: 158–164.

Notes

1. There is a 40-year decline in voter participation. For example, for 18–24 year olds, only 32% voted in 1998 as opposed to 50% in 1964; of the 18–19 year olds, only 11% voted. In addition, interest is waning in keeping up to date with political affairs: 58% in 1964 with a drop to 26% in 1998.

2. I say this with caution as the latest Wingspread conference is testimony to the shining examples of enthusiasm and hope related to student leaders' activism.

Reflection and Discussion

1. Consider a right or freedom that you particularly value and imagine it being taken away. How would you express yourself?

2. Most people would agree that service to others is important, but it can also take time away from a student's studies. From your perspective, weigh the positives and negatives of time devoted to community involvement.

Writing Matters

1. Williams believes strongly that Gandhi's life and the examples he set are still relevant today. Which parts of her article do you find most applicable or relevant to you? Which seem distant from your concerns? Discuss some of the significant changes that have occurred since Gandhi's time (1869–1948). How would someone who wanted to practice his philosophy have to adjust to them?

2. Examine Williams' logic that citizens are responsible for the actions of their government. What prominent examples can you cite of citizens expressing

themselves in protest over government policy? Are these acts of courage or duty? How do you respond to those who say that protests accomplish little? When, if ever, are the risks worth the potential repercussions?

Student Power

Student activism has a long history.
- As far back as the mid-19th century, students and professors in Germany, Italy and France altered the political direction of their countries, while students in the US spoke out against slavery.
- In the first part of the 20th-century, student leaders studying in the Netherlands and England inspired nationalist movements that forced the Dutch from Indonesia and Britain from India.
- Although student movements have often identified with Marxism and ideas from the left, in the period after World War I, many students in Italy and Germany supported Hitler and Mussolini.
- Reform-minded 20th-century students in Latin America helped transform higher education by insisting on widespread change.
- In the US, the student anti-war protests of the 1960s were preceded by student activism in the 1930s that focused on the Spanish Civil War and opposition to American involvement in World War II.
- More recently, student movements in Islamic countries have confirmed the continuing power of religion as a force, particularly when combined with nationalism.

Source: Philip G. Altbach, *Youth Activism: An International Encyclopedia*, 2005

Generation We and the 2008 Election

Ruy Teixeira, *futuremajority.com*, November 17, 2008

Ruy Teixeira is a Visiting Fellow at the Brookings Institution and the author of several books, including The Emerging Democratic Majority.

How invested were you in the US presidential campaigns of 2008?

With the election of Barack Obama, we are moving into a new political era. Spearheading the arrival of this new era is the Millennial generation (born 1978–2000). In a very short time, the Millennials have had a huge impact on our politics, an impact that will only grow in years to come. Nowhere has that impact been more obvious than in this

November's election. Millennials came out in very large numbers and overwhelmingly supported Barack Obama, as well as Democrats down the ticket. The progressive inclinations of this generation are now crystal clear.

2   This report provides a detailed analysis of Millennials' turnout, voting preferences and attitudes in this election, supplemented where appropriate with data from earlier surveys and studies. The portrait that emerges from this analysis is of a progressive generation for whom the 2008 election is just an opening bid on their desire for change. The Millennial earthquake has begun and American politics will never be the same.

3   *Note: This analysis builds on extensive previous research on Millennials supporting the book* Generation We: How Millennial Youth Are Taking Over America And Changing Our World Forever *by Eric Greenberg. That research and the book itself are all available for free download at the Gen We website.*

Millennial Turnout and Civic Engagement

4   The 2004 election was the first election in which the 18–24 year old age group was completely composed of Millennials and in which the 18–29 year old group was dominated by Millennials. In that election, Census data indicate that 18–24 year olds increased their turnout 11 points to 47 percent of citizens in that age group and 18–29 year olds increased their turnout 9 points to 49 percent. These increases were far, far higher than among any other age group.

5   In 2006, Millennials also increased their turnout levels relative to the last congressional election. Census data show that 18–29 year olds (almost all Millennials at this point) increased their turnout from 23 percent to 26 percent of citizen-eligible voters, a 3 point gain relative to 2002. This gain was once again higher than among any other age group.

6   The 2008 elections continued this pattern. To begin with, turnout of 18–29 year olds skyrocketed in this year's primaries, about doubling overall. And in the November general election, exit poll data showed the 18–29 year old group (now composed exclusively of Millennials) increasing its share of voters from 17 to 18 percent. Based on extrapolations from these data[1] (the Census data for this election will not be available for many months), 18–29 year old turnout increased from 4–5 percentage points. This is quite an impressive performance in an election where overall turnout went up only a little over 1 percent.[2] Indeed, 18–29 year old turnout performance was so relatively strong

that it accounts for about 60 percent of the overall increase in votes in this election.

This uninterrupted series of turnout increases augurs well for Millennials' ability to impact politics in the future. This is especially so since 18–29 year old Millennials, at 18 percent of voters, are already larger than the senior vote (16 percent of voters), a group typically treated as being exceptionally influential by political observers. But Millennials, even at this early stage, outweigh them.

Moreover, the 18 percent figure actually understates the current level of Millennial influence on the electorate. This is because the 18–29 year old group does not include the oldest Millennials, the 30 year olds who were born in 1978. Once they are figured in, a reasonable estimate is that Millennials were around 20 percent of the vote in this election.

This figure will steadily rise as more Millennials enter the voting pool. In 2008, about 55 million Millennials were of voting age and roughly 48 million were citizen-eligible voters. Between now and 2018, Millennials of voting age will be increasing by about four and half million a year. And in 2020, the first Presidential election where all Millennials will have reached voting age, this generation will be 103 million strong, of which about 90 million will be eligible voters. Those 90 million Millenial eligible voters will represent just under 40 percent of America's eligible voters.[3]

These trends mean that every election up until 2020 will see a bigger share of Millennial voters both because more of them will be eligible to vote and because the leading edge of the Millennials will be aging into higher turnout years. Thus, in 2012, there will be 74 million Millennials of voting age and 64 million Millennial eligible voters, 29 percent of all eligible voters. Assuming that Millennials' relatively good turnout performance continues (but not that it gets any better), that should translate into roughly 35 million Millennials who cast ballots in 2012 and an estimated 26 percent of all voters.

By 2016, there will be 93 million Millennials of voting age and 81 million Millennial eligible voters, 36 percent of all eligible voters. This should produce an estimated 46 million voting Millennials, representing 33 percent of all voters. And in 2020, those 90 million Millennial eligible voters should translate into 52 million Millennial votes, representing 36 percent of all votes cast in that election.

Moreover, because more and more Millennial voters will be aging into their higher turnout years after 2020, the proportion of Millennials among voters should continue to rise for a number of elections, despite the fact that all Millennials will already be in the voting pool. For example, by 2028, when Millennials will be ages 28–50, their share of voters should be about 38 percent, 2 points higher than in 2020. Not surprisingly, given these high voter participation levels, the Millennial generation is also notable for its high levels of civic engagement in other areas. For example, volunteerism is unusually high among Millennials. According to UCLA's American Freshman survey— conducted for the last 40 years, with several hundred thousand respondents each year—83 percent of entering freshmen in 2005 volunteered at least occasionally during their high school senior year, the highest ever measured in this survey. And 71 percent said they volunteered on a weekly basis.[4]

13   They are also more politically engaged. In the 2006 American Freshman survey, more freshman reported they discussed politics frequently as high school seniors (34 percent) than at any other point in the 40 years covered by the survey. And, in a December, 2006 Pew Research Center Gen Next study, 18–25 year old Millennials (corresponding to birth years 1981–88 at the time of the survey) are running about 10 points higher than Gen X'ers at the same age on following what's going on in government and in level of interest in keeping up with national affairs.

14   Similarly, in a January, 2007 Pew Research Center survey, 77 percent of 18–29 year olds said they are interested in local politics, up 28 points from 49 percent in 1999—the highest increase of any age group surveyed. The survey also found that 85 percent of 18–29 year olds report they are "interested in keeping up with national affairs," a 14 point increase from 71 percent in 1999 and nearly the same level of interest as adults of all ages (89 percent.)

15   Millennials also come out well in measures of election-related political engagement. Looking back at the 2004 election, the University of Michigan's National Election Study (NES), found that 18–29 year olds in 2004 (an age group dominated by Millennials, who were 18–26 at the time), were either higher or matched previous highs on a wide range of political involvement indicators, when compared to 18–29 year olds in previous elections. These indicators included level of interest in the election, caring a good deal who wins the election, trying to influence others' vote, displaying candidate buttons or stickers, attending political meetings and watching TV programs about the campaign. (The 2008 NES which will provide comparable data for this election will not be available until late spring of 2009.)

16   The most recent survey findings confirm this pattern of high civic engagement, especially as it pertains to the intersection of technology and politics. The most thorough data come from the Harvard Institute of Politics' (IOP) Fall, 2008 survey of 18–24 year old Millennials, completed

in early October, just one month before this year's election. In that survey, 52 percent said they had signed an online petition, 27 percent had written an email or letter advocating a political position, 24 percent had contributed to an online political discussion or blog advocating a political position, 22 percent had attended a political rally, 16 percent had donated money to a political campaign or cause and 14 percent had volunteered on a political campaign for a candidate or issue.

Facebook and Myspace have become major outlets for political 17 engagement among Millennials. In the IOP survey, two-thirds said they had a Facebook account and, of that group, 36 percent said they had used Facebook to promote a political candidate, idea or event. The analogous figures for Myspace were 60 and 18.

Data from another recent survey provide more detail on this 18 emerging online political engagement among Millennials. In a mid-October Democracy Corps/Greenberg Quinlan Rosner Research survey of 18–29 year olds, 53 percent said they had watched a campaign commercial online; 45 percent said they had read a political blog; 39 percent had visited a campaign or candidate-sponsored website; 30 percent had forwarded a political video to a friend or family member; 28 percent had sent or forwarded emails about a candidate or campaign; 25 percent had forwarded a campaign commercial to a friend or family member; and 23 percent said they had signed up as a friend of a candidate on Facebook, Myspace or a similar social networking site.

It's also worth noting that nonpolitical civic engagement like vol- 19 unteerism continues at high levels among broad groups of Millennials (as noted earlier, volunteerism in the last year of high school has reached record levels). In the IOP survey, 47 percent of 18–24 year old Millennials reported they had volunteered for community service in the last year. And political discussion, which has also reached record levels among high school seniors, remains high among these older Millennials: 58 percent said they had discussed the Presidential campaign with someone just in the last day.

There is also some evidence there is an additional reservoir of civic 20 engagement among Millennials yet to be tapped. In the IOP survey, 76 percent said that if a friend or peer asked them to volunteer for a community service they considered worthy, they would do so; the analogous figures for attending a political rally or demonstration and volunteering on a political campaign were 63 and 47 percent respectively. In addition, 59 percent said they would be interested in engaging in some form of public service if the new President made a call to do so to young Americans (as Kennedy did in 1961).

Finally, the IOP survey amply documents the extent to which 21 Millennials have strongly positive attitudes about the potential of political engagement. For example, 69 percent thought political engagement was an effective way of solving important issues facing the country and 67 percent thought such engagement was an effective way of solving important issues facing their local community; the analogous figures for community volunteerism were 68 and 81.

22   In addition, 72 percent disagreed that "politics is not relevant to my life right now"; 84 percent disagreed that "it really doesn't matter to me who the president is"; 53 percent disagreed that "people like me don't have any say about what the government does"; 59 percent disagreed that "political involvement rarely has any tangible results"; and 60 percent disagreed that "it is difficult to find ways to be involved in politics." In addition, 68 percent agreed that "running for office is an honorable thing to do"; the analogous figures for community service and getting involved in politics were 89 and 64.

23   But it's important to stress that these are attitudes about the *potential* of political engagement. As surveys have persistently documented, Millennials believe today's government and political leaders are typically falling far short of their potential to do good and solve problems. In the IOP survey, 69 percent agreed that "elected officials seem to be motivated by selfish reasons"; 74 percent agreed that "politics has become too partisan"; and 67 percent agreed that "elected officials don't seem to have the same priorities that I have." These concerns will have to be addressed and overcome for Millennial activism to reach its full potential.

Millennial Voting and Partisanship

24 The progressive inclinations of the Millennial generation have been apparent for awhile. In 2006, 18–29 year olds overall voted 60–38 Democratic, with the 18–24 year old group (all Millennials) going 59–38 Democratic, while the 25–29 year olds (all Millennials but the 29 year olds) were 60–39 Democratic. These identical margins among the 18–24 year olds and 25–29 year olds point to great generational consistency among the Millennials.

25   In light of this generational consistency, it's interesting to note that in 2004, when 18–24 year olds were all Millennials but 25–29 year olds were mostly not, we did not see consistency across the two age groups. The all-Millennial 18–24 year olds voted 56–43 Democratic for president while the older, mostly non-Millennial 25–29 year old group voted only 51–48 Democratic.

26   In 2008, 18–29 year olds, now all Millennials, voted Democratic by a stunning 66–32 margin. And just as in 2006, we see remarkable generational consistency: 18–24 year olds voted 66–32 Democratic

while 25–29 year olds voted 66–31 Democratic. Essentially no difference.

Obama's support among 18–29 year olds was remarkably broad, 27 extending across racial barriers. He carried not just Hispanic 18–29 year olds (76–19) and black 18–29 year olds (95–4) but also white 18–29 year olds (54–44). Obama's 10 point advantage among white 18–29 year olds contrasts starkly with his 15 deficit among older whites. . . .

The voting inclinations of the Millennials, hugely important in this 28 election, could become even more so over time. If Millennials remain oriented as they are and maintain the generational consistency they have shown so far, the simple process of cohort replacement—more Millennials moving into the electorate and taking the place of older voters—will increase the Democrats' margin over the GOP by an additional two and a half percentage points in 2012 and then by another two and a half points in 2016. . . .

[They are] assure[d] of a dramatic impact on our society in the 29 decades to come. The 2008 election is truly just the beginning of that impact, which is likely to reshape our world in profound and positive ways. Given the scale of the challenges we face, the Millennial earthquake could not come at a better time.

Endnotes

1. Extrapolations from Center for Information and Research on Civic Learning and Engagement (CIRCLE), "Turnout Rises to at Least 52 percent," November 7, 2008. Exit poll extrapolations of youth turnout have generally tracked the Census data well; see CIRCLE, "The Youth Vote 2004," CIRCLE Working Paper 35, July, 2005 for useful comparisons.
2. Michael McDonald, "2008 Unofficial Voter Turnout," US Elections Project, November 9, 2008.
3. Estimations in this and subsequent paragraphs based on author's analysis of 2008 Census National Population Projections by single years of age, 2008 NEP exit poll sample composition and 2004 Census Voter Supplement data by single years of age.
4. Some data sources indicate that rates of volunteering among Millennials may actually have been highest right after, and presumably in reaction to, 9/11—but differences in question wording and population surveyed prevent a definitive judgment on this possibility.

Reflection and Discussion

1. Teixeira's article is packed with data—numbers, percentages, dates. In the political arena, how much attention should we devote to numbers and

percentages, polls and surveys? Explain whether we should focus more on the numbers or the issues. In what ways can the two be treated separately?

2. Teixeira argues that the youngest voting cohort has played a pivotal role in recent US elections. What evidence did you see that people your age made a difference? How confident are you that the political influence of the Millennial generation is growing and on what do you base that confidence?

Writing Matters

1. The overall tone of Teixeira's article is upbeat and optimistic yet he also includes information that some readers could use to undermine his thesis. Locate this information and argue whether it strengthens or weakens his case. In essays that you've written, when have you acknowledged opposing data or points of view? How did you frame those parts of your essay in order to let readers know that you still stood firmly behind your thesis?

2. The IOP survey found that most respondents said they would volunteer community service or attend a political rally if a friend or peer invited them. If they are so easily swayed into action, why do they not take the initiative themselves?

FIGURE 4.2 How much sympathy do you have for those who complain but do not vote?

Reflections of a Non-Political Man

Sven Birkerts, *Readings,* 1999

Sven Birkerts has published several books including An Artificial Wilderness: Essays on 20th Century Literature *and* The Electric Life: Essays on Modern Poetry. *He teaches at Mount Holyoke College in Massachusetts.*

Have you ever been accused of being not political enough? Too political? How did you respond?

I have a friend who wants me to be more political. He doesn't specify, but I know what he means: He wants me to do things, take conspicuous stances, have a more engaged posture in the world. And he's right. That is, he must be right—otherwise why would I feel such a prickling of guilt whenever he brings the subject up? And these days he seems to bring it up all the time. When he does I naturally become defensive; I scramble toward the familiar silence of not being understood. 1

This same friend, in an effort to raise my consciousness, has now asked me to write for him an essay on Noam Chomsky's and Edward Herman's latest book, *Manufacturing Consent.* In the face of such sincere concern for the fitness of my soul, I could not think of a way to refuse. I confess, too, that I hoped the book would make a change in me. It's not that I want to be nonpolitical, it's just that I am. I would give a great deal to be able to lay to rest the sickly guilt that moves through me whenever I face up to my own ineffectuality, my refusal to take any direct action against the waste, corruption and oppression that are around us like tethers. 2

So I read. And I read with care. Slowly, marking passages with a pencil. I paused—sometimes I made myself do so—over statistics confirming one outrage after another. I made every effort to understand, to impress on myself what this really meant in the world beyond the words. And I took pains to track the progress of Chomsky's argument: I marveled at the cool fury of the prose. I could see Chomsky's determination to avoid all rhetoric, to let the facts speak for themselves. Reading, I felt a deep respect for the dedication and will required to wage a campaign for truth in the face of near-universal deafness. I thought, too, about the points I would make and the sections I would cite to push those points home. I read, I marked, I plotted. And when I came to an end of it, I found that I stood squarely before an obstacle in myself: I could not possibly discuss this book, these ideas, in the necessary terms. 3

4   Not because I was not persuaded; not because I do not believe that Chomsky is doing a hero's work; not because the information does not need to go out to every person who thinks about anything more consequential than Friday's twilight doubleheader at Fenway Park—but because I was not an adequate vessel for Chomsky's vision. I would have to pretend to a stance or perspective that I could assent to intellectually, but that I had not earned with my heart. Indeed, the more I soaked myself in the information, and the more I thought about the implication of the analysis that Chomsky sets out—how the whole empire of our communications is tacitly and implicitly geared to furthering the vested interests of US imperialism—the more I found myself coiling back upon my own blockage: my inability, unwillingness, to put myself forward in meaningful political action on behalf of anything. The two—Chomsky's thesis and my response—are very separate things, but as I read they became one. The book and its author became in my mind a single emblem of engaged activism before which I was struck dumb.

5   I faced the difficult fact: I will do nothing overt to further causes I believe in—I will do nothing political. An awful admission. Certainly there is no dearth of causes, all of them asking for our most committed support. Greenpeace, Amnesty International, pro-choice mobilization, anti-apartheid organizations, nuclear freeze campaigns. What is wrong with me that I cannot bestir myself to do anything more than sign an occasional petition, write out a small check?

6   I discussed my sense of handicap with my friend. He suggested that the problem was not mine alone, that it seemed to afflict a great many people, prominent among them the writers, artists and thinkers that one might expect would be closer to such consciousness and involvement. We went back and forth debating possible reasons, considering everything from cultural narcissism to spiritual detachment in the service of art, but we were not able to solve the matter. I promised him that if I could not write the essay he had assigned, I would instead set down my reasons for failure.

7   I would like to write about this inactivity, this political paralysis of mine, honestly. I would like to write about it without lapsing into the clever, cynical mode that comes to me so readily when I get defensive. But I am, of course, defensive. Somewhere not all that deep within I know that the blockage represents a failing. No, I correct myself: I don't know this, I only suspect it. And I would like to—I think I would like to—change myself, to think my way through to an understanding of things out of which response—action—would result naturally. For I know that nothing could be more false, and wrongheaded, than a rash effort on my part to set things right by simply deciding to do something. To go march at Seabrook, say.

But how to work through this tangle? First, I ought to make a clear 8 distinction between political passivity (or paralysis) and political apathy. I am not apathetic. Certainly not about the thousand-and-one ills of the world. If I am apathetic about anything, it's political process: activity. But no, even that is not quite right. For I have great admiration for those people who feel the compulsion to act out their beliefs and who find meaningful ways to do so. I see newsreel footage of demonstrators being carted away from nuclear power plants or dumping sites and I envy them. I find myself wishing that I, too, knew my convictions in such a bodily—complete—fashion. Nothing stops me from joining the march—but I do not join. I applaud others; I cannot make myself act.

The obvious defense, the first that comes to mind, is that these 9 activities are ultimately useless, that they will not stay the course of the world or stop the powers that be from enacting their schemes. This I can readily discard: for even if the protests availed nothing, they would still send a signal to those powers that they cannot simply railroad their designs into place; they cannot expect that everyone consents. And this is a necessary statement.

As it happens, such an argument is beside the point anyway. 10 Protest and activism have brought about a great number of improvements in our collective situation. They hastened the withdrawal of troops from Vietnam; they brought about important legislative victories for blacks; they have put tremendous social and economic pressure on the South African government to end apartheid policies; they have forced the shutdown of flawed nuclear facilities, and so on. The charge of uselessness will not stick.

So, what stops me from signing up, from going to work on behalf 11 of some cause that is especially important to me? In part, I know, that answer has to do with the sheer complexity of the offenses. I feel that a total situation—I mean a mesh made up of social and economic components, a labyrinth congruent with the deeper structures of society— begs a total response. And a total response is impossible for any individual. I could not give myself wholeheartedly (and what other kind of giving of oneself is there?) to the fight to preserve the snail darter while knowing that apartheid and plutonium dumping were in full swing elsewhere. That is, I could not psychologically do this. Logic, of course, protests—one cannot do everything; one should not therefore do nothing. I may not be able to solve all of the problems of the world (which is what I would, with my monstrous egotism, like to do), but I could put my voice and body on the line and do some good on behalf of some small part of the web. Others would be doing the same for other parts—perhaps some collective results could be achieved.

12   The logic is incontestable, but I remain inert. I must search further into myself. If what stops me from taking action is not apathy—and I believe I am not apathetic—then maybe the culprit is laziness. I squirm a bit as the beam of self-scrutiny probes at the crannies of the soul. Yes, to be sure, laziness is there in the character makeup. Or, to raise it to the dignity of a Deadly Sin: sloth. But pointing the finger there does not bring the matter to an end. For sloth is a disease of the will. And I have to own that I am only slothful in certain areas of my life. When I want or will something, I can be tirelessly active. So, my sloth in these political matters must point to some more or less unconscious refusal in myself. I am overtaken by sloth because for some reason I do not want to partake. Why not?

13   Selfishness? The belief that an expenditure of energy and thought will not net me commensurate return? That I will be giving out more than I get back? Maybe. It's not as though I haven't made those calculations, balancing off the time and caloric output required just to swell the ranks of a given demonstration by my humble numerical presence. Couldn't that energy be better spent elsewhere?

14   I may be getting closer. That is, I recognize the defensive logic as one I make use of when guilt afflicts me. I didn't go to take my stand at such and such a rally because I reckoned my time was better spent doing what I do. I hasten to clarify this. You see, I have to deem what I do—think, read, write—to be a part of the overall struggle. Not, perhaps, of the immediate political struggle, but the larger one, which works to ensure the survival of spirit, free inquiry, humanness—value—in a world where these qualities are under threat. There is no way to speak of this without sounding pompous or holier-than-thou. Trying to be serious about these ultimate things carries that risk. . . .

15   Why, then, looking now from the positive side, do I insist on remaining politically passive?

16   I find two reasons, and they are, in a manner of speaking, joined at the hip. The first is that I do not ultimately believe that there is a division between the political sphere of life and the others, however we might name them. Rather, I see the various levels of perception, action, and consequence as interfused; they form, as does the psyche itself, a continuum. And it is therefore fundamentally—existentially and ontologically—false to mark out one such area—the political—as requiring us especially. Such a view, I realize, does nothing to end apartheid or put food into the mouths of the starving, and it will need further exploration. But let me first spell out the other, linked, reason.

17   My second belief, put most simply, is that human behavior not only functions along a continuum, with all its parts in relation, it also obeys what might be called hydraulic principles. That is, an excessive

pressure at one point must result in diminution elsewhere. Energy given over to works is energy withdrawn from the work. Time consecrated to mailing petitions (and it's not just time, it's the energy of the devotion) is time taken from reflection on the larger condition of things. . . .

My place, then, is at the desk with my books and thoughts. I have 18 to try to do what I can to explore ideas and tendencies. Some part of this activity necessarily impinges upon the terrain of the "political," and insofar as it does I hope that my words promote the humane values, that they exert some small influence on people who do act. But who can say how these indeterminate forces move through the world?

As I write this, I realize that there is a point I have been meaning to 19 make, namely, that the commitment I claim for myself assumes the long view. That is, that I think of these values as continuities, and that I will for myself complete identification with their substance. This, no less than the "processing" I spoke of, calls for an absolute focus of energy and will. I mention this because in the course of thinking about this subject I have more than once looked back to the period of the late '60s. Not only because it was an era of conspicuous and directed political intensity, but also because I now see what happened to a great many members of my generation. Far too many of my peers have gone from vociferous front-line activism ("Free Huey!" and "If you're not part of the solution, you're part of the problem") to careers in the corporate mecca. They are now functionaries in the big machine that runs on only so long as it can exploit a class of have-nots. Well, there's politics, too. They had views and voices, and they gave them over when the prevailing winds shifted. They sold out. And they were able to do so because their convictions, though genuine, though vocally expressed, were shallowly rooted. Have they not undone twice over what they accomplished when they had righteousness in their hearts?

What consequences, then, can I claim for my brand of inactivity? A 20 hard question to answer. I have not put food into one hungry person's mouth. But neither have I knowingly aided any of those who amass their profits by taking it away. (To be sure, I have consumed my share of societal goods and services—I am implicated.) I have not fought to close down any power plants. I have not overtly worked to end policies of apartheid or US involvement in the political process of Central American countries. What have I done? Well, I have tried through teaching and writing to influence the perspectives of others; I have labored through the same channels to expose rhetoric and meretriciousness in writing, and to uphold examples of what is meaningful and sustaining—this in the belief that there is a continuum between words and mental processes and actions in the world. I have abstained from giving any comfort or solace to the bureaucrat. I have tried to live through the daily muddle with consistency and mental clarity. I have done everything to follow the promptings of the deeper muse. And all of this has left me very little for politics in the more immediate sense of the word. Probably I am not disqualified from urging on others the analysis of Chomsky and Herman, but the assignment happened to give me the pretext I needed for combing out these gnarled thoughts and protestations. They are not every person's thoughts. If they were, there would be little hope for the struggle to better the world. I hope that no one reads me as recommending the kind of stasis I am condemned to. I could not bear it if I somehow abetted the cause of our mutual enemy—the taker, exploiter, liar, polluter, rhetorician.

Reflection and Discussion

1. Birkerts confesses to being nonpolitical, but he says he is not apathetic. How much is your attitude like his?
2. Respond to the first-person point of view that Birkerts uses. How effective is it?

Writing Matters

1. Despite being nonpolitical, Birkerts mentions "the waste, corruption, and oppression that are around us like tethers." How do we as citizens address these concerns if we don't get involved in the political process? Is it true that "if you're not a part of the solution, you're a part of the problem"? What legitimate reasons can you cite for students not voting, for example? What needs to change before students get more involved with political matters on their campuses, in their communities and in the world?
2. Birkerts claims that his contributions to the world lie in other areas—thinking clearly and trying to influence people through his teaching and writing. How worthy are these causes? Do they offset his inability to be more political? How would you evaluate the author's contributions?

MAKING CONNECTIONS

1. Generation Me or Generation We? Critically review the articles in this chapter that focus on the attitudes and civic engagement of Millennials. Do Millennials volunteer more because they care more or because they need so many volunteer hours for school? How do you reconcile surveys suggesting

that they have a sense of personal responsibility for the community with their still-low voter turnout? Compared to their parents, are Millennials more or less engaged in their communities, or are they equally engaged, but in different ways? Based on these articles, additional research and your own experience, write an essay analyzing the political involvement of Millennials, suggesting how their differences will change the way we work together as communities and as a nation.

2. How do activist students differ from their less-involved peers? Interview two or three students who participate in campus organizations that engage in political or social action and two or three students who don't to find why they are or are not involved. Compare their answers to each other and to the motivating factors discussed in this chapter. Were the involved students engaged for "the right reasons"? For example, some people might want to give back to the community while others seem more interested in gaining experience or accumulating academic credits. Are these different motivations necessarily contradictory? How might the "wrong reasons" change the nature and results of their participation?

3. Significant change—whether personal or systemic—can be time consuming and messy, accompanied by sustained opposition. Cite examples of changes in our society that have been difficult and describe the disagreements that the participating parties experienced. What role did compromise play? What can happen when communication breaks down? To what extent is dissent or disobedience of established law acceptable? Research this topic in order to gain a clearer perspective on how change comes about in American society.

4. Faculty, administrators and students often have very different perspectives, which sometimes makes it difficult for all parties to agree on policies affecting the campus. Select an issue like how much influence students should have on campus and interview people from all sides. What kinds of agreements and disagreements did you discover and how do you explain them? What would you recommend in order for all the parties involved to understand one another better, both for this and other issues?

TAKING ACTION

1. Write an editorial for your campus newspaper expressing your opinions on service learning courses at your college. As you develop your response, consider some of these questions: Do students like yourself know what service learning opportunities are available on your campus? Do these kinds of courses enhance the learning experience or add to the burdens already on students? Should they be promoted more visibly? Should a service learning course (or courses) be optional or a graduation requirement for all students? When possible, refer to specific courses and departments as well as comments from other students.

2. Sample the archives of your student newspaper and note the topics that are covered. Which are relevant to you? Which ones aren't? Which issues get too much coverage? Which aren't covered enough? Based on your research, write a letter to the paper expressing your opinions specifically and clearly.

Chapter 5

Volunteerism—
Is It for You?

At the heart of volunteerism is the concept of free will—that the volunteers choose to serve with no obligation or significant remuneration. Yet our government demands more and more that volunteers fill in for services previously provided by paid professionals. Many schools require a certain number of community service hours or else inform students that colleges require applicants to volunteer. Employers find that "volunteer" projects build teamwork and generate free publicity, so they are often willing to pay employees their regular salaries to serve the community. How is the experience changed when it is no longer purely voluntary?

Yet even those freely choosing to serve do so with a reward in sight, if nothing more than a sense of accomplishment. People often say that givers always get back more than they contribute, but what exactly does this mean? What about when giving becomes difficult? Does the quality of the contribution affect the quality of the volunteer experience? In truth, some volunteers cause more problems than they solve. What are the lasting effects of volunteerism on the volunteers, those they serve and society as a whole?

BEFORE YOU READ

Who in your family volunteers? What experience have you had as a volunteer? Did you do it because you had to? Did it turn out the way you expected? Would you volunteer again? What has been your experience as the recipient of services from volunteers? Would you prefer to have had a professional take care of you?

171

Fixing? Helping? Or Serving?

Stanley Goldberg, *Templeton Power of Purpose Awards,* 2004

Stanley Goldberg, a professor of communicative disorders at San Francisco State University, received a Templeton Power of Purpose Award for this essay in 2004.

How do you feel about spending time with people who are near death?

1   "We're going to ask you to fall in love with people who'll leave you within months or even weeks. Then we're going to ask you to do it again and again."

2   It was the first day of my volunteer training session at the Zen Hospice Project. The sessions were run by its founder, Frank Ostaseski who's devoted his life to serving the dying and training people similarly committed to their care. It was an unnerving concept. How would it be possible to allow myself to fall in love with someone, knowing with certainty, they would be leaving me within a very short period of time? As Frank continued talking, I wondered if I would have permitted myself to fall in love with my wife of 35 years if I knew she would die within weeks or months after our first meeting. Most likely, I would have pulled back, in spite of the intense feeling I had knowing her for only a few hours. I wouldn't have allowed myself to enter a relationship that would result in the loss I knew would be coming. But here was someone asking me to do it, not once, but repeatedly. Before I had a chance to come to terms with his first statement, he uttered a second and more difficult one.

3   "There's a distinction between 'fixing,' 'helping,' and 'serving.'"

4   In my mind, I didn't see any difference. I viewed all three as identical. As a speech-language pathologist I thought I had been doing these three things simultaneously for the past 25 years.

5   "When you fix, you assume something is broken. When you help, you see the person as weak. But when you serve, you see the person as intrinsically whole. You create a relationship in which both parties gain. The purpose of hospice is to serve."

6   While the distinctions were deceptively simple, they are fundamental to understanding intentions. I realized for my entire professional career, I was a "fixer" and "helper." Someone who could look at a problem a child had and either find a solution or minimize its effects. I now was being asked to place a defining characteristic of my identity on a shelf and assume a new role, a "server." Instead of continuing

explaining with words, Frank pulled out a stack of 100 black and white photographs of people who died in hospice over the past year.

"I'd like you to intently look at each one before passing them to the 7 person on your right. Everyone here has already died, but imagine they're still alive. Just think about your reactions to what you're seeing. Then we'll talk."

As we looked at the beautiful photographs of people who were in 8 the process of dying, my first reaction was to do everything in my power to help them. At about the 50th photograph, I realized there was nothing here to fix. In spite of my knowledge and experience, their condition would only progress, ending in death. Everyone would still die in spite of all my efforts, in spite of anyone's efforts. Nobody would have been able to fix or help. All that was possible was to serve. I was beginning to have a theoretical understanding of "service." But I've come to believe that theory is the lowest level of understanding. The next up involves the concept's application. I saw that often during our training. I was able to watch experienced volunteers serving the dying. But the highest level of understanding is when you're engaged in what you thought you knew either through theory or observation. I didn't have to wait long for that to happen. It occurred during my first week as a volunteer.

"There are so many of you," she wrote on the small erasable slate 9 outlined with yellow plastic flowers.

"I know," I said. "We multiply like bunnies." 10

Cindy was referring to the number of volunteers at the Guest 11 House. She tried to laugh, but only the right side of her face and lips moved in a slight upward direction. The surgeon had removed her cancerous pharynx and tongue, and created a stoma, which is an opening in the front of her throat to breathe. Neither food nor water could be taken by mouth, since it would enter her lungs and immediately suffocate her. To prevent it from happening before the planned reconstructive surgery was performed, her mouth was wired closed and food, water, and medicine were administered through a tube directly into her stomach. Unfortunately, the tumor spread rapidly and surrounded the carotid artery. Reconstruction wasn't possible and her prognosis was poor. For two years, Anna, her mother, was with her constantly, taking care of every need. As her condition worsened, she could no longer care for her 57-year-old daughter in their one bedroom apartment. They came to the Guest House to spend their last weeks together.

The Guest House is a restored Victorian home in San Francisco 12 with space for five residents who are not expected to live for more than six months. The actual stay rarely exceeds two, with many leaving us within weeks of arriving. Located on a residential street, there is no indication anything remarkable is going on inside. There are no signs, and to enter, you ring a doorbell as you would with most homes. For each five-hour shift, two volunteers and an attendant, either a Certified Nurse's Aide or a Home Health-Care Worker, are upstairs with the residents. Sometimes an additional volunteer is downstairs cooking. Since most volunteers do one weekly shift, there were about 40 who cover the house weekly between 8:00 AM and 10:00 PM every day.

13   During the first two weeks, Cindy was still alert enough to communicate by using her slate and gestures. There were many things she didn't need to say. Often a look was sufficient. A movement of her head towards Anna meant she would like to talk with me without her mother present.

14   "Anna, why don't you take a break? You can have a nice cup of tea downstairs. Cindy and I will be fine together."

15   "Are you sure?" Anna said looking anxiously towards Cindy.

16   Cindy gestured towards her mother, as if shooing a child out of a room. She left and Cindy just shook her head. By the third week, it was difficult to write.

17   "Lonely when I'm gone," she wrote.

18   "I know. We're all doing whatever we can to prepare her. I think the social worker is trying to find a support group when you leave."

19   She just shook her head and laid it back on her pillow while straightening her blanket. Cindy was meticulous about her appearance, even as she approached death. When I came the following week for my Thursday shift, I learned she had refused to take any more nourishment or water. She said it made her nauseous. In hospice, the wishes of the residents are paramount, whether it involves something we think is trivial, like the placement of flowers in their room, or something serious such as refusing food. For the volunteers and staff it was irrelevant why she chose not to receive nutrients. Choices are respected.

20   After she was no longer eating and grew weaker, her need for modesty became a problem. During the first two weeks of her stay at the house, when clothes or bed linens needed to be changed, Cindy would allow only female volunteers to be present. Initially, it wasn't a problem, since if only male volunteers were available, she was able to support herself in bed or move with minimal help to a chair or commode. As her weight dropped to less than 80 pounds and muscles atrophied, it became difficult for her to move or remain in a position for the attendant alone to clean or change her. Anna often wouldn't have the strength to assist. As Cindy's health continued to deteriorate and our friendship increased, modesty was replaced by practicality. There came a time when there were no female volunteers on my shift and the attendant asked for my assistance in changing Cindy.

"It's OK Cindy, don't be embarrassed, look who it is," Anna kept 21 repeating.

She turned and smiled at me. She didn't need any reassurance. We 22 had become friends and confidants over the past few weeks. Most of our conversations involved gestures and nods. Neither of us was embarrassed the first time I helped in cleaning her body. Afterwards, it was just another thing we did together, no different then having a conversation or me sitting quietly at her bedside holding her hand. Most of the time I would hold her while the attendant cleaned. These were very intimate moments, where she was utterly helpless. During the last week of her life, the bedsores on her back became extremely painful. When changing her shirt, I supported her as she sat on the edge of the bed. After everything was completed, she refused to lie back down. Squeezing my hand firmly, she indicated with her head she wanted to continue sitting.

I had been standing at the edge of the bed gently holding up her 23 back with my hand, avoiding touching the sores near the base of her spine. I decided to sit close so my entire arm could support her.

"Is that OK?" I asked. 24

She slowly nodded her head with her eyes closed. Although I 25 thought it would be fine even before I asked, I never assume anything with residents. Each is unique in their needs. There is no such thing as uniformity in dying. What pleases one resident angers or causes pain to another. I usually was right when interpreting Cindy's needs since I was spending most of my time at the House with her and Anna. In addition to my regular shift, at least once a week I would spend the night sitting next to her so Anna could rest. As I held her, I noticed she began leaning on me. As I felt my right side support her entire body, the words and music of Bill Withers' song "Lean on Me" formed in my mind.

Sometimes in our lives, we all have pain, we all have sorrow.
But if we are wise, we know that there's always tomorrow.
Lean on me, when you're not strong and I'll be your friend.
I'll help you carry on, for it won't be long 'til I'm gonna
need someone to lean on.

Gradually I went from supporting to cradling. I couldn't tell when 26 our positions changed, but it was a difference noticed by both her mother and the attendant. No one spoke. My left hand held hers. As the pain increased, so did the strength of her grip.

Please swallow your pride, if you have things you need to borrow.
For no one can fill those needs that you won't let show.

Just call on me brother when you need a hand.
We all need somebody to lean on.

27   As I cradled her body with my right arm, her tension began to diminish. As it did, her grip also changed. It became soft and almost caressing. Occasionally, she would release her grip and lovingly move her fingers over mine. I felt honored serving her and being allowed to share such a profound experience near the end of her life.

If there is a load you have to bear that you can't carry,
I'm right up the road, I'll share your load if you just call on me.
Call me if you need a friend.
Call me.

28   As I sat with her, I didn't see a person whose body was ravished by cancer. I felt I was in the presence of a complete individual who graciously was allowing me to share a profound experience. She was letting go of everything and relying on my presence to get her through intense physical pain and the uncertainty of the journey she would soon begin. She stayed in my arms for over 30 minutes, with me occasionally stroking her forehead and gently rocking her. In some ways it reminded me of the times when my son and daughter were infants and I would hold them while they slept. For them, helplessness was the beginning of their lives. For Cindy, who was two years younger than me, it signaled the end.

29   When I try to explain that every day I leave the Guest House I feel I've received more than I gave, most people think I'm being unduly modest.

30   "It's a mitzvah (blessing) what you do," my Jewish friend would say.

31   "We're very proud of you," my family repeatedly tells me.

32   "You've been a blessing to us," families of the dying say through tears.

33   Most people who don't do it, view serving as a sacrifice. Something altruistic and totally giving. Nothing can be further from the truth. Few understand that serving someone as they approach death is incredibly rewarding. It's like having an endless supply of water being poured into a small bucket. There is no way it can contain the cascade. When I leave a resident's room, I often remember one of the classic Monty Python sketches where a man is stuffing himself with whatever food is placed in front of him. As his gluttony increases, so does the size of his body. It becomes enormous. When he lies back in his chair, covered with food he couldn't put into his mouth, a voice is heard from off-stage.

34   "Wouldn't you like a little mint?"

"No," the man groans, "I'll burst." 35

"Ah, come on, just one little mint," the voice pleads. 36

"Well OK," the man responds. "Just one." 37

A hand places the mint in the man's mouth. As he's savoring it, 38 he literary explodes. I often feel that way when I'm serving a resident. I'm unable to contain everything that's given to me. But just like the gluttonous man, I can't resist additional mints. Those who I serve become my teachers, providing me with lessons about living that are transforming. Every time I leave a resident's room I leave with a greater understanding of life and my place within it. The same feeling occurs regardless if I was feeding, talking, changing bed linens, cleaning their body, listening, or just quietly sitting at the bedside.

When I sat with Cindy the next week, she would occasionally open 39 her eyes and make hand movements towards the end of her bed. I had no idea what they meant. Before I left I kissed her on the forehead, saying goodbye for what I knew was the last time.

"I'm going to miss you very much. You've meant a lot to me and 40 everyone else in the house. Thank you for what you've taught me. I love you and we'll watch over Anna. Have a good journey."

I didn't know if she heard me. There was no visible sign she did. 41 But I've been told people, who are near death and appear to be unaware of their surroundings, are able to hear and understand what is being said to them. I was no longer concerned with Frank's statement that he was going to ask us to fall in love with people who would leave us within weeks or months. After serving Cindy, I knew I would do it again and again. Two days after I saw Cindy all of the volunteers received the following email.

> Cindy died peacefully this morning, pronounced at 8:15 AM.
>
> Anna was at her side and Irma was also there at 7:30 when she took her last breath. Tom, the volunteer with HBB who has been visiting daily, had been here most of the evening and part of the night. Judy from HBB stopped in around 1 AM to check on Cindy and give support to Anna.
>
> Cindy did not want to have the ceremonial bath done, so Hanna and Carrie bathed and dressed her in the clothes that Anna had set out. We surrounded her with candles and the flowers from her room. Cindy has a "Mona Lisa" smile on her face!
>
> The mortuary will be here around 10:30 this morning, as Cindy's wish was to be picked up immediately. All are welcome to join us in honoring her leaving at that time.

Thanks, again, for all the support and love you have given Cindy and Anna.

Blessings, Laurie

42   Serving gives purpose to life. Yes, it benefits others. But it's unique among all other human activities in what it does to those who practice it. In spite of what you give, you receive significantly more. I helped Cindy in the dying process, but in return, without asking, she taught me the importance of letting go of what no longer works. Being involved in her death brought me to that third level of understanding. Every resident I've served has been my teacher. Lessons are never requested. They just occur. If I listen carefully, I receive them. Metaphorically, they say "Listen, this is important." Often, they have the subtlety of a sledgehammer. Some I immediately understand. Others, I'm still struggling with. But all move me forward in my understanding of life.

43   For many people, these lessons are rare occurrences. For those involved in service, they happen everyday. Serving a person results in a stripping away of agendas and egos. Pema Chodron said that having an ego was like a very fat person trying to get through a very narrow door. It's possible, but painful. Serving our residents is an egoless event, as I imagine it is in all other forms of service. Things that are peripheral to being human dissolve into their needs and fears. I remember a question I asked Frank.

44   "How do you know what's the right thing to say or do? With my clients, if I say something wrong or even stupid, I know I can fix it next week. But with the dying, there may not be a next week."

45   Without any hesitation he said, "You've been doing these things your entire life. Not just as a therapist, but as a human being. If you're present, you'll know the right thing to do, you'll just know."

46   He was right. The defensive layers of armor which for years insulated me from both pain and compassion fell away. And the most amazing thing is I can't understand how I became a more authentic human being with so little effort. Something happened to me as I served. I liken it to a caterpillar metamorphosing into a butterfly. She doesn't choose to change, it just happens. Becoming a better human being isn't difficult. In fact, I didn't even have to try. All I did was to serve. I think the transformation had to do with how the residents treated me. Emptying a urinal or listening to someone's fear of dying brought an equal amount of gratitude. To be so loved and appreciated by someone you're serving changes the soul.

47   When I serve I view everyone as intrinsically whole. As someone who is no different than me. As someone who deserves every bit of

compassion and happiness I wish for myself. That's the beauty of service. I am them and they are me. The idea is embodied in the Tibetan concept of equanimity, where you look into the soul of another human being, and see yourself. In hospice we hope our service leads to a peaceful and dignified death for residents. Sometimes it does, other times it doesn't. But you always grow regardless of the outcome. You grow through your intentions. Whether I place a box of tissues closer to the weak hands of a resident, clean a commode, or guide a friend along her final journey, my intention is always the same—to serve people as if I was them.

I recently visited my daughter in New York City. As we walked 48 through Greenwich Village on a cold winter day, we came upon a children's pocket park on 6th Avenue and Minetta Lane. Within the park was a small cinder block building that probably housed children's playground items. As we passed by I was impressed by the wonderful scene painted by the children on the building's wall. I kept looking at it as we walked until I noticed a quote by a well-known educator written in a child's hand. It was the author of the quote that caused me to stop. But it was the words that kept me there.

> *Service is the rent we pay for living. It is the very purpose of life and*
> *Not something you do in your spare time.*

As I review what I have gained by serving the dying, and how it 49 has given purpose to my life and changed me, I realize I'm not paying enough rent.

Reflection and Discussion

1. Goldberg faced many challenges as he cared for Cindy. Which would be hardest for you?
2. What other volunteer opportunities would be similar to care of the dying, asking you to "fall in love with people who'll leave you within months"?

Writing Matters

1. The distinction between "fixing," "helping" and "serving" applies to more than just hospice care. Think of a time someone tried to assist you at a time of great need. What attitude did that person take? Describe the experience, showing how the person fixed, helped or served, and the ways that attitude affected your experience.
2. Goldberg is an expert in his field and certainly could serve others well by providing his professional services for free, yet he volunteers for hospice work, bringing tea, listening, helping clean and clothe a dying person. Would he have helped more by providing free treatment to children with serious communicative disorders? Was he right to make this choice?

"Alternative" Spring Breaks: Helping Poor and Homeless

Jay Rey, *Buffalo News,* March 11, 2006

Jay Rey is a staff reporter at the Buffalo News.

What did you do last spring break? Is it something you'd be proud to tell your children about?

1 Spring break has arrived for thousands of local college students, packing up and heading south for a good time.

2   Swimsuit. Check.

3   Suntan lotion. Check.

4   Hammer and nails. Huh?

5   Chugging beer next to the pool in Florida or sunbathing on a beach in Mexico still may be spring-break tradition, but using the mid-semester time off to help the poor and homeless isn't so unusual either. Canisius College students are leaving Sunday to lend a hand in impoverished Appalachia. Students at Hilbert College left Friday for a five-day service trip to rural South Carolina. And last year's hurricane devastation may have motivated more college students to head to the Gulf Coast. Ten percent of St. Bonaventure's student body has been cleaning up in the Gulf this week during the school's break. "We're gutting houses, cleaning up mold, cutting down trees in the way," St. Bonaventure freshman Ayshia Welsh said by cell phone. "We're basically doing a deep cleaning of the town."

6   That experience is still far from the norm, and each year there's concern the traditional fun-and-sun spring break excursions are getting out of control. Eighty-three percent of young women polled agreed spring break trips involved binge-drinking, while nearly three-quarters of them said it results in increased sexual activity, an American Medical Association survey released this week showed. But as many as 33,000 college students from across the nation are believed to be taking part in community service trips during spring break, estimates the Florida-based nonprofit Break Away, which helps campuses organize trips. These students—from colleges big and small, public and private—grab their work gloves and head to rural towns, urban neighborhoods and overseas locations.

7   Nearly 300 St. Bonaventure students, faculty and alumni fanned out this week to five locations along the Gulf Coast. Small groups from Alfred State College, Daemen College and the University at Buffalo's

School of Social Work also will spend next week immersed in the cleanup effort in the coastal region. "It's beyond words how bad it is down here," said James Mahar, a finance professor, who helped organize the St. Bonaventure trip. "You can't believe what you see—and what you don't see. There's nothing." Welsh, from Elma, is in Biloxi, Miss., where she has been sleeping in a tent behind a church. She and her group work through the morning, break for lunch, and then continue their cleanup until early evening. She grabs dinner and a quick rinse off in outdoor showers before calling it a day.

Help from MTV

"Rather than just doing something for myself, I thought I'd do something to help other people," Welsh said. 8

These "alternative" breaks started about 15 years ago, when some 9 students grew tired of the excessive and risky behavior at spring-break trips, said Jill Piacitelli, executive director of Break Away. The Katrina-ravaged Gulf contributed to more students volunteering this year, she said. MTV also helped draw attention to the alternative spring-break movement, by hooking up with the United Way to send students to help in the Gulf.

At Canisius College, about 70 students and staff will help the poor 10 and elderly at six locations in West Virginia, Kentucky and South Carolina, a spring-break trip the school has offered for 15 years, said Joe Van Volkenburg, a campus minister at Canisius. "We have found word spreads among our students," Van Volkenburg said. "If students come away with a good experience, they tell their friends and participation begins to grow." The Canisius students will help build or paint homes, or maybe tutor kids. The experience will cost them $285 to help pay for their food, lodging and transportation.

It's "Eye-Opening"

"A lot of people think you're nuts," said John Loeser, a Canisius junior, 11 who will be making his third trip. "But if you go on this trip with an open mind, and an open heart, you're transformed. It's an eye-opening experience, especially for the student who doesn't get beyond the campus here in Buffalo."

A dozen students from Hilbert College in Hamburg embarked 12 Friday on the school's most extensive alternative spring break. They will work through a Catholic outreach center to help with home repairs and after-school programs in a small, poor town in South Carolina. "It was time to take Hilbert's volunteer efforts beyond the limits of

Western New York," said Sister Jacqueline Benbenek, Hilbert's director of campus ministry.

13   Welsh, the freshman from St. Bonaventure, admits a more relaxing spring break in a warmer climate was an enticing thought after a long semester. But now that she's in Biloxi, she doesn't want to leave. "Honestly, if I hadn't already paid for this semester I would have stayed," Welsh said. "There's so much to do."

Reflection and Discussion

1. How do these alternative activities fit the purpose of a break?
2. If these students wanted to make a difference, why aren't they helping out nearer to their home or campus?

Writing Matters

1. Why would students say they were transformed? How does this activity become something more than just helping out and then going back to business? If you have participated in an alternative break or a similar program at another time, explain this from your own experience; otherwise, find out by researching on the Internet or interviewing people who have had this opportunity.
2. The American Medical Association survey shows most young women believe that spring break translates into problem drinking and increased sex, yet certainly these students could have a restful and safe spring break without resorting to one of these volunteer alternatives. Discuss the problems students have with spring break, looking at underlying causes and ways to address them.

Why Young People Are Volunteering in Record Numbers

The Center for Information & Research on Civic Learning & Engagement, *Around the CIRCLE: Research & Practice,* November 2005

CIRCLE conducts research on the civic and political involvement of young adults, focusing on areas that have practical applications to promote youth engagement.

When have you been required to "volunteer"? Why did you do it?

1   It has been well documented that young people today are volunteering at unprecedented rates. A new CIRCLE Working Paper by Lewis A. Friedland and Shauna Morimoto examines the motivating factors

behind this rise in volunteering. The researchers found that for middle- and upper-middle-class high school students "résumé-padding" is one of the motivating factors driving the increase in volunteering. According to Dr. Friedland, "Much of the reported volunteerism was shaped by the perception that voluntary and civic activity is necessary to get into any college; and the better the college (or, more precisely, the higher the perception of the college in the status system) the more volunteerism students believed was necessary. Many of the middle- and upper-middle-class youth are explicitly volunteering for the purpose of what they themselves called 'résumé-padding.'" In addition to the résumé-padding, the study finds that several other factors are motivating the rise in volunteer activity, and these factors vary by class and racial position, ideological disposition, and religious involvement. Finally, the report contains a typology of youth volunteering.

The study is based on detailed interviews of almost 100 residents of Madison, Wisconsin, between the ages of 14 and 19, sampled from various schools and community centers. Madison is a city with robust civic engagement, so the sample included a wide variety of civic behaviors. 2

Increased Pressure to Attend College Reshapes Civic Motivators

Surveys have found that high school students of all classes, with virtually no significant racial, ethnic, or gender differences, expect to attend college. According to Dr. Friedland, "We found that students recognize that their future life chances rest on 'college,' whether defined as the local community college, the lesser state university, a public flagship, or the 'best' private schools, much as an earlier generation depended on a high school diploma." This realization in turn has created anxiety among high-school-aged youth about how they can improve their chances for college admission. Under these circumstances, young people of all classes are approaching service as (in part) an instrumental price to pay for college admission. 3

Moreover, the research shows that young people do not understand the criteria for admission to the different types of higher education. Young people interviewed in the study widely believed that significant service is a requirement for admission to all types of schools, including technical colleges and state schools in which a moderate GPA virtually guarantees admission. However, these service expectations only come into play in genuinely selective schools, those with an admissions rate of 50 percent or less, and even here the amount of service only becomes a major criterion in highly selective schools. 4

Nevertheless, the researchers found that a kind of "service inflation" has spread downward in the class structure.

Typology of Youth Volunteers

5 Alongside of the résumé-padding, however, the researchers did find significant other forms of activity, with different motivations that themselves varied by class and racial position, ideological disposition, and religious involvement. Following is a typology of volunteers developed from the interviews:

1. The first type Friedland and Morimoto identify is college bound youth, of the middle- and upper-middle-classes. They produce the majority of service-based volunteerism. These are the young people most engaged in résumé-padding for college, and they often do so self-consciously, with awareness of their own motives and little or no sense that this instrumental orientation compromises their motives. For example, one student said he does "as much service learning as I can because they like that apparently." Asked where he got this impression he replied: "I don't know, it's just what a lot of my graduating friends have told me. The more service-learning, the more community service you have, like the better you look and the more it'll count for your bad GPA or whatever."

2. A subtype of the middle-class résumé-padders are well-integrated college bound youth, often from civically- or politically-oriented middle- and upper-middle-class families, who have articulated ideological or moral motivations for engaging in civic or political activity. These young people are also engaged in résumé-padding, but their motives are mixed. They simply assume that these activities are what they should do, and need to do, but also have other motivations.

Young Adults as Volunteers
- Some seek out volunteer work, but most respond to an invitation to serve.
- Forty percent of today's 15- to 25-year-olds volunteer, more than any other age group.
- High school volunteer experiences, discussion and debate greatly influence the civic engagement of young people.

Scott Keeter, Cliff Zukin, Molly Andolina, Krista Jenkins, *The Civic and Political Health of the Nation: A Generational Portrait, September 19, 2002*

3. A further subtype of résumé-padders are those whom Friedland and Morimoto call "civic youth." They are young people engaged in explicit and highly civic activities, for example membership on

youth boards. From the outside, they would be identified as among the most highly civic young people in the community, and indeed in many respects they are. But their motives are also complex, linked to both résumé-padding and social position.

4. A fourth type, religious young people, varied in their motives, some engaging in civic activity out of an explicit sense of religious duty, either to God or to their church community. For others, although religious motives and institutions were a significant part of the background and language, civic and community activity seemed to be linked to résumé-padding motives.

5. Another type the researchers identified were working and lower-class young people, often minorities, that they encountered in community based clubs, and neighborhood after-school centers. These young people had strong community orientations that seemed to go beyond immediate self-interest to an expressed interest in "helping the community" and, specifically, helping the younger children, their brothers and sisters, and neighborhood children, to build a better life.

6. A subset of the sample were politically engaged youth, with explicitly anti-establishment orientations, that sometimes were ideological, but often seemed visceral, linked to an awareness of the unfairness of their life situation. Although the stereotype of radical youth may be those who are from more privileged, middle- and upper-middle-class backgrounds, many were from working and lower-middle-class families.

7. Finally, there was a loose type that Friedland and Morimoto call cultural rebels, with a loose cultural antiauthoritarianism that expressed itself in cultural identification with movements like hip-hop, or certain variants. Both motives and forms of engagement are diffuse.

Transmitting Civic and Social Capital

The report concludes that the changing motivations behind volunteering could have implications for future civic capital. Dr. Friedland notes, "If the normative connections to community that may have characterized civic engagement in the past are, indeed, becoming hollowed out in a middle-class under enormous pressure to retain its position, the transmission of social and civic capital across generations may be more precarious than survey data alone indicate." The full report, entitled "CIRCLE Working Paper 40: The Changing Lifeview of Young People: Risk, Résumé Padding, and Civic Engagement," can be downloaded from www.civicyouth.org. [6]

Reflection and Discussion

1. Review the seven types of high school volunteers identified by Friedland and Morimoto. Where did you and people you know fit in these categories? How did your different motivations manifest in your approach to volunteer work, if at all?

2. The researchers were quite surprised at the mistaken perception that extensive volunteer work and service learning were needed to get into any college, particularly since this misunderstanding led students to spend hours doing things they would otherwise not do. Where do such misunderstandings come from? Why wouldn't students check out the facts?

Writing Matters

1. Should community service be required for high school graduation? Is service given voluntarily the same as service done in pursuit of a diploma or college admissions? Evaluate the value of community service to a teenager as well as any ill effects caused by making it mandatory and decide whether school districts should adopt this policy.

2. With a group, develop a questionnaire to capture the information needed to categorize students into the types defined by the study and determine how their motivation affected their experience as volunteers. Interview 30 or more students and collate the results. How similar are your subjects to those in the CIRCLE study? Analyze some aspect of your results in detail—for example, the effect of initial motivation on the volunteer experience, the applicability of the CIRCLE categories—and report on their implications. You may wish to review the complete report for some ideas on questions to ask.

Putting the "National" in National Service

John McCain, *Washington Monthly,* October 2001

Decorated veteran John McCain is the senior senator from Arizona and has been a candidate for president of the United States.

What does the phrase "national service" mean to you?

1   America is witnessing a welcome blooming of popular culture chronicling the contributions of the generation that lived through the Depression and vanquished fascism. From *Saving Private Ryan* to Tom Brokaw's *The Greatest Generation* to Stephen Ambrose's *Band of Brothers,* Americans are hungry to learn about the heroic service of our parents

and grandparents. Some of the commentary surrounding this positive trend, however, has been wistful, even pessimistic. While rightly celebrating the feats of the World War II generation, many pundits bemoan the lack of great causes in our day and doubt whether today's young people would be willing to make the sacrifices necessary to meet such challenges, even if they existed.

I believe these commentators have it wrong. During the last presidential race, I had the privilege of traveling the country and meeting vast numbers of young people. I cannot express how impressed I was. With energy and passion as contagious as it was inspiring, these young Americans confided their dreams and shared their aspirations, not for themselves alone, but for their country. Their attitude should come as no surprise. Though today's young people, according to polls, have little faith in politics, they are great believers in service. Indeed, they are doing volunteer work in their communities in record numbers—proof that the urge to serve runs especially deep in them. Indeed, most Americans share this impulse, as witnessed after last month's terrorist attacks, when thousands of Americans lined up to give blood and assist in rescue efforts. It is time we tapped that urge for great national ends.

And it is not true, as the cynics suggest that our era lacks great causes. Such causes are all around us. Thousands of schools in our poorest neighborhoods are failing their students and cry out for talented teachers. Millions of elderly Americans desperately want to stay in their homes and out of nursing facilities, but cannot do so without help with the small tasks of daily life. More and more of our communities are being devastated by natural disasters. And our men and women in uniform are stretched thin meeting the vital task of keeping the peace in places like Bosnia and Kosovo.

Beyond such concrete needs lies a deeper spiritual crisis within our national culture. Since Watergate, we have witnessed an increased cynicism about our governmental institutions. We see its impact in declining voter participation and apathy about our public life—symptoms of a system that demands reform. But it's a mistake, I think, to believe that this apathy means Americans do not love their country and aren't motivated to fix what is wrong. The growth of local volunteerism and the outpouring of sentiment for "the greatest generation" suggest a different explanation: that Americans hunger for patriotic service to the nation, but do not see ways to personally make a difference.

What is lacking today is not a need for patriotic service, nor a willingness to serve, but the opportunity. Indeed, one of the curious truths of our era is that while opportunities to serve ourselves have exploded—with ever-expanding choices of what to buy, where to eat, what to read, watch, or listen to—opportunities to spend some time serving our country have narrowed. The high cost of campaigning keeps many idealistic people from running for public office. Teacher-certification requirements keep talented people out of the classroom. The all-volunteer military is looking for lifers, not those who might want to serve for shorter tours of duty.

6   The one big exception to this trend is AmeriCorps, the program of national service begun by President Bill Clinton. Since 1994, more than 200,000 Americans have served one-to-two-year stints in AmeriCorps, tutoring school children, building low-income housing, or helping flood-ravaged communities. AmeriCorps members receive a small stipend and $4,725 in college aid for their service. But the real draw is the chance to have an adventure and accomplish something important. And AmeriCorps' achievements are indeed impressive: thousands of homes constructed; hundreds of thousands of senior citizens assisted to live independently in their own homes; millions of children taught, tutored, or mentored.

7   Beyond the good deeds accomplished, AmeriCorps has transformed the lives of young people who have participated in its ranks. They have begun to glimpse the glory of serving the cause of freedom. They have come to know the obligations and rewards of active citizenship.

8   But for all its concrete achievements, AmeriCorps has a fundamental flaw: In its seven years of existence, it has barely stirred the nation's imagination. In 1961, President John F. Kennedy launched the Peace Corps to make good on his famous challenge to "[a]sk not what your country can do for you, but rather what you can do for your country." Since then, more than 162,000 Americans have served in the Peace Corps, and the vast majority of Americans today have heard of the organization. By contrast, more than 200,000 Americans have served in AmeriCorps, yet two out of three Americans say they have never heard of the program.

9   If we are to have a resurgence of patriotic service in this country, then programs like AmeriCorps must be expanded and changed in ways that inspire the nation. There should be more focus on meeting national goals and on making short-term service, both civilian and military, a rite of passage for young Americans.

Service Economy

10   National service is an issue that has been largely identified with the Democratic Party and the left of the political spectrum. That is unfortunate, because duty, honor, and country are values that transcend ideology. National service, both civilian and military, can embody the virtues of patriotism that conservatives cherish.

More than a decade ago, the patron saint of modern conservatism, 11
William F. Buckley, Jr., offered an eloquent and persuasive conservative
case for national service. In the book *Gratitude*, Buckley wrote,
"Materialistic democracy beckons every man to make himself a king;
republican citizenship incites every man to be a knight. National service, like gravity, is something we could accustom ourselves to, and
grow to love."

Buckley was right, but it's fair to say that it took a while before we 12
conservatives accustomed ourselves to the idea. Indeed, when Clinton
initiated AmeriCorps in 1994, most Republicans in Congress, myself
included, opposed it. We feared it would be another "big government
program" that would undermine true volunteerism, waste money in
"make-work" projects, or be diverted into political activism.

We were wrong. Though AmeriCorps' record is not untarnished, 13
the overall evidence for its effectiveness is hard to deny. For instance,
AmeriCorps members tutored over 100,000 first-through-third graders
during the 1999–2000 school year. On average, those children scored
significantly higher on reading performance tests than would otherwise have been expected, according to Abt Associates, an independent
evaluation firm. Having seen results like these—and having often seen
AmeriCorps members work on the ground—more and more of my
GOP colleagues have changed their minds about the program. Forty-
nine of 50 governors, 29 of them Republicans, signed a letter last year
urging Congress to support AmeriCorps. One of the signers was then-
Texas Governor George W. Bush. As president, Bush put forth a budget
that keeps AmeriCorps at its current level of members—the ultimate
sign that national service today has truly bipartisan support.

Part of what conservatives admire about AmeriCorps is that it 14
strengthens "civil society"—the rich web of neighborhood, nonprofit,
and faith-based groups outside of government that provide services to
those in need. This is built into the decentralized design of the program. Most AmeriCorps funding is in the hands of state governors,
who give it to their National and Community Service Commissions,
who in turn make grants to local nonprofits, who then recruit and hire
AmeriCorps members. The vast majority of AmeriCorps members are
thus "detailed" to work for organizations like Habitat for Humanity,
the Red Cross, or Big Brothers/Big Sisters. They become, in effect, full-
time, paid staff members of these often-understaffed organizations.

Rather than elbowing out other volunteers, as many of us feared, 15
AmeriCorps members are typically put to work recruiting, training,
and supervising other volunteers. For instance, most of the more than
500 AmeriCorps members who work for Habitat for Humanity spend
less time swinging hammers themselves than making sure that

hammers, nails, and drywall are at the worksite when the volunteers arrive. They then teach the volunteers the basic skills of how to hang drywall. As a result, studies show that each AmeriCorps member generates, on average, nine additional volunteers.

16   The ability to provide skilled and motivated manpower to other organizations is what makes AmeriCorps so effective. But it also creates a problem. AmeriCorps members often take on the identity of the organizations they're assigned to. In the process, they often lose any sense of being part of a larger national service enterprise, if they ever had it at all. Indeed, staffers at nonprofit groups sometimes call AmeriCorps headquarters looking for support for their organizations, only to find out that *their own salaries* are being paid by AmeriCorps. It's no wonder most Americans say they have never heard of the program. And a program few have heard of will obviously not be able to inspire a new ethic of national service.

17   I believe AmeriCorps needs to be expanded and changed, in ways that do not alter those aspects of the program that make it effective, but that build greater *espirit de corps* among members and encourage a sense of national unity and mission.

18   There is no doubt that this can be done because some smaller programs within AmeriCorps are already doing it. One example is City Year, an AmeriCorps effort that began in Boston and is now operating in 13 American cities. City Year members wear uniforms, work in teams, learn public speaking skills, and gather together for daily calisthenics, often in highly public places such as in front of city hall. They also provide vital services, such as organizing after-school activities and helping the elderly in assisted-living facilities.

19   Another example is AmeriCorps' National Civilian Community Corps, a service program consciously structured along military lines. NCCC members not only wear uniforms and work in teams, as City Year members do, but actually live together in barracks on former military bases, and are deployed to service projects far from their home base. This "24/7" experience fosters group cohesion and a sense of mission. AmeriCorps' NCCC members know they are part of a national effort to serve their country. The communities they serve know that, too.

20   In April of last year, when the Mississippi's flood waters threatened the town of Camanche, Iowa, an AmeriCorps NCCC team was brought in to coordinate volunteers and help plug leaks in the town's levee. "This AmeriCorps crew has probably single-handedly saved $1 million to $1.5 million worth of property damage since they've been here," Camanche Public Works Director Dave Rickertsen told the *St. Louis Post Dispatch.* NCCC teams also helped out last year after

floods in Ohio and Florida, a hurricane in North Carolina, and forest fires in six western states, providing disaster relief to an estimated 33,500 people. This year they've been dispatched to help combat nine floods and dozens of forest fires.

When not providing disaster relief, NCCC teams often work in national parks, clearing overgrown trails and rebuilding cabins. In the spring, they help Habitat for Humanity run its Collegiate Challenge, a program that convinces thousands of college students each year to spend their spring breaks not in bars in Ft. Lauderdale but building homes for low-income families.

In May of last year, one NCCC crew descended on the home of Stella Knab, an 80-year-old former cleaning lady, now confined to a wheelchair. Knab lived with her handicapped son in New Orleans' Bywater district, in a decrepit house with cracked plumbing and rotted wood floors with holes big enough for neighborhood rats to pay visits. The NCCC team moved Knab and her son into a motel for two weeks, and in partnership with a local nonprofit group, the Preservation Resource Center, completely gutted and rebuilt the interior of her house. "It was pretty scary. I really can't imagine someone living like this," Paula Dora, 23, one the AmeriCorps members, told *The New Orleans Times-Picayune.* "It felt more like the Third World than it did the 'Land of the Free.' It feels so good to be able to make such a difference."

Only about 1,000 of AmeriCorps' 50,000 members are a part of NCCC. City Year accounts for another 1,200. Congress should expand these two programs dramatically, and spread their group-cohesion techniques to other AmeriCorps programs. Indeed, the whole national service enterprise should be expanded, with the ultimate goal of ensuring that every young person who wants to serve can serve. Though this will require significantly more funding, the benefits to our nation will be well worth the investment. At the same time, we must encourage the corporate sector and the philanthropic community to provide funding for national service, with federal challenge grants and other incentives.

We must also ask our nation's colleges to step up to the plate and more aggressively promote service. Currently, only a small fraction of college work-study funds are devoted to community service, far less than what Congress originally intended when it passed the Higher Education Act in 1965. Congress must encourage universities to comply with the intent of the act to promote student involvement in community activities.

We should also be concerned by the growing gap between our nation's military and civilian cultures. While the volunteer military has been successful, fewer Americans know and appreciate the sacrifices and contributions of their fellow citizens who serve in uniform. The military is suffering severe recruitment problems.

26   In the past, it has been a rite of passage for our nation's leaders to serve in the armed forces. Today, fewer and fewer of my congressional colleagues know from experience the realities of military life. The decline of the citizen-soldier is not healthy for a democracy. While it is not currently politically practical to revive the draft, it is important to find better incentives and opportunities for more young Americans to choose service in the military, if not for a career, then at least for a limited period of time.

27   For example, an important responsibility of our armed services is peacekeeping around the world. Often, this involves non-military activities such as constabulary work. The military should explore whether short-term enlistees could fulfill these responsibilities, freeing other personnel to perform more traditional military duties.

28   We should also undertake a campaign to revive Reserve Officer Training Corps (ROTC) on college campuses across the country. On many campuses, ROTC was expelled as a result of protests during the Vietnam War. One result has been an ever-declining number of college graduates choosing military service as a career. Congress should consider linking financial aid to the willingness of colleges to allow ROTC back on campus. It is truly outrageous that some colleges receive federal aid while forbidding access to an organization that promotes the defense of our freedoms.

29   In America, our rights come before our duties, as well they should. We are a free people, and among our freedoms is the liberty to care or not care for our birthright. But those who claim their liberty but not their duty to the civilization that ensures it live a half-life, indulging their self-interest at the cost of their self-respect. The richest men and women possess nothing of real value if their lives have no greater object than themselves.

30   Success, wealth, celebrity gained and kept for private interest—these are small things. They make us comfortable, ease the way for our children, and purchase a fleeting regard for our lives, but not the self-respect that, in the end, matters most. Sacrifice for a cause greater than self-interest, however, and you invest your life with the eminence of that cause.

31   Americans did not fight and win World War II as discrete individuals. Their brave and determined energies were mobilized and empowered by a national government headed by democratically elected leaders. That is how a free society remains free and achieves greatness. National service is a crucial means of making our patriotism real, to the benefit of both ourselves and our country.

Reflection and Discussion

1. Why do people say we have no "great causes" when McCain can easily list a handful?
2. McCain decries "the decline of the citizen-soldier," suggesting that we might welcome volunteers to the armed forces, promising them jobs in non-military positions. How would this type of arrangement give the enlistees the military experience McCain looks for?

Writing Matters

1. Should Congress indeed withhold financial aid from students at schools without ROTC? What are the strongest arguments for and against such a rule?
2. McCain sees military service and community service as two sides of the same coin. In what ways are they alike and different? How much do you agree with him?

Doing Disservice: The Benefits and Limits of Volunteerism

Drake Bennett, *American Prospect,* October 2003

Drake Bennett is a freelance writer living in Boston and a former Prospect writing fellow.

What can be wrong with volunteering?

No matter what we do, those of us in our 20s can't seem to measure up to the Greatest Generation. That bygone nation of joiners, providers and world-beaters, in the standard story, puts to shame today's sad assemblage of narcissists and whiners. Gone are the days when the United States, stung by a Japanese sneak attack, rose up to shrug off the Great Depression and cohere into a fighting force of Riveting Rosies and Private Ryans. Political scientist Robert Putnam called our grandparents "the long civic generation."

Of course, the September 11 attacks did arouse a general sense of solidarity and national duty. According to the Progressive Policy Institute, there were, for example, three times as many volunteers for the national service program AmeriCorps as available slots. And despite the conventional wisdom that America's young are less civically engaged than their parents and grandparents, the reality is that young America is awash in community service. High-school and college community-service activities have never been more extensive. Many would build on this trend and dramatically expand existing service opportunities; some would even make a stint doing national service mandatory.

3   It's a venerable idea. For its supporters, national service does triple duty, shaping productive, selfless citizens and filling unmet social needs while creating a shared sense of national identity. As William James bracingly put it in a 1910 essay, "To coal and iron mines, to freight trains, to fishing fleets in December, to dishwashing, clothes-washing, and window-washing, to road-building and tunnel-making, to foundries and stoke-holes, and to frames of skyscrapers, would our gilded youths be drafted off, according to their choice, to get childishness knocked out of them, and to come back into society with healthier sympathies and soberer ideas."

4   President Bush himself has caught the national service bug. In his 2002 State of the Union address, he proposed expanding AmeriCorps by 50 percent, adding nearly $300 million to national service spending and creating spots for 2 million Americans in the country's national service programs by some unspecified date. Characteristically, there has been no follow-up. In fact, the House of Representatives voted down an emergency $100 million infusion for cash-strapped

FIGURE 5.1 In 2003, hundreds of former, current, and prospective AmeriCorps volunteers rallied to get funding for AmeriCorps.

AmeriCorps. As the memoirist-turned-service-advocate Dave Eggers wrote in a heartbroken *New York Times* op-ed, "Congress and the White House have turned their backs on these volunteers."

But the zeal of national service proponents is undimmed. The war on terrorism and its massive security needs, they argue, demand manpower of the sort that only a domestic army of community servants can supply. And the sense of threat has added urgency to discussions of national identity and solidarity, both issues that national service promises to address. The terrorist attacks only brought into relief a trend that has been accelerating for several years: In a growing number of states and school districts, community service is a requirement for high-school graduation, and "service learning" is the pedagogy of the day. 5

As a veteran of City Year—the community-service organization upon which then-President Bill Clinton based AmeriCorps—and one who counts my year of service a formative and productive one, I'm not sure that this epidemic of volunteerism is entirely a welcome trend. For starters, compulsory volunteering is a contradiction in terms. Also, systemic government solutions rather than piecemeal acts of goodwill better address many of the problems that volunteers tackle. If hospitals and libraries increasingly rely on volunteers, it's because reduced federal appropriations are starving institutions that depend on public funding. In this context, well-intentioned young people who fill the gap are enablers of the attack on public services. 6

Moreover, much of what's done by volunteers has a tacit politics that volunteerism may inadvertently conceal. If you volunteer in a soup kitchen or help the homeless, you should also be working to eliminate the causes of homelessness. That enterprise, of course, logically leads to social change and to politics as the necessary instrument of change. But many volunteer organizations, either because of their tax status, their funding sources or their necessary nonpartisanship, take great pains to eschew politics. A few years ago, when students affiliated with Phillips Brooks House, Harvard University's pre-eminent community-service institution for undergraduates, came out in support of the school's "living wage" campaign, they earned a rebuke from the university's new president, Lawrence Summers, for taking what he judged to be an overly partisan stand. 7

Local service projects—George Bush Senior's "thousand points of light"—fragment political energy. Yale Law School professors Bruce Ackerman and Anne Alstott, in their 1999 book, *The Stakeholder Society*, take contemporary liberals to task for their unwillingness to tackle the enormous and central problem of wealth inequality in favor of "a thousand lesser policies." Universal service seems to be a pretty good example of just that. Unlike conservatives, modern liberals are unafraid to 8 use the government to take care of what the market can or will not. But to rely on an army of young amateurs to deal with societal needs seems a strangely indirect way to go about it. If inner-city schools are struggling, isn't the solution to give them more money for their infrastructures and teacher salaries instead of spending the money on an at best lightly trained conscript?

9   In addition, employers in both the public and private sectors, gifted with a national service corps of nearly 4 million, would be sorely tempted to use this pool of cheap, captive labor to phase out salaried (and benefited) employees. As Service Employees International Union lobbyist Skip Roberts dryly notes, "That might be the only reason why it might appeal to anyone in the White House." But what of the character-building aspect of it? It's undeniable that some young people would have their first taste of service in such a program. However, with a vast majority of high schools participating in community service (83 percent, according to a 1999 study by the US Department of Education), most students have already been exposed to the concept. And so far, research has failed to link even voluntary service with increased civic engagement. A recent study by the National Association of Secretaries of State found that youth who performed service were no more likely to be involved in politics than their nonvolunteering peers. The fact is, Americans between the ages of 15 and 25 already volunteer more than any other age group; but they also vote far less (and the number of voters continues to shrink). According to a 2002 study released by the University of Maryland's Center for Information & Research on Civic Learning & Engagement (CIRCLE), young Americans are also less likely than their (admittedly also pretty disengaged) elders to have participated in traditional forms of civic engagement—writing a letter to their congressman or newspaper, for example, or marching in a demonstration or volunteering for a political campaign.

10   When asked about this, the apolitical young respond that politics is, in effect, useless. Thomas Ehrlich is a former board member of the Corporation for National Service and a current scholar at the Carnegie Foundation for Teaching and Learning who studies civic engagement and service learning. He has found that "one of the reasons kids give [for their apolitical tendencies] is that they don't see a chance to make a difference. They can tutor a kid in school, clean up a park, serve in a community kitchen and feel that they're making a difference. But trying to change the political process in their community, much less the country—they don't see that happening."

11   Tellingly, the CIRCLE study found that the civic activities young people preferred were individual or nongovernmental: buying a

certain brand because they agreed with its values, for example, or donating to a charity. After all, as Michael Delli Carpini, a scholar of civic life and the dean of the University of Pennsylvania's Annenberg School for Communication, has noted, "Civic engagement has become *defined* as the one-on-one experience of working in a soup kitchen, clearing trash from a local river or tutoring a child once a week. What is missing is an awareness of the connection between the individual, isolated problems these actions are intended to address and the larger world of public policy." To enshrine what is in effect institutionalized volunteerism in a federal program could very well end up merely reinforcing the idea that acts of kindness, random or not, rather than governmental action, are the solution to society's ills.

And that is the central paradox of national service: It is big government for people who don't like big government—the counterpart of government support for local "faith-based" social services, or for traditional marriage as the cure for poverty. The current national service debate is really a holdover from the Clinton administration. 12

While liberals are rightly ambivalent about national service, it has gained supporters among self-styled "national greatness" conservatives, thinkers like William Kristol and David Brooks who are concerned with restoring America's sense of purpose and grandeur. For them, government is meant not so much to govern, or even to solve social ills, but to inspire and provide its citizens with a Teddy Roosevelt–like sense of resolve and destiny. Brooks, for example, has argued that what the federal government needs to focus on is building grand monuments and institutions like the Library of Congress. 13

Universal service would surely be an institution, and it would provide lots of people with a sense of purpose. But surely that's setting the bar pretty low for a federal program. As Tocqueville pointed out in the 1830s, America has always had a rich social fabric of voluntary institutions. The point of government is not to keep its citizens busy living lives of vigorous action but to do what markets cannot. Yet active government requires an activist public agenda, which in turn depends on activated voters. If there's a paucity of civic engagement among the young, it is less in the area of volunteering than in taking seriously the enterprise of citizenship. 14

Reflection and Discussion

1. When young volunteers fill jobs that were cut out of the budget, Bennett calls them "enablers," a term used for friends and family who, for example, cover up for alcoholics and drug addicts. How are these volunteers "enablers"?

2. Thomas Ehrlich says that young people eschew politics in favor of volunteer work, which they believe allows them to make a difference. What drives this preference—political impotence, ignorance, impatience?

Writing Matters

1. Should Congress provide more funding for AmeriCorps? Evaluate the value given for the money spent, considering any other qualitative intangibles that are relevant.
2. Many social service agencies and their volunteers fear taking political action lest they lose funding, yet Bennett suggests that they must work for change, not just fill a need. How much time should volunteers work toward political change to eliminate the problems they are most concerned with?

Voluntary Work and the Needs of Strangers

Richard Sennett, *New Statesman*, January 27, 2003

Richard Sennett teaches sociology at the London School of Economics and Massachusetts Institute of Technology. He is the author of several books on the sociology of culture, including Respect in an Age of Inequality, *from which this article is excerpted.*

Have you ever helped someone in need (or been helped) and found that the help was misinterpreted as a sign of friendship?

1 When the young John Maynard Keynes resigned from the India Office in 1908, his superior wrote back: "I have never been quite able to satisfy myself that a government office . . . is the best thing for a young man of energy and right ambitions. It is a comfortable means of life. . . . But it is rarely exciting or strenuous and does not make sufficient call on the combative and self-assertive elements of human nature." Others less ambitious had to be pushed, as security degenerated into complacency. The Indian writer Amit Chaudhuri evokes that degeneration in describing an office given over to "a time-tested culture of tea-drinking, gossip and procrastination. . . . It was, in a sense, a relaxing place to be in, like withdrawing to some outpost that was cut off from the larger movements of the world."

2 The institutions which replaced rigid bureaucracy in the later 20th century made fewer social demands on those who worked within; these same light institutions transformed the provision of welfare. Both

those who leaped and those who were pushed found they had lost something in this transformed world, whatever its freedoms; they had lost a way to structure mutual respect.

During the boom of the 1980s and 1990s, flat, short organizations 3 proved better, throughout the private sector, at seizing opportunities than firms based on the traditional bureaucratic pyramid. In 1965, IBM had 23 standardized links in its chain of command; by 2000, only seven degrees of formal separation stood between the bottom and the top. Despite the end of the boom—and the need for more stable relations with suppliers, investors and dedicated employees—flat, short institutions have entrenched themselves. No global business can be done without them, no new firm will ever be created on the principle of lifetime employment. More ominously, the flat, short company has become a model for organizations in civil society.

"Short," in welfare reform, means a state reducing its responsibili- 4 ties by replacing permanent or fixed guarantees with more temporary acts of help. The most dramatic example in America and western Europe is the cut in the duration of unemployment benefits. Short welfare diminishes government responsibility and shifts the management of fate back on to the individual. The result, as the policy analyst Patrick Dunleavy argues, is to create inequalities between passive dependants and more independent consumers of welfare. The first require guidance; the second require only resources. Into the first category falls a 90-year-old struggling to manage his or her pension investments, into the second that same person 40 years before. Into the first category fall the perplexed immigrant couple trying to choose a school for their children in London, into the second fall the parents who have lived in London all their lives. Reformers tend to offer the first group a poorer quality of service.

Further, the flat, short structure can concentrate power. In suppos- 5 edly "devolved" systems of welfare, central government determines how much localities can spend, rather than what every citizen needs. Hollowing out a welfare bureaucracy reduces the interpretative communication between layers which marks the bureaucratic pyramid. "Need" becomes an abstraction, a number, a datum instantly assessed from the top rather than a negotiable human relationship.

Demand greater than supply pushes up profits in a business, but 6 produces misery in a welfare state. This is one reason for diminishing welfare demand by putting welfare clients to work. But there is another: work has long seemed character-building, increasing both self-esteem and respect from others. In the case of homeless adolescents, access to work has indeed provided profound emotional as well as material support, a strengthening of self-esteem shown in numerous studies. Adults on welfare who had the capacity to work but not the opportunities respond similarly well to these programs.

7   Yet the work these new workers do complicates the issue of mutual esteem and respect. Though some parts of American government have experimented with training former welfare clients for viable, skilled jobs with a future, the work available is more often low-skill service labor in flexible businesses: work in fast-food restaurants, or as contract-term guards, or as temporary hospital aides. The ways of working in these organizations are, for the middle class as well as for the poor, not very cohesive.

8   In pyramids, people who loyally served the institution were meant to be rewarded for their loyalty. Now seniority, service and loyalty have fewer claims on firms. In *Only the Paranoid Survive*, the ex-president of the Intel Corporation declares: "Fear of competition, fear of bankruptcy, fear of being wrong, and fear of losing can all be powerful motivators. How do we cultivate fear of losing in our employees? We can only do that if we feel it ourselves." Detachment makes sense in such organizations. People are meant to treat work as an episodic activity, a series of tasks as one jumps from place to place.

9   Flat, short forms of work tend to forge weak bonds of fraternity among workers. The social analyst Robert Putnam has found, for instance, that co-workers account for fewer than 10 percent of friendships in America; when people are asked to whom they would turn to discuss an important issue, fewer than half listed a single co-worker. Moreover, the flexible work world tends to breed passivity in its bottom echelons. In an unstable institution, where people have no viable claims on the organization, they tend to keep their heads down in order to survive. The sociologist Jill Andresky Fraser calls this "emotional detachment as a survival strategy."

10   These social deficits of short, flat organizations apply particularly to new, needy workers at the bottom. New workers have trouble forming support networks in such workplaces; the climate of detachment, institutional distrust and passivity is not good for learning how to work. Their problems are sharpened because the last and lowest hired are often the first fired; without expensive employment assistance, these entry-level jobs can prove particularly demoralizing to workers who formerly relied on welfare. The problems faced by those in welfare-to-work point to a basic fact about all flexible organizations: their social bonds are weak. Many observers have concluded that community life will have to make up for this social deficit.

11   Classical sociology contrasts *Gesellschaft* and *Gemeinschaft*—the first naming merely function, the second more emotionally full relations between people. The contrast is between the behavior of strangers

and that of neighbors, between big places and small ones, between behavior which emphasizes rules and behavior more spontaneous in character. Many modern welfare reformers prefer *Gemeinschaft*; it seems a less demeaning context of care.

But this contrast is too simple. Successful welfare "in the commu- 12 nity" often has to operate by impersonal and rigid rules. One of the most effective youth organizations in Chicago, the Chicago Area Project, began in the 1930s and, for several generations, did street work with delinquents, work which required sharply honed skills. Adolescent criminals frequently try to "wind up" social workers, for instance, by being as sullen or aggressive as possible, trying to provoke the adults into losing control. Responding emotionally would spell disaster.

The adults who learnt how to cope with this on the streets were not 13 locals, but outsiders who had drawn over the years on the accumulated knowledge of others. The time required to make such programs work is not that of casual, daily life. A contemporary program for young drug addicts in Paris presupposes about 18 months to establish an effective network of contacts with the community of drug addicts, and then about five years to wean them individually off drugs.

In Chicago as in Paris, good street work requires a planned nar- 14 rative whose denouement is exit from crime, if not from addiction; the Chicago Area Project looks highly bureaucratic to an outsider because this long exit requires the help of doctors, legal advice, as well as financial support for the offenders and occasionally for their families. To eschew formal bureaucracy is often, in effect, to provide little help.

The American preference for spontaneous and voluntary forms of 15 communal welfare has religious roots. Protestantism pushed face-to-face communication in the direction of intimate revelation—to reveal oneself, and to experience the revelations of others, became a kind of final test of mutual respect.

In the 1830s, Tocqueville noted how far this revelatory intimacy 16 had advanced: what the American volunteer gets from good works is a personal relationship. In his view, charity had become the means to the end of creating small, local communities.

The danger is to mistake charity for friendship—a confusion which 17 attended American poor-visiting in the 19th century. The bourgeois American "friends" often sought to form face-to-face relations with the poor they visited, more so than in Britain. More modern forms of American volunteerism have been similarly personal, as in the "big brother" organizations which provide role models and surrogates for missing fathers. But very few friendships can bear the weight of providing sustained help. Just as a refusal to respond to provocation or manipulation is an impersonal, professional skill, so the long-term, intensive commitment of time to a client cannot follow the deepening of intimacy in a friendship; the caseworker hopes that eventually the client will be able to loosen the bond.

18   The characteristic figure of American welfare since Tocqueville's time has been the local volunteer, and the social history of volunteering has turned largely around the ways volunteers themselves had to discover and deal with the possible confusions of help and friendship. The importance of sorting out what it means to volunteer has grown, in recent years, as the "reform" of big, pyramidal institutions has progressed: ever more burdens are thrown on the volunteer's shoulders. And the superficiality and instability of social relations in much of modern work makes the idea of community service seem even more important.

19   Today, the American volunteer has become a fairly well-defined social figure. As elderly people live longer and in better health, their willingness to volunteer has indeed grown, while students and young people increasingly do public service projects as part of their education. But individuals in the 30–50 age group, particularly those in their thirties, donated their time significantly less in 1998, than in, say, 1975.

20   This gap is sometimes explained by the increasing pressures of work. But that explanation alone is not enough. By emphasizing the virtue of the voluntary act, originating in individual desire, Protestant welfare runs up against the problem of individuals who do not want to give, or to participate in the public realm.

21   When he coined the term "individualism" in the second volume of *Democracy in America,* Tocqueville drew out this problem in the most dramatic way. Individualism, he argued, consists in love of family and friends, but indifference to any social relations beyond that intimate sphere. Social equality only makes the problem of individualism worse: because most people seem the same as oneself in tastes, beliefs and needs, it seems one can and should leave it to them to deal with their own problems.

22   Voluntary organizations are an institutional counterweight to individual, egalitarian indifference to others. Today, the amount of wealth the US puts into non-profit charities and foundations is staggering— about 12 times the rate of contributions in Britain. However, while in both America and Europe the total amounts given to the not-for-profit sector are growing, the amounts contributed per individual are falling; it is the wealthy few who are swelling the coffers. At the end of the great economic boom of the 1990s, Americans donated less per head than they did in 1940, at the end of the Great Depression.

So the individual impulse to give remains an issue; those individu- 23
als most likely to give are people who then volunteer for community
service. In the US, one study has found that most "institutional kindness" comes from volunteers who want to transform something in
their own characters, adding to themselves and their experiences of
others what they cannot find in the cold world of functional or rational
relationships. Another has shown how voluntary organizations attract
recruits by promising, indeed demanding, changes in their "core
selves."

The political analyst Robert Putnam has drawn a distinction 24
between what he calls "bonding" and "bridging" social relationships.
Bonding relationships consist of those associations which are "inward-
looking and tend to reinforce exclusive identities and homogeneous
groups." This is the realm of face-to-face; it remains strong. Bridging
relationships are "outward-looking and encompass people across
diverse social cleavages." This is the civic realm of strangers, and it is
growing ever weaker.

The difference comes into focus in considering blood donations. In 25
all western societies, these rise dramatically during times of war or
national attack; people spontaneously "bridge." In more tranquil
times, American rates of blood donation have declined—from 80 units
to 62 units between 1987 and 1997—whereas in Britain they have held
up. The British sociologist Richard Titmuss, in *The Gift Relationship*
(1970), categorized donors into different types from A, "the donor who
sells his blood for what the market will bear," to H, the altruistic donor
who most closely approximates "in social reality the abstract concept of
a 'free human gift.'" American donors spanned the spectrum from A to
H. British donors were more clustered at the free-gift end. More than
70 percent came from families in which no one had been a blood recipient; they were not returning blood their kin had used. Nor did they
have any idea where or to whom their blood would go: there could be
no face-to-face interaction with recipients. In Titmuss's view, civil society is strong when that interaction is not needed, weak when the gift is
personalized.

Following Titmuss, other sociologists looked at breast milk. 26
Because breast milk—given mostly to prematurely born infants—is
hard to express and requires repeated sessions to accumulate in usable
amounts, its donation is far more arduous than gifts of blood. Again
the rate of donation is higher in Britain than in America, and most
donors, write the researchers, know that "donations are for unnamed
strangers without distinction of age, sex, medical condition, income,
class, religion or ethnic group."

27   None of this should be taken as evidence that Americans are selfish: they point, rather, to a structural problem in the American communal model. On the positive side, this model encourages personally fulfilling activities such as mentoring; on the negative side, it creates an impediment to perceiving and taking seriously the needs of strangers. It could be said the dilemma is peculiarly American, a compensation for lack of a viable, more impersonal public realm. But the context is global rather than national. The spread of flexible institutions of work is more than an American phenomenon; so is the effort to restructure welfare along new bureaucratic lines. Both arouse the desire for a compensating, countervailing community.

28   Volunteering is, however, a poor remedy for binding strangers together, or dealing with social complexities. It lacks what might be called an architecture of sympathy—a progressive movement up from identifying with individuals one knows to individuals one doesn't know. The prerequisite of autonomy is missing too: the willingness to remain strangers to one another in a social relationship. The Dutch sociologist Abram de Swaan has argued that the civilizing functions of the welfare state require the "generalization of interdependence" in societies. Yet the sphere of mutual regard is too small, too intimate, when the volunteer is taken to be the ideal figure providing care to others. Saying this is not to denigrate volunteers, but rather to criticize the idealization of these "friends" when something other than friendship is required.

29   Just as welfare reformers have celebrated local volunteers, they have also attacked public service workers—and indeed the very ethos of public service. For the past quarter-century, more largely, the honor of public service work has been slighted.

30   Those subject to this onslaught have defended their self-respect by asserting the value of useful rather than flexible labor. In a recent investigation into public service work in Britain (in which I took part), a London street sweeper declared: "On Mondays I certainly get job satisfaction. It's the worst day for rubbish because there's only a skeleton staff on at weekends. When I look back at the street I've just done and all the piles of rubbish are gone and it's clean, I'm pleased." A dog handler for the customs services who sniffs out drugs with her pooch says: "I feel valued both by my employer and the public. People know it is a worthwhile job, stopping drugs coming into the country."

31   The defense mounted by these public service workers focuses not just on one's value to the organization, nor just on one's value to the general public, but on the act of doing something useful. Usefulness takes on the characteristics of craftwork, characteristics which include an egoistic involvement in the task itself. People simply believe that the work is worth doing.

American public service workers share these values, but American social workers tend to stay in public service for much shorter lengths of time than their British counterparts; their rates of turnover have steadily increased in the past generation. The increasingly flat and short practices of healthcare are driving doctors in both countries out of public health services. In both America and Britain, there is now an enormous Sargasso Sea of floating part-time teachers who move in and out of the profession. 32

Service to others certainly matters to public service workers, but the craft aspect of usefulness helps people to persevere under conditions in which their honor is frequently impugned. The work itself provides objective standards of feeling oneself worthwhile. The street sweeper likes a clean street, the handler of drug-sniffing dogs likes handling dogs. 33

Focusing on the craft of useful work separates this kind of caregiving from compassion. It does not turn on pity for those in need. The craft dimensions of useful work serve as a caution against the error of believing that doing good necessarily entails self-sacrifice. Usefulness must, by contrast, have an inherent value, a focus on a specific object, which gives the service worker satisfaction. 34

Pyramidal bureaucracies could provide everyone a place and a proper function, see them as whole human beings, though at the cost of denying them participation. The institutional innovations of our time do not place people stably, and do not see people whole. In compensation, people may seek to connect to others, voluntarily, locally, face to face. A social void may indeed be filled this way. But there is no solution to the problem of welfare here. 35

Reflection and Discussion

1. Think of the organizational structures of the groups you've volunteered with. Are they large national or international groups or small local agencies? How did the size and structure affect your satisfaction?
2. Robert Putnam says that our relationships are strong with those similar to us, but weak with those unlike us. To what extent do you think this is true? How does this affect our willingness and ability to help others?

Writing Matters

1. Most people see volunteering as a way to understand what others are going through, yet Sennett argues that this is not true, at least in America. Analyze Sennett's argument and decide whether volunteering helps or hinders us in developing knowledge and empathy for those in need.

2. Sennett sees donations to charity as a parallel to volunteerism. To what extent does this analogy work? Where does it fail and why?

MAKING CONNECTIONS

1. Should some form of short-term national service be required for young people? Research what is done in other countries, finding out the requirements as well as the long-term effects on the citizens, and argue for or against this type of program in the United States.

2. McCain points out the Higher Education Act of 1965 intended to use a substantial portion of college work-study funds for community service. Research this act and discover why this isn't being done. What could happen in your community if work-study students could provide tutoring or other help?

3. Many worthy organizations have difficulty finding volunteers. Pick one and analyze the material it uses to recruit volunteers based on what you have learned in this chapter. Does it ask for unreasonable commitments or qualifications? How well does it communicate its mission and the benefits it offers volunteers? Conclude your analysis by recommending the changes needed to promote more volunteerism more effectively.

4. Reflect on the connection between volunteerism and the strength of civic and community relationships. How much does volunteer work build a strong and connected community, bridging differences? How much does it reflect the existing strength of the community?

TAKING ACTION

1. What's your passion? Research local volunteer opportunities that will use your current skills and let you work toward your career. Don't be satisfied with a routine posting ("someone to help at the humane society"); look carefully to determine what work you could do that would help you and your client agency most. Put together a brief résumé, pointing out your qualifications for this ideal volunteer position, and send it with a cover letter asking for a chance to volunteer in a specific way.

2. Many organizations offer opportunities to volunteer for a single day. Sign up for one and engage in the experience as both a committed volunteer and as a researcher studying the volunteer experience. Write about your experience in depth, describing the volunteer agency, other volunteers, the work itself and the people served. Whether you choose the form of a personal essay (like Goldberg's) or an ethnography (like the full CIRCLE) report, reflect on the meaning of the experience for everyone involved.

Maybe Heroism Isn't Dead

Modern tragedies—9/11, Hurricane Katrina—touch our lives and hearts in two ways, uniting us through compassion for the victims while inspiring us with the courage of those who risk everything to bring aid. Without an immediate victim needing a daring rescue, though, many people find it hard to call anyone a hero; our cynicism focuses on flaws, not strengths. But, as Jiřina Šiklová notes, "Heroism is either an immediate reaction on behalf of another human being or community . . . or a conscious long-term endeavor to achieve a specific goal that is deemed important enough to be worth sacrifice of other values, including one's life." The long, slow work of this second type of heroism does not engender the immediate rewards of the death-defying rescue, yet still requires courage and commitment to make a better world. When standing up for a principle involves self-sacrifice or even danger, are the rewards worth the risks? Can one person really make a difference? What qualities must a hero have besides courage?

BEFORE YOU READ

Think of your heroes, those magical people who have inspired you since earliest childhood. Which of them still inspire you? What has caused you to drop some of them from your pantheon? How have your attitudes toward heroes and heroism changed over the years?

Heroes I Have Taught—and Who Have Taught Me

M. Garrett Bauman, *Chronicle of Higher Education,* December 12, 2003

Award-winning essayist M. Garrett Bauman teaches writing at Monroe Community College in New York.

What do you know about your classmates in this and other courses? What assumptions might you have about those you don't know well?

1   David was gaunt and bony-faced, and the sole of one shoe flapped loosely as he walked. In his first paper for my writing class, he wrote about living in a halfway house among abandoned buildings on a street littered with liquor bottles and hypodermic needles. At night, drive-by shootings and sirens inspired his nightmares. To support himself, he commuted an hour by bus to flip burgers for minimum wage. Hunger gnawed him, and only concentrating on studies focused his mind. He apologized for missing one class—he didn't have bus fare. When I offered to help him find financial aid, pride blazed in his eyes: "I don't want free things. I gotta do this myself. I'm going to be different now."

2   By midsemester I'm worn down by makeup-obsessed women tittering like preteens, groggy party dogs who stumble unprepared into class, and students who think the purpose of education is to *have* a shiny grade pinned on them. Then there are students like David—those whom I can only call heroic. The word has been overused in recent years. It should mean more than either helpless suffering or simple victory. Heroism entails extraordinary effort at great cost to oneself. Heroes lose more often than they win because they struggle against such daunting odds.

3   Some students, more commonly in community colleges, must overcome intense poverty or psychological trauma just to do their academic work. "Milo" was a refugee from Bosnia. In one essay he described watching as his father, wife, and child were murdered during a raid on his village. Vowing revenge, Milo ambushed his enemies—anyone from the other side. "Anyone," he repeated cryptically. "I could not kill them enough. I became the devil I hated." He wept as he handed in the paper, reluctant, I think, to release the blind rage that had propped him up for years.

4   A paper is a simple thing. A thousand pass under my eyes each semester. Yet writing this one was a courageous act by a man who faced himself without excuses, who was steeled to make an accounting before rejoining mankind. I admired Milo for allowing college to touch

that private place. How little do professors suspect what our assignments really require of students who have decided to take us at our word and use college to redefine themselves. It is ironic that after years of trying to awaken students to intellectual life, I need to be reminded of how powerful ideas are.

And ideas matter more deeply to some students than professors 5 know. On the first day of class, Leo told us that he was 78 years old. "I have colon cancer," he said. "I have to get my college education now." Later he informed me that surgeons had removed his rectum, so he hoped that I would excuse any "emergency situations." In class Leo debated passionately, admired other students' insights, and sought to continue discussions with them after class. He glowed as though ideas were a dose of vitamins. When a few students were unprepared, he told them, "I wish I had your years in my tank. I'm not going to be on this earth much longer to make it better. But you will. Are you going to know what you need to know?" I worried that they might regard him as a moralizing grouch, but they accepted his rebuke like a friendly jab in the arm.

Leo died a few months after our course ended, a semester short of 6 graduation. But I'm more proud of his courage than sad for his loss. He gives me a reason to believe that learning can be heroic—when it pushes the boundaries of what we have been. As long as we stretch our edges, we keep death at bay. And Leo, I believe, will get his opportunity to help the world through some of the young people he affected.

Some struggling students find their mentors in books. I recently 7 assigned Frederick Douglass's account of his years in slavery. Since Douglass had lived not two miles from our campus, I thought it might be too-familiar material. But before our first discussion, I received a recorded phone message: "This is Robyn. It's 2 AM. I know you're not there, but I had to talk to you. I'm reading Douglass, and he knocked me cold." She had read a passage in which he comforts himself after a vicious whipping. He says that he is not the only slave in the world, that today's misery may increase his future happiness, that he will persevere. "Do you think that's true?" Robyn asked. "It's like he wrote it for me, to put me in my place. If he can say that after what he went through, so can I."

A superb student in a previous class, she was drawn and nervous 8 this term. When I casually inquired about her demeanor, she drew me aside. A month before classes began she had been raped. It had been brutal and devastating, but she decided to prosecute. "I am not going to let him get away with it," she vowed. Since then, she had battled flashbacks and bouts of rage, self-loathing, and hypnotic dazes. Still, she insisted, "I'm not going to let him take college from me. I will get the work done." She had so far, but the legal procedures sapped her, violated her again. During one agonizing night, Douglass had whispered consolation.

9   A few days later, Robyn phoned. "I have to miss class today. He's on campus."

10   "The—"

11   "He was watching me. I have to tell security and get an order of protection." She hung up before I could ask if she was safe. Safe! Would she ever feel safe again?

12   I don't know how Robyn's story will end. For now she's hanging on. It's not fair that she has to battle such demons to concentrate on literature. But her effort has sensitized her to her studies. In her quest for an explanation for her wound, a philosophy to help her live, Robyn feels the passion and courage behind what, to many students, are mere words: "I listen to a simple sentence a teacher says, and it has the whole world inside. Everything means so much." Some of her work is flat, but much of it is truly inspired. She is using college as a rope to climb from the pit.

13   Often, heroic effort warps a person in unflattering ways. Luis is easy to dislike. He slumps in the back corner and when called on simply shakes his head. He packs his bag 15 minutes before class ends. I know his quirks because he flunked my composition class last term— slamming his final paper into the trash as he stormed out. I ask why he took me again, and he stares directly in my eyes.

14   "I'm sorry about the way I acted. Sometimes, man, I get so angry and don't know what to do with it. I wanted you again." I'm not sure if that was a compliment or a promise to finish me off.

15   Last term Luis resisted exploring his inner landscape. This time he charged into it. His first paper examined a lyric by the rapper DMX: "To live is to suffer, but to survive, that's to find meaning in the suffering." He developed the quotation by describing his own quest for meaning. Luis's mother was a prostitute, an "alcoholic, crackhead, and heroin freebaser." She adored his sister, lavishing designer clothes and jewelry on her while sending Luis to school in clothes so unwashed and ragged that bullies picked on him. Luis struggled to figure out why this had happened to him.

16   "I knew I didn't deserve it," he wrote. "I was just a little kid." To save himself he "became a cold-hearted S.O.B.," lashing out violently when pressure built. Fleeing home at 15, he became a loner who vowed, "There is no such thing as love, at least not for me."

17   Recently he met his mother on the street—in a wheelchair, emaciated, nearly bald, her flesh covered with red lesions, blind in one eye. She had contracted AIDS. She pointed at Luis: "It's your fault I'm here. If you didn't desert me. . . ."

The meaning that Luis found in suffering was this: He decided that there was no wrong or right, only learning. You can't pick out what you want to believe but must see what's really there. He vowed to embrace all things, to learn through his suffering. Sophocles, who created some of the earliest tragic *heroes*, would surely nod in agreement.

This semester, Luis still dresses in hip-hop style and has his classroom tics, but he's working at his courses, pulling A's and B's. He has become an officer in the local Latino club. But even if he were earning C's, it would be a heroic achievement.

For many students, getting to class is an odyssey beset with malevolent gods. It is unfair that they *have* to fight living monsters and inner demons to read a book. One consolation is that such struggles often intensify the value of their academic work. How strange that so many students grudgingly slog through assignments that don't touch them, while others, laboring in the dark nights of their souls, save themselves with the same pages. They are the ones who pursue the most dangerous goal of education—the reshaping of their lives.

Reflection and Discussion

1. Most often we think of heroes as acting to benefit others, yet the students in this article are struggling for their own education. Must heroism help others?
2. Why does Bauman say that "the most dangerous goal of education" is "reshaping" your life?

Writing Matters

1. The student called David refused to get financial aid, saying "I gotta do this by myself. I'm going to be different now." Think how self-sufficiency develops in yourself and other people you have known. Under what circumstances could David's determination be considered heroic? When would it be self-defeating?
2. Bauman says that Leo taught him that "learning can be heroic." Do you agree? Support your position using examples of heroism and learning from your own experience and the lives of others.

Jesuit Greg Boyle, Gang Priest

Carol Ann Morrow, *St. Anthony Messenger,* August 1999

Former teacher Carol Ann Morrow has written extensively on spirituality and social justice and now works as editor of Youth Update.

What experience have you had with gangs, directly or indirectly?

1   It helps to have connections if you want to meet the Rev. Greg Boyle, S.J.—gang connections. Father Greg doesn't have much time to tell his story . . . Why? Because he gives—and gives and gives—his time, his energy and his influence (known in the neighborhood as "juice") to the young people of the Pico/Aliso District in East L.A.

2   Pico Gardens and Aliso Village, sometimes called "The Projects," is the largest tract of subsidized housing west of the Mississippi. This huge piece of social engineering hasn't worked out so well. It's poor, crowded and packed with gangs.

3   Some of Pico/Aliso overlaps Boyle Heights (different era, different Boyle). Within those 16 square miles, 60 gangs claim 10,000 members, Hispanic and black. This equals violence and plenty of action at the Hollenbeck division of the Los Angeles Police Department—if Father Greg Boyle doesn't get there first.

4   In two days hanging around Father Greg's office, a modest though vividly painted storefront on L.A.'s East First Street, G-Dog or G, as the kids affectionately call the Jesuit, reveals life in a very fast lane. The priest's office—nine feet square maximum—is a windowless, unfinished drywall box in the epicenter of the 600-square-foot headquarters of Jobs for a Future (JFF). He has an open door in—and an open door beyond—to other offices, storage for Homeboy Industries silk-screened items and the only bathroom. Traffic through Greg's doorway feels as hectic as the L.A. freeway system.

5   Father Greg requests, "Hold my calls." But when a prison inmate gets a chance to phone, the priest reneges, "Well, let me take just this one. . . ." A young man comes by—dressed for success—to tell his happy story and thank Father Greg for the contact, the clothes, a job, a hope. With Greg on the phone and me in the visitor's chair, the young man preens back and forth between the front and back doors of this short runway. He and the priest exchange a complex handshake, a triumphant smile, a thumbs-up. No words seem necessary. Pride is evident in both son—and father. Father Greg is surrogate parent to hundreds of Hispanic youth, many the children of Latino immigrants.

6   The office is crammed with memorabilia which I study while he's on the phone. Official framed certificates, plaques and news clippings hang next to drawings by—and photos of—neighborhood youth. Latin American artifacts and activist posters jockey for wall space with strong, distinctive samples of graffiti wall art. The colorful sketches Father Greg has pinned to the wall have no ominous overtones, however. His poorly lit office is bright with evidence of love.

How can Father Greg take time to talk about what's already hap- 7
pened when more is happening—right now? How can he speak of his
dreams when young dreamers are lined up outside the door? "So—
what do you want to know?" he asks as he hangs up the phone, signs
some kind of permission slip for a girl's school function, hollers out
with pseudo-sternness, "No more calls!" and tries to fit the story of his
life into the 10 minutes before he dashes to another appointment.

Irish-American Jesuit Homeboy

Gregory Boyle is one of eight children. His father, third-generation 8
Irish-American, worked in a family-founded dairy in Los Angeles
County. His mom worked to keep track of her large family. When the
young Greg graduated from L.A.'s Loyola High School in 1972, he
decided to become a Jesuit and was ordained a priest in 1984.

To this observer, it would seem that the Jesuit's every assignment 9
(pre- and post-ordination) would present major hurdles for most
middle-class Americans: hospice, soup kitchen, prison, Latin America,
the South Bronx. For Father Greg, each contributed to the pastoral
awareness he brought to his 1986 assignment as pastor of Dolores
Mission. He wanted to be a Jesuit because the Order has a social-activist
bent. He wanted, he had said, to work with the poor. Dolores Mission is
certainly that. The parish is within walking distance of downtown Los
Angeles, yet constitutes another economic and social hemisphere.

It's been a bumpy 13 years for Father Greg, including a year and a 10
half away from the neighborhood after his six years as pastor were concluded. Some people didn't want him to come back after his sabbatical,
but they weren't the young men—and young women—who constituted
the priest's primary focus: gang members and other kids on the edge.

When he returned in 1994, his assignment was to concentrate 11
exclusively on job development and related ministries with neighborhood gangs—and not on the other urgencies Los Angeles's poorest
pastorate had required of him. JFF is more than enough to stress a
much larger staff than the seven the agency employs.

Is he tired? It seems a logical question, given the pace observed in 12
just two days! The 45-year-old Jesuit answers, "I don't expect to be
doing this forever, but I love it and it gives me life. Like this morning—
I'm coming from court and a kid flags me down and he's wearing his
shirt unbuttoned, a nice dress shirt, nice pants. He's got a tie and he's
waving it. 'Do my tie,' he's begging. So I pull over because it's an emergency. I do his tie and he looks great and I say, 'You know what, Johnny.
I'm proud of you!' Johnny turns around and says, 'Me, too!'"

13   When he isn't fixing ties or talking on the phone, Father Greg may be in court—as he was this morning—or visiting the 14 detention centers where he celebrates Mass on a rotating basis, or out raising funds through a combination of great stories, hard truths and gospel witness. He might be out on the street. He might be writing letters, since he answers every letter from a local youth in detention. This averages about 40 a month, reports Celeste Fremon, in her . . . 1995 biography, *Father Greg & the Homeboys*. Her book is based on two years of following G-Dog around in good times and bad.

14   Ms. Fremon, journalist, mother, advocate for Greg and the kids known as homeboys . . ., has heard the Los Angeles Police Department complain vociferously about Father Greg. They think he harbors and supports criminals. She has attended some of the many gang-member funerals over which Father Greg's presided. She's heard—and reported—the objections of police officers who say he glorifies gang membership by allowing Church burials for these young people. Greg sees a funeral as a great personal heartache but also a significant teaching moment, a time when other homies might let down their defenses and listen.

15   Celeste Fremon sees Father Greg as one of the neighborhood's greatest hopes. She describes Pico/Aliso as a war zone. She sees gang leaders as the kids with the "most intelligence, social skills, leadership capacity and the ability not to blink in the face of danger." She says that the Jesuit hasn't brought peace to Pico/Aliso but he has brought change. He has brought such an infusion of love that some young men "have finally become strong enough to save themselves," the concluding sentence of Ms. Fremon's book. . . .

At Central Headquarters

16   Father Greg has brought other dynamic and dedicated people to work at Jobs for a Future. Emily Castillo, Norma Gillette, John Tostado and Carlos Vasquez are also hard at work during the days [I visit] JFF's First Street offices.

17   These staff members do what it takes to get kids working. Just what is that? Emily arranges for a "Clean Slate," which at JFF means getting tattoos removed. White Memorial Hospital doctors cooperate in this venture. Norma develops résumés and matches those résumés with job opportunities. She is scouring the want ads when I arrive, circling possibilities.

18   John and Carlos are job developers and case managers for youth in their early days of employment. They write letters of recommendation.

They visit businesses to see how they can connect the energy of their clients with the goals of businesspeople.

JFF helps its clients get the clothes they need to make that all- 19 important first impression. Father Greg spent part of this interview on the phone checking his credit balance, apparently finding the totals disappointing. "A million and one kids need clothes to get to jobs and stuff like that," he says, happily exasperated by a positive problem. Gilbert, a neighborhood youth now employed, is new at his job and "still pretty pushed for clothes." White T's and black Dickey work pants, de rigueur in the neighborhood, are—for that very reason—seldom admired in the workplace. Father Greg and other staff members also serve as tie-knot tutors and are happy to add that to their résumés.

To ensure employment opportunities, Father Greg began 20 Homeboy Industries, which markets T-shirts, sweats, mugs and hats bearing the Homeboy logo. All these items are imprinted by Homeboy Silkscreen, a for-profit subsidiary.

A visit to the silkscreen operation and to Homeboy Bakery—both 21 hot as blazes on an L.A. August afternoon—finds members of rival gangs sweating side by side, learning skills they can use and building a résumé that can also boast of their punctuality, reliability and ability to cooperate. While the bakery employs only 10 on a shift, young men can begin there, learn and move on. The men I see have no time to talk. They are intent on creating loaves of fragrant, yeasty, gourmet bread.

Carlos Vasquez explains that these are transitional, training busi- 22 nesses, but both appear to be succeeding. The bakery, oddly enough, failed as a tortilla supplier, but is getting good press in its current rein- carnation as a supplier to fine restaurants with Frisco Baking Co. as dis- tributor. KPWR, an L.A. hip-hop FM station, has given the bakery $150,000 through its Knowledge Is Power Foundation. It also engages the silk-screeners to make logo T's.

Since [my] visit to Jobs for a Future, three more companies are in 23 place: Homeboy Landscaping, Homeboy Cleaning Service and Homeboy Artesania. . . .

Why These Gangs?

The Los Angeles Police Department's anti-gang program is called 24 Operation Hammer. The general approach is to get gang members off the street and into jail. Father Greg calls it the "full-incarceration method" which he contrasts with his own "full-employment strategy."

25   What explains this powerful and dangerous phenomenon of youth gangs? Father Greg says, "It's a sense of belonging. There's not something that pulls kids into gangs so much as something that pushes them. It's not so much what lures or attracts them but what pushes them out of the four walls that should be holding them in—and don't."

26   He continues, "The kid is sort of pushed out at home and then gravitates around this group. He's not so much, 'Wow, doesn't that look attractive.' It's not, because they will join a gang and they'll have to watch their back forever. They'll endanger the lives of their loved ones and it goes on and on. None of it is very attractive. But if there's abuse or alcohol or neglect or if the parents aren't around," kids look for a place they can belong.

27   They are high-spirited young people, wary but clever and charming. Armando Avecedo has a tattoo on his neck in Chinese characters. Why? He explains, "So not everyone can read it." How does it translate? "Trust no woman," he says deadpan, his dark eyes delighting in the irony of telling so many his secret.

28   "We are prone as a society to demonize and reject these kids and not want to help them," laments Father Greg. "What if we really were to deal with the problem rather than just resign ourselves to warehousing the consequences? What if we were just to say yes to kids rather than insist that kids just say no to gangs? We want adults to be able to say yes to these kids, to offer them a way to get on with their lives. They've been through a lot. I've never met a victimizer who wasn't first victimized. So you have to deal with that compassionately as Jesus would."

Imagining a Future

29 Jobs for a Future—and the mission of Greg Boyle—is premised on just that: a belief in the future, a future for each and every young person in the projects. Father Greg works with kids whose homes are broken, whose parents are unemployed, who have dropped out of school, who say they "ain't got no future." To them, the Jesuit says, "I can see your future! Trust me!" He explains that much of his ministry is to imagine a future that the kids can't see—and help that future materialize.

30   I ask for a success story: kids employed, kids grown and out of the projects, kids living the American dream. He points to young men—like Fernie, pictured on the cover—working around the office, answering the constantly ringing phones, packaging Homeboy Industries orders, showing up for work, being "go-fers," being counted. "All the different gangs are represented right now in our office," he observes.

"Not only does society need to put a human face on gangs but enemies also need to put a human face on one another," he adds.

Still Father Greg is hesitant to speak in terms of success. "I feel 31 called to be faithful, not successful," he says. "I feel called to be faithful to an approach and to a certain wisdom about who these kids are. I believe that if they are given a chance, then they'll thrive and they'll begin to imagine a future for themselves."

What would this future look like? "Obviously, we want peace in 32 the community. We want the kids to have a sense of who they are in God's eyes. They're such damaged kids in the sense that they haven't had much love or support at home. That affects their sense of themselves, of who they think they are.

"They think they're the bad son. I keep telling them over and over, 33 'You are the son that any parents would be proud to claim as their own.' That's the truth. That's not some fantasy. As soon as they know that they're exactly what God had in mind when God made them, then they become that. Then they like who they are. Once they can do that—love themselves—they're not inclined to shoot somebody or hurt somebody or be out there gang-banging."

They are the prized—if prodigal—sons. Jesuit Greg Boyle extends 34 to them—and to many a homegirl as well—the accepting arms of a loving father.

Reflection and Discussion

1. Morrow feels that most middle-class Americans would have trouble working with poor, sick and dying people. Why would she consider the challenges of this work to be class-specific? Why would Boyle look at it as training?

2. Look at the things that Boyle and JFF do, not what they say. What do these actions tell us about how they feel about those they help?

Writing Matters

1. Both Boyle and the police risk their lives when they face gang members, yet Morrow has singled out Boyle as a hero. Compare the work of Boyle and the police and decide which is more heroic, supporting your choice with examples from the article.

2. Boyle says that he is "called to be faithful, not successful." Is it enough to be faithful to what we believe in? When can mere faithfulness (without regard to success) be a form of cowardice? Under what circumstances is faithfulness heroic?

Heroism and Biology

Robert Winston, *Manchester Guardian,* October 24, 2002

Lord Winston is Professor of Fertility Studies at Imperial College, London University, and Director of NHS Research and Development for Hammersmith Hospital. The author of several books, he is a regular presenter on BBC science series.

When have you had a heroic impulse?

1   Imagine that the human body has, like a thriller movie, an internal soundtrack. Think of the film, perhaps of the killer about to pull back the shower curtain, or jump out from under the stairs. But we always know beforehand that something terrible is about to happen. How do we know? From the music or the lighting, of course, the shrill chords, silence or shadows that build up the tension in advance.

2   Our body has a version of this same scenario. It is highly adept at preparing us for the fright before we know it is there. The brain, in moments of danger, is wired to perceive before it thinks, indeed to register at lightning-fast speed. In a threatening situation, proper thinking takes far too long. The fear reflex is unencumbered by choice or consideration; it pre-empts rational or logical perception. Our most primal emotion—to advance or retreat, fight or flight—is triggered so fast that thought and awareness are veritable deserters at the frontline of the battle for survival: they don't even get a look-in.

3   Yet we may be in danger of creating a misconception. "Fear" is a word loaded with pejorative connotations. We talk of being "paralyzed with fear," "dumb-struck" with fear, fear leaving us "stock-still." This paralysis may be an inherited response from our time on the savannah. Threatened by a large predator, our best strategy would have been to remain like a statue and avoid detection.

4   Sometimes we may even be scared "witless." Yet wit, as we have seen, isn't even close enough to the action in the first place. Our use of language links fear with some sense of stationary helplessness. In biological terms, however, nothing could be further from the truth. Inside the body all hell is breaking loose. The brain and the autonomic nervous system—the controller of the gut, blood vessels, glands and lungs—have gone into overdrive, triggering a hormonal cascade, starting the body's race to a finishing line that represents a readiness to operate at—or even beyond—the extremes of physical capacity.

5   Fear may be at the root of cowardice; it may make us run faster and further from danger than seems possible. But fear also sanctions the

flip-side to the flight instinct: fight. Fear allows us to perform incredible feats of survival and endurance—we all have heard the occasional tale of someone who has wrestled a huge crocodile, or knocked-out a fully grown black bear with a left jab, or even the grandmother who has lifted a pick-up truck to pull a trapped child from under a wheel. Yes, fear may be the father of cowardice. But perhaps it gives birth to a second son, an Abel to the Cain. Fear could also be a parent of heroism.

But is heroism instinctual? Could we isolate genes which predispose us to heroic actions? It is not an easy task to untangle the altruistic impulse. Instincts are not designed to make us better people, nor are they designed to promote the good of the species as a whole. In fact, they are not designed at all, they have come about through natural selection, through pursuit of genetic success. Traits that enhance the chances of survival and reproduction of those genes are going to proliferate. All of which presumably means that, where the motivations of the modern-day hero may be unclear, we know that his ancestor may have acted for himself alone. 6

For an act to be defined as heroic we normally understand it as involving some form of personal danger. The hero puts him or herself at risk. And examples of risk-taking in both humans and animals are much more widespread than we might at first think. 7

Take the Trinidadian guppy, our first member of nature's extreme sportsmen's club. When a predator nears a school of guppies, one or two especially intrepid males will slowly approach the intruder, inspecting it for signs of danger—in essence playing a very treacherous game of "chicken." And generally the guppy feels more disposed to do this when a female is near. Alternatively, there is the Arabian babbler, another thrill-junky. Often, the male babbler announces his presence to predators by shouting at them—in essence an invitation to "Catch me if you can!" Again, the watchful female appears instrumental. These instances are examples of risk-taking for the universally popular purpose of attracting a mate, to propagate our genes and hence our species. Amotz Zahavi, professor of zoology at the institute for nature conservation research at Tel Aviv University, studied the babbler for many years and termed this behavior the "handicap principle": risky behavior is a perfect way of advertising high-quality genes. 8

Taken to extremes, this represents what 1930s biologist Sir Ronald Fisher described as "runaway sexual selection"—a vicious circle that ends up building magnificent mate-attracting traits which may, paradoxically, be a handicap to survival. (We see other examples of this phenomenon in the overgrown antlers of the red deer, or most famously, the ludicrous encumbrance of the peacock's tail). For humans, the peacock's tail comes in the form of risk, prowess, status 9 and wealth. It's about showing our potential for consumption, boasting about our prowess. The risk instinct has perhaps now become so ingrained that it is a fundamental element of human psychology, whether or not we are looking for a mate. Human beings delight in excess, find more and more ways of putting themselves in jeopardy, and adopt as many expensive handicaps as they can find.

10   So an element of heroism may come down to sex. Men are frequently more likely to do "heroic" things when watched by an attractive female. The biology of sexual selection influences all kinds of risky behavior and people get excited by the sexiness of heroic action. Hollywood bases much of its industry on this simple truth. But if suddenly this all sounds rather cynical—great acts of human kindness reduced to an exploitative tactic for enhancing one's attractiveness to the opposite sex—then do not worry unduly, there is still perhaps some hope for our altruistic hero. The most self-interested drive in human psychology, sex, may indeed be heavily involved in the most selfless acts of heroism. But the key word here is "involved." Sexual selection does not run the show. In the rich and unpredictable world of human behavior, while the presence of our genes is always felt, no one is their prisoner.

11   Most of us harbor a hope that pure altruism, unaffected by any selfish impulse, exists in human life. It almost seems a matter of pride that we find evidence of apparently selfless acts of heroism, of people putting their own lives in jeopardy in order to save the lives of those with whom they have no connection. We need to understand what happens in the crucial moment of decision to enable them to overcome the powerful instincts to save themselves at the expense of all else. Put simply, why do people bother helping anyone else at all?

12   In order to answer this question, we must look at our most basic attitudes. Do we have any impulse for collaboration? Evolutionary psychologists John Tooby and Leda Cosmides have proposed a theory known as the Big Mistake Hypothesis. They assert that, because we evolved in small, kin-based groups on the Pleistocene savannah, we have a predilection for cooperation with all members of any given social circle. On the savannah, the tribe would have been related by blood, or at least by "marriage"—that is sexual or child-raising partnerships. Our modern minds, ever influenced by our evolutionary history, adapt the savannah to the complex social structures of today, and as a consequence, we "mistake" wider society for kin. So cooperation in today's world is a maladaptive by-product of kin selection.

13   As a result, we cannot completely get out of the habit of helping those around us, even though now the benefits are far less, since there is no specific self-interest in helping strangers who do not share a significant proportion of our genes. And strangers do not have a genetic

interest in helping us or returning a favor either, which means we may—and let's face it, often do—get suckered into helping someone and getting nothing in return. If it is in the hero's nature not to care about reward, then perhaps in our everyday actions, we see the germ of the altruistic impulse.

Virtually every aspect of our lives depends wholly on cooperation 14 and trust and therefore, of course, taking risks. Language, for example, is an astounding feat of cooperation. Is cooperation part of our evolutionary psychological makeup, is it hard-wired into our brains? Has natural selection resulted in our instincts developing to the extent that altruistic action is no longer an alien concept?

The primatologist Frans de Waal calls it a profound paradox that 15 "genetic self-advancement at the expense of others—which is the basic thrust of evolution—has given rise to remarkable capacities for caring and sympathy." I am not sure that it is a paradox, but it is certainly ironic. Self-interest may be the defining characteristic of natural selection, but it does not define all human behavior; nor I think, does it give a complete picture of human instinct. Human emotion and value possibly can travel beyond the cold calculus of evolution.

Nearly all of us are capable of empathy; most of us feel guilt. We are 16 all responding to a moral code that determines our emotions, but heroism often goes beyond that code, and pure altruism is uncommon. Even if we have altruistic intentions, we may lack the courage to see them through. So where altruism exists, it must be treasured. It has its instinctual roots in an ability to understand the pleasure and pain experienced by others; it will be nurtured by our upbringing and our moral environment. Ultimately, though, it is our capacity to combine instinct, emotion and reason that gives us the facility to perform heroism's remarkable acts.

Reflection and Discussion

1. To what extent do you agree that men are more likely to act heroically in front of a desirable mate? What would be the equivalent behavior in women?

2. Think of some examples of human "runaway sexual selection," which Winston finds manifest in risk-taking and status-seeking. How much do you think this behavior is instinctual? How much is conscious?

Writing Matters

1. Winston contends that people get sexually excited by heroic risk-taking, which forms the basis for many a successful film. Evaluate this assertion in the context of action movies that you are familiar with. What else might make viewers delight in courageous action heroes?

2. While de Waal finds it paradoxical that "genetic self-advancement at the expense of others—which is the basic thrust of evolution—has given rise to remarkable capacities for caring and sympathy," Winston finds it "ironic." Carefully analyze the meaning of those two terms and explain which best fits your understanding of this phenomenon.

Nobel Peace Prize

Since 1901, a committee has met to award the Nobel Peace Prize "to the person who shall have done the most or the best work for fraternity between nations, for the abolition or reduction of standing armies and for the holding and promotion of peace congresses." Some of the laureates have worked directly for peace by mediating disputes or facilitating disarmament, others through their humanitarian efforts and work for human rights. Which of the prize winners below are you familiar with?

2007	Intergovernmental Panel on Climate Change and Albert Arnold (Al) Gore Jr.
2006	Muhammad Yunus and the Grameen Bank
2005	Mohamed El Baradei
2004	Wangari Maathai
2003	Shirin Ebadi
2000	Kim Dae-jung
1998	John Hume and David Trimble
1997	Jody Williams
1996	Carlos Filipe Ximenes Belo and José Ramos-Horta
1995	Joseph Rotblat
1994	Yasser Arafat, Shimon Peres and Yitzhak Rabin
1993	Nelson Mandela and F.W. de Klerk

Source: The Nobel Foundation, 2006

What Is a Hero?

Peter H. Gibbon, *A Call to Heroism: Renewing America's Vision of Greatness,* 2002

Historian and educator Peter H. Gibbon traveled around the country interviewing students and experts on the meaning of heroes and heroism for the 21st century.

How close are you to your heroes? How many are distant contemporary or historical figures? How many are people you know personally?

For most of human history, *hero* has been synonymous with *warrior.* 1
Although we often link these words today, we do have an expanded, more inclusive definition of *hero* than the one we inherited from the Greeks. Modern dictionaries list three qualities in common after the entry *hero:* extraordinary achievement, courage and the idea (variously expressed) that the hero serves as a "model" or "example"—that heroism has a moral component.

Today, extraordinary achievement is no longer confined to valor in 2
combat. As well as military heroes, there are humanitarian heroes, cultural heroes, political heroes. Thomas Edison lit up the night. Harriet Tubman rescued slaves. Thomas Jefferson wrote the Declaration of Independence. Beethoven is a hero of music, Rembrandt of art, Einstein of science.

Likewise, courage means many things besides physical bravery: 3
taking an unpopular position, standing up for principle, persevering, forging accomplishment out of adversity. After her life was threatened, activist Ida B. Wells continued to condemn lynching. Franklin Roosevelt battled polio. Helen Keller transcended blindness and deafness.

The moral component of the meaning of heroism—and, I believe, the 4
most important one—is elusive. . . . In dictionaries, *heroic* is an adjective of praise. . . . The *Oxford English Dictionary* uses the phrase "greatness of soul". . . . [which] I believe . . . to be a mysterious blend of powerful qualities summarized by Shakespeare in *Macbeth* (*IV.iii.91*–94), where he describes the "king-becoming graces" as:

> . . . *justice, verity, temp'rance, stableness, Bounty, perseverance,*
> *mercy, lowliness, Devotion, patience, courage, fortitude.*

When Nelson Mandela received an honorary degree from 5
Harvard University in a special ceremony in September 1998, the seniors sat in the front rows. My son, who was among them, commented that there was an aura about Mandela, something about being in his presence that evoked a surprisingly powerful response. I believe the response he was describing is awe, which washed over many people attending the ceremony that afternoon and came from contemplating Mandela's extraordinary achievement, his profound courage, and his greatness of soul. I find it significant that the heroes in American history with the most staying power, like Abraham Lincoln and George Washington, had this same greatness of soul. And I find it encouraging that the three people *Time* magazine

picked as the most influential of the twentieth century—Albert Einstein, Mohandas Gandhi, and Franklin Delano Roosevelt—each had this quality.

6   Heroes, of course, do not have extraordinary achievement, courage, and the qualities that comprise greatness of soul in equal abundance, but I argue that the more of them one has, the higher one is in the pantheon. And if you take an antonym for each of Shakespeare's "king-becoming graces," you come up with a pretty good definition of what a hero is *not:* unjust, untruthful, intemperate, unstable, stingy, wavering, vengeful, arrogant, capricious, impatient, cowardly, and volatile.

7   The greatest burden the word *hero* carries today is the expectation that a hero be perfect. In Greek mythology, even the gods have flaws. They are not perfect but rather hot-tempered, jealous, and fickle, taking sides in human events and feuding among themselves.

8   The Roman historian Plutarch wrote some of the earliest biographies of heroes: *Lives of the Noble Grecians and Romans.* For hundreds of years these biographies were enormously influential in European and American education. . . . [These] were not hagiographies; in each he reminds us that an exemplary life has never been a perfect life, and we learn from his subjects' vices as well as their virtues. For example, in his treatment of the Roman statesman Cato the Elder (one of George Washington's heroes), Plutarch praises Cato for his frugality and integrity, and for being a good father and husband, but rebukes him for boasting about his achievements and mistreating his slaves. Plutarch acknowledged the flaws of the men he wrote about, but in the main he admired their many accomplishments.

9   In America today we have come to define the person by the flaw: Thomas Jefferson is the president with the slave mistress, Einstein the scientist who mistreated his wife, Mozart the careless genius who liked to talk dirty. These definitions lodge in our minds—especially if they relate to sex—and become the first and sometimes the only thing we remember.

10   As a society, we need to explore a more subtle, complex definition of the word *hero,* suitable for an information age, one that acknowledges weaknesses as well as strengths, failures as well as successes—but, at the same time, one that does not set the bar too low. We need to portray our heroes as human beings but let them remain heroic. Yes, Lincoln liked bawdy stories, was politically calculating, and suffered from melancholy. But he also exhibited astonishing political and moral courage, led our nation through its greatest crisis, and always appealed to the "better angels of our nature." . . .

"Very good, Gary: 'A hero is a celebrity who did something real.' "

FIGURE 6.1 What's the difference?

Source: © The New Yorker Collection 1990, William Hamilton, from cartoonbank.com.
All Rights Reserved.

A Hero by Any Other Name?

As I travel around the country talking to students, I have been asked 11
many times, "Can't a celebrity be a hero?" A celebrity can be a hero but,
by definition, a celebrity is simply someone who is famous. Are celebrities usually heroes? It is hard to combine the qualities of heroism with
the values of today's entertainment industry.

In the media, the word *hero* is often used interchangeably with 12
legend, icon, and *idol.* . . . The name of a popular news magazine program
that profiles famous people is *Headliners and Legends.* A recent issue of a
pension fund magazine introduced a new advertising campaign with
the headline "Icons, Thinkers and Everyday Heroes." Questions about
distinctions among these words surface all the time in my audiences.

Legendary stories have always swirled around heroes. Since the 13
age of Homer, legends flourished in societies that had low levels of formal education and slow means of communication. Often embroidered
more elaborately after death, legends enhanced the status of mere mor-
tals. Today newscasters and talk show hosts do use the word *legend* to
describe a fanciful story that has been woven into someone's history

but more often to describe some giant of the entertainment industry, like John Wayne, or some athletic superstar, like Babe Ruth. A legend is someone about whom stories have been generated by fans and publicists, someone who has become larger than life, someone around whom an aura of mystery has gathered.

14   Legends have a powerful emotional pull. We crave colorful, romantic stories. At the same time, an egalitarian, highly educated, information-rich society erodes legends and makes it harder to have heroes. Legendary history flourished in nineteenth-century America; contemporary historians believe it is their duty to distinguish legend from fact. We now have hundreds of books with titles like *Penetrating the Lincoln Legend* and *Stonewall Jackson: Soldier and Legend*. In a fact-based scientific society, people prefer their heroes to stand tall and strong without the help of legends.

15   Used liberally in advertisements and the entertainment industry, the term *icon* originally meant an image of a saint. This is still true in the Eastern Orthodox Church, but in our more secular world an icon need not be a saint. In computer listings under the keyword icon are books on Saint Basil the Great and Sir Thomas More. There are also books on Che Guevara, Frank Sinatra, Mae West, and the Harley-Davidson motorcycle. *Icon* has become a fashionable word, applied to anyone or anything that some group will venerate, for whatever reason.

16   Less trendy, *idol* shares with *icon* the quality of worship. In the Bible, an idol is a false god, like the Golden Calf that Moses strikes down in the book of Exodus. *Idol* is often linked to immaturity; matinee idol, teen idol, rock idol are common blends. Idolatry implies slavish devotion, uncritical veneration, the kind of adulation found in cults. . . .

17   [T]he word *mentor* has lately become a strong competitor of *hero*. Like hero, the word *mentor* comes to us from the Greeks. In the *Odyssey*, Mentor was the tutor of Odysseus' son, Telemachus. Both in its origin and in contemporary use, *mentor* means teacher or adviser. A mentor is someone who has knowledge we would like to have or who, in corporate terms, can show us the ropes. A mentor "takes on" a novice: a student, a protégé, the junior associate in a law firm. We usually know our mentors and learn from them through conversation, imitation, and instruction. Beethoven is a hero of music, our music teacher a mentor.

18   Marian Wright Edelman, president of the Children's Defense Fund in Washington, DC, told me in a phone interview that she was inspired by Sojourner Truth, who rescued slaves, and Alva Myrdal, who fought for peace and social justice. All groups of young people "are in desperate need of heroism," she said, but most of our heroes are "quiet role models working hard for their communities.". . .

[I]n their everyday lives Americans look to their neighborhoods for 19 their heroes. Today, many Americans define heroes as decent people who sacrifice or try to make a difference. They name streets after local World War II veterans, parks after teachers, bridges after local politicians and philanthropists. Rejecting historical and public figures, who may have feet of clay or a skilled public relations expert, they democratize the word *hero* and jettison the Greek notion of the hero as superhuman and godlike.

When I wrote to John Updike to ask about his views on heroes, he 20 referred me to a book of his, *Picked-Up Pieces,* where I found a statement he made in an interview for *Life* magazine in 1966: "The idea of a hero is aristocratic. You cared about Oedipus and Hamlet because they were noble and you were a groundling. Now either nobody is a hero or everyone is. I vote for everyone." . . .

The definition of *hero* remains subjective. What is extraordinary 21 can be debated. Courage is in the eye of the beholder. Greatness of soul is elusive. Inevitably there will be debates over how many and what kinds of flaws a person can have and still be considered heroic.

Nevertheless, today we are reluctant to call either past or present 22 public figures heroic. We are fearful they might be illusory, falsely elevated by early death or good spin doctors or the vagaries of history. The twentieth century has taught us well that leaders once thought heroes can turn out to be tyrants. And the tacit assumption that a hero is supposed to be perfect has made many Americans turn away from the word—and the concept—altogether. The contemporary preference for words like *role model* and *mentor* and the shift from the recognition of national to local heroes are part of the transformation of the word *hero* that occurred in the second half of the twentieth century.

There is something appealing about a society that admires a range 23 of accomplishments, that celebrates as many people as possible, that looks beyond statues of generals on horseback into small towns and the obscure corners of history for its heroes. Making *hero* more democratic, however, can be carried to an extreme. It can strip the word of all sense of the extraordinary. It can lead to an ignorance of history, a repudiation of genius, and an extreme egalitarianism disdainful of high culture and unappreciative of excellence.

We need role models and mentors and local heroes; but by limiting 24 our heroes to people we know, we restrict our aspirations. Public heroes—or imperfect people of extraordinary achievement, courage, and greatness of soul whose reach is wider than our own—teach us to push beyond ourselves and our neighborhoods in search of models of excellence. They enlarge our imagination, teach us to think big, and expand our sense of the possible.

References

Homer. *The Odyssey,* Translated by W.H.D. Rowse. Signet Classics, 1999.

Plutarch. *Makers of Rome: Nine Lives of Plutarch.* Penguin Books, 1965.

Reflection and Discussion

1. Think of someone who has touched you by "greatness of soul." How did this person affect you?
2. Gibbon suggests that there is a trend to consider heroism to be aristocratic, thinking it undemocratic to single people out for great courage, achievement and "greatness of soul." Explain why you agree or disagree with this position.

Writing Matters

1. Gibbon says that celebrities aren't usually heroes because today's entertainment industry values may be in conflict with heroism. What values would he be talking about? Given the amount of time many people spend following these celebrities, what does this say about our society?
2. In ancient times, Gibbon notes, heroes were known to be flawed. Later, he makes a distinction between heroes and legends. Yet the ancient flawed heroes are often best known for their legendary exploits. Why do you think so many people today find it difficult to accept flawed heroes? Should we be less concerned with historical accuracy? What is wrong (if anything) with being inspired by legend?

Heroines and Role Models

Maxine F. Singer, *Science,* July 19, 1991, from a commencement address at Barnard College

Maxine F. Singer is an award-winning biochemist and former president of the Carnegie Institution of Washington.

Look at the race, gender, ethnicity and talents of the people you look up to. How much do you need your heroes and role models to be like you?

1   The label "role model" is well intended, and the concept is useful. Yet, the term is bothersome. Why?

2   Young women in the 1930s and '40s, when I grew up, had real heroines. Isadora Duncan and Martha Graham were among them. Their extraordinary talents made dance into an original art form. They

initiated schools, had followers, were leaders; their unconventional personal lives were romantic. Heroines, yes, but role models? Most American women of my generation could not have imagined an unconventional personal life, and most lacked the talents of Duncan and Graham, not to mention their courage.

Marie Curie was another heroine of ours. The biography of Curie, written by her daughter Eve, inspired scientifically inclined young women in an age when heroism still mattered and not many women were scientists. Through the book, and the famous movie based on it, we were touched by the image of Marie and Pierre Curie stirring great vats of pitchblend in their dark shed of a laboratory. Nor could anyone forget that this hard physical work led to two Nobel Prizes: one in physics in 1903, shared by Marie and Pierre Curie with Antoine Bequerel, and another in 1911, for Marie alone in chemistry for the discovery of radium.

The description in Eve Curie's book is of a heroine, not a role model. No young American woman could imagine the sacrifice of the lonely years Marie Curie spent in Poland as a governess, sending money to her sister who was studying medicine in Paris, saving what was left for her own eventual opportunity to study. And none of us would want to emulate her disregard for the known dangers of radiation, a disregard that ended in the destruction of her life.

Still, these heroines are more worthy exemplars than contemporary women occupying the roles to which young American women aspire. For one thing, a heroine is distant while a role model's proximal reality encourages too close scrutiny and a destructive mimicry of both public and private behavior. More importantly a heroine is, by definition, known for courage and nobility of purpose, thereby uplifting our own ambitions out of narrow, self-centered concerns.

Why then do young women now speak so often of role models and so rarely of heroines? Why are heroines and even heroes so out of fashion? Nobility of purpose is not currently admired; our society is afraid that following such a leader will extract too high a cost from us as individuals or as a nation. Rather, we deny greatness and seek instead a false image of equality. In our compulsive effort to make everyone ordinary we assume license to delve into personal matters, from the trivial to the profound; unsurprisingly, the glorious images are tarnished. And for those who are truly great, where the effort to make them ordinary cannot succeed, we strive to make them evil. Not even the giants of our world can escape. Consider the sad efforts to tarnish Martin Luther King's image, as if that could undermine his greatness.

Technology makes this program easier. Television is unforgiving in its ability to reveal the personal flaws of everyone from athletic stars to

FIGURE 6.2 Isadora Duncan: An unlikely hero for a scientist?

scientists. Modern high-speed journalism sometimes seems to make the whole world into a soap opera.

8   People have always known that heroines and heroes are imperfect. But they chose to ignore the warts so that the greatness could inspire new achievement. We are all diminished by the disappearance of heroism. Role models will be for naught if there are no heroines and heroes from whom to learn about courage, about noble purpose, about how to reach within and beyond ourselves to find greatness.

9   Young women now have more freedom to shape themselves than young women anywhere or at anytime in history. That freedom is a lonely and difficult burden, but it is also a blessing. The burden cannot be conquered nor the blessing realized by standing in anyone's shadow. But both can be achieved by standing on the shoulders of the great heroines.

Reflection and Discussion

1. Why would Singer, a scientist, include two famous modern dancers among her heroines? How could their exploits and achievements inspire her?

2. What does Singer mean when she says "we deny greatness and seek instead a false image of equality"? Why do you agree or disagree with her?

Writing Matters

1. As a society, we have largely abandoned gender-specific terms for professions and roles, often by adopting new, neutral terms (flight attendant instead of steward or stewardess). Sometimes, though, women have taken on the term previously reserved for men; female movie stars, for example, proclaim their seriousness by calling themselves actors rather than actresses. Singer, nonetheless, uses the term *heroine* rather than *hero* throughout this piece. Other than gender, how do heroines differ from heroes? Can a woman be a heroine but not a hero? If we value gender equality, should we retain the word *heroine* or abandon it in favor of *hero* or a new term, such as Maya Angelou's *shero*?

2. Select someone whom you consider to be either a role model or a hero/heroine. Explain why this person is one but not the other, referring to this article and using examples of the person's actions and character.

The Ambivalence of Political Courage

Jason A. Scorza, *A Review of Politics,* Autumn 2001

Jason Scorza, an award-winning teacher of philosophy and political science at Farleigh Dickinson University, provides resources for activists on his blog www.swiftlytiltingplanet.org.

How courageous, if at all, were the 9/11 terrorists? What about suicide bombers?

The Deadly Beauty of Courage

Courage is a beautiful word which calls to mind countless images of 1
daring, heroism, and noble self-sacrifice. Joan of Arc was brave. So, in a different sense, were Sir Thomas More, Martin Luther King, Jr., and Steven Biko. Socrates, according to some accounts, was the bravest man who ever lived.[1] Celebration of this fiery disposition is an important, even ubiquitous, feature of contemporary culture, and is particularly evident in popular film, television, and fiction, where heroes must, above all, be brave, even if they also are arrogant, brutal, and

otherwise without charm. But the glorification of courage is also a fixture of popular news coverage, where, on any given day, the requisite courage of the hero may be attributed to a firefighter, professional ball player, sick child, Red Cross relief worker, or even a family dog. For all its beauty, however, *courage* is also a potentially deadly word that can inflame violent passions. While this sometimes may be for the sake of freedom, justice, or equality, all too often it is merely for the sake of courage itself, and the thrill of facing danger and surmounting fear.

2   When given a political role or context, the beauty of courage is not diminished. Indeed, its beauty may be enhanced when associated with great and glorious deeds played out on the public stage. It is not surprising, therefore, to find that courage was once widely esteemed in both eastern and western political thought. Confucius, Plato, Aristotle, Cicero, and, of course, Machiavelli all reserve important places for this virtue in their visions of politics. Unfortunately, the deadliness of the word *courage* is also much more pronounced when considered in a political context. The language of courage . . . and numerous expressions signifying cowardice (e.g., spinelessness, gutlessness, fecklessness, etc.) has always been an effective means for motivating people.[2] Political leaders from Pericles to Winston Churchill to Ronald Reagan have recognized in this language a means to inspire, unite, and galvanize citizens, tapping and releasing their energy into the realm of politics. Sadly, many people especially some *men* respond almost without thinking to invocations of courage and accusations of cowardice, making them that much easier for political leaders to manipulate and direct against enemies and scapegoats.[3]

3   So powerful is the language of courage that, even as it is employed in the service of politics, it simultaneously marks or inscribes itself upon the political culture of a society. All too often this serves only to make the political behavior of members of that society more combative, aggressive, bellicose, and, of course, much more deadly. When politics is transfigured in this manner, the virtue of courage can begin to eclipse other important political and moral dispositions, such as toleration, compassion, reasonableness, and civility, leaving a society bereft of these admirable and useful qualities.[4] Hence, by attempting to appropriate the language of courage for the purposes of politics, politics, ironically, can find itself appropriated and disfigured by the language of courage.

4   This may be one reason although it is not the only reason why the word *courage* has all but disappeared from the lexicon of liberal political thought. Montesquieu himself was acutely aware of its visceral appeal when he suggested that it is usually the worst, most destructive forms of heroism that attract people.[5] This also may be one reason why

liberal political theorists, today, seldom identify courage as an important quality of leadership or citizenship. . . . [W]riting very much in the spirit of Montesquieu, [Richard] Rorty explains that "even if the typical character types of liberal democracy *are* bland, calculating, petty, and unheroic, the prevalence of such people may be a reasonable price to pay for political freedom."[6]

Political Courage and Political Responsibility

. . . I want to think more about whether liberalism should recognize   5 courage as an ordinary virtue of a free people. To accomplish this, I want to consider the *relative* appeal for liberalism of three conceptions of political responsibility, each of which is closely associated with the virtue of courage, both in the history of political thought and in the popular political imagination. These three views—patriotic citizenship, pragmatic leadership and conscientious citizenship—are, in one sense, rivals, capable of promoting misunderstanding, friction, and even conflict among their respective enthusiasts, who may admire courageous political behavior, but only when it conforms to one not all of these views. However, in another sense, these three views may actually entail one another, in so far as each provides checks against the potential excesses and internal flaws of the others. Indeed, when at least some citizens in a political community embrace each view as a model for their own political conduct, their courageous efforts may tend to *complement* each other within a political culture in which they also are rivals.

The Courage of Patriotic Citizens

Patriotic citizenship is most commonly associated with citizens who   6 are also soldiers, and, therefore, must confront fear and face danger on the battlefield, fighting, killing, and sometimes dying for their country. It is not surprising, therefore, that the practice of patriotic citizenship is often understood to require courage. . . . For the citizen-soldier, courage can be inspired and sustained by a chauvinistic love of country, although it may also flow from a love of the liberty that one shares with one's countrymen. Pericles, for instance, recognizes the importance of patriotism for promoting courage in citizens. Indeed, his Funeral Oration was a piece of political rhetoric calculated to produce this passion in his listeners, so that they would be willing to fight on against Sparta. Addressing the Athenians, Pericles declared:

> You must daily fix your gaze upon the power of Athens and
> become lovers of her, and when the vision of her greatness has

inspired you, reflect that all this has been acquired by men of courage who knew their duty and in the hour of conflict were moved by a high sense of honor, who, if ever they failed in any enterprise, were resolved that at least their country should not find herself deserted by their valour, but freely sacrificed to her the fairest offering it was in their power to give.[7]

7   The enormous popularity of contemporary films such as *Saving Private Ryan* (1998) and *The Patriot* (2000) suggests that the idea of patriotic citizenship remains an important part of contemporary political culture. . . . So honored in today's culture are soldiers who fight and die in the service of their country that politicians are generally reluctant to criticize any military action when troops are in the field. And when they do criticize such actions, they usually are extremely careful only to criticize other politicians, who put "our boys" in harm's way, and never the conduct of the soldiers themselves, even when it deserves rebuke.

8   It is indisputable that modern liberal societies are well served, at least sometimes, by the courage of patriotic citizen-soldiers, especially when this courage is directed on behalf of an admirable goal, such as national self-defense or the protection of the defenseless. However, patriotic citizenship also has a distinctive internal defect. Specifically, the blind loyalty that can inform and sustain the courage of the citizen-soldier often involves a more or less unexamined trust in one's political system and a more or less unquestioned confidence in the judgment of political and military leaders. This confidence, unfortunately, can cause patriotic citizen-soldiers to commit acts that they would not necessarily commit if they had been able (or willing) to subject their orders to their own moral sense. Thus, the courage of patriots is easily misdirected and betrayed by shortsighted or unscrupulous political leaders and, therefore, represents an enormous source of political power for leaders, who may or may not use it wisely or ethically.

The Courage of Pragmatic Leaders

9 The second conception of political responsibility—pragmatic leadership—involves an idealized view of the political leader, usually an officeholder, who faces danger or disgrace by making difficult decisions, sometimes setting aside personal moral scruples on behalf—ostensibly—of the common good. . . .

10   The courage of political leaders continues to be widely admired.[8] For contemporary American readers, the idea of courageous and pragmatic leadership is most famously and memorably described in John F. Kennedy's *Profiles in Courage* (1956). Although this is not a work of

political theory, and lacks conceptual rigor, it accurately captures (through historical accounts) a view of the courage of leaders that continues to have a powerful hold on America's popular political imagination. Kennedy's view of pragmatic leadership celebrates the ability of officeholders, such as John Quincy Adams, Daniel Webster, and Sam Houston, to resist pressure by constituents, colleagues, parties, and special interests, bravely setting aside even their own self-interest and political aspirations, in order to perform the duties required of their offices.

Like Machiavelli, Kennedy understood that there are times when 11 duties of office will conflict with an officeholder's own personal ethical beliefs. For example, when Kennedy praises the political courage of Daniel Webster—with reference to Webster's critical support for the Compromise of 1850—he acknowledges that Webster's vote for stability and national unity was also a vote against the ideals of liberty, equality, and human dignity which Webster himself embraced.[9] The most objectionable aspect of the Compromise, from the perspective of Webster's Massachusetts constituents, was the strengthening of the existing Fugitive Slave Law, which made it unlawful for citizens to refuse to participate in the apprehension of runaway slaves. Although Webster was much maligned by his constituents for his perceived betrayal not only of their principles but also his own avowed beliefs, he is nevertheless regarded as an exemplar of courage by Kennedy and others who admire and embrace the idea of pragmatic leadership.

The courage of pragmatic leadership is sustained not by loyalty, as 12 is that of patriotic citizenship, but, rather, by an often amoral commitment to official duty. Thus, its distinctive internal flaw is that an officeholder may inadvertently and, perhaps, with the best of intentions, become a force not for progress and social justice but, rather, as Webster may have been, for injustice and the status quo. Some people think that the practice of political courage requires an absolute commitment to personal ethical principles on the part of officeholders. However, an officeholder whose courage is informed and sustained solely by personal ethical principles is not practicing pragmatic leadership but is instead practicing a kind of political responsibility, and displaying a kind of courage, more commonly associated with conscientious citizens who are not officeholders.[10]

The Courage of Conscientious Citizens

Conscientious citizenship involves a romantic view of the stubbornly 13 idealistic citizen who faces danger and fear and rises above "mere" politics as an activist, reformer, conscientious objector, whistleblower, or gadfly. This is yet another view of political responsibility that has been closely associated with courage, both in the history of political thought and in popular culture. . . . Among modern theorists, both Ralph Waldo Emerson and Henry David Thoreau have argued that courage helps individuals resist the pressures (and temptations) of social conformity, enabling citizens to stick to their own principles, whatever they may be.

14   Courage, in the context of conscientious citizenship, can be understood to be a virtuous constraint on political thought, political conversation, and political action. Hence, conscientious citizens try to think, converse, and act with courage, whenever they think about politics, converse about politics, or act in the public sphere. For conscientious citizens, courage is a virtue that helps them bring order to their own political lives, no matter how limited or extensive their political involvement is.

15   When ordinary citizens think conscientiously (and courageously) they try to view the problems of their community, country, or world through their own actions and omissions, rather than as situations and events alien to themselves. When thinking in this manner an individual situates oneself in the complex social problems and controversial public ethical questions that confront one's society and tries to discern whether or not these problems and questions convey upon oneself a personal responsibility to act or speak. Whether they do or not, it takes courage to discover precisely what one's political or social responsibilities are. Citizens must struggle against the temptation to flee from freedom and responsibility, as well as against the inclination to avoid learning enough about social problems or public ethical questions to think, say, or do anything about them.

16   Conscientious citizenship also involves a willingness to be challenged by claims of possible duties, which, in turn, requires a willingness to participate in political conversations. When a person converses conscientiously (and courageously) that individual speaks frankly rather than timidly to others about social problems and public ethical questions, without worrying about how one's words will be received. Such an individual must also listen to frank speech about social problems and public ethical questions without worrying about whether this speech will make difficult or dangerous claims upon one. This is not easy, even in private settings among friends and colleagues. All at once, one fears the exposure of one's ignorance, differences of opinion, or indifference of opinion. Similarly, it can be very painful to listen to speech which is critical of oneself or which claims that one is required to perform difficult or dangerous duties.

17   Sometimes the practice of conscientious citizenship culminates in courageous direct action, or in conscientious refusal to act (which is,

itself, a kind of action). When ordinary citizens act conscientiously (and courageously), they do not wait for a crowd to join but, rather, act directly in the public sphere, thus dissolving, at least partially, the problem of collective action and collective inaction.

It is important to note that most political action by ordinary citizens is rather unheroic, primarily because the practice of politics in a modern liberal state is itself, predominantly, unheroic. Indeed, liberal politics seeks to reduce the need for courageous and conscientious political action by individuals, relying instead on practices such as voting, attending town meetings, and lobbying one's congressperson. Making courageous political activity a regular fixture of politics as, for instance, Arendt does defeats the purpose of liberal politics, which is to enable individuals to pursue self-determined projects in an environment that is characterized by freedom, stability, and basic justice.[11]

Therefore, only very rarely will the practice of conscientious citizenship lead people to act courageously or put them directly in harm's way, as the followers of the Reverend Martin Luther King, Jr., and the young students who opposed the Milosevic regime in Yugoslavia were put in harm's way. The need for courageous direct action may arise only once or twice (or not at all) in any given individual's lifetime, and usually only after many less demanding avenues of political remedy have been exhausted. Even so, courageous direct action remains a pregnant possibility of conscientious citizenship.

However, once an individual begins to practice conscientious citizenship, through courageous political thought, conversation, or action, it may carry one away. And it is in getting carried away that the potentially deadly internal defect of conscientious citizenship lies. In conscientious citizenship, there is the potential both for fanaticism, which closes potentially open minds, and for solipsism, which can make one forget about the reality of other persons. Indeed, when focusing exclusively on one's principles, other people, including those one wants to help, can become little more than the means for relieving one's guilty conscience. Intoxicated by the romantic appeal of courageous political action, and blinded by their own ideals, conscientious citizens can be as dangerous for a liberal society as blindly loyal citizen-soldiers or amoral politicians.

Notes

1. Socrates displayed courage as a soldier (by saving the life of Alcibiades during the battle of Delium), as an officeholder (by opposing the unconstitutional trial of the *strategoi* while taking his turn presiding over the Athenian council), and as an ordinary citizen (first, by refusing to

participate in the assassination of Leon of Salamis and, later, by refusing to abandon or renounce his philosophical explorations). For Plato's account of the courage of Socrates see *Laches* 187e-188; *The Apology* 28e-29a; and *Symposium* 219a-221b. For discussion of Plato's own view of courage, see Aristide Tessitore, "Courage and Comedy in Plato's *Laches*," *Journal of Politics* 56 (1994): 115–33.

2. The word *courage is* derived from the French word *coeur* ("heart"), and was, perhaps, originally associated with chivalry. Other names for courage have different derivations and connotations. For instance, "bravery" comes from the Italian word *bravo* (a thug or hired assassin). Some philosophers still make something of these distinctions. Walton, for instance, suggests that courage stripped of its lofty purpose and normative content is mere bravery. See Walton, *Courage*, p. 98. However, in ordinary usage, the differences between the various names for courage have become indistinct, even as our thinking about the nature of courage has become muddied. The question of what, exactly, courage is, and whether courage can be said to have strong normative content, has been reopened. This question cannot be closed merely by reference to etymology.

3. This problem was identified by Thomas Hobbes, who explained, in a protoliberal moment, how the passion of courage defined as "sudden anger"—along with the kindred passions of honor and glory, could be used by political leaders to overcome the rational self-interest of citizens to avoid civil discord. See Thomas Hobbes, *Leviathan* [1651] (New York: Viking Penguin, Inc., 1968), pp. 123, 157.

4. As Amelie Rorty explains, "Psychologically, the magnetizing dispositions of courage typically diminish the force of other highly desirable categorical dispositions" (Rorty, "The Two Faces of Courage," in *Mind in Action* [Boston: Beacon Press, 1981, p. 301).

5. Montesquieu writes: "L'héroïsme que la Morale avoue ne touche que peu de gens. C'est l' héroïsme qui détruit la Morale qui nous frappe et cause notre admiration" (Montesquieu, "Mes Pensées," *Oeuvres Complètes*, ed. Roger Caillois [Paris: Bibliothèque de la Pléiade,1949], I:1305). ["The heroism that morality favors does not affect that many people. It is the heroism that destroys morality that affects us and causes our admiration."]

6. Richard Rorty, "The Priority of Democracy to Philosophy," in *The Virginia Statute for Religious Freedom*, ed. Merrill Peterson and Robert Vaughan (Madison: University of Wisconsin Press, 1988), 269.

7. Thucydides, *History of the Peloponnesian War*, trans. C.F. Smith (Cambridge, MA: Harvard University Press, 1991), II.43.1.

8. For instance, public opinion surveys reveal that American citizens still perceive courage to be an important quality of political leadership. One recent national survey found that 82.7 percent of Americans believe that courage is an extremely important or very important characteristic of leaders, while only 3.4 percent believe courage to be either not very important or not important at all. Courage ranked higher than charisma, forcefulness, and

religiousness, but slightly below good judgment, honesty, and fairness. See Institute for Research in Social Science, University of North Carolina at Chapel Hill, USA Today Study Number 3023 (May 1987).

9. John F. Kennedy, *Profiles in Courage* [1956] (New York: Harper and Row, Publishers, 1964), p. 60.

10. Although Kennedy sometimes refers to the responsible and unselfish officeholder as "conscientious," I prefer to reserve this term to describe persons who follow their personal moral principles rather than official duties which can, themselves, be inconsistent with these principles.

11. Consider Arendt's account of the centrality of courage to political life. Arendt writes, "The connotation of courage, which we now feel to be an indispensable quality of the hero, is in fact already present in a willingness to act and speak at all, to insert one's self into the world and begin a story of one's own" (*Human Condition*, Chicago: University of Chicago Press, 1958, p. 186).

Reflection and Discussion

1. What does Scorza mean by "the deadly beauty of courage"? What effect is created by his use of dramatic negative terms to describe a quality we most often consider positive?

2. While most would agree that we may need courage to speak up on social and political issues, Scorza claims it requires courage even to become knowledgeable about these problems and listen to others. Why does he believe this? How much do you agree with him?

Writing Matters

1. Scorza believes that there is an "internal defect" in the courage of soldiers and others he calls "patriotic citizens." Consider the actions of soldiers in wars you are familiar with. How dangerous can this defect be? What conditions, if any, increase the danger that the soldiers may act immorally out of blind loyalty?

2. In what ways do you fit Scorza's definition of "conscientious citizen"? In what ways do you not? What would you have to do to meet his standard? Why would you make these changes or choose to remain less "conscientious"?

MAKING CONNECTIONS

1. Must courage be selfless? The Carnegie Hero Fund excludes those who act out of personal or professional duty, as well as those whose actions also benefit themselves in any way. Critique this policy, explaining how it fits or conflicts with your views.

2. What is it that makes us admire the faithfulness of a Greg Boyle, the pacific civil disobedience of Mahatma Gandhi and the righteous action of Martin

Luther King, Jr., in much the same way that we look up to military heroes, the Spartans at Thermopylae, the Texans at the Alamo, Congressional Medal of Honor winners? Compare the qualities of civil and military heroes. Why do we now look at all of them as heroes?

3. Several evolutionary theories posit a genetic basis for the development of altruism. Research them and identify which, if any, best fit your understanding of human behavior. If altruism is indeed instinctual, how can it be considered "noble"?

4. In literature and popular culture, we come across characters and individuals who are described as "anti-heroes." Investigate this term and apply it to a character in a book or film. What qualities do anti-heroes have that separate them from heroes? What makes them appealing to a particular audience? Which are more attractive to you and why?

TAKING ACTION

1. Who is your hero? Write an essay showing why that person is a hero, including careful consideration of the definitions of hero found in the readings for this chapter. Now, get your hero recognized: There are annual awards for heroes that take open nominations, but there are other ways to get your hero acknowledged. Many organizations—schools, churches, charities, businesses, government agencies—issue commendations, formal certificates of appreciation. Research ways to get your hero recognized and adapt your essay into a nomination.

2. This chapter has focused on people who didn't set out to be heroes, but rather wanted to right a wrong, save some people or some thing from extinction or make something better, yet through their work they changed the world. Look around you—what calls you to take action? Write a plan describing a problem and proposing steps to solve it, and then present your proposal to a likely sponsor.

Media—Mirrors or Makers of Change?

The producers of TV news, reality shows and advertising often claim that they merely reflect society, showing people as they are, offering what they ask for. But in America today, no one is immune (and few are indifferent) to the transformative powers of media. Overtly and covertly, the media influence everything from personal appearance to political choice. Understanding how the media shapes opinion can produce a clearer picture of ourselves and our place in our communities.

The Culture of Television

Television is one of the most formative influences of modern life, affecting not only what we buy and whom we vote for but how we relate to one another. Though questions about television's social impacts have been debated for years, there is always a new wrinkle, another twist, because TV is constantly changing. Reality TV, for example, is not new but its popularity has exploded, and its myriad forms have produced effects most people would not have anticipated just a few years ago. While we can easily acknowledge some of the ways we are influenced by this type of television content, we seldom consider how we are affected by the experience of spending so many hours as viewers rather than as active participants. Perhaps one reason why studying television is so fascinating is that when we examine it, we are also examining ourselves.

BEFORE YOU READ

How much TV do you watch and how important is it to you? Do you usually watch alone or with others? How often do you talk about TV programs with family or friends? Do you think any particular types of television are more "beneficial" than others? How can TV affect a person's self-image? How about his or her goals?

FIGURE 7.1 In the 1950s, television brought families together.

Take a Break from TV—Yeah, Right

Ana Veciana-Suarez, *The Houston Chronicle,* April 19, 2006

Ana Veciana-Suarez was born in Cuba and writes a syndicated column for the Miami Herald. *Her novels include* The Chin Kiss King *and* The Flight to Freedom.

How old were you when you started watching TV? What limits, if any, did your parents impose on TV watching?

Heard of the Great American Smokeout, that national event that gets 1 smokers to quit for a day—and maybe forever? It's been going on for three decades, with a modicum of success. TV Turnoff Week, which starts Monday, hopes to garner some of the same results: getting addicted Americans to kick the habit. I have to wonder, though, what might be more difficult to relinquish: nicotine or screen. I'm not being facetious, either.

In the living room, bedroom, kitchen and just about everywhere 2 else, including the minivan, is the pervasive white noise of our lives, the flickering backdrop, the easy prop and the ready pal. Where once our ancestors gathered around the flames of a miraculous fire, then in the welcoming warmth of the kitchen, we now collect ourselves around the television set. All morning I've been trying to recall a family get-together where the darn thing wasn't on, but my mind draws a blank. Come to think of it, TV tends to serve as decoration, like an impressive ice sculpture, in other parties I attend. Several of my friends flip it on as soon as they get home from work, a gesture as automatic as opening the front door. TV is the surrogate hug from the spouse who's working late, the companion that won't whine about having a hard day. I even know of children who insist they need it to fall asleep: our modern version of the bedtime story.

3   Obviously we need a TV Turnoff Week. Or two or three. This year it happens to come at a propitious time because of a brouhaha unwittingly launched by some children's organizations. The creators of *Sesame Street* just released a new line of videos aimed at babies as young as six months, a move that has outraged many child-development experts who have spent the last decade trying to get parents to fire the electronic baby-sitter, particularly for the tiniest tots. The *Sesame Beginnings* DVDs are supposed to be watched by parents with the kiddies, but this has not quieted the ire of some, who point out that the American Academy of Pediatrics advises against TV for children under two. (The reasons are many and, to me, obvious, but if you doubt, check out www.aap.org.)

4   Of course, this *Sesame Street* version is simply the latest entry in a growing market of videos for infants. In 1998, the British show *Teletubbies*, aimed at the two-and-under set, premiered on PBS, prompting the AAP to recommend that parents avoid television for that audience. Nevertheless, other companies—think Disney's *Baby Einstein*—have entered the estimated $100-million-a-year market. It's no wonder that, as we rope babies into TV life even before we introduce them to juice and cereal, we have become a nation that must be weaned by gimmick and threat. Of course it's not just TV. Almost any screen sucks up our attention these days. Our electronic blankies organize our lives, tether us to the office, keep us in touch and provide us with round-the-clock music and commentary.

5   TV Turnoff Week deals with one, just one, kind of screen. A grassroots project with the support of more than 65 national organizations, it simply wants to balance the scales. This year, on average, US children will spend more time with TV (1,023 hours) than in school (900 hours). All grown up, the average American watches four hours a day. In contrast, parents spend 38.5 minutes in meaningful conversation with their kids. Sure, going cold turkey, even for a week, may sound extreme to the obsessed among us, but think of all the other things you can do.

6   Shhh! Isn't that the sound of conversation?

Reflection and Discussion

1. Compare the time you spend watching television to other forms of entertainment you indulge in. If you were to stop watching screens for an entire week, what would your life be like? What would you gain and lose?

2. Examine the language Veciana-Suarez uses in her article. Which words in particular attracted your attention and how do they help establish her point of view? Think about who her audience is and decide how well the language fits with those who are most likely to read her article. In what part of the newspaper would you expect to find her piece and what does that say about the kind of article it is?

Writing Matters

1. Go to the website Veciana-Suarez mentions and investigate the concerns of the American Academy of Pediatrics about children under two watching TV. Then read reviews of TV shows and DVDs intended for children under two, such as the *Sesame Beginnings* series. Argue for or against children under two years of age watching TV and make a recommendation to a parents' group based on your findings.

2. Write a piece similar to Suarez's but adopt a different point of view—one much more critical of television (or screens) or one extolling the positives of watching TV. Include not only your habits but those of people around you.

Image Slaves: Everybody Wants to Be on Television

Alison Hearn, *Bad Subjects,* June 2004

Alison Hearn is an assistant professor at the University of Western Ontario. She has written extensively on culture, media and politics as well as visual and tele-visual theory.

How do you feel about TV shows like *American Idol* and *Survivor* or similar ones?

Part One

The question isn't "are they the right color to be slaves?" but "are they vulnerable enough to be enslaved?" The criteria of enslavement today do not concern color, tribe or religion; they focus on weakness, gullibility and deprivation.

—Kevin Bales, *Disposable People*

1.

1   I'm in Boston at a popular bar called The Rack. The bar is full of young adults, only they're not drinking or eating or chatting each other up. They are all sitting at tables writing intently. These 18- to 24-year-olds are not studying for exams in this famous college town; they are filling out applications to audition for an MTV "real movie" called *The Real Cancun*.

2   I slide in next to some kids at a booth and introduce myself. I have a tape-recorder with me, am middle-aged and, I assume, reasonably legitimate-looking. But, before I get a chance to explain my project and directly ask for their consent, one of them says "YES! I'd love to be interviewed, what do you want to know?" The others perk up and pay attention. I sense they think this is part of the audition. What the hell, I figure, so I turn the recorder on and ask for their names. They all reply eagerly, sitting up straight, flipping their hair, and, with cadences down pat, like car salesmen trying to close a deal, they offer me their best pitch:

3   "My name's John and I'm a 20-year-old Boston native with a great sense of humor and an adventuresome spirit."

4   "I'm Jenny. I'm planning to be a nurse, but being in this movie is my destiny! It would be a dream come true . . . "

5   "Hi, I'm Matt. I'm 19 years old and I really feel I have something special to share with the world . . . "

6   I feel assaulted by shiny happy people; these guys are showing me their well-rehearsed personas and offering them up to me for my own use. I hesitate and then set the record straight. "OK look, I'm an academic," I confess, "chances are really good it will be a few years until any of the results of this research sees the light of day, if at all. Any quotes I use will be anonymous, and, sadly, there won't be any photos in the book I'm working on."

7   Beat. "Oh. Ummm. Well that's cool. What do you want to know?" says John. And the interview begins.

2.

8   "Reality" now sits alongside "comedy" or "drama" as a major genre in broadcast television. The networks have entire divisions devoted to "reality" with VPs in charge. Six out of the twelve top-rated programs last season in US primetime were "reality" shows; with *American Idol*'s Tuesday and Wednesday night shows repeatedly capturing the top two spots. "Reality" is now an Emmy category.

9   Never mind that no one really knows what, exactly, the generic term "reality" refers to—game show, soap opera, action-adventure,

drama, sports. "Reality" has made over the industry in an incredibly short period of time, economically, textually and culturally. Industry people recognize that the term "reality television" signifies, not generic coherence, but common modes of production: these shows use "real people" or "non-actors" as their talent, in some instances "real contexts" for sets, and, on occasion, amateur or non-professionally produced video tapes for their content. Chad Raphael has called these things "nontraditional labor and production inputs." Producers of reality television series routinely bypass unionized labor.

In the simplest sense, "reality television" names a set of cost- 10 cutting measures in television production brought in by management as a response to the economic pressures faced by broadcast television trans-nationally. Some of these pressures include increased competition in media markets and growing audience fragmentation, legislative deregulation, the weakening of public broadcasting, and, specifically in the case of American-based broadcast television, spiraling costs associated with the inflated demands of already existing media celebrities. The no-brainer solution to broadcast television's economic woes involves lowering production costs by self-consciously deploying the fantasy-image economy already in place to entice "outsiders" to offer up their labor for free.

The economy of reality television is certainly the reason for its rise 11 to prominence. It is cheap to produce and easy to sell, and the supply of labor is apparently endless. Everybody wants to be on television.

3.

"Pretty much everything I do is as if I'm being watched anyway."
—Mike, a 20-year-old student from Salem State College

Over and over again in the interviews I conduct that day in Boston, and 12 in subsequent interviews, potential reality show contestants claim they don't really care about the money; they only want the fame. These folks line up for hours, longing for the "life-altering experience" of being a part of TV-land, hoping to generate a saleable image-commodity for themselves.

The reason for this desire for fame is clear enough. We live in the 13 age of phantasmagoric capital, as Ernest Sternberg calls it, where image, not information, is the driving force in the market. Workers understand that our labor involves self-production in the form of persona. Just as we accept the loading up of goods with evocative emotions and meanings by advertisers, we understand that we, ourselves, must also consciously self-present in concrete and meaningful ways. It's just as important to "be seen" as a good nurse, executive, flight attendant, as to actually do the tasks that make up the job; "the capacity for calculated posing" is a routine job requirement. Sternberg argues that notoriety and recognition serve as "proxy indicators" of personal ability in this new economy of the image. If a person is well known, then their persona-producing capacity must be good; therefore they must be a good bet—a good worker, a good hire.

14   Since 1953 American courts have recognized fame as property with market value. A person's fame is seen not as a part of their identity, but rather as a commodity they have labored to produce; it is their "publicity right." A person's fame or "publicity right" is deemed to be fully alienable and descendible. Celebrity Joe Piscopo had to give away half of his publicity rights to his ex-wife in a divorce case. Whenever he trades on his name she gets half the profit. David Bowie issued Bowie Bonds in 1997—securities based on the very fact of his fame. Tiger Woods made 50 million dollars in endorsement deals in the year 2000. Fame is big business.

15   Reality television is the fast lane to fame. Why work as a wage slave when the promise of big payoff from being on TV is only an audition away?

Part Two

"[T]he new slavery appropriates the economic value of individuals while keeping them under complete coercive control—but without asserting ownership or accepting responsibility for their survival."

—Bales

4.

"Welcome to the coliseum. Here's your net and your trident. Get to work."

—Reality show producer to casting agent

16 The first round of auditions for *The Real Cancun* are conducted in groups of eight kids. The casting agent gathers them up and initiates a modified game of "I never-ever"—a college drinking game where someone names something they haven't ever done, and, if you have done it, you must drink a shot. In this case, people are asked to simply raise their hand. The casting agent starts, "I've never ever had a threesome." Within minutes these complete strangers are revealing incredibly

intimate details of their lives. One guy is obsessive compulsive and has to keep wiping himself down with wet-naps during sex. One girl once woke up naked on a beach, miles from her hotel, during spring break with no memory of what had happened. One guy confesses to having had every sexually transmitted disease possible except AIDS. These kids are locked in a pitched battle to sell their most personal stories and experiences to the casting agent.

While the kids are working on trading their mundane selves in for 17 shiny new image-commodities, the casting agents are looking for "eye candy with issues." They see their job simply as casting good potential "characters," pretty people with good "life-story arcs"—a conflicted back-story that remains unresolved and the desire to "work through their issues" in the future, preferably in front of millions of people. "Non-pretty" people are chosen only if they are "telegenically ugly," like Kramer on Seinfeld.

The casting process is rigorous and involves detailed question- 18 naires, lengthy on-camera interviews, and psychological and background checks. The one-on-one interviews are intense, usually lasting over an hour. One casting agent confesses:

"It's a very one-way pulling of information out of people, and 19 when someone tells you something tragic or something like that, you get this weird mixture of emotions. You think 'wow that's really interesting and it'll be great for the show' and you're happy, but then you feel sorry for the person at the same time. It can be confusing. It's very intimate. You feel almost like a psychiatrist without any of the responsibility."

Reality television contestant contracts are notoriously exploitative. 20 Participants trade away the rights to their identities almost entirely for the chance to enter the star-making machinery of the television industry. An outtake from an *American Idol* contract reads:

"I hereby grant to Producer the unconditional right throughout the 21 universe in perpetuity to use, simulate or portray my name, likeness, voice, singing voice, personality, personal identification or personal experiences, my life story, biographical data, incidents, situations, events which heretofore occurred or hereafter occur. . . . Other parties . . . may reveal and/or relate information about me of a personal, private, intimate, surprising, defamatory, disparaging, embarrassing or unfavorable nature that may be factual and/or fictional."

Idol franchise king-pin Simon Fuller signs all the *Idol* finalists 22 (in all the *Idol* competitions all over the globe) to exclusive agreements with his recording, management and merchandising companies. Contestants must agree to allow their likenesses to be used for sponsorships and endorsements, whether or not they themselves support the particular service or product. In this way 19 Entertainment manages all potential aspects of these contestants' careers. Nineteen Entertainment can opt-out of its agreements at any time with all but the winners of the competition. The contestants, however, cannot. It's been estimated that Fuller earned $60 million in 2003.

23   The confidentiality clauses on reality television contracts are also ironclad. These shows depend on contestants remaining mum about the show's outcome until the airdate. The contracts threaten severe punishment for any such breach. The contracts also prevent contestants from disclosing anything at all about the working conditions on the show, the producers, the series as a whole, or the broadcast network. In other words, they are contractually obligated to have had nothing but a "great time" during the filming. *American Idol* contestants are liable for five million dollars should they say anything about their experience on the show. *American Idol* Rueben Stoddardt: "Without the show we wouldn't be recording artists. But we did a lot of commercials, dawg. We were exploited but not exploited. It just taught us a lot about the business. *American Idol* is what we like to call a crash course on the entertainment industry."

5.

"I just don't get what makes someone else more interesting
than me. I mean everyone has something valuable to offer,
right? How come these TV guys get to decide?"

—John, a 20-year-old Boston native, after his failed audition

24   Humiliation is foundational to reality television. It certainly marks its current labor practices. The TV industry enacts strategies of what contemporary management literature calls "corporate seduction." These "seductive socialization programs," use status as their carrot—merely by creating categories of inclusion and exclusion—"you are one of the chosen few out of a great field of candidates, we want you." In this way loyalty is created and any number of abuses can be done to the worker once loyalty is won and the seduction is complete. As Roy Lewicki writes, "if the seduction has worked it feels like free choice, and the organization does not have to kick you; you kick yourself."

25   More and more of people are voluntarily "kicking themselves" for the benefit of the image industry, hoping to generate their own individualized image-token in return. Paid nothing, often asked to foot their own bills for the privilege of subjecting themselves to the colonizing gaze of the camera, and captive to the interests of the owners who generate the terms of their "fame," these "actively engaged" audience

bodies have become, in a most explicit way, the sensuous raw material which the image industry cannibalizes to perpetuate its own interests.

The degree to which humiliation is blatantly enacted in the shows 26 themselves varies. Sometimes it is simply implied. The recent spate of home and body makeover shows presumes "original humiliation" on the part of their participants and then offers deliverance from it. But, more often, the performance of humiliation is overt—such as in the recent *What's Hot* show—in which judges use laser pointers to highlight the flaws in contestant's bodies. Humiliation is clearly the draw in the recent spate of *Candid Camera*–type shows like *Punked* or the *Jamie Kennedy Experiment*, in which celebrities and regular folks get humiliated in a good-natured kind of way. In other instances, such as the weekly ritual of "voting off" characteristic of both *American Idol* and *Survivor*, the humiliation involved is less obvious because it has been naturalized. The contestants who get voted off have simply been subject to the Darwinian process of survival of the fittest. They just didn't play the game well enough. These show's narratives make a virtue out of those who can successfully withstand the exclusion, judgment and heartless assessment of others, and use their own ability to manipulate to "win." More simply, they rehearse, over and over again, the story of sacrifice, pain, and exploitation required by life under capital.

Humiliation also marks the experience of watching reality televi- 27 sion. Anecdotal responses often involve repulsion and shock at, both, the inane concepts behind the shows ("They're doing what? Chaining 50 midgets together to pull an airplane? Sending people to boot camp? Trying to break up couples? Making people live out in the bush for a year? Locking a group of strangers in portables for three months?") and at having watched them. In spite of these reactions, however, we seem to be drawn to the shows—like "flies to a glue-pot"—like passing motorists to a car wreck. Pleasure and humiliation are elided when we watch. Reality shows summon their viewers to ignore any initial shock or dismay, and to adopt, what Susan Sontag has called, a form of "professionalized looking." This kind of looking is engendered by the commodity system; it involves seeing through the lens of cold fiscal calculation. Reality television links this form of perceptual cruelty to the experience of cultural pleasure.

At the level of production, text, and reception, then, reality televi- 28 sion shows perform, mine, and enforce a general cultural ethos of humiliation and masochism. Reality television reinforces at every level the terms of the masochistic contract offered us by techno-capital; non-unionized, mostly non-paid workers are enlisted through strategies of corporate seduction and the promise of fame, to produce stories that legitimate the broader ethos of the corporate regime that gave birth to them. Once on the shop floor workers are contractually obligated to comply with a version of reality fully delineated and controlled by their employers. Reality television programs might best be understood as the ideological sweatshops of techno-capital; their participants are its paradigmatic docile bodies.

6.

"Dear friend, I give you what you need, but you know the
conditio sine qua non; you know the ink in which you have to
sign yourself over to me; in providing for your pleasure,
I fleece you."

—Marx, Economic and Philosophical Manuscripts

29 A few weeks after the interviews at The Rack, Jenny, the student nurse, calls me on my office phone: "I was just wondering whether you need anything else from me, you know, for your book thing." I explain to her that I have what I need from her, but thanks. I ask her how her audition went: "Oh, I didn't get past the first round. Some other girl in my group totally hogged all the attention. But I'm gonna go to the *American Idol* auditions in NYC, and I've sent a tape into *Real World*, so I'm still hoping. I still believe it's my destiny."

30   NewsCorps, Viacom, Disney and General Electric all posted record profits in 2003. The television sectors of these corporations, Fox, CBS, ABC, NBC respectively, showed profit growth ranging from 6 to 14 percent. Reality shows such as *Survivor, American Idol,* and *The Apprentice* were routinely in the top 10-rated shows. Ad rates and revenues have increased. There can be no doubt that the reality television format is producing increased corporate earnings. But what else is being produced?

31   The phenomenon of reality television represents the increasing trend toward the corporate colonization of the "real." In the rhetorical use of the term "real" to name the process of capture by the television camera and production as its subject, these shows work to legitimate a "post-real" world—a world driven by the interests of corporate capital, mediated by new technology. In their colonization of the concepts of identity, relationship, meaningful interactivity, reality television shows work to construct and reinforce a system of cultural value, which involves the active production of the self as a saleable image-commodity. This process of self-commodification is both summoned and exploited by the media industries. In Kevin Bales' words, reality television's

labor practices involve a system of control where "people become completely disposable tools for making money." In this age of image-capital, reality television produces the image-slave.

Reflection and Discussion

1. How would you characterize the attitudes of the would-be contestants at the beginning of the article?
2. Hearn gives some reasons why people today, especially young people, are fascinated with image and fame. What other reasons might help explain this phenomenon?

Writing Matters

1. Watch an episode of a reality television show, carefully looking for evidence that would support or refute Hearn's contention that "Humiliation is foundational to reality television." Why do viewers enjoy the way contestants are treated? How would you respond to being treated in a similar way on national television? To further develop your response, you might watch the program with someone else and add that person's reactions to the program.
2. Hearn is boldly critical of the relationship between reality TV power brokers and those who aspire to be contestants. If you agree with her, explain why, supplementing the parts of the article you find weakest and adding points. If you disagree, write a rebuttal of her article, pointing out where her judgments may be faulty or her logic weak. Argue for the legitimacy of reality TV, defending those who participate as contestants as well as those who watch.

Television by the Numbers

99	percent of American households that have televisions
2.24	average number of televisions per household in the US
1,680	number of minutes per week that the average American child watches TV
3.5	minutes per week of meaningful conversation between parents and children
73	percent of parents who want to limit their children's TV viewing

Source: Nelson Herr, *Television and Health*, 2001.

Watching TV Makes You Smarter

Steven Johnson, *New York Times Magazine,* April 24, 2005

Steven Johnson is the author of several books including Everything Bad Is Good for You *and* All God's Creatures.

How do you feel about the effects of television on a person's intelligence?

The *Sleeper* Curve

SCIENTIST A: Has he asked for anything special?
SCIENTIST B: Yes, this morning for breakfast . . . he requested something called "wheat germ, organic honey and tiger's milk."
SCIENTIST A: Oh, yes. Those were the charmed substances that some years ago were felt to contain life-preserving properties.
SCIENTIST B: You mean there was no deep fat? No steak or cream pies or . . . hot fudge?
SCIENTIST A: Those were thought to be unhealthy.

—From Woody Allen's *Sleeper*

1   On January 24, the Fox network showed an episode of its hit drama *24*, the real-time thriller known for its cliffhanger tension and often-gruesome violence. Over the preceding weeks, a number of public controversies had erupted around *24*, mostly focused on its portrait of Muslim terrorists and its penchant for torture scenes. The episode that was shown on the 24th only fanned the flames higher: in one scene, a terrorist enlists a hit man to kill his child for not fully supporting the jihadist cause; in another scene, the secretary of defense authorizes the torture of his son to uncover evidence of a terrorist plot.

2   But the explicit violence and the post–9/11 terrorist anxiety are not the only elements of *24* that would have been unthinkable on prime-time network television 20 years ago. Alongside the notable change in content lies an equally notable change in form. During its 44 minutes—a real-time hour, minus 16 minutes for commercials—the episode connects the lives of 21 distinct characters, each with a clearly defined "story arc," as the Hollywood jargon has it: a defined personality with motivations and obstacles and specific relationships with other

characters. Nine primary narrative threads wind their way through those 44 minutes, each drawing extensively upon events and information revealed in earlier episodes. Draw a map of all those intersecting plots and personalities, and you get structure that—where formal complexity is concerned—more closely resembles *Middlemarch* than a hit TV drama of years past like *Bonanza*.

For decades, we've worked under the assumption that mass culture 3 follows a path declining steadily toward lowest-common-denominator standards, presumably because the "masses" want dumb, simple pleasures and big media companies try to give the masses what they want. But as that *24* episode suggests, the exact opposite is happening: the culture is getting more cognitively demanding, not less. To make sense of an episode of *24*, you have to integrate far more information than you would have a few decades ago watching a comparable show. Beneath the violence and the ethnic stereotypes, another trend appears: to keep up with entertainment like *24*, you have to pay attention, make inferences, track shifting social relationships. This is what I call the *Sleeper* Curve: the most debased forms of mass diversion—video games and violent television dramas and juvenile sitcoms—turn out to be nutritional after all.

I believe that the *Sleeper* Curve is the single most important new 4 force altering the mental development of young people today, and I believe it is largely a force for good: enhancing our cognitive faculties, not dumbing them down. And yet you almost never hear this story in popular accounts of today's media. Instead, you hear dire tales of addiction, violence, mindless escapism. It's assumed that shows that promote smoking or gratuitous violence are bad for us, while those that thunder against teen pregnancy or intolerance have a positive role in society. Judged by that morality-play standard, the story of popular culture over the past 50 years—if not 500—is a story of decline: the morals of the stories have grown darker and more ambiguous, and the antiheroes have multiplied.

The usual counterargument here is that what media have lost in 5 moral clarity, they have gained in realism. The real world doesn't come in nicely packaged public-service announcements, and we're better off with entertainment like *The Sopranos* that reflects our fallen state with all its ethical ambiguity. I happen to be sympathetic to that argument, but it's not the one I want to make here. I think there is another way to assess the social virtue of pop culture, one that looks at media as a kind of cognitive workout, not as a series of life lessons. There may indeed be more "negative messages" in the mediasphere today. But that's not the only way to evaluate whether our television shows or video games are having a positive impact. Just as important—if not more important—is the kind of thinking you have to do to make sense of a cultural experience. That is where the *Sleeper* Curve becomes visible.

Televised Intelligence

6 Consider the cognitive demands that televised narratives place on their viewers. With many shows that we associate with "quality" entertainment—*The Mary Tyler Moore Show*, *Murphy Brown*, *Frasier*—the intelligence arrives fully formed in the words and actions of the characters on-screen. They say witty things to one another and avoid lapsing into tired sitcom clichés, and we smile along in our living rooms, enjoying the company of these smart people. But assuming we're bright enough to understand the sentences they're saying, there's no intellectual labor involved in enjoying the show as a viewer. You no more challenge your mind by watching these intelligent shows than you challenge your body watching *Monday Night Football*. The intellectual work is happening on-screen, not off.

7 But another kind of televised intelligence is on the rise. Think of the cognitive benefits conventionally ascribed to reading: attention, patience, retention, the parsing of narrative threads. Over the last half-century, programming on TV has increased the demands it places on precisely these mental faculties. This growing complexity involves three primary elements: multiple threading, flashing arrows and social networks. . . .

8 Critics generally cite *Hill Street Blues* as the beginning of "serious drama" native in the television medium—differentiating the series from the single-episode dramatic programs from the 50s, which were Broadway plays performed in front of a camera. But the *Hill Street Blues* innovations weren't all that original; they'd long played a defining role in popular television, just not during the evening hours. The structure of a *Hill Street* episode—and indeed of all the critically acclaimed dramas that followed, from *thirtysomething* to *Six Feet Under*—is the structure of a soap opera. *Hill Street Blues* might have sparked a new golden age of television drama during its seven-year run, but it did so by using a few crucial tricks that *Guiding Light* and *General Hospital* mastered long before.

9 Bochco's genius with *Hill Street* was to marry complex narrative structure with complex subject matter. *Dallas* had already shown that the extended, interwoven threads of the soap-opera genre could survive the weeklong interruptions of a prime-time show, but the actual content of *Dallas* was fluff. (The most probing issue it addressed was the question, now folkloric, of who shot J.R.) *All in the Family* and *Rhoda* showed that you could tackle complex social issues, but they did their

tackling in the comfort of the sitcom living room. *Hill Street* had richly drawn characters confronting difficult social issues and a narrative structure to match.

Since *Hill Street* appeared, the multi-threaded drama has become 10 the most widespread fictional genre on prime time: *St. Elsewhere, L. A. Law, thirtysomething, Twin Peaks, NYPD Blue, E.R., The West Wing, Alias, Lost.* (The only prominent holdouts in drama are shows like *Law and Order* that have essentially updated the venerable *Dragnet* format and thus remained anchored to a single narrative line.) Since the early 80s, however, there has been a noticeable increase in narrative complexity in these dramas. The most ambitious show on TV to date, *The Sopranos,* routinely follows up to a dozen distinct threads over the course of an episode, with more than 20 recurring characters. . . .

The Case for Confusion

Shortly after the arrival of the first-generation slasher movies— 11 *Halloween, Friday the 13th*—Paramount released a mock-slasher flick called *Student Bodies,* parodying the genre just as the *Scream* series would do 15 years later. In one scene, the obligatory nubile teenage babysitter hears a noise outside a suburban house; she opens the door to investigate, finds nothing and then goes back inside. As the door shuts behind her, the camera swoops in on the doorknob, and we see that she has left the door unlocked. The camera pulls back and then swoops down again for emphasis. And then a flashing arrow appears on the screen, with text that helpfully explains: "Unlocked!"

That flashing arrow is parody, of course, but it's merely an exag- 12 gerated version of a device popular stories use all the time. When a sci-fi script inserts into some advanced lab a nonscientist who keeps asking the science geeks to explain what they're doing with that particle accel- erator, that's a flashing arrow that gives the audience precisely the information it needs in order to make sense of the ensuing plot. ("Whatever you do, don't spill water on it, or you'll set off a massive explosion!") These hints serve as a kind of narrative hand-holding. Implicitly, they say to the audience, "We realize you have no idea what a particle accelerator is, but here's the deal: all you need to know is that it's a big fancy thing that explodes when wet." They focus the mind on relevant details: "Don't worry about whether the babysitter is going to break up with her boyfriend. Worry about that guy lurking in the bushes." They reduce the amount of analytic work you need to do to make sense of a story. All you have to do is follow the arrows.

By this standard, popular television has never been harder to fol- 13 low. If narrative threads have experienced a population explosion over the past 20 years, flashing arrows have grown correspondingly scarce. Watching our pinnacle of early 80s TV drama, *Hill Street Blues,* we find there's an informational wholeness to each scene that differs markedly from what you see on shows like *The West Wing* or *The Sopranos* or *Alias* or *ER.* . . .

14   The deliberate lack of hand-holding extends down to the microlevel of dialogue as well. Popular entertainment that addresses technical issues—whether they are the intricacies of passing legislation, or of performing a heart bypass, or of operating a particle accelerator— conventionally switches between two modes of information in dialogue: texture and substance. Texture is all the arcane verbiage provided to convince the viewer that they're watching Actual Doctors at Work; substance is the material planted amid the background texture that the viewer needs make sense of the plot. . . .

Even Bad TV Is Better

15 Skeptics might argue that I have stacked the deck here by focusing on relatively highbrow titles like *The Sopranos* or *The West Wing,* when in fact the most significant change in the last five years of narrative enter- tainment involves reality TV. Does the contemporary pop cultural landscape look quite as promising if the representative show is *Joe Millionaire* instead of *The West Wing?*

16   I think it does, but to answer that question properly, you have to avoid the tendency to sentimentalize the past. When people talk about the golden age of television in the early 70s—invoking shows like *The Mary Tyler Moore Show* and *All in the Family*—they forget to mention how awful most television programming was during much of that decade. If you're going to look at pop-culture trends, you have to compare apples to apples, or in this case, lemons to lemons. The relevant comparison is not between *Joe Millionaire* and *MASH*; it's between *Joe Millionaire* and *The Newlywed Game,* or between *Survivor* and *The Love Boat.*

17   What you see when you make these head-to-head comparisons is that a rising tide of complexity has been lifting programming at the bot- tom of the quality spectrum and at the top. *The Sopranos* is several times more demanding of its audiences than *Hill Street* was, and *Joe Millionaire* has made comparable advances over *Battle of the Network Stars.* This is the ultimate test of the *Sleeper* Curve theory: Even the junk has improved.

18   If early television took its cues from the stage, today's reality pro- gramming is reliably structured like a video game: a series of competi- tive tests, growing more challenging over time. Many reality shows borrow a subtler device from gaming culture as well: the rules aren't fully established at the outset. You learn as you play.

On a show like *Survivor* or *The Apprentice*, the participants—and 19
the audience—know the general objective of the series, but each
episode involves new challenges that haven't been ordained in
advance. The final round of the first season of *The Apprentice*, for
instance, threw a monkey wrench into the strategy that governed the
play up to that point, when Trump announced that the two remaining
apprentices would have to assemble and manage a team of subordinates who had already been fired in earlier episodes of the show. All of
a sudden the overarching objective of the game—do anything to avoid
being fired—presented a potential conflict to the remaining two con-
tenders: the structure of the final round favored the survivor who had
maintained the best relationships with his comrades. Suddenly, it wasn't
enough just to have clawed your way to the top; you had to have made
friends while clawing. The original *Joe Millionaire* went so far as to
undermine the most fundamental convention of all—that the show's
creators don't openly lie to the contestants about the prizes—by induc-
ing a construction worker to pose as man of means while 20 women
competed for his attention.

Reality programming borrowed another key ingredient from 20
games: the intellectual labor of probing the system's rules for weak
spots and opportunities. As each show discloses its conventions,
and each participant reveals his or her personality traits and background, the intrigue in watching comes from figuring out how the
participants should best navigate the environment that has been
created for them. The pleasure in these shows comes not from
watching other people being humiliated on national television; it
comes from depositing other people in a complex, high-pressure
environment where no established strategies exist and watching
them find their bearings. That's why the water-cooler conversation
about these shows invariably tracks in on the strategy displayed on
the previous night's episode: why did Kwame pick Omarosa in that
final round? What devious strategy is Richard Hatch concocting
now? . . .

The Rewards of Smart Culture

The quickest way to appreciate the *Sleeper* Curve's cognitive training is 21
to sit down and watch a few hours of hit programming from the late
70s on *Nick at Nite* or the SOAPnet channel or on DVD. The modern
viewer who watches a show like *Dallas* today will be bored by the
content—not just because the show is less salacious than today's soap
operas (which it is by a small margin) but also because the show contains far less information in each scene, despite the fact that its soap-opera

structure made it one of the most complicated narratives on television in its prime. With *Dallas,* the modern viewer doesn't have to think to make sense of what's going on, and not having to think is boring. Many recent hit shows—*24, Survivor, The Sopranos, Alias, Lost, The Simpsons, E.R.*—take the opposite approach, layering each scene with a thick network of affiliations. You have to focus to follow the plot, and in focusing you're exercising the parts of your brain that map social networks, that fill in missing information, that connect multiple narrative threads.

22   Of course, the entertainment industry isn't increasing the cognitive complexity of its products for charitable reasons. The *Sleeper* Curve exists because there's money to be made by making culture smarter. The economics of television syndication and DVD sales mean that there's a tremendous financial pressure to make programs that can be watched multiple times, revealing new nuances and shadings on the third viewing. Meanwhile, the Web has created a forum for annotation and commentary that allows more complicated shows to prosper, thanks to the fan sites where each episode of shows like *Lost* or *Alias* is dissected with an intensity usually reserved for Talmud scholars. Finally, interactive games have trained a new generation of media consumers to probe complex environments and to think on their feet, and that gamer audience has now come to expect the same challenges from their television shows. In the end, the *Sleeper* Curve tells us something about the human mind. It may be drawn toward the sensational where content is concerned—sex does sell, after all. But the mind also likes to be challenged; there's real pleasure to be found in solving puzzles, detecting patterns or unpacking a complex narrative system.

23   In pointing out some of the ways that popular culture has improved our minds, I am not arguing that parents should stop paying attention to the way their children amuse themselves. What I am arguing for is a change in the criteria we use to determine what really is cognitive junk food and what is genuinely nourishing. Instead of a show's violent or tawdry content, instead of wardrobe malfunctions or the F-word, the true test should be whether a given show engages or sedates the mind. Is it a single thread strung together with predictable punch lines every 30 seconds? Or does it map a complex social network? Is your on-screen character running around shooting everything in sight, or is she trying to solve problems and manage resources? If your kids want to watch reality TV, encourage them to watch *Survivor* over *Fear Factor.* If they want to watch a mystery show, encourage *24* over *Law and Order.* If they want to play a violent game, encourage *Grand Theft Auto* over *Quake.* Indeed, it might be just as helpful to have a rating system that used mental labor and not obscenity and violence as its classification scheme for the world of mass culture.

Reflection and Discussion

1. Why do many reports about heavy TV watching focus on negative effects?
2. Johnson compares the plot lines of some TV programs to the complexities found in certain video games. What similarities do you see? What differences?

Writing Matters

1. Elaborate on Johnson's premise that watching TV programs with complex plots can contribute to cognitive development. Which of his examples do you agree with most and why? Which do you disagree with? Choose other cognitively challenging programs and explain your choices.
2. Johnson argues that older, simpler TV programs were modeled after live theatre while contemporary television programs, reality shows included, have been influenced by the structure of video games. How accurate is his comparison between video games and present-day TV programs? Cite some video games that have been particularly influential and explain their effects. In what other ways have video games influenced television?

Tuning In, Tuning Out

Robert Putnam, *Political Science and Politics,* December 1995

Robert Putnam has taught at Stanford, MIT and Harvard. He is probably best known for his book Bowling Alone.

What are your reactions when you hear television criticized?

Several years ago I conducted research on the arcane topic of local government in Italy (Putnam 1993). That study concluded that the performance of government and other social institutions is powerfully influenced by citizen engagement in community affairs, or what (following Coleman 1990) I termed *social capital.* I am now seeking to apply that set of ideas and insights to the urgent problems of contemporary American public life.

By "social capital," I mean features of social life—networks, norms, and trust—that enable participants to act together more effectively to pursue shared objectives. Whether or not their shared goals are praiseworthy is, of course, entirely another matter. To the extent that the norms, networks, and trust link substantial sectors of the community and span underlying social cleavages—to the extent that the social capital is of a "bridging" sort—then the enhanced cooperation is likely to serve broader interests and to be widely welcomed. On the other hand, groups like the Michigan militia or youth gangs also embody a kind of social capital, for these networks and norms, too, enable members to cooperate more effectively, albeit to the detriment of the wider community.

3   Social capital, in short, refers to social connections and the attendant norms and trust. Who benefits from these connections, norms, and trust—the individual, the wider community, or some faction within the community—must be determined empirically, not definitionally.[1] Sorting out the multiple effects of different forms of social capital is clearly a crucial task, although it is not one that I can address here. For present purposes, I am concerned with forms of social capital that, generally speaking, serve civic ends.

4   Social capital in this sense is closely related to political participation in the conventional sense, but these terms are not synonymous. Political participation refers to our relations with political institutions. Social capital refers to our relations with one another. Sending a check to a PAC is an act of political participation, but it does not embody or create social capital. Bowling in a league or having coffee with a friend embodies and creates social capital, though these are not acts of political participation. (A grassroots political movement or a traditional urban machine is a social capital intensive form of political participation.) I use the term "civic engagement" to refer to people's connections with the life of their communities, not merely with politics. Civic engagement is correlated with political participation in a narrower sense, but whether they move in lock-step is an empirical question, not a logical certitude. Some forms of individualized political participation, such as check writing, for example, might be rising at the same time that social connectedness was on the wane. Similarly, although social trust—trust in other people—and political trust—trust in political authorities—might be empirically related, they are logically quite distinct. I might well trust my neighbors without trusting city hall, or vice versa.

5   The theory of social capital presumes that, generally speaking, the more we connect with other people, the more we trust them, and vice versa. At least in the contexts I have so far explored, this presumption generally turns out to be true: social trust and civic engagement are strongly correlated. That is, with or without controls for education, age, income, race, gender, and so on, people who join are people who trust.[2] Moreover, this is true across different countries, and across different states in the United States, as well as across individuals, and it is true of all sorts of groups.[3] Sorting out which way causation flows—whether joining causes trusting or trusting causes joining—is complicated both

theoretically and methodologically, although John Brehm and Wendy Rahn (1995) report evidence that the causation flows mainly from joining to trusting. Be that as it may, civic connections and social trust move together. Which way are they moving?

Bowling Alone: Trends in Civic Engagement

Evidence from a number of independent sources strongly suggests that America's stock of social capital has been shrinking for more than a quarter century. 6

- Membership records of such diverse organizations as the PTA, the Elks club, the League of Women Voters, the Red Cross, labor unions, and even bowling leagues show that participation in many conventional voluntary associations has declined by roughly 25% to 50% over the last two to three decades (Putnam, 1995, 1996).
- Surveys of the time budgets of average Americans in 1965, 1975, and 1985, in which national samples of men and women recorded every single activity undertaken during the course of a day, imply that the time we spend on informal socializing and visiting is down (perhaps by one quarter) since 1965, and that the time we devote to clubs and organizations is down even more sharply (probably by roughly half) over this period.[4]
- While Americans' interest in politics has been stable or even growing over the last three decades, and some forms of participation that require moving a pen, such as signing petitions and writing checks, have increased significantly, many measures of collective participation have fallen sharply (Rosenstone and Hansen 1993; Putnam 1996), including attending a rally or speech (off 36% between 1973 and 1993), attending a meeting on town or school affairs (off 39%), or working for a political party (off 56%).
- Evidence from the General Social Survey demonstrates, at all levels of education and among both men and women, a drop of roughly one-quarter in group membership since 1974 and a drop of roughly one-third in social trust since 1972.[5] Moreover, . . . slumping membership has afflicted all sorts of groups, from sports clubs and professional associations to literary discussion groups and labor unions. Only nationality groups, hobby and garden clubs, and the catch-all category of "other" seem to have resisted the ebbing tide. Furthermore, Gallup polls report that church attendance fell by roughly 15% during the 1960s and has remained at that lower level ever since, while data from the National Opinion

Research Center suggest that the decline continued during the 1970s and 1980s and by now amounts to roughly 30% (Putnam 1996). . . .

7   With due regard to various kinds of counter-evidence, I believe that the weight of the available evidence confirms that Americans today are significantly less engaged with their communities than was true a generation ago.

8   Of course, lots of civic activity is still visible in our communities. American civil society is not moribund. Indeed, evidence suggests that America still outranks many other countries in the degree of our community involvement and social trust (Putnam 1996). But if we compare ourselves, not with other countries but with our parents, the best available evidence suggests that we are less connected with one another. . . . This is the mystery I seek to unravel here: Why, beginning in the 1960s and accelerating in the 1970s and 1980s, did the fabric of American community life begin to fray? Why are more Americans bowling alone?

Explaining the Erosion of Social Capital

9   Many possible answers have been suggested for this puzzle. . . . I have discovered only one prominent suspect against whom circumstantial evidence can be mounted, and in this case, it turns out, some directly incriminating evidence has also turned up. . . . The culprit is television.

10   First, the timing fits. The long civic generation was the last cohort of Americans to grow up without television, for television flashed into American society like lightning in the 1950s. In 1950 barely 10% of American homes had television sets, but by 1959 90% did, probably the fastest diffusion of a technological innovation ever recorded. The reverberations from this lightning bolt continued for decades, as viewing hours per capita grew by 17–20% during the 1960s and by an additional 7–8% during the 1970s. In the early years, TV watching was concentrated among the less educated sectors of the population, but during the 1970s the viewing time of the more educated sectors of the population began to converge upward. Television viewing increases with age, particularly upon retirement, but each generation since the introduction of television has begun its life cycle at a higher starting point. By 1995, viewing per TV household was more than 50% higher than it had been in the 1950s.[6]

11   Most studies estimate that the average American now watches roughly four hours per day.[7] Robinson (1990b), using the more conservative time-budget technique for determining how people allocate

their time, offers an estimate closer to three hours per day, but concludes that as a primary activity, television absorbs 40% of the average American's free time, an increase of about one-third since 1965. Moreover, multiple sets have proliferated: by the late 1980s, three quarters of all U.S. homes had more than one set (Comstock 1989), and these numbers too are rising steadily, allowing ever more private viewing. In short, as Robinson and Godbey (1995) conclude, "television is the 800-pound gorilla of leisure time." This massive change in the way Americans spend our days and nights occurred precisely during the years of generational civic disengagement.

Evidence of a link between the arrival of television and the erosion of social connections is, however, not merely circumstantial. The links between civic engagement and television viewing can instructively be compared with the links between civic engagement and newspaper reading. The basic contrast is straightforward: newspaper reading is associated with high social capital, TV viewing with low social capital. 12

Controlling for education, income, age, race, place of residence, work status, and gender, TV viewing is strongly and negatively related to social trust and group membership, whereas the same correlations with newspaper reading are positive. . . . [In] every educational category, heavy readers are avid joiners, whereas . . . heavy viewers are more likely to be loners.[8] Viewing and reading are themselves uncorrelated—some people do lots of both, some do little of either— . . . (controlling for education, as always) "pure readers" (that is, people who watch less TV than average and read more newspapers than average) belong to 76% more civic organizations than "pure viewers." Precisely the same pattern applies to other indicators of civic engagement, including social trust and voting turnout. "Pure readers," for example, are 55% more trusting than "pure viewers."[9] 13

In other words, each hour spent viewing television is associated with less social trust and less group membership, while each hour reading a newspaper is associated with more. An increase in television viewing of the magnitude that the United States has experienced in the last four decades might directly account for as much as one-quarter to one-half of the total drop in social capital, even without taking into account, for example, the indirect effects of television viewing on newspaper readership or the cumulative effects of "life-time" viewing hours.[10] 14

How might television destroy social capital? 15

Time displacement: Even though there are only 24 hours in everyone's day, most forms of social and media participation are 16 positively correlated. People who listen to lots of classical music are more likely, not less likely, than others to attend Cubs games. Television is the principal exception to this generalization—the only leisure activity that seems to inhibit participation outside the home. TV watching comes at the expense of nearly every social activity outside the home, especially social gatherings and informal conversations (Comstock et al 1978; Comstock 1989; Bower 1985; and Robinson and Godbey 1995). TV viewers are homebodies.

17   Most studies that report a negative correlation between television watching and community involvement . . . are ambiguous with respect to causality, because they merely compare different individuals at a single time. However, one important quasi-experimental study of the introduction of television in three Canadian towns (Williams 1986) found the same pattern at the aggregate level across time: a major effect of television's arrival was the reduction in participation in social, recreational, and community activities among people of all ages. In short, television is privatizing our leisure time.

18 **Effects on the outlooks of viewers:** An impressive body of literature, gathered under the rubric of the "mean world effect," suggests that heavy watchers of TV are unusually skeptical about the benevolence of other people—overestimating crime rates, for example. This body of literature has generated much debate about the underlying causal patterns, with skeptics suggesting that misanthropy may foster couch-potato behavior rather than the reverse. While awaiting better experimental evidence, however, a reasonable interim judgment is that heavy television watching may well increase pessimism about human nature (Gerbner et al 1980; Dobb and MacDonald 1979; Hirsch 1980; Hughes 1980; and Comstock 1989, 265–69). Perhaps, too, as social critics have long argued, both the medium and the message have more basic effects on our ways of interacting with the world and with one another. Television may induce passivity, as Postman (1985) has claimed, and it may even change our fundamental physical and social perceptions, as Meyrowitz (1985) has suggested.

19 **Effects on children:** TV occupies an extraordinary part of children's lives—consuming about 40 hours per week on average. Viewing is especially high among pre-adolescents, but it remains high among younger adolescents: time-budget studies (Carnegie Council on Adolescent Development 1993, 5, citing Timmer et al. 1985) suggest that among youngsters aged 9–14 television consumes as much time as

all other discretionary activities combined, including playing, hobbies, clubs, outdoor activities, informal visiting, and just hanging out. The effects of television on childhood socialization have, of course, been hotly debated for more than three decades. The most reasonable conclusion from a welter of sometimes conflicting results appears to be that heavy television watching probably increases aggressiveness (although perhaps not actual violence), that it probably reduces school achievement, and that it is statistically associated with "psychosocial malfunctioning," although how much of this effect is self-selection and how much causal remains much debated (Condry 1993). The evidence is . . . not yet enough to convict, but the defense has a lot of explaining to do. . . .

Conclusion

Revolutions in communications technologies have profoundly affected 20 social life and culture, as the printing press helped bring on the Reformation. [Ithiel de Sola] Pool concluded that the electronic revolution in communications technology, whose outlines he traced well before most of us were even aware of the impending changes, was the first major technological advance in centuries that would have a profoundly decentralizing and fragmenting effect on society and culture. Pool hoped that the result might be "community without contiguity." As a classic liberal, he welcomed the benefits of technological change for individual freedom, and, in part, I share that enthusiasm. Those of us who bemoan the decline of community in contemporary America need to be sensitive to the liberating gains achieved during the same decades. We need to avoid an uncritical nostalgia for the Fifties. On the other hand, some of the same freedom-friendly technologies . . . may indeed be undermining our connections with one another and with our communities. . . . [O]ne of Pool's most talented protégés, Samuel Popkin (1991, 226–31) has argued that the rise of television and the correlative decline of social interaction have impaired American political discourse. The last line in Pool's last book (1990, 262) is this: "We may suspect that [the technological trends that we can anticipate] will promote individualism and will make it harder, not easier, to govern and organize a coherent society."

Pool's technological determinism was "soft" precisely because he 21 recognized that social values can condition the effects of technology. In the end this perspective invites us not merely to consider how technology is privatizing our lives—if, as it seems to me, it is—but to ask whether we entirely like the result, and if not, what we might do about it. But that is a topic for another day.

Notes

1. In this respect I deviate slightly from James Coleman's "functional" definition of social capital. See Coleman (1990):300–321.

2. The results reported in this paragraph and throughout the paper, unless otherwise indicated, are derived from the General Social Survey. These exceptionally useful data derive from a series of scientific surveys of the adult American population, conducted nearly every year since 1972 by the National Opinion Research Center, under the direction of James A. Davis and Tom W. Smith. The cumulative sample size is approximately 32,000, although the questions on trust and group membership that are at the focus of our inquiry have not been asked of all respondents in all years. Our measure of trust derives from this question: "Generally speaking, would you say that most people can be trusted, or that you can't be too careful in dealing with people"; for this question, N = 22390. For evidence confirming the power of this simple measure of social trust, see Uslaner (1995). Our measure of group membership derives from this question: "Now we would like to know something about the groups or organizations to which individuals belong. Here is a list of various organizations. Could you tell me whether or not you are a member of each type?" The list includes fraternal groups, service clubs, veterans' groups, political clubs, labor unions, sports groups, youth groups, school service groups, hobby or garden clubs, social fraternities or sororities, nationality groups, farm organizations, literary, arts, discussion or study groups, professional or academic societies, church-affiliated groups, and any other groups. For this question, N = 19326. Neither of these questions, of course, is a perfect measure of social capital. In particular, our measure of multiple memberships refers not to total groups, but to total *types* of groups. On the other hand, "noise" in data generally depresses observed correlations below the "true" value, so our findings are more likely to understate than to exaggerate patterns in the "real world."

3. Across the 35 countries for which data are available from the World Values Survey (1990–91), the correlation between the average number of associational memberships and endorsement of the view that "most people can be trusted" is r .65. Across the 42 states for which adequate samples are available in the General Social Survey (1972–1994), the comparable correlation is r .71. Across individuals in the General Social Survey (1972–1994), controlling for education, race, and age, social trust is significantly and separately correlated with membership in political clubs, literary groups, sports clubs, hobby and garden clubs, youth groups, school service groups, and other associations. The correlation with social trust is insignificant only for veterans groups, labor unions, and nationality groups.

4. The 1965 sample, which was limited to nonretired residents of cities between 30,000 and 280,000 population, was not precisely equivalent to the later national samples, so appropriate adjustments need to be made to

ensure comparability. For the 1965–1975 comparison, see Robinson (1981, 125). For the 1975–1985 comparison (but apparently without adjustment for the 1965 sampling peculiarities), see Cutler (1990). Somewhat smaller declines are reported in Robinson and Godbey (1995), although it is unclear whether they correct for the sampling differences. Additional work to refine these cross-time comparisons is required and is currently underway.

5. Trust in political authorities—and indeed in many social institutions—has also declined sharply over the last three decades, but that is conceptually a distinct trend. As we shall see later, the etiology of the slump in social trust is quite different from the etiology of the decline in political trust.

6. For introductions to the massive literature on the sociology of television, see Bower (1985), Comstock et al. (1978), Comstock (1989), and Grabner (1993). The figures on viewing hours in the text are from Bower (1985, 33) and *Public Perspective* (1995, 47). Cohort differences are reported in Bower (1985, 46).

7. This figure excludes periods in which television is merely playing in the background. Comstock (1989, 17) reports that "on any fall day in the late 1980s, the set in the average television owning household was on for about eight hours."

8. In fact, multiple regression analysis, predicting civic engagement from television viewing and education, suggests that heavy TV watching is one important reason why less educated people are less engaged in the life of their communities. Controlling for differential TV exposure significantly reduces the correlation between education and engagement.

9. Controlling for education, 45% of respondents who watch TV two hours or less a day and read newspapers daily say that "most people can be trusted," as compared to 29% of respondents who watch TV three hours or more a day and do not read a newspaper daily.

10. Newspaper circulation (per household) has dropped by more than half since its peak in 1947. To be sure, it is not clear which way the tie between newspaper reading and civic involvement works, since disengagement might itself dampen one's interest in community news. But the two trends are clearly linked.

References

Bower, Robert T. 1985. *The Changing Television Audience in America.* New York: Columbia University Press.

Carnegie Council on Adolescent Development. 1993. *A Matter of Time: Risk and Opportunity in the Nonschool Hours: Executive Summary.* New York: Carnegie Corporation of New York.

Comstock, George, Steven Chaffee, Natan Katzman, Maxwell McCombs, and Donald Roberts. 1978. *Television and Human Behavior.* New York: Columbia University Press.

Comstock, George. 1989. *The Evolution of American Television.* Newbury Park, CA: Sage.

Condry, John. 1993. "Thief of Time, Unfaithful Servant: Television and the American Child," *Daedalus* 122 (Winter): 259–78.

Dobb, Anthony N., and Glenn F. Macdonald. 1979. "Television Viewing and Fear of Victimization: Is the Relationship Causal?" *Journal of Personality and Social Psychology* 37: 170–79.

Gerbner, George, Larry Gross, Michael Morgan, and Nancy Signorielli. 1980. "The 'Mainstreaming' of America: Violence Profile No. 11," *Journal of Communication* 30 (Summer): 10–29.

Hirsch, Paul M. 1980. "The 'Scary World' of the Nonviewer and Other Anomalies: A Re-analysis of Gerbner et al.'s Findings on Cultivation Analysis, Part I," *Communication Research 7* (October): 403–56.

Hughes, Michael. 1980. "The Fruits of Cultivation Analysis: A Re-examination of the Effects of Television Watching on Fear of Victimization, Alienation, and the Approval of Violence." *Public Opinion Quarterly* 44: 287–303.

Meyrowitz, Joshua. 1985. *No Sense of Place: The Impact of Electronic Media on Social Behavior.* New York: Oxford University Press.

Pool, Ithiel de Sola. 1990. *Technologies Without Boundaries: On Telecommunications in a Global Age.* Cambridge, MA: Harvard University Press.

Popkin, Samuel L. 1991. *The Reasoning Voter.* Chicago: University of Chicago Press.

Postman, Neil. 1985. *Amusing Ourselves to Death: Public Discourse in the Age of Show Business.* New York: Viking-Penguin Books.

Robinson, John. 1990b. "I Love My TV." *American Demographics* (September): 24–27.

Robinson, John, and Geoffrey Godbey. 1995. *Time for Life.* College Park, MD: University of Maryland. Unpublished manuscript.

Timmer, S. G., J. Eccles, and I. O'Brien. 1985. "How Children Use Time." In *Time, Goods, and Well-Being,* ed. F. T. Juster and F. B. Stafford. Ann Arbor, MI: University of Michigan, Institute for Social Research.

Williams, Tannis Macbeth, ed. 1986. *The Impact of Television: A Natural Experiment in Three Communities.* New York: Academic Press.

Reflection and Discussion

1. In the not-so-distant past, most homes had only one television and families often watched it together. What has been gained and lost by the disappearance of television viewing as a shared experience? In what contexts do you still like to watch TV with someone else?

2. If you were to watch television less, what would you do with the extra time?

Writing Matters

1. How valid is Putnam's claim that television is largely to blame for Americans' declining membership in groups outside the home? How important is participation in community affairs? What problems do you anticipate if we become increasingly isolated? What can people do to avoid it?

2. Putnam suspects that television encourages pessimism and passivity. To what extent do you agree or disagree? Watch an evening of television, starting with the network news and continuing on through the most popular shows during prime time. Cite specific examples to support or refute Putnam's conclusion. Consider verifying your findings with a similar experiment conducted on a different night.

Does Television Erode Social Capital?

Pippa Norris, *Political Science and Politics,* September 1996

Pippa Norris is associated with the Kennedy School of Government at Harvard University.

Would you characterize yourself as either pro or anti-TV? Somewhere in the middle? Why?

In "Tuning In, Tuning Out: The Strange Disappearance of Social 1 Capital" Robert Putnam develops a powerful indictment of American television . . . argu[ing] that television in America has contributed decisively towards the erosion of social capital and civic engagement. "Social capital" is understood as the dense networks of norms and social trust which enable participants to cooperate in the pursuit of shared objectives. Putnam argues that the more we connect with other people, on a face-to-face basis within the community, the more we trust them (Putnam 1994, 1995a; see also Brehm and Rahn 1995).

The puzzle which Putnam seeks to explain is why America's stock 2 of social capital has been shrinking for more than a quarter century, as demonstrated by the decline in membership of social groups and voluntary associations, and in many forms of collective political participation such as attending town meetings, or working for political parties (Putnam 1995a). After considering a wide range of factors which could have led towards civic disengagement in America, including trends in the structure of the economy, changes in the family, and the growth of the welfare state, Putnam argues that this trend has been closely associated with the arrival of television. Based on analysis of the General Social Survey data from 1974–94, controlling for a range of demographic factors like education, age and income, the study found that the amount of television viewing was strongly and negatively related to social trust, group membership, and voting turnout, whereas the same correlations with newspaper readings were found to be positive (Putnam 1995b, 678). The effects of television have been most marked, it is argued, upon the post-war generation. Putnam claims that television has destroyed social capital most obviously through displacing social and leisure activities outside the home, but he also suggests, based on secondary studies (Gerbner et al. 1980), that television may have produced a more misanthropic view of the world among viewers. . . .

3   Yet . . . many of the attacks on the media are drawn in black-and-white terms, as though there is one television experience, rather than multiple channels and programs, and one audience, rather than different types of viewers. There has been surprisingly little attempt carefully to establish the antecedent factors which condition the media's ability to shape the public's trust and civic engagement. In particular we do not know whether the public is affected by the simple amount of television viewing, as Putnam (1995b) claims, or whether the contents of what people watch is equally important. All things being equal, we might expect that viewers who were devoted to the *The Newshour with Jim Lehrer,* C-SPAN, and *Nightline* might end up as rather well-informed citizens who were well-equipped to become engaged in public life. In other countries like Britain there seems to be a positive link between regularly watching the television news and levels of political knowledge, participation, and efficacy (Norris 1996). From a wealth of previous research in political communications we might also expect that the characteristics of the people who receive the news might condition how they are influenced: for example, partisans might be expected to be less persuadable than independents. Nor have we clearly disentangled the relationship between different indicators of declining support for the American political system. Too often trends over time in social trust, confidence in government, civic engagement, and political participation are banded together without analyzing whether these factors are actually linked. Yet the relationship may not be straightforward. For example, observers often blame declining confidence in government for the fall in electoral participation, yet studies have found that trusting citizens are not more likely to vote, engage in campaign activities, or be interested in politics (Citrin 1974; Rosenstone and Hansen 1993). Theoretically these factors may be unrelated, so that the media may perhaps produce a more skeptical public without any

significant consequences for political activism. In the light of this debate, the aim of this paper is to reexamine the impact of the media on civic engagement and political participation in America. . . .

The Media and Political Participation

We can start by examining how far the use of different media sources is 4 related to types of political activism, without any controls for the social background of viewers and readers. The initial results of this analysis . . . confirm the thesis that the amount of time people spent watching television was significantly correlated with every type of political participation. Across every category, the more people watched, the less active they were. Those who had joined organizations like a sports club or church group, for example, spent about 2.5 hours per day watching television, compared with 3.3 hours for non-members. Moreover heavy viewers also proved less interested in national and local community politics, and less likely to engage in political discussions.

Yet the results also demonstrate that the amount of television 5 which people watch gives only a partial insight into the effects of the media. If we turn to the content of what people watched the picture changes. Those who regularly tuned into the network news were significantly more likely to be involved in all types of political activity, and the relationship between watching public affairs programs on television and civic engagement proved even stronger. This indicates that we should not blame television watching per se for political disengagement, as Putnam suggests (1995b), but rather the contents of what people are watching. Those who are tuning into network news and current affairs programs are also heavily engaged in public life. Newspaper readership was even more significantly related to activism, although interestingly those who regularly tuned into talk shows on radio did not seem to be stimulated to participate in other forms of politics. . . .

The Media and Political Attitudes

In addition to the direct effects on civic engagement, critics have com- 6 monly charged television with producing a cynical and ill-informed public, alienated from government and the community in which they live. In order to examine some of the evidence for this charge we can compare the political interest, sense of political efficacy, and political knowledge of different media users. Again we rely upon the battery of items which Verba et al. (1995: Appendix B) use for scaled measurement. The measurement of interest includes interest in local community affairs as well as in national politics. The knowledge scale includes correct answers to eight items, including name-recognition of representatives and awareness of some constitutional issues and concepts. Political efficacy measures how far citizens felt that they could influence local and national government, with a four-item scale. Since these attitudes could also be expected to vary according to social background, these are entered into the regression models used earlier. . . .

7   [A]gain education and income consistently proved to be significant indicators of political attitudes, as many studies have found, while age and race were also related to political knowledge. Turning to the measures of media use, reading newspapers was positively associated with knowledge, efficacy and interest, indeed the strongest predictor of these attitudes in the equation. Just as consistently, the hours people spent watching television was negatively associated with these attitudes: people who watch a great deal of television know less about politics, feel less able to affect government, and are less interested in politics. To this extent, the common charge against the medium was sustained, although the direction of causality has to remain an open question. Yet watching public affairs programs on network news was associated with greater interest in politics, and those who watched the news also had a higher sense of efficacy. We need further analysis of these attitudes, with better measures of what programs people were watching, and panel survey data, to start to disentangle this relationship further.

Conclusions

8   Critics have commonly attacked television for a host of ills in American society, ranging from violence among children to racism, illiteracy, alienation, and lack of civic involvement. The pervasiveness of television culture throughout American society has made it an easy target for those of the right and left who feel it is the cause of the malaise in public life. Yet the very pervasiveness, like the air around us, makes it particularly difficult to establish the truth of the charges.

9   The analysis presented in this study suggests that the relationship between civic engagement and television viewership is more complex than sometimes suggested. While the amount of television viewing does seem to support the Putnam thesis, other evidence regarding what American viewers tune into suggests that watching news, and particularly current affairs programs from *Nightline* to *60 Minutes* does not seem to be damaging to the democratic health of society, and may even prove beneficial. In short, the charge that television is the root cause of the lack of confidence and trust in American democracy seems on this basis (in the weaker version) unproven, and (in the stronger claim) to be deeply implausible.

We get, from American television, a diversity of channels, pro- grams and choices. If some choose C-SPAN, *Meet the Press* and *CNN World News*, they are likely to end up somewhat more interested in the complex problems and issues facing American government at the end of the twentieth century. Could we be better informed and more involved? Of course. But compared with most democracies America is already high as a nation of joiners, with a dense network of civic associations. And it is not self-evident that turning off the television, and talking with our neighbors, or even going bowling, is necessarily the best way of addressing the long-term problems of confidence in American government or trust in a deeply-divided American society.

References

Brehm, John and Wendy Rahn. 1995. "An Audit of the Deficit in Social Capital." Unpublished paper.

Citrin, Jack. 1974. "Comment: The Political Relevance of Trust in Government." *American Political Science Review*. 68: 973–88.

Gerbner, George, Larry Gross, Michael Morgan and Nancy Signorielli. 1980. "The Mainstreaming of America." *Journal of Communication* 30:10–29.

Norris, Pippa. 1996. "Political Communication in Election Campaigns: Reconsidering Media Effects." In *British Elections Parties Yearbook,* eds. Colin Railings et al. London: Frank Cass.

Putnam, Robert. 1995a. "Bowling Alone, Features Revisited." *The Journal of Democracy*. 6(1):65.

Putnam, Robert. 1995b. "Tuning In, Tuning Out: The Strange Disappearance of Social Capital in America." *PS: Political Science & Politics*. 27(4):664–683.

Putnam, Robert. 1994. *Making Democracy Work.* Princeton, NJ: Princeton University Press.

Rosenstone, Steven J. and John Mark Hansen. 1993. *Mobilisation, Participation and Democracy in America.* New York: Macmillan.

Verba, Sidney, Kay Lehman Schlozman and Henry E. Brady. 1995. *Voice and Equality: Civic Voluntarism in American Politics.* Cambridge, MA: Harvard University Press.

Reflection and Discussion

1. Norris says "social capital" has to do with how much we trust others. Generally, the more time we spend in the presence of other people, the better we know and trust them. Cite some examples from your own experience that either confirm or deny this relationship.

2. Norris notes that both the right and left sides of the political spectrum have been critical of television. Why would politicians be so universally anti-television?

Writing Matters

1. The question that Norris addresses is whether or not television is a strong influence on the civic involvement of Americans. Given the date of the article, television may have been a more important part of people's lives than it is now. What about the time people spend at their computers? Are e-mailing, video games and the Internet replacing television watching? Conduct interviews and do some research to confirm your ideas. To what extent are these activities keeping people from experiencing direct human contact with others?

2. Norris claims that what TV viewers watch is as important as how much they watch. To what extent do you agree with her? Decide on a period of time—several days, for example—and keep track of your TV viewing habits. Then arrange the shows you watch into categories. What kinds of shows predominate? How aware were you of these trends before you began your experiment? What conclusions can you come to about the kind of TV you prefer? What, if anything, does this say about your tastes, personality or interests?

The *CSI* Effect

Kit R. Roane and Dan Morrison, US *News and World Report,*
May 2, 2005

Kit R. Roane and Dan Morrison are journalists who have written for many publications on a variety of subjects, including the war in Iraq.

Why are TV crime shows popular? Why has *CSI*, in particular, been so successful?

1   A disappointed jury can be a dangerous thing. Just ask Jodi Hoos. Prosecuting a gang member in Peoria, Ill., for raping a teenager in a local park last year, Hoos told the jury, "You've all seen *CSI*. Well, this is your *CSI* moment. We have DNA." Specifically, investigators had matched saliva on the victim's breast to the defendant, who had denied touching her. The jury also had gripping testimony from the victim, an emergency-room nurse, and the responding officers. When the jury came back, however, the verdict was not guilty. Why? Unmoved by the DNA evidence, jurors felt police should have tested "debris" found in the victim to see if it matched soil from the park. "They said they knew from *CSI* that police could test for that sort of thing," Hoos said. "We had his DNA. We had his denial. It's ridiculous."

2   Television's diet of forensic fantasy "projects the image that all cases are solvable by highly technical science, and if you offer less than

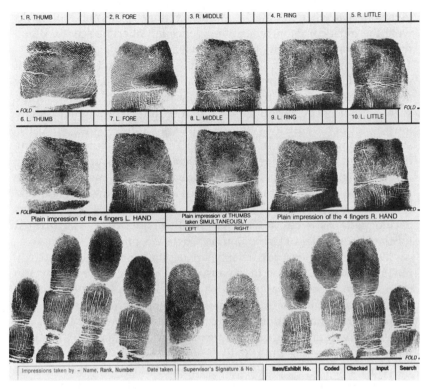

FIGURE 7.2 "There is nothing more deceptive than an obvious fact."
Sherlock Holmes

that, it is viewed as reasonable doubt," says Hoos's boss, Peoria State's Attorney Kevin Lyons. "The burden it places on us is overwhelming." Prosecutors have a name for the phenomenon: "the *CSI* effect."

Some of the "evidence" the *CSI* shows tout—using a wound to make a mold of a knife, or predicting time of death by looking at the rate at which a piece of metal might rust—is blatant hokum, experts say. But more and more, police and prosecutors are waking up to the need to cater to a jury's heightened expectations. That means more visual cues, with PowerPoint and video presentations, and a new emphasis during testimony on why certain types of evidence haven't been presented. If there are no fingerprints in evidence, more prosecutors are asking investigators to explain why, lest jurors take their absence as cause for doubt.

The same goes for DNA or gunshot residue. Joseph Peterson, acting director of the Department of Criminal Justice at the University of Illinois-Chicago, says DNA is rarely culled from crime scenes and analyzed. Crime scenes today are much like they were in the 1970s,

Peterson says, when his studies found that fingerprints and tool marks were the most common types of evidence left at crime scenes. Blood was found only 5 percent of the time, usually at murder scenes.

5   Like crime scenes, many crime labs also haven't changed that much—at least in one respect. Many are still understaffed, and they often don't receive all of the relevant physical evidence from the crime scene, either because police investigators don't know what they're looking for or because they figure—possibly wrongly—that the case is strong enough without it. A crime lab's bread and butter is testing drugs found at crime scenes, doing toxicology screens, and comparing fingerprints. DNA matches are way down the list, mainly because they're time consuming and expensive. How much time? A Cape Cod trash hauler gave police a DNA sample in March 2004. The lab was backlogged. Last week, after it was finally analyzed, he was arrested for the 2002 murder of fashion writer Crista Worthington.

6   Defense attorneys, predictably, are capitalizing on the popularity of shows like *CSI*, seizing on an absence of forensic evidence, even in cases where there's no apparent reason for its use. In another Peoria case, jurors acquitted a man accused of stabbing his estranged girl-friend because police didn't test her bloody bedsheets for DNA. The man went back to prison on a parole violation and stabbed his ex again when he got out—this time fatally.

7   The *CSI* effect was raised in the acquittal last month of actor Robert Blake in the murder of his wife. The L.A. district attorney called the jurors "incredibly stupid," but jurors noted that the former *Baretta* star was accused of shooting his wife with an old Nazi-era pistol that spewed gunshot residue. Blake's skin and clothes, a juror told *US News*, had "not one particle."

On Thin Ice

8   Still, forensic evidence and expert testimony can add a lot of weight. Confronted with a possible fingerprint or DNA match, many defendants will plead guilty instead of risking a trial and the possibility of a heavier penalty.

9   At trial, many juries tend to believe forensic experts and the evidence they provide—even when they shouldn't. Sandra Anderson and her specially trained forensic dog, Eagle, are a case in point. Dubbed a canine Sherlock Holmes, Eagle and his trainer were the darlings of prosecutors and police across the country. They appeared on TV's *Unsolved Mysteries* and headlined forensic science seminars. The dog seemed to have a bionic nose, finding hidden traces of blood evidence, which Anderson duly corroborated in court. In one case, Eagle's

million-dollar nose gave police enough for a search warrant after he found damning evidence in the house of a biochemist suspected of murdering his wife. Plymouth, Mich., Police Lt. Wayne Carroll declared at the time: "Before we brought that dog down there, we were on thin ice." Anderson and Eagle, however, were frauds. After she admitted planting blood on a hacksaw blade during the investigation of the suspect, Azizul Islam, he was granted a new trial last year. It was one of several cases in which Anderson faked evidence. She is now serving a 21-month prison term after pleading guilty to obstruction of justice and making false statements. Lawyers and forensic experts say Anderson is just one of the more bizarre cases of forensic specialists lying under oath, misreading test results, or overstating evidence.

In recent years, the integrity of crime labs across the country, 10 including the vaunted FBI crime lab, have come under attack for lax standards and generating bogus evidence. One problem is that crime labs don't have to be accredited. All DNA labs seeking federal funding will have to be accredited by next year, but roughly 30 percent of the publicly funded crime labs operating in the United States today have no certification, a recent Justice Department study found. The FBI's lab gained accreditation in 1998, after it was embarrassed by a series of foul-ups. A Houston lab sought accreditation this year, following a scandal that has so far resulted in the release of two men from prison and cast doubt on the lab's other work.

Dozens of coroners, crime lab technicians, police chemists, forensic 11 anthropologists, crime-reconstruction experts, and other forensic specialists, meanwhile, have been fined, fired, or prosecuted for lying under oath, forging credentials, or fabricating evidence. It's hard to find anyone in law enforcement who can't recite a story of quackery on the stand or in the lab. Forensic practitioners say the popularity of the field may make things even worse, noting that new forensics-degree programs are cropping up all over the place, some turning out questionable candidates. "For some reason, the forensic sciences have always had their fair share of charlatans," says Max Houck, director of the Forensic Science Initiative at West Virginia University. "Because of the weight the analysis is now given, professional ethics and certification of labs has never been more important." . . .

Even accredited crime labs, however, can make mistakes. Most 12 publicly accredited labs gauge their proficiency through declarative tests, where lab workers know they're being tested. Although most labs do well on such tests, some experts question their ability to judge labs' day-to-day performance. And even in declarative tests, deficiencies can be glaring. According to 2004 proficiency results from one private testing service reviewed by *US News*, a few labs failed to properly match samples on simple DNA tests, mysteriously came to the right result after making the wrong interpretation of the data, or accidentally transposed the information from one sample onto another. In a ballistics test, one lab matched a slug with the wrong test gun.

13   Such errors can have real-world consequences in court. In 1999, a Philadelphia crime lab accidentally switched the reference samples of a rape suspect and the alleged victim, then issued a report pointing to the defendant's guilt. Last year, a false fingerprint match led the FBI to wrongfully accuse an Oregon lawyer—and converted Muslim—of complicity in the al Qaeda-linked Madrid train bombings. The FBI later blamed the foul-up on the poor quality of the fingerprint image. "There are a number of cases that deal with what on the surface ought to be dead-bang evidence," says Fisher. "But it turns out it was the wrong result. Improper testing or improper interpretation of data left the innocent convicted."

14   For all the setbacks and scandals, science has made considerable progress in the courts since the advent of forensic investigation. In the 1600s, the evidence against two London "witches" accused of causing children to vomit bent pins and a two-penny nail was . . . a bunch of bent pins and a two-penny nail. So it must have seemed fairly revolutionary in the 1800s when a Brussels chemist named Jean Servais Stas devised a way to separate a vegetable poison from the stomach of a countess's brother to prove how he had been killed. Or when an English investigator around the same time solved the case of a murdered maid by matching a corduroy patch left in the mud at the crime scene to the pants of a laborer working some nearby fields.

"Obvious" Problems

15 That doesn't mean forensics can always be believed, however, even when the data are accurate. As Sherlock Holmes said, "There is nothing more deceptive than an obvious fact." DNA is a case in point. While DNA testing is the most accurate of the forensic sciences, experts can make vastly different interpretations of the same DNA sample. Criminal justice experts say most lawyers and judges don't know enough about any of the forensic sciences to make an honest judgment of the veracity of what they are told. Prosecutor Mike Parrish in Tarrant County, Texas, decided to get a second opinion on his DNA evidence in a capital murder case three years ago after the local police lab amended its result to more strongly link his suspect to the crime. Suspicious, Parrish had the sample reanalyzed by the county medical examiner, whose results were much less definitive. In the end, Parrish said, because of the conflicting DNA reports, he chose not to seek the death penalty.

Other forensic tests are even more open to interpretation. 16
Everything from fingerprint identification to fiber analysis is now coming under fire. And rightly so. The science is inexact, the experts are of no uniform opinion, and defense lawyers are increasingly skeptical. Fingerprint examiners, for instance, still peer through magnifying glasses to read faint ridges.

Many of these techniques and theories have never been empirically 17
tested to ensure they are valid. During much of the past decade, coroners have certified the deaths of children who might have fallen down steps or been accidentally dropped as "shaken baby" homicides because of the presence of retinal hemorrhages—blood spots—in their eyes. Juries bought it. Noting that new research casts grave doubt on the theory, Joseph Davis, the retired director of Florida's Miami-Dade County Medical Examiner's Office and one of the nation's leading forensics experts, compares proponents of shaken-baby syndrome to "flat Earthers" and says its use as a prosecution tool conjures up "shades of Salem witchcraft" trials.

The list goes on. Ear prints, left behind when a suspect presses his 18
ear to a window, have been allowed as evidence in court, despite the fact that there have been no studies to verify that all ears are different or to certify the way ear prints are taken. The fingerprint match, once considered unimpeachable evidence, is only now being closely scrutinized. The National Institute of Justice offered grants to kick-start the process this year. Other "experts" have pushed lip-print analysis, bite-mark analysis, and handwriting analysis with degrees of certainty that just don't exist, critics say.

Microscopic hair analysis was a staple of prosecutions until just a 19
few years ago and was accorded an unhealthy degree of certitude. "Hair comparisons have been discredited almost uniformly in court," says Peterson of the University of Illinois-Chicago. "There are many instances where science has not come up to the legal needs," adds James Starrs, professor of forensic sciences and law at George Washington University. Everyone, including the jury, wants certainty. But it seldom exists in forensics. So the expert, says Starrs, "always needs to leave the possibility of error."

Reflection and Discussion

1. As a result of their TV habits, jurors seem to be expecting more "hard evidence." What other examples can you think of that demonstrate the effects of television on everyday life situations?
2. Crime shows that attempt to be realistic often oversimplify or exaggerate. What are some possible reasons?

Writing Matters

1. When television shows like *CSI* begin influencing the attitudes and opinions of jurors, what problems do you see for the American criminal justice system? Who is more likely to benefit—victims or those accused of crimes? What do judges and attorneys need to do in order to assure that jurors accurately assess evidence in criminal cases?

2. Inspired by what they watch on television, many students are being attracted to majors in criminal justice and courses in chemistry and forensics. How many students do you know whose career choices seem to be influenced by popular culture—TV shows, movies or music videos? What advice would you give to those whose career goals seem based more in fantasy than reality? What kinds of checks are important when deciding on a job or profession?

MAKING CONNECTIONS

1. Review the articles in this chapter that include some of the effects of television on children. How do these positions compare to the way television affected you when you were a child? As a parent or mentor, what rules or guidelines would you establish with respect to TV viewing for children of different ages? What would you do to either emulate or alter the guidelines your parents established for you? To explain your rationale for these rules, use, if you wish, additional research and illustrations from your own experience.

2. What is the future of television? What direction do you see it moving in and what changes do you anticipate? What do you make of the trend toward programs with multi-layered plots and multiple characters? What about reality TV and song and dance competitions? Crime and sports programming? How will the Internet, cell phone and video games affect what happens to television?

3. Research the role of the Federal Communications Commission and argue whether its regulatory powers should be expanded or curtailed. What is its fundamental purpose and how well has it lived up to it? What past decisions has this commission made that you agree or disagree with and why? How do you respond to the point of view that Americans need supervision of broadcast media? How well has the FCC handled children's exposure to questionable television and Internet content? How do you feel about decisions the FCC has made (or not made) regarding media consolidation?

4. Will Rogers is credited with saying "All I know is what I read in the papers." What if this same equation were adapted to apply to television? Compare television to print sources for news, culture and entertainment. Which does a better job of keeping people informed? Culturally aware? Entertained? What information or experiences would people miss who only watched television? What about if they only read and never watched TV? If you had to choose between reading and watching TV, which would you select and why?

5. Books, movies, plays and TV have used television as subject matter in both serious and comic ways. Select two works that focus on television and describe how it has been treated in both. What similarities and differences do you see? What is each saying about television or those who watch it? Which do you find to be most effective and why?

TAKING ACTION

This chapter highlights just a few of the criticisms leveled at television: that it contributes to social disengagement, pessimism, poor time management, distractedness, a lack of physical activity. Concentrate on one or two of these problems (or another that you are aware of) and develop a plan of action.

Television station managers help influence the programming content of their stations; advertisers are sensitive to public opinion regarding the shows they support with their ads; members of the Federal Communications Commission pay attention to viewer feedback, especially when they get strong opinions about what kind of TV young people are exposed to. Choose one of these sources and write a well-reasoned letter explaining how you feel about a particular television show or trend in television. Decide either what we need more of or what should be curtailed or eliminated. Be as specific as possible.

With enough planning, this activity could be part of a report on consumer advocacy. You could include the reply to your letter (or lack of a response) in an evaluation of how well consumers are being heard in our society.

Body Image—If You Don't Like It, Change It

We live in a society which places unrelenting emphasis on appearance, inundating us with images of seemingly perfect celebrities, pointing out flaws previously unmentionable in polite company, directly challenging us to take action. "Replace that unsightly bulge with a six-pack!" Plastic surgery, once exclusively the domain of wealthy women, has now become the choice of the average woman, teens, and even a rapidly growing percentage of males, as they, too, have been caught up in the frenzy to improve their appearances. How can people maintain a positive sense of self while facing standards and expectations that seem impossible to attain?

BEFORE YOU READ

How satisfied are you with your looks? How does your appearance help or hurt you in your personal and professional relationships? Have you refrained from doing something because you didn't think you looked good enough?

FIGURES 8.1 AND 8.2 Perfect beauty? Think again. The photo on the left is untouched; the one on the right has been digitally altered to smooth the skin and hair, whiten the teeth and shape the eyebrows.

Pretty Unreal

Julie Mehta and Polly Sparling, *Current Health 2,* January 2005

Julie Mehta, a freelance journalist, has had articles published in Parenting, Woman's World *and* Current Health *and is working on her first novel. Polly Sparling is a senior editor for* Hudson Valley Magazine.

How old were you when you started to think critically about your appearance? Can you remember a specific comment or incident that triggered this?

A sultry blond stares back from a magazine ad, her miniskirt revealing 1 long, slender legs. An underwear model looms large on a billboard, flaunting his six-pack abs. A rock star sprawls across a CD cover, a belly-button ring decorating her toned stomach.

And then there's you. You pass a mirror and glance at your image. 2 What do you see? Maybe there's a zit on your forehead. Maybe the jeans that fit great last week now feel snug. You've heard it before: Nobody's perfect.

What's a person to think? Perfect images of perfect celebrities are 3 everywhere. It's enough to make anyone feel insecure or envious. "The media sets up impossible comparisons. Whether you're watching sitcoms or music videos or looking through magazines, the images you're seeing are airbrushed and enhanced," said Shari Graydon, author of *In*

Your Face: The Culture of Beauty and You. "And research shows that the more time kids spend with image-based media, the worse they feel about themselves."

Falling Short

4 Seeing all those artificially perfected images can hurt your body image—the way you see and feel about your body and the way you think others see you. From cartoon characters to movie stars, you have probably been exposed to messages about what is considered attractive as far back as you can remember. Those messages can seriously mess with your body image.

5   "I think the media has a big impact," 16-year-old Erika, of Scottsdale, AZ, told *Current Health.* "It sets the standard—says thin is in. If the media wasn't saying skinny is appropriate, people wouldn't feel like they need to be so thin." According to Graydon, wanting to be thinner is a huge issue for many girls, while boys feel increasing pressure to be more buff. Boys look at singers such as Usher and realize they'll never have those abs—or the screaming female fans that go with them. In extreme cases, girls develop eating disorders and boys turn to steroids in an effort to achieve an ideal that isn't real.

"It's All Fake"

6 Celebrities and models are in the business of looking good, and they get a lot of help. Many follow special diets, and others have personal trainers who work with them for several hours a day. Just because they look fit doesn't mean they're healthy, though. Extreme diets can cause health problems, and compulsive workouts can lead to injury.

7   Despite models' best efforts, many still don't look "good enough" for the industry. "One hundred percent of fashion photos are retouched," said Brad Adams, a New York City photographer whose retouching service works with advertising agencies. "Usually the eyes and teeth are whitened, makeup and skin problems corrected, and hair cleaned up. Models are already thin, but I've done jobs where even skinny models are made to look skinnier."

8   Movie stars also receive the "digital diet" treatment, says a woman at another New York retouching service. "Even celebrity snapshots like those in *People*—the paparazzi shots—are retouched." She explains that Photoshop, a widely used software program, can digitally narrow hips or add to cleavage and make almost any change look realistic. "It's all fake," she added. "Nobody really has skin like that. All human beings have pores and get zits, and once they get rid of those, they have wrinkles."

Pursuit of Perfection

Why is everything touched up these days? "Magazines are supported 9 by ads, and ads are about selling you a product," said author Jessica Weiner, who travels the country speaking to middle school and high school students about body image. "If you feel good about yourself, how many products will you buy? So [advertisers] have to make you feel like you need what they're selling by using unrealistic images." On a more basic level, the woman from the New York retouching company points out, "people like flawless and perfect images."

What, exactly, is perfection? "Different cultures and times define 10 beauty differently," said Graydon. "In North America, large breasts are popular. But in Brazil, [women] get plastic surgery to have smaller breasts and bigger butts. And in Uganda and Peru, heavier women are seen as beautiful." Even in this country, ideals of beauty have shifted widely from generation to generation, from the voluptuous Marilyn Monroe in the 1950s to the waif-thin Kate Moss in the 1990s.

Ripple Effect

Perhaps you don't care what the media say you should look like. Still, 11 you may be indirectly influenced by it through friends and family. "A lot of girls that I know always complain about their bodies," said Ashley, 14, of Wallingford, CT. "It drives me crazy when they compare themselves to other people that they see in school or on TV."

Family members can also be culprits. If they constantly diet or 12 pump up, you may follow their example—especially if they are concerned about your weight. "A lot of parents have gone through being teased and don't want their kids to go through that," said Kimber Bishop-Yanke, who runs self-esteem camps for girls in Detroit. "I see parents who are concerned their kids are getting fat, but it's normal to eat more and gain weight during puberty. It's just part of growing up."

Of course, no one said growing up is easy. "I'm not fat, but I'm not 13 skinny either," said 13-year-old Jordan, a seventh grader from Baton Rouge, LA. "I think I have big thighs, and when I wear shorts they stick out. A lot of kids tease me, but I try not to care so much."

Girls seem particularly prone to body-image issues. "When I was 14 younger, it was harder because I wanted to fit in so much," admitted Natalie, 17, of Humphrey, NE. Erika from Scottsdale added, "I'm in cheer, and most of my friends want to lose weight." She says she has dieted before and goes to the gym several times a week. Meanwhile, her classmate, Aliraza, 15, says he has never really worried about his looks. "I'm pretty sure girls have a lot more pressure when it comes to appearance."

15   Tim, a 14-year-old from New York City, agrees there is less pressure on boys than girls but says, "There is still some pressure—to be more buff." Experts, such as Roberto Olivardia, are starting to pay more attention to the effects of media pressure on boys. Olivardia, an instructor at Harvard University, co-wrote the book *The Adonis Complex: The Secret Crisis of Male Body Obsession,* which details a disorder among men that the authors call "bigorexia." Considered the reverse of anorexia, bigorexia occurs when a guy sees himself as puny no matter how muscular he is. Symptoms may include excessive time spent working out, constant grooming and mirror checking, and anabolic steroid use.

16   Bigorexia is one type of body dysmorphic disorder (BDD), a medical condition that equally affects males and females. BDD is an ongoing obsession with some small or imaginary problem with one's body. About one of every 50 people suffers from the condition.

Being True to You

17 Ultimately, body image has a lot more to do with your mind than your body. Self-esteem plays a huge role in body image, so the better you feel about yourself, the more likely it is you'll like what you see in the mirror. Whether you're slim or curvy, lanky or big, the keys to looking your best are eating right, exercising regularly, and feeling good inside.

18   "You're not your nose or butt or hair on a good or bad day," said Graydon. As a practical matter, "most people are way too distracted by their own imperfections to focus on yours," she added. What it all comes down to is that your body is your home for life. Given enough time, you may look back and laugh at the way you once fixated on your body's "flaws." Natalie couldn't agree more. "As you get older, you get to be more comfortable with who you are, and you learn to be happy with yourself." Why not start by loving your body—and yourself—now?

Nip and Tuck: Teen Plastic Surgery

19 Last year in the United States, more than 300,000 teens age 18 or younger had some sort of cosmetic work done. The most common procedures among teens were rhinoplasty (nose job), otoplasty (ear pinning), and skin enhancements such as chemical peels and microdermabrasion, usually to minimize acne scars.

20   Were teens following the example of so-called reality TV shows, including *Extreme Makeover, The Swan* and *I Want a Famous Face?* The shows don't tell the whole story. "They emphasize results but don't show much of the cost, recovery, and potential risks," said Joseph Serota, a Colorado plastic surgeon.

Reflection and Discussion

1. Have you ever wanted to look like a celebrity? Which one? What have you done to increase the resemblance?
2. Where do you get the idea of what you think you should look like: friends, family, television, magazine, movies or something else? Which of these sources has the greatest influence on you? Why?

Writing Matters

1. Mehta and Sparling suggest we should just start loving ourselves the way we are. How easy is that to do? What are the advantages of self-acceptance? What are the disadvantages? Discuss the struggle of trying to fit in against wanting to be true to yourself.
2. How does television treat the imperfect? Record three hours of television shows of a particular type (for example, drama, reality, comedy or news). Categorize the people based on appearance and gender. In what ways, if any, are more attractive characters treated differently from those who are less attractive? What role does gender play in these differences?

The Price of Perfection

Robin Marantz Henig, *Civilization,* May/June 1996

Robin Marantz Henig is a freelance writer and book author, specializing in the medical and science fields.

To what lengths have you gone to improve your appearance? What steps have been the most painful, expensive, dangerous, foolish?

Il faut souffrir pour etre belle;

One must suffer to be beautiful.

—Anonymous

Before 1992, when they were taken off the market because of questions   1
about long-term health risks, silicone implants had been inserted into the chests of more than a million American women. A small minority of these were cancer patients undergoing breast reconstruction after a mastectomy. But the vast majority were perfectly healthy women who simply wanted to be bustier. Why were these women so willing to undergo risky surgery and endanger their well-being for the sake of a

bigger bra size? How had they succumbed to the idea that they had to be beautiful in order to succeed, and that there was only one way to be beautiful?

2   These women were part of a long line of women—and, on occasion, men—who for centuries have undergone mutilating or dangerous procedures in the quest for beauty. Their methods have varied with changing ideals of beauty and new techniques to shift, stretch and rearrange their bodies. Over the centuries, women have mauled and manipulated just about every body part—lips, eyes, ears, waists, skulls, foreheads, feet—that did not quite fit into the cookie-cutter ideal of a particular era's fashion. In China, almost up until World War II, upper-class girls had their feet bound, crippling them for life but ensuring the 3- or 4-inch-long feet that were prized as exquisitely feminine. In central Africa, the Mangbettu wrapped the heads of female infants in pieces of giraffe hide to attain the elongated, cone-shaped heads that were taken to be a sign of beauty and intelligence. During the Renaissance, well-born European women plucked out hairs, one by one, from their natural hairlines all the way back to the crowns of their heads, to give themselves the high, rounded foreheads thought beautiful at the time.

3   The long history of beauty-by-mutilation makes us rethink today's frenzied search for the ideal female body. The current epidemic of anorexia, face-lifts and liposuction is often thought of as unique to the late 20th century. So we tend to blame uniquely modern institutions for these trends, particularly the fashion industry and Hollywood. Fashion magazines tout a single image of beauty, that of a dewy-eyed, slim-hipped 14-year-old dressed to look like a grownup. Movies and TV shows feature actresses who, with the exception of an occasional Roseanne, all look the same. When actress Pamela Lee enhances her curves, when Cher undergoes dozens of cosmetic surgeries, other women tend to assume that they should try to look that way, too. And with the price of many of the most brutal operations now set at about the cost of a 10-day Caribbean cruise, the quest for physical perfection has moved from the salons of Beverly Hills to the living rooms of Middle America.

4   This dogged pursuit of female beauty, however it is defined and to whatever lengths women go to achieve it, has been with us for so long that it suggests there is some evolutionary advantage to being vain. In the struggle for a male's attention, the woman who dominates may be the one who preens in the right way. She believes that in the state of nature, a male will mate with the female who seems as if she would make the best mother, one who looks youthful and healthy. So in evolutionary terms, the women who come closest to

this nubile ideal are the ones who will have the most reproductive success.

The crazed quest for beauty at any cost has led to some bizarre practices along the way. Consider, for instance, the highs and lows of fashions regarding a woman's breasts. In ancient Greece and again in 14th-century Europe, breasts were hidden and tightly bound. The ideal torso was a flat torso, an ideal that reemerged for the flappers of the 1920s and the mod models, like Twiggy, of the 1960s. Among the Circassians in the Caucasus region of Asia—reputed to be the most beautiful women in the world because of their symmetrical features and lily-white skin—a young girl was sheathed tightly in leather garments from before puberty until the day she was married. On her wedding night, the bridegroom ritualistically cut apart the leather with his hunting knife. "After that, the breasts were allowed to grow—if, indeed, they were still disposed to," note Arline and John Liggett in *The Tyranny of Beauty*. "What was cheerfully ignored was that many women became anemic, frequently consumptive, and that a great many died."

By the mid-1800s, Rubenesque curves were back. A well-rounded bosom was something to be proud of—and something to be artfully enhanced with clever undergarments. Breasts were powdered, perfumed and painted to appear as fair as the face and neck. Middle-aged women even drew delicate blue veins on their breasts to make their skin look as translucent as a maiden's.

Around this time, falsies first became popular. Originally they were made of wax or stuffed cotton, but these stiff shapes just lay on the chest and failed to move with the wearer. Within a few years, more natural-looking falsies came on the market, made of wire or inflatable rubber, and these, according to one French firm's advertisements, were capable of "following the movements of respiration with mathematical and perfect precision."

In 1903, an iconoclastic Chicago surgeon named Charles Miller opened a cosmetic-surgery practice in which he experimented with new methods of surgical breast enlargement. Miller opened up women's chests and inserted, according to his own account, "braided silk, bits of silk floss, particles of celluloid, vegetable ivory and several other foreign materials." There is no record of how his patients reacted, physically or emotionally, to their stuffed breasts.

When stylish women put their breasts under cover again in the 1920s, they used constricting devices like the one from the Boyish Form Brassiere Company of New York, guaranteed to "give you that boy-like flat appearance." Some women actually folded their breasts, squashing them as close as possible against the rib cage and holding them there with elastic binding. Then the pendulum swung once again. By the 1950s, breasts were back. And this time, 20th-century technological know-how was able to provide far more sophisticated solutions for those who didn't measure up. At first, the only women who surgically enlarged their breasts were professional entertainers. Carol Doda, a topless cocktail waitress from San Francisco, was one of the pioneers. In the late 1950s, she became an instant celebrity when she boosted her bosom to a size 44DD with 20 shots of liquid silicone.

10   "Enthusiasm for this method waned," notes Kathy Davis in *Reshaping the Female Body: The Dilemma of Cosmetic Surgery*, "when it was discovered that paraffin or silicone injected directly tended to migrate to other parts of the body, causing cysts and necrosis [death] of the skin. Sponges made of terylene wool, polyvinyl or polyethylene were then introduced to replace the injections. These new materials were an improvement, but they often hardened, protruded or caused fluid to accumulate in the breasts, which then had to be drained."

11   Despite the vagaries of vanity, which changed the notion of ideal breast size every few decades, one factor has held relatively constant: Most cultures, through the centuries, have wanted their women to be slim. Anorexia may seem to be a uniquely late-20th-century disease, but the sad truth is that going to great lengths to be thin is nothing new.

12   In ancient Greece, mothers wrapped their newborn daughters tightly in bands of wool or linen for the first six months or more, in hopes of elongating their proportions to the willowy, slim ideal of the time. And in England in 1665, a health pamphlet titled "To Reduce the body that is too fat to a mean and handsome proportion" noted that one handy technique for losing weight was bloodletting. Overweight women, according to this pamphlet, should be bled "largely, twice a year, the right arm in the spring, the left in the autumn"—an eerie precursor to today's binging-and-purging syndrome known as bulimia. For the nether regions that still bulged too much, the pamphlet advised using "ligaments to bind those passages where the member is supplied with nourishment." In the 1930s, desperate women actually swallowed tapeworms to lose weight; the opera diva Maria Callas is said to have been one such reducer.

13   For those who could not drop all the pounds they wanted to, undergarments came to the rescue. The most notorious—and perplexingly long-lived—of these was the corset. In one form or another, women subjected themselves to wearing corsets for over 500 years, from their introduction during Chaucer's time until far into the Victorian age.

14   The first corset, or cotte (from the French word *cote,* meaning "rib"), was made of two pieces of linen fabric stiffened and held

together with paste. Later, corsets became far more cumbersome, involving 2-inch-wide wooden boards and even heavy lead breastplates. By the 19th century, the corset had become a portable torture chamber made of rubber and strips of whalebone, pieces of which might easily protrude from their casings and pierce a woman's skin. It was designed to be worn so tightly that women tended to faint, unable to breathe deeply enough to get sufficient oxygen to their brains.

To many observers, corsets were obviously foolhardy and poten- 15 tially dangerous. In the British medical journal *The Lancet,* an 1868 article stated flatly that "the mischief produced by [a corset] can hardly be over-estimated. It tends gradually to displace all the most important organs of the body while by compressing them it must, from the first, interfere with their functions."

Yet the feminine ideal at the time remained a slender "wasp- 16 waisted" figure with an 18-inch waist—a size that virtually no woman past puberty could attain without some heavy-duty assistance. This involved not only corseting but also its sadistic extension, tight-lacing. This extreme form of compression is how the servant Mammy squeezed Scarlett O'Hara into her ball gown in *Gone with the Wind,* pulling and straining at the crisscrossing ribbons that held the corset closed at the back.

No woman could tight-lace herself alone, not only because the 17 laces tied up in the back, but also because the woman's natural instinct for self-preservation would likely prevent her from applying the kind of pressure needed to attain that 18-inch ideal. Most required the assistance of their maids (tight-lacing was the madness of the upper classes), their mothers or at the very least their bedposts. Sometimes the recalcitrant flesh fought back so mightily that it required two helpers, one to tighten the laces while the other held the subject in place with her foot. Tight-lacing, writes Lois W. Banner in *American Beauty,* "may have been a primary cause of the uterine and spinal disorders widespread among 19th-century women." Today, there are surgical alternatives to tight-lacing, including liposuction and tummy tucks. But removing excess fat and skin isn't enough for everyone: Cher even went to the extremes of undergoing an operation to remove two perfectly healthy ribs—and so accentuate her tiny waistline.

Less drastic measures, using laser surgery, are also now allowing 18 women to erase the facial "imperfections" that have troubled them for generations. In the Elizabethan age many women, in search of skin that looked like porcelain, whitened their faces using ceruse, a potentially lethal combination of vinegar and lead. Queen Elizabeth I used ceruse so consistently that it eventually ate pits into her skin, causing her to pile the paint on in thicker and thicker layers in hopes of camouflaging the growing damage. This, in turn, only led to more corrosion, and the Virgin Queen's face was ultimately so ravaged that she ordered all mirrors banned from the palace. (Arline and John Liggett write that Elizabeth's servants exploited the ban on mirrors in a wickedly mischievous way: Every morning they painted the queen's face white with ceruse, but they painted her nose "a cruel crimson.")

19   By the mid-1800s, face paint was thought to be cheap and tawdry, so ladies who wanted to achieve the porcelain look "naturally" took to swallowing whitening potions made of vinegar, chalk or arsenic, the last of which is poisonous even in tiny amounts. Arsenic was also the base for Fowler's Solution, a topical cream prescribed for teenage acne in that period. But like Retin-A a century later, Fowler's not only dried up pimples but also gave a translucent tone to the skin, so some fashionable women used it as a facial cosmetic.

20   Women unwittingly courted blindness, too, in their beauty quest. The ancient Egyptians, Romans and Persians tried to make their eyes glitter by using drops of antimony sulfide. The drops often dried up the tear ducts, though, and eventually destroyed vision. In the 16th and 17th centuries, women used eye drops made of belladonna (also known as deadly nightshade) to dilate their pupils. But while it had the desired effect of making their eyes look dewy, interested and excited, the drops also robbed these women of the normal pupil-shrinking reflex that keeps bright light away from the delicate retina. Modern experts believe that by continuously dilating their pupils, these women may have predisposed themselves to the potentially blinding eye condition of glaucoma.

21   Chemicals used to make blondes out of brunettes also proved far more dangerous than their users first suspected. In the 19th century, British women used a solution made of poisonous oxalic acid to change their hair color. They believed that dark hair was caused by an excess of iron in the system, and the acid was thought to neutralize iron. They mixed an ounce of oxalic acid in a pint of boiling water, soaked their hair thoroughly, and went out into the sunshine to let it dry. This procedure was repeated, according to one pamphlet of the day, "until it begins to affect the skin when it must be discontinued, otherwise the hair will fall out."

22   In Venice, the recipe for hair lightening involved a mixture of bisulfate of magnesia and lime. A paste made of these ingredients could be "very effectual in bleaching the hair," wrote one Venetian with tongue firmly in cheek, "and also for burning it away entirely, together with the skin and brains, if there are any, beneath it."

23   Manipulations of the skeleton proved to be every bit as disfiguring as some of the chemicals applied to the skin and hair. The most

notorious and long-lasting practice of bodily mutilation for the sake of beauty was the foot-binding of Chinese girls.

Foot-binding went far beyond wrapping bandages around the feet 24 and hoping they did not grow. It was something more akin to Cinderella's stepsisters cutting off their own heels and toes to fit into the dainty glass slipper. Beginning at about the age of 5, a girl's foot was virtually folded in two, and a 10-foot-long bandage was wrapped tightly around it to force the toes down toward the heel as far as possible. The child could not move without doubling over in a graceless and largely futile effort to walk without putting any weight on her feet. Her feet eventually lost all blood supply, which turned the skin blue; portions of the soles and toes might actually drop off. Mercifully, these deadened feet usually—though not always—ended up without any sensation at all. In order to keep the young girls from tearing off the maddening bandages, many families kept their daughter's hands tied to a pole.

Every two weeks, the girl's feet would be squeezed into a new pair 25 of shoes, one-fifth of an inch smaller than the pair before. After several years of this, the girl's bones were sufficiently crippled and deformed to keep the feet stunted at the desired 3-inch "golden-lotus" length.

"My foot felt very painful at the start," recalled one woman, whose 26 account was related in *The Tyranny of Beauty*. "The heel of my foot became odoriferous and deteriorated. Because of the pain in my foot, my whole body became emaciated. My face color changed and I couldn't sleep at night." But this woman put up with the agony, because she was convinced that "no one wanted to marry a woman with big feet."

Western cultures, while not going to quite the same extreme as the 27 Chinese, also revered a small female foot; indeed, that is what the Cinderella story is all about. Women wear shoes that are tight, pointy-toed and high-heeled because they make feet look small, even though they also hurt. High heels are bad not only for the feet but also for the entire body. The woman's torso is not designed to hobble about on its toes; stiletto heels can lead to abnormally shortened calf muscles, stretched spines and chronic back pain.

Just as painful as stunting the growth of one part of the body is 28 exaggerating the growth of another—a practice that has been widespread in Asia and Africa. Many African peoples have inserted plates into young women's lips to enlarge them, or weighed down their earlobes with heavy hoops so that the lobes eventually brush the shoulders. Some contemporary observers think that such practices began as a way to make African women less appealing to the slave traders headed to the New World, but they gradually became accepted as standards of beauty for other members of the tribe.

29   Among the Padaung people of early-20th-century Burma, the ideal of female beauty involved a greatly elongated neck, preferably 15 inches or more. This was accomplished by fitting girls with a series of brass neck rings. At a very young age, girls began by wearing five rings; by the time they were fully grown they were wearing as many as 24, piled one on top of another. Even today, Burmese refugees in northern Thailand continue to stretch their daughters' necks, since the bizarre stretching has become something of a tourist attraction. The weight of the rings leads to crushed collarbones and broken ribs, and the vertebrae in the neck become stretched and floppy. Indeed, these women wear the rings round-the-clock because, without them, their stretched-out necks are too weak to support their heads.

30   What many of these beauty trends have in common is that they forced women into positions of frailty, with their impossibly long necks, impossibly tiny feet, impossibly small waists. And the highest-achieving women have tended to be those most susceptible to the lure of the ideal; their Perfectionist streak made them want to attain every goal society deemed worthy, no matter how ludicrous it might be. This might explain why Queen Elizabeth I, whose comprehensive classical education was rare for a girl in her day, fretted over her hair and her complexion like a teenager preparing for a ball. And it might explain why Hillary Rodham Clinton, arguably one of the most powerful women in the United States, was willing to jazz up her looks in the 1980s with contact lenses and peroxide for the sake of her husband's political career—and why she careens through hairdos the way other women change their shoes.

31   One question today, of course, is why women respond to these images in a way that is different from men. How many men take Arnold Schwarzenegger's body personally? While cosmetic surgery is increasing among American males, it is still primarily the province of women, as is the self-loathing that often results in women who fail to look the way they believe they are supposed to look. In surveys that ask men and women, or boys and girls, questions like "What do you think about your body?" females reveal a distorted and inferior body image far more commonly than do males.

32   There might be an evolutionary explanation for this difference. Sex researchers Masters and Johnson found that while men are highly susceptible to visual cues in their sexual arousal, women respond more to other senses. Evolutionary biologists tell us that men are attracted to women because of the way they look, while what attracts women is not so much a man's looks as evidence of his wealth, status and power. So maybe it follows that women would be more susceptible to the prevailing idea of what it means to look desirable—they have more at stake.

Aside from trying to look good for men, women have traditionally tried to impress one another, casting sidelong glances to see how they compare with the other females in the cave, the harem, the secretarial pool or the executive boardroom. From this perspective, face-lifts and tummy tucks are just another way to keep up with the competition, no more significant than a move from long skirts to short ones. And modern surgical techniques have made changing a bust line almost as easy as adjusting a hemline.

Feminist writer Susan Faludi offers a more political interpretation. She writes in *Backlash: The Undeclared War Against American Women* that as women achieve greater economic power, the prevailing ideal of female beauty becomes more and more passive and childlike. "The beauty standard converges with the social campaign against wayward women," she writes, "allying itself with 'traditional' morality; porcelain and unblemished exterior becomes proof of a woman's internal purity, obedience, and restraint." To Faludi, a change in the prevailing standard of beauty toward a more girlish look—as happened in the 1960s and again in the 1990s—is a sure sign that, politically, women have become too threatening.

Since before Cleopatra's day, women have been judged by the way they look, and they have struggled mightily to make themselves look the way they want to be judged. To expect this to change as women become more powerful is simply naive. Gloria Steinem—a highly accomplished author and publisher, a noted feminist leader and, not incidentally, a very attractive woman—confessed in her recent autobiography to harboring profound self-doubt about the way she looks. If Steinem feels that way, it is hardly surprising that others do too. Perhaps Elizabeth I was onto something after all. Maybe the only way for women to look ahead is to banish all mirrors from the palace.

Reflection and Discussion

1. Place our culture's attitude toward beauty in Henig's historical perspective. In what ways are Americans more focused on appearance than people in the countries she mentions? In what ways less?
2. Henig says that most societies "have wanted their women to be slim," yet much art—from primitive to classical to modern—has celebrated women that are by no means thin. What would explain this apparent difference?

Writing Matters

1. Men are more sensitive to visual clues, so, Henig speculates, women may follow beauty trends out of the biological drive to attract a mate for

reproduction. Evaluate this theory, considering how fashion trends come and go, and that many of these trends may inhibit reproduction.

2. Faludi suggests that fashion trends serve as a sort of counterweight to women's economic strength—when women are more powerful, they are expected to look weaker and more childlike. Explore and assess this theory: How would these fashion trends arise—on a personal level, through a form of unspoken consensus or from a sort of conspiracy? Why would powerful women be so susceptible? What trends does Faludi's theory explain? Where are the gaps?

For You, My Lovely, A Facelift

Natasha Singer, *New York Times*, December 29, 2005

Natasha Singer, a 2002 Woods Hole Ocean Science Journalism Fellow, writes on fashion and style for the New York Times.

How would you feel if someone gave you a gift certificate for a nose job? What would you do?

1   Last year Helena Rasin's grandmother gave her $200 for Christmas. This year her grandmother gave her a new nose. "A nose job is the best Christmas present ever because you'll have it forever," Ms. Rasin, 25, a drug company representative in Los Angeles, said two weeks ago while at home recuperating from her rhinoplasty. "It's not like some sweater you don't like and have to take back to the store. Even with the bandages still on, I can already tell I look cuter."

2   For a denizen of a looks-centric milieu like Los Angeles, Ms. Rasin, who emigrated from Ukraine in 1992, may seem like a plastic surgery late bloomer. Many of her peers had their noses bobbed back in high school and did not get cosmetic procedures this year, Ms. Rasin said. Instead they gave them to family members. "It's kind of in now, it's kind of hip this year to give surgery," Ms. Rasin said.

3   December has always been a busy month for plastic surgeons, whose schedules fill with patients seeking a little streamlining before the holiday party season or in advance of body-baring beach vacations. But this year, rather than going under the knife themselves, an increasing number of people conferred nips and tucks upon their loved ones, doctors say. Children financed $15,000 face-lifts for their parents. Sisters shelled out $500 for each other's Botox treatments. And wives sent husbands to cosmetic dentists for $40,000 sets of porcelain tooth veneers.

But among some doctors and social critics the idea of buying loved 4 ones new and improved body parts raises moral and psychological questions about the consequences of amending someone else's appearance, especially if the gift was not requested. Critics worry that giving friends or relatives permanent body alterations could negatively affect romantic relationships or family dynamics, and some doctors turn away as many as one in three patients out of concern they are being pressured to undergo the procedures. Gift giving may also cause patients to overlook the medical risks involved in cosmetic procedures. "It is an unlikely possibility, but these are presents you could die from," said Virginia L. Blum, the author of *Flesh Wounds: The Culture of Cosmetic Surgery.*

Since the 1970s affluent parents have quietly arranged for their 5 teenage daughters to have nose jobs during the holiday vacation. But overt gifts of plastic surgery between adults were almost unheard of before the advent of television shows like *Extreme Makeover* four years ago. The exact number of people buying cosmetic procedures for others is unknown. But in a survey of about 100 facial surgeons conducted by the American Academy of Facial Plastic and Reconstructive Surgery, 49 percent said they had seen patients in 2004 who received cosmetic surgery as a gift, up from 31 percent in 2001. The practice goes on year round, thanks to birthdays and anniversaries, but seems to peak during the Christmas and Hanukkah season.

"We're seeing more and more women in their 20s and 30s who have 6 loose tummies and hollow breasts as a result of having babies," said Dr. Linda Li, a plastic surgeon in Beverly Hills, CA. "The women want to restore themselves by having surgery, and their husbands are giving it to them." Dr. Li, a regular on the makeover show *Dr. 90210,* said she has about 30 new patients this month who are receiving surgery as a gift. Some have appointments for $7,000 breast augmentations. Others, she said, will have multiple surgeries in a single session: a $23,000 combination of a tummy tuck, liposuction, breast implants and eye lifts, for instance. "The way we view cosmetic surgery has really changed," Dr. Li said. "If you can shop for your own new tummy, new chest and new teeth, you can buy them for someone else too."

Costs
- Botox: $376 per injection
- Tooth-whitening: $600–$1,000
- Dental veneers: $700–$2,500 per tooth
- Liposuction: $1,500–$6,000
- Breast implants: $3,000–$8,000
- Face lift: $5,000–$15,000

But some people wince at the idea that cosmetic treatments might 7 become gifts as sought after as Xbox video game consoles or iPod nanos. As cosmetic enhancement enters the realm of consumer goods, critics say, it becomes part of the competitive sport that is shopping. Keeping up with the Joneses becomes keeping up with their noses. "We have a desperate need to get our flat screen TVs, our updated electronics, our liposuction and our breast implants to keep up with the lives of the rich and famous," said Sean Jablonski, a supervising writer for *Nip/Tuck*, the fictional plastic surgery show that dissects the underbelly of cosmetic culture. A recent episode featured Santa Claus wanting to endow a comely elf named Circe with double-D breast implants. "Plastic surgery is now so accepted and infused in our social landscape that we can broach improving someone else as long as it's wrapped as a gift," Mr. Jablonski said.

8   Many doctors say surgical gift giving reduces medicine to a service industry as accessible as fast food. And that may cause patients to overlook the fact that any invasive operation can have complications, including infection, scarring, brain damage (from anesthesia) and death. "Cosmetic surgery has slipped so far away from the realm of serious medicine that buying it seems as trivial as purchasing a garment or a hairdo," said Dr. Adam Searle, the president of the British Association of Aesthetic Plastic Surgeons.

9   This month he and his colleagues sent out a press release excoriating a British plastic surgery chain called Transform Medical Group for offering gift certificates for everything from lip augmentation to liposuction. Dr. Searle said buying gift certificates for any medical procedure, be it plastic surgery or a hernia operation, is inappropriate. American plastic surgery societies condemn selling gift certificates for procedures, although they condone them for skin care products or doctors' consultations. "A decision to have plastic surgery should be between a patient and a doctor," and not commercialized with gift certificates, said Dr. Mark L. Jewell, a plastic surgeon in Oregon who is the president of the American Society for Aesthetic Plastic Surgery.

10   Television shows like *Extreme Makeover* and *The Swan* may inspire viewers to bestow enhanced body parts upon one another, said Dr. Richard Ellenbogen, a plastic surgeon in Beverly Hills. "The wish-fulfillment format of these television shows has made it comfortable for people to give surgery to each other," he said. "You give the gift to your wife or your girlfriend and she becomes the swan."

11   But just as makeover shows enumerate a person's purported faults before correcting them, a person who offers a cosmetic procedure to a loved one may implicitly criticize the recipient's looks. "All along you've been thinking that your own perky and not so smallish breasts are fine," said Daphne Merkin, an author in New York City whose book *Dreaming of Hitler* contains essays on beauty and identity. "Then someone says, 'Honey, I'm going to improve you by giving you new breasts.' I presume this could lead to a divorce. No one is going to be flattered by such a gift because a judgment is being made about you."

Ms. Blum, an associate professor of English at the University of Kentucky in Louisville, said makeover shows have turned Americans into would-be surgeons who constantly examine one another for signs of aging. "The makeover shows have made us feel safer about insulting each other's body parts because correction seems just around the corner," she said. 12

Some recipients are unenthusiastic about the gift of surgery. Last month a man who wanted to give his girlfriend breast implants took her for a consultation with Dr. Peter B. Fodor, a plastic surgeon in Los Angeles who is the immediate past president of the American Society for Aesthetic Plastic Surgery. Dr. Fodor said he turned the couple away because he could tell by the woman's body language, and by her concern that big implants might cause her breasts to sag, that her boyfriend was trying to coerce her into the procedure by paying for it. "If she gets new breasts she doesn't want just for the boyfriend's sake and then the relationship ends, it will be hell for her in every way," Dr. Fodor said. "If she keeps the implants, they will remind her of him. If she has the implants removed, she will have big scars." He said he turns down about 30 percent of gift surgery patients. "Gifts only work if the patient would have wanted the surgery anyway." 13

Often it is the patient who seeks the gift of a lift. Take Grace Gao Macnow, the 54-year-old owner of Graceful Services Spa in Midtown Manhattan. For several years she had been telling her daughter, Li Huang, that she wanted cosmetic surgery to reduce the wrinkles around her eyes and mouth. This month Ms. Huang spent about $15,000 on a mini face-lift and eyelid lifts for her mother, she said. "If I can make her happy, money is not an issue," said Ms. Huang, who just opened her own spa downtown. "Now my mother is showing off, telling our relatives that her daughter really cares about her because I bought her a face-lift." Dr. Robert C. Silich, the plastic surgeon who performed Ms. Macnow's face-lift this month, said he found it "sweet that the daughter is giving this as a gift." 14

But Ms. Blum said the idea of gift surgeries reminded her of old diamond advertisements that had slogans like "Show her how much you love her." "The idea was the bigger the diamond, the bigger your love," Ms. Blum said. "It was brilliant marketing. Are gift procedures the surgical equivalent?" 15

Reflection and Discussion

1. What's the difference between gift certificates for Botox and those for a facial? Between giving a woman new clothes, different from what she usually wears, and offering her a tummy-tuck?

2. How acceptable is cosmetic surgery among the people you know? Do people proudly point out the work they have done? Do they criticize others for having or not having plastic surgery? How do you feel?

Writing Matters

1. Consider the various makeover shows, from the simple fashion and style changes of *What Not to Wear* and *How Do I Look?* to the other end of the spectrum with *Extreme Makeover* and *I Want a Famous Face.* Under what circumstances are people helping friends by nominating them for these shows? When are they insulting the friend? Have these shows changed the nature of what is acceptable to say about another's appearance?

2. What messages are sent by the various cosmetic surgery gifts mentioned: rhinoplasty, Botox, breast implants, tooth veneers? What about procedures to hide the natural body changes that come from pregnancy? Looking at these gifts, discuss what values are important to the givers, the recipients and our society.

Mirror, Mirror on the Wall . . . Are Muscular Men the Best of All?

Nancy Clark, *American Fitness,* January/February 2004

Nancy Clark, M.S., R.D., offers private nutrition consultations to athletes of all levels in Brookline, MA, and is the author of a number of nutrition books for competitive athletes.

Think of boys you have known personally and the literary characters you have read about. Have all of them been satisfied with the way they looked?

1   Muscle dysmorphia is a new syndrome emerging behind gym doors. You might notice it in your gym's weight room. Some weightlifters pathologically believe their muscles are too small. They have poor body image (i.e., are ashamed of, embarrassed by and unhappy with their bodies) and a passionate desire to not only build muscle, but also avoid gaining fat. This preoccupation with building muscles manifests itself in excessive weightlifting (e.g., spending four or more hours per day at the gym), attention to diet (e.g., consuming protein shakes on a rigid schedule), time spent "body-checking" (e.g., looking in mirrors, CDs, window reflections, etc.), excessively weighing themselves (i.e., 10 to 20 times per day), too little time spent with family and friends and, not uncommonly, anabolic steroid use.

s this overconcern with body size a new obsession? Perhaps. In the few years, we have been increasingly exposed to half-naked, mus- male bodies (e.g., Calvin Klein underwear ads). Evidently, even exposure to these images can affect a man's view of his body. In a ? of the media's effect on male body image, a group of college men ?d advertisements featuring muscular men, while another group ?d neutral advertisements without partially-naked male bodies. ? the men (unaware of the hypothesis being tested) were given a image assessment. Those exposed to the muscular images ?d a significantly greater discrepancy between the body they ide- ?ant to have and their current body size (Leit, Gray and Pope ? Another study suggests up to a third of teenage boys are trying ?n weight to be stronger, fitter, attain a better body image and per-form better in sports (O'Dea and Rawstone 2001).

The irony is while college-age men believe a larger physique is more attractive to the opposite sex, women report desiring a normal-sized body. In a study of men from the United States, Austria and France, the subjects were shown a spectrum of body images and asked to choose:

- the body they felt represented their own
- the body they would ideally like to have
- the body of an average man their age and
- the male body they felt women preferred.

The men chose an ideal male body that was about 28 pounds more muscular than their current bodies. They also reported believing women prefer a male body with 30 pounds more muscle than they currently pos-sessed. Yet, an accompanying study indicated women actually preferred an ordinary male body without added muscle (Pope 2000).

At the 2003 Massachusetts Eating Disorders Association's (MEDA) annual conference, Dr. Roberto Olivardia shared his research on ado-lescent boys' body image. Olivardia is a psychology instructor at Harvard Medical School and co-author of *The Adonis Complex: The Secret Crisis of Male Body Obsession* (Free Press, 2000). The title alludes to Adonis, the Greek god who exemplifies ideal masculine beauty and desire of all women. Olivardia explained that adolescence is a time for exploring "Who am I?" Without a doubt, so much of who a teen is, is defined by his body. Because today's boys have been exposed from day one to GI Joe action figures, Hulk Hogan and Nintendo's Duke Nukem, they have relentlessly received strong messages that muscular bodies are desirable. Those at risk for muscle dysmorphia include adolescent boys who were teased as children about being too fat or short. Individuals at highest risk are those who base their self-esteem solely on their appearance.

6   In our society, muscularity is commonly associated with masculinity. According to Olivardia, compared to ordinary men, muscular men tend to command more respect and are deemed more powerful, threatening and sexually virile. Muscular men perceive others as "backing off" and "taking them seriously." Not surprisingly, men's desire for muscles has manifested itself in a dramatic increase in muscle (and penile) implants.

7   Olivardia expressed concern the "bigger is better" mindset can often lead to anabolic steroid use. He cited statistics from a study with 3,400 high school male seniors: 6.6 percent reported having used steroids; more than two-thirds of that group started before age 16 (Buckley et al. 1988). Olivardia regrets males commonly use steroids in secrecy and shame. "Men will tell someone they use cocaine before they admit to using 'juice.'" This commonly keeps them from seeking help.

"Daddy doesn't have a job. Daddy goes to the gym."

FIGURE 8.3 When does personal fitness become an obsession?

Steroids carry with them serious medical concerns: breast enlarge-   8
ment, impotence, acne, mood swings, risk of heart disease, prostate
cancer, liver damage and AIDS (from sharing needles)—not to mention
sudden death, although it may occur 20 years from current use. "Roid
rage," the fierce temper that contributes to brutal murders and violence
against women, is an immediate danger.

What's the solution? According to Olivardia, young men need edu-   9
cation about realistic body size to correct the distorted thought "if some
muscle is good, then more must be better." They might also need treatment for obsessive-compulsive disorder. Sadly, most men believe they
are the only ones with this problem and, thereby, take a long time to
admit needing therapy. When they do, too few programs exist to help
them explore the function this obsession serves in their lives—a sense
of control. They mistakenly believe control over their bodies equates to
control over their lives.

References

Buckley, W.E., et al. "Estimated prevalence of anabolic steroid use in high
   school seniors." *JAMA, 260* (1988):3441–5.

Leit, R.A., Gray, J.J. and Pope, H.G. "The media's representation of the ideal
   male body: A cause for muscle dysmorphia?" *International Journal of Eating
   Disorders, 31* (April 2002):334–8.

O'Dea, J.A. and Rawstone, P. "Male adolescents identify their weight gain
   practices, reasons for desired weight gain, and source of weight gain
   information." *Journal of American Dietetic Association, 101*, no. 1 (January
   2001):105–7.

Pope, H.J., et al. "Body image perception among men in three countries."
   American Journal of Psychiatry, 157 (August 2000):1297–301.

Reflection and Discussion

1. Clark cites studies which show that college-aged men want to be more
   muscular to attract women, yet women prefer less muscular, more normal
   men. What could explain this discrepancy?

2. In the past, males usually did a fair amount of physical labor which built
   their muscles naturally, but now many do little more than carry a heavy
   backpack. How much of the bodybuilding trend can be attributed to the
   need to exercise to counteract our sedentary lifestyle?

Writing Matters

1. Many boys have been influenced by sports stars, applying their youthful
   single-mindedness to activities that brought them closer to their idols.

Consider how many boys have spent weeks breaking in baseball gloves, days and nights practicing free throws, living, breathing and eating nothing but their sport. In what ways is the bodybuilding trend just more of the same? In what ways is it different? At what point does this focus become a harmful obsession and what, if anything, should be done about it?

2. Obsessive body building is a relatively recent problem which Clark says gives young men a sense of control over their lives. Evaluate this premise to see if it explains this phenomenon. What has changed in our society? What makes these men feel they lack control? How did people get a sense of control in the past?

"Thinspiration": Online Websites Promote Eating Disorders

Alana Semuels, *Pittsburgh Post-Gazette*, June 22, 2005

Alana Semuels reports on health issues.

How thin is too thin?

1   Pictures of sickly thin models and tips about how to hide her anorexia greeted Shannon Bonnette every time she surfed the Web five years ago. Bonnette visited the sites out of curiosity more than anything else—after 15 years with an eating disorder, she didn't need any tips. But the girls on the sites were a community of sorts; they were all going through a similar illness, and all felt misunderstood. Bonnette, who is from Erie and now lives in Conneaut, Ohio, even started her own Web site, where she kept a journal of her experiences dealing with anorexia. She would get e-mails from people who supported her honesty in talking about her site, even though it was difficult to read.

2   Bonnette, who now runs a Web site to support people recovering from eating disorders, has been on both sides of a controversy that has been building over the past few years with the growth of "pro-ana" and "pro-mia" Web sites that promote, respectively, anorexia and bulimia, and of Web sites that are geared towards recovery. On one side are doctors who worry that these sites might trigger eating disorders in young people on the brink of the disease, or worsen the medical state of people who already have eating disorders. On the other are the sites' organizers, who argue that they provide a community for all those who feel isolated by their illness, and that warnings on their sites are meant to dissuade anyone who cannot handle their content. That's part of the problem with these sites: doctors think they may

perpetuate the illness, while visitors don't see their problem as an illness at all.

Anorexia as a Lifestyle?

"The very core of the belief that backs these sites is that eating disorders are a lifestyle choice and not an illness," said Dr. Rebecka Peebles, an instructor in adolescent medicine at Lucille Packard Children's Hospital in Palo Alto, CA. A disclaimer on one popular site reads: "This is a pro-ana Web site. That means this is a place where anorexia is regarded as a lifestyle and a choice, not an illness or disorder. There are no victims here."

As a doctor who looks at the medical complications of anorexia, Peebles does not agree with this assessment. She's done some preliminary studies of the effects of these Web sites and suggests that they can be detrimental to the health of those who visit them. Peebles and medical student Jenny Wilson surveyed 64 patients who had been seen for treatment of eating disorders and 91 parents of such patients. Although they acknowledge that the sample size is small, they found that almost 40 percent of the patients had visited pro-eating disorder Web sites, and 38 percent had visited pro-recovery sites.

Who Carefully Studies the Shapes of Models?

- Forty-three percent of women who are extremely dissatisfied with their own bodies
- Seventeen percent of women who are extremely satisfied with their own bodies
- Nineteen percent of all men surveyed

Source: "The 1997 Body Image Survey," *Psychology Today,* February 1997

People who used the sites had more hospitalizations because of their eating disorder, and were spending less time on schoolwork than patients who did not visit the sites. Over 60 percent of the patients who visited the pro-ana sites had learned weight loss techniques from the sites, and more than 30 percent of patients had learned similar techniques from postings made by other patients on the pro-recovery sites. Peebles also thinks that these sites might attract teens in particular, because many pro-eating disorder sites feature disclaimers warning the "weak-hearted" not to enter—a red flag of sorts that something is off-limits, and therefore, worth checking out.

The Problem of Support

But while the sites might affect some people negatively, Shannon Bonnette says they provided her with a valuable avenue of support. Anorexia was a part of her identity that isolated her from others. "I just figured it was the way I was going to die," she said. Her parents had taken her to the Cleveland Clinic for treatment, and she saw a counselor on her college campus, but she didn't think that the doctors she talked to knew anything about eating disorders.

7   Even during the worst times of her illness, the ability to put her experiences on the Web were valuable. She says her postings were more real and gritty than what she read in the recovery community, where everything was focused on the positive. "Therapists and doctors who think that they know it all, they don't know it all," she said. Because of the Web sites, "people going through it feel a whole lot less lost."

8   It's true that these Web sites can provide a community of sorts, and a place for people to share their experiences of going through a difficult disorder, said Stanford's Peebles. Eating disorders in general are isolating, she said, and often people who are ill are restricted from physical activities or school, and if they're in treatment, they spend more time at home, and inevitably, on the computer. Peebles even has patients who cannot or will not express their feelings in person, but will refer her to their pro-ana Web sites where they write about what they've been up to. "I'd like people to discuss their feelings openly," she said, "but it's a fuzzy line. It's difficult."

9   Some of her patients epitomize this line—they are proud of being "pro-ana" and of their Web sites, but when she asks them if they would want their mothers or sisters going on the sites, they respond with an emphatic "no."

Wanting to Get Well

10 Whether they provide support or worsen the medical conditions of people with eating disorders, the sites affect people in vastly different ways. Depending on whether a person is anorexic, or recovering, or on the brink of developing the disease, the sites could be a source of help, or the trigger that plunges her into a deadly disease. But since they're on the Internet, there's no way to cater them specifically to a certain group of people, no matter how much the disclaimers on the sites might try.

11   While there are Web sites out there that promote eating disorders, and those that encourage the road to recovery, people with eating disorders will often go to the ones that support their illness because some, by definition, have mixed feelings about getting better. "One of the diagnostic criteria for the illness is denial of the seriousness of the illness," said Marsha Marcus, a psychiatry professor at the University of Pittsburgh School of Medicine. "By definition they are made anxious about thinking of relinquishing the illness."

Do We Really Need Skinny Models?

A study of 800 university students found that women who are dissatisfied with their own bodies get depressed after seeing the unrealistically thin models who are so often used in advertising, but normal-sized attractive models are just as effective in selling products and do not trigger depression.

Source: "Research Backs 'Normal Size' Models in Ads," *Life Style Extra*, August 31, 2005

The sites might trigger eating disorders in vulnerable individuals, 12 she said. While she doesn't think that Web sites can cause or cure a serious disorder, Marcus knows that eating disorders stem from a complex combination of forces. In some ways, the support they might provide is countered by the way they encourage people to stay thin or maintain an eating disorder. Some sites, such as Bonnette's, try to provide the support network without the negative aspects of some sites.

Strangely, it was a pro-ana Web site that helped her recover; after 13 reading the complaints and journals of girls who just wanted to lose a few more pounds, to get below 100 or 96 or 94, she just got sick of it all. She began to realize that the postings never changed, and that no one ever got any better. With this thought, she started to give healthy eating a try.

But Bonnette's case is by no means a common means of recovery 14 from eating disorders. She was lucky—she is 26 now and gave birth to a baby this spring. Her site now straddles a fine line—it isn't pro-ana, nor does it constantly urge people to recover, she said. It doesn't contain the pictures of thin models or the diet tips present on some sites, but it provides links to some of those sites, as well as sites that help people through recovery. While her site has been criticized as being pro-ana, she thinks it is an invaluable source of information for people with eating disorders and those who want to discover. It's not like some of the negative sites that are over-the-top, she says. "There's definitely a line," she said. "As with everything, there's a good and a bad."

Reflection and Discussion

1. Anorexia nervosa can lead to severe physical illness and even death and is often connected to other serious psychological problems ranging from depression to sexual abuse. On the other hand, some pro-ana websites give clear evidence that their owners are not true anorexics; for example, the owners list lifetime low weights that are normal or even heavy. Who should determine what is a lifestyle choice and what is a disease?

2. Many parents, even parents of anorexics, are unaware of their children's Internet activity. What can and should parents do, if anything, to protect their children online?

Writing Matters

1. On the Internet, look at some pro-ana websites, looking in particular at the photos they use for "thinspiration." How different are these images from those that you see every day in broadcast and print media? Do you find these images attractive? Do they inspire you to lose weight? Discuss how prior knowledge and emotions affect our interpretations.
2. Many web-hosting services have contracts that allow them to shut down sites that they deem harmful, so Yahoo! and MSN, for example, no longer allow pro-ana sites. Yet Bonnette and others have found support from this web community, and anorexics pick up tricks even from recovery sites. Should pro-ana websites be banned? If so, should the recovery sites also be stopped?

The Ugliness Problem

Dan Seligman, *Forbes*, August 15, 2005

Dan Seligman is a columnist for Forbes.

If you get on a bus, would you prefer to take a seat next to an ugly person or an attractive one?

1 A sizeable and growing body of literature attests to the fact that homely people confront disadvantages not only in the competition for spouses but in many other areas of life. They have lower incomes than handsome types. When accused of crime, they tend to be dealt with more harshly by judges and juries. One recent report, sorrowfully dwelt upon by *New York Times* columnist Maureen Dowd, concludes that less attractive children are discriminated against by their own parents. (Parents are alleged to be less mindful of the safety of unattractive tots.)

2 In most academic venues and popular media the reaction has been to emphasize the irrational thinking that underlies discrimination against the ugly. The alternative perspective, about to be advanced on this page, questions whether the discrimination really is so irrational.

3 The classic article about the economic effects of physical appearance, published in the December 1994 *American Economic Review*, was written by Daniel S. Hamermesh (University of Texas, Austin) and Jeff

E. Biddle (Michigan State). It relies on three studies (two American, one Canadian) in which interviewers visited people's homes, asked the occupants a lot of questions about their education, training and job histories, and discreetly (one hopes) rated each man or woman on physical attractiveness. The ratings were on a scale of one (best) to five (worst). In the larger of the two American samples 15% of interviewees were rated "quite plain" or "homely"—categories four and five.

Hamermesh and Biddle found that men in the top two categories 4 enjoyed incomes 5% above those of men rated merely average in appearance. The unfortunate fellows in the two bottom categories were paid 9% below the average. The results for women workers were somewhat similar, except that the workplace effects were smaller. The study controlled for differences in education, experience and several other factors affecting pay but did not measure (and thus did not adjust for) intelligence. Hamermesh and Biddle agree that it's rational to pay more for good looks in some occupations, e.g., salesperson, but deny that this explains much of the pay gap. They leave you thinking that the basic dynamic is pure employer discrimination—a simple preference for good-looking people.

Their paper says nothing about the policy implications of this per- 5 spective, but in a recent conversation with Hamermesh I discovered that he is sympathetic to ugly people who want laws to bar the discrimination.

But is it entirely irrational to view ugly people as generally less 6 competent than beautiful people? It is hard to accept that employers in a competitive economy would irrationally persist in paying a premium for beauty—while somehow never noticing that all those lookers were in fact no more intelligent and reliable than the ugly characters being turned down. In the standard economic model of discrimination put forward years ago by Gary Becker of the University of Chicago, employers who discriminate irrationally get punished by the market, i.e., by competitors able to hire competence at lower rates.

The mating practices of human beings offer a reason for thinking 7 beauty and intelligence might come in the same package. The logic of this covariance was explained to me years ago by a Harvard psychologist who had been reading a history of the Rothschild family. His mischievous but astute observation: The family founders, in 18th-century Frankfurt, were supremely ugly, but several generations later, after successive marriages to supremely beautiful women, the men in the family were indistinguishable from movie stars. The Rothschild effect, as you could call it, is well established in sociology research: Men everywhere want to marry beautiful women, and women everywhere want socially dominant (i.e., intelligent) husbands. When competent men marry pretty women, the couple tends to have children above average in both competence and looks. Covariance is everywhere. At the other end of the scale, too, there is a connection between looks and smarts. According to Erdal Tekin, a research fellow at the National Bureau of Economic Research, low attractiveness ratings predict lower test scores and a greater likelihood of criminal activity.

8   Antidiscrimination laws being what they are, it is sometimes difficult for an employer to give intelligence tests or even to ascertain criminal histories. So maybe the managers who subconsciously award a few extra points to the handsome applicants are rational. Or at least not quite as stupid as they look.

Reflection and Discussion

1. Look at the way the article is structured. Where does Seligman give his own position? How does he prepare the reader to be open to his point of view?
2. Daniel S. Hamermesh and Jeff E. Biddle found only 15% of the people interviewed were "quite plain" or "homely." What kinds of things would you include to define these terms? Does this number seem high or low to you?

Writing Matters

1. Consider Seligman's evidence. If more attractive people are smarter and uglier people are more criminal, why would it be wrong to use physical attractiveness as a criterion for any job?
2. The "Rothschild effect" refers to the history of one of the wealthiest families in the history of the world, yet Seligman equates the gradual beautification of this family as the result of competent men marrying pretty women. In what other ways might the Rothschild fortunes have affected this?

MAKING CONNECTIONS

1. Which of the articles on body image and advertising influenced you the most? Why? How might advertising executives respond to some of the more controversial claims made in these articles? Discuss how you personally have been affected by the physical perfection of people in the media. Explain how you were influenced when you were younger as opposed to how you feel now.
2. Compare the different ways men and women see their bodies. What signs indicate that men can no longer get along without paying attention to the way they look? Is age at work here? Refer to specific influences in the media and popular culture which are changing how men view their bodies.

3. Investigate the prevalence of perfection in the media. Review several similar works (e.g., three fitness magazines or three makeover television shows) geared toward people of your age and gender that include health and nutrition advice. Make a tally of all the images presented, in advertising as well as in the magazine articles or actual television shows. How many are perfect or almost perfect men or women? How many seem to be average-looking? Ugly? What percent are fat or short? Analyze their editorial content on health and nutrition. How consistent are the content and the images? Report on the messages you find in your media sample, analyzing your findings in light of the issues raised in this chapter.

4. Pick a style trend of any kind and interpret its political and social implications. You may look at fashion, makeup, body sculpting, plastic surgery—any change to appearance that has been popularized. Has it arisen from the street or was it dreamt up by merchandisers and promulgated by the media? Does this trend affect both genders equally? Has it become common across socioeconomic and cultural classes or is it confined to a limited group? What does the trend say about the influence of the individuals who have adopted it?

5. In *Manhood in America,* sociologist Michael Kimmel sees both the obsession with bodybuilding and the problem of obesity as symptoms of our inability to balance our lives. Evaluate this thesis as an explanation for many of the trends discussed in this chapter, artificial means to obtain artificial looks. What would need to change to achieve both balance and acceptance?

TAKING ACTION

Many organizations have garnered attention for their causes by issuing awards that wrap their message in memorable prose, touting their heroes, castigating their villains. For years, the Center for the Study of Science in the Public Interest (www.cspinet.org) issued annual "Harlan Page Hubbard Lemon Awards" for "misleading, unfair and irresponsible" advertising. Improbable Research (www.improb.com/ig/), in association with a number of student organizations, grants Ig Nobel Awards for scientific achievements that "cannot or should not be reproduced."

Which issue or issues raised in this chapter concern you most—the impossible body images promoted in the media, anorexia, bigorexia, plastic surgery, preference for attractive people? Or do you believe that people are making too much of a natural desire to look as good as we can?

Create your own awards, targeting either good or bad examples or a combination of both, coming up with at least five categories. Give your organization a name—political action groups often start with just one or two people naming themselves, designing letterhead so they can send official-looking correspondence. If possible, create a website announcing these awards, giving you the ability to include links and artwork illustrating the work you are recognizing.

Write a press release announcing your awards to send to at least five publications. Press releases are written in a journalistic style, in a specific format:

1. Start with the heading: FOR IMMEDIATE RELEASE
2. Follow with the heading "Contact Information:" where you give the name of your organization, your name, mail address, email address and telephone number.
3. Write a short (no more than 10 words), catchy, informative title.
4. Make sure the first paragraph tells who, what, where, when, why and how.
5. Write the rest of the body with the most important information first. (Journalists call this the inverted pyramid.)
6. End with background information about your organization, with a reference for further information (perhaps a website).
7. Make the last line ###, indicating the end of the release.

Like schoolwork, press releases are double-spaced, printed in black on white paper and carefully proofread.

Chapter 9

Dirty Secrets—What We Don't Know and Why

We live in an age which previous generations could not have imagined, an age in which the answers to countless questions are only a click away. But with all this new information come new challenges—not only about how to sort through the data, but how to evaluate it and know what to trust. For example, we can applaud reporters, editorialists and bloggers for bringing situations to light and still have nagging questions about objectivity or intent. Mistrust grows when people learn that they have been misled, yet if we automatically suspect all government representatives, all advertisers, all authorities, how do we negotiate the hundreds of daily decisions that make up our lives? Is living with a sense of "healthy skepticism" our best bet?

BEFORE YOU READ

Where do you get your news? How about health and product information? How much confidence do you have in the sources that provide this information? What is your confidence (or lack of it) based on? To what extent do you trust the government to tell you the truth? What about businesses?

FIGURE 9.1 How open should a democracy be?

Whitewash at Ground Zero

Carl Pope, *Sierra Magazine,* January/February 2004

In 1992, Carl Pope was named Executive Director of the Sierra Club, the most prominent environmental organization in the United States.

What health dangers would you associate with the collapse and cleanup of the World Trade Center towers in New York?

1   Why would our government lie to us about something this big? Immediately after the collapse of the World Trade Center, scientists at the EPA gathered as much data as they could on the health risks caused by the fires and airborne debris. Based on that research, the agency quickly drafted a press release warning of high asbestos levels in lower Manhattan, and of risks to "sensitive populations" such as the elderly and asthmatics. The EPA also intended to caution property owners that

their homes and businesses would need professional cleanup to remove asbestos, heavy metals, and other contaminants.

But when the EPA ran its press release by the White House, it was rejected for fear it would hamper the "return to normalcy." Even while Bush expressed compassion for the victims and support for the rescue workers and residents of lower Manhattan, including a dramatic visit to Ground Zero, his White House spin doctors took their blue pencils to the agency's announcement. Rather than the EPA, the White House–controlled National Security Council was put in charge of the final release, with the rationale that it had expertise in weapons of mass destruction.

"Our tests show that it is safe for New Yorkers to go back to work in New York's financial district," announced the rewritten statement, released on September 16. The reference to sensitive populations was deleted. The asbestos warning was replaced with an assurance that "ambient air quality meets OSHA [Occupational Safety and Health Administration] standards and consequently is not a cause for public concern." OSHA standards, however, assume limited hours in a workplace, as well as appropriate protective equipment. The need for professional contractors to clean homes and offices was watered down to a general recommendation that people should follow instructions from city officials.

Two years later, in August 2003, the EPA's Office of Inspector General concluded that the findings had been manipulated: "Competing considerations, such as national security concerns and the desire to reopen Wall Street . . . played a role in EPA's air quality statements." (Another "competing interest," apparently, was the desire to downplay New York's need for federal help and to protect the president's cherished tax cuts. When New York officials complained that promised federal aid was slow in coming, White House budget director Mitch Daniels accused them of playing "money-grubbing games.")

The inspector general's report came too late for thousands of people like Pat Moore, who cleaned up the three feet of dust and debris in her apartment herself because "no one told us about the possible risks." It was too late for the Ground Zero workers, 78 percent of whom, according to Mount Sinai Hospital, suffered from lung ailments. A private testing firm found asbestos levels of 850,000 fibers per square centimeter in the Woolworth Building, just across from city hall—more than eight times the level considered to be "high." Other tests found heavy asbestos loads in a stairwell used by employees of the Securities and Exchange Commission. Robert Gulack, senior counsel for the SEC, who developed bronchitis after the attack, charged that the stairwell had been recontaminated by the failure to clean the exterior of the building. "They rushed us back into contaminated playgrounds and schools and places of business," Gulack said. "They took it upon themselves to decide what we would be told, and what might be too upsetting for us to know." And when New York City firefighters asked to have their stations tested for toxic contamination, the administration refused.

6   The EPA responded to the furor over the inspector general's report in the same way the Bush administration responds to all criticism: by refusing to admit that anything had ever gone awry. Even in retirement, former EPA administrator Christie Whitman continued to be a good soldier for the administration that had routinely ignored her and overridden her agency's scientists. She blamed the rescue workers themselves for their failure to wear protective equipment: "If they had worn the devices," she told the *New York Post*, "we'd see a lot less problems."

7   "When she said that everything was OK, the firefighters believed those statements," shot back Steve Cassidy, the head of the firefighters' union. "For her to say now that we are responsible is outrageous."

8   In his confirmation hearings to succeed Whitman as EPA administrator, Utah governor Mike Leavitt (R) was questioned about the scandal. Would the Bush administration provide funding to complete the cleanup of lower Manhattan? Would it provide long-term health monitoring and care for those who had been exposed to toxic pollutants because they had relied on the EPA's doctored public statements? Leavitt's nonresponsive answers led several senators to put his nomination on hold while they awaited an explanation of why the federal government deliberately misled those on the front line of the first battle in the war against terrorism. It never came.

9   If the EPA and the White House are willing to lie about something as visible, and emotionally uniting, as Ground Zero, how can we trust what they tell us about pollution in our own neighborhoods?

Reflection and Discussion

1. Pope begins by accusing the American government of lying. What was your first response to this claim?
2. How important was it for New Yorkers and all Americans to resume their daily lives after September 11, 2001? What could have happened if the original report by the Environmental Protection Agency had been released?

Writing Matters

1. Pope claims that the Bush administration manipulated information about air quality at Ground Zero. The supposed purpose was to avoid widespread panic, but a thorough cleanup of toxins would have cost billions. In this

situation, what was more important—people's health or money? What could have resulted if, for example, the New York Stock Exchange had been forced to close or relocate? What about commerce and travel in and out of New York? Ultimately, what decisions would you have made and why?

2. The end of the article suggests a significant breach of trust on the part of the government. In what ways has reading "Whitewash at Ground Zero" changed your ideas about the government's concern for your well-being? How much confidence do you have that community, state or federal officials are consistently telling the truth? What dangers, if any, do you see in being too skeptical? What recommendations do you have for Americans concerned about their health and safety?

They Die Piece by Piece

Joby Warrick, *Washington Post*, April 10, 2001

Joby Warrick, a reporter for the News & Observer, *won a Pulitzer Prize in 1996 for reporting on the environmental and health hazards of the hog industry in North Carolina.*

How much do you think about where your food comes from?

It takes 25 minutes to turn a live steer into steak at the modern slaughterhouse where Ramon Moreno works. For 20 years, his post was "second-legger," a job that entails cutting hocks off carcasses as they whirl past at a rate of 309 an hour. The cattle were supposed to be dead before they got to Moreno. But too often they weren't. "They blink. They make noises," he said softly. "The head moves, the eyes are wide and looking around." Still Moreno would cut. On bad days, he says, dozens of animals reached his station clearly alive and conscious. Some would survive as far as the tail cutter, the belly ripper, the hide puller. "They die," said Moreno, "piece by piece."

Under a 23-year-old federal law, slaughtered cattle and hogs first must be "stunned"—rendered insensible to pain—with a blow to the head or an electric shock. But at overtaxed plants, the law is sometimes broken, with cruel consequences for animals as well as workers. Enforcement records, interviews, videos and worker affidavits describe repeated violations of the Humane Slaughter Act at dozens of slaughterhouses, ranging from the smallest, custom butcheries to modern, automated establishments such as the sprawling IBP Inc. plant here where Moreno works. "In plants all over the United States, this happens on a daily basis," said Lester Friedlander, a veterinarian and formerly chief government inspector at a Pennsylvania hamburger plant.

"I've seen it happen. And I've talked to other veterinarians. They feel it's out of control."

3   The US Department of Agriculture oversees the treatment of animals in meat plants, but enforcement of the law varies dramatically. While a few plants have been forced to halt production for a few hours because of alleged animal cruelty, such sanctions are rare. For example, the government took no action against a Texas beef company that was cited 22 times in 1998 for violations that included chopping hooves off live cattle. In another case, agency supervisors failed to take action on multiple complaints of animal cruelty at a Florida beef plant and fired an animal health technician for reporting the problems to the Humane Society. The dismissal letter sent to the technician, Tim Walker, said his disclosure had "irreparably damaged" the agency's relations with the packing plant. "I complained to everyone—I said, 'Lookit, they're skinning live cows in there,'" Walker said. "Always it was the same answer: 'We know it's true. But there's nothing we can do about it.'"

4   In the past three years, a new meat inspection system that shifted responsibility to industry has made it harder to catch and report cruelty problems, some federal inspectors say. Under the new system, implemented in 1998, the agency no longer tracks the number of humane-slaughter violations its inspectors find each year. Some inspectors are so frustrated they're asking outsiders for help: The inspectors' union last spring urged Washington state authorities to crack down on alleged animal abuse at the IBP plant in Pasco. In a statement, IBP said problems described by workers in its Washington state plant "do not accurately represent the way we operate our plants. We take the issue of proper livestock handling very seriously."

5   But the union complained that new government policies and faster production speeds at the plant had "significantly hampered our ability to ensure compliance." Several animal welfare groups joined in the petition. "Privatization of meat inspection has meant a quiet death to the already meager enforcement of the Humane Slaughter Act," said Gail Eisnitz of the Humane Farming Association, a group that advocates better treatment of farm animals. "USDA isn't simply relinquishing its humane-slaughter oversight to the meat industry, but is— without the knowledge and consent of Congress—abandoning this function altogether."

6   The USDA's Food Safety Inspection Service, which is responsible for meat inspection, says it has not relaxed its oversight. In January, the agency ordered a review of 100 slaughterhouses. An FSIS memo reminded its 7,600 inspectors they had an "obligation to ensure compliance" with humane-handling laws. The review comes as pressure grows on both industry and regulators to improve conditions for the

155 million cattle, hogs, horses and sheep slaughtered each year. McDonald's and Burger King have been subject to boycotts by animal rights groups protesting mistreatment of livestock.

As a result, two years ago McDonald's began requiring suppliers 7 to abide by the American Meat Institute's Good Management Practices for Animal Handling and Stunning. The company also began conducting annual audits of meat plants. Last week, Burger King announced it would require suppliers to follow the meat institute's standards. "Burger King Corp. takes the issues of food safety and animal welfare very seriously, and we expect our suppliers to comply," the company said in a statement.

Industry groups acknowledge that sloppy killing has tangible con- 8 sequences for consumers as well as company profits. Fear and pain cause animals to produce hormones that damage meat and cost companies tens of millions of dollars a year in discarded product, according to industry estimates. Industry officials say they also recognize an ethical imperative to treat animals with compassion. Science is blurring the distinction between the mental processes of humans and lower animals—discovering, for example, that even the lowly rat may dream. Americans thus are becoming more sensitive to the suffering of food animals, even as they consume increasing numbers of them. "Handling animals humanely," said American Meat Institute President J. Patrick Boyle, "is just the right thing to do."

Clearly, not all plants have gotten the message. A *Post* computer 9 analysis of government enforcement records found 527 violations of humane-handling regulations from 1996 to 1997, the last years for which complete records were available. The offenses range from overcrowded stockyards to incidents in which live animals were cut, skinned or scalded. Through the Freedom of Information Act, the *Post* obtained enforcement documents from 28 plants that had high numbers of offenses or had drawn penalties for violating humane-handling laws. The *Post* also interviewed dozens of current and former federal meat inspectors and slaughterhouse workers. A reporter reviewed affidavits and secret video recordings made inside two plants. Among the findings:

- One Texas plant, Supreme Beef Packers in Ladonia, had 22 violations in six months. During one inspection, federal officials found nine live cattle dangling from an overhead chain. But managers at the plant, which announced last fall it was ceasing operations, resisted USDA warnings, saying its practices were no different than others in the industry. "Other plants are not subject to such extensive scrutiny of their stunning activities," the plant complained in a 1997 letter to the USDA. . . .

- At an Excel Corp. beef plant in Fort Morgan, CO, production was halted for a day in 1998 after workers allegedly cut off the leg of a live cow whose limbs had become wedged in a piece of machinery. In imposing the sanction, US inspectors cited a string of violations in the previous two years, including the cutting and skinning of live cattle. The company, responding to one such charge, contended that it was normal for animals to blink and arch their backs after being stunned, and such "muscular reaction" can occur up to six hours after death. "None of these reactions indicate the animal is still alive," the company wrote to USDA.
- Hogs, unlike cattle, are dunked in tanks of hot water after they are stunned to soften the hides for skinning. As a result, a botched slaughter condemns some hogs to being scalded and drowned. Secret videotape from an Iowa pork plant shows hogs squealing and kicking as they are being lowered into the water.

10   USDA documents and interviews with inspectors and plant workers attributed many of the problems to poor training, faulty or poorly maintained equipment or excessive production speeds. Those problems were identified five years ago in an industry-wide audit by Temple Grandin, an assistant professor with Colorado State University's animal sciences department and one of the nation's leading experts on slaughter practices. . . .

11   Grandin now conducts annual surveys as a consultant for the American Meat Institute and McDonald's Corp. She maintains that the past four years have brought dramatic improvements—mostly because of pressure from McDonald's, which sends a team of meat industry auditors into dozens of plants each year to observe slaughter practices. Based on the data collected by McDonald's auditors, the portion of beef plants scoring "acceptable" or better climbed to 90 percent in 1999. Some workers and inspectors are skeptical of the McDonald's numbers, and Grandin said the industry's performance dropped slightly last year after auditors stopped giving notice of some inspections. Grandin said high production speeds can trigger problems when people and equipment are pushed beyond their capacity. From a typical kill rate of 50 cattle an hour in the early 1900s, production speeds rose dramatically in the 1980s. They now approach 400 per hour in the newest plants. "It's like the *I Love Lucy* episode in the chocolate factory," she said. "You can speed up a job and speed up a job, and after a while you get to a point where performance doesn't simply decline—it crashes."

12   When that happens, it's not only animals that suffer. Industry trade groups acknowledge that improperly stunned animals contribute to

worker injuries in an industry that already has the nation's highest rate of job-related injuries and illnesses—about 27 percent a year. At some plants, "dead" animals have inflicted so many broken limbs and teeth that workers wear chest pads and hockey masks. "The live cows cause a lot of injuries," said Martin Fuentes, an IBP worker whose arm was kicked and shattered by a dying cow. "The line is never stopped simply because an animal is alive."

A "Brutal" Harvest

At IBP's Pasco complex, the making of the American hamburger starts 13
in a noisy, blood-spattered chamber shielded from view by a stainless steel wall. Here, live cattle emerge from a narrow chute to be dispatched in a process known as "knocking" or "stunning." On most days the chamber is manned by a pair of Mexican immigrants who speak little English and earn about $9 an hour for killing up to 2,050 head per shift.

The tool of choice is the captive-bolt gun, which fires a retractable 14
metal rod into the steer's forehead. An effective stunning requires a precision shot, which workers must deliver hundreds of times daily to balky, frightened animals that frequently weigh 1,000 pounds or more. Within 12 seconds of entering the chamber, the fallen steer is shackled to a moving chain to be bled and butchered by other workers in a fast-moving production line. The hitch, IBP workers say, is that some "stunned" cattle wake up. "If you put a knife into the cow, it's going to make a noise: It says, 'Moo!'" said Moreno, the former second-legger, who began working in the stockyard last year. "They move the head and the eyes and the leg like the cow wants to walk."

After a blow to the head, an unconscious animal may kick or 15
twitch by reflex. But a videotape, made secretly by IBP workers and reviewed by veterinarians for the *Post*, depicts cattle that clearly are alive and conscious after being stunned. Some cattle, dangling by a leg from the plant's overhead chain, twist and arch their backs as though trying to right themselves. Close-ups show blinking reflexes, an unmistakable sign of a conscious brain, according to guidelines approved by the American Meat Institute. The video, parts of which were aired by Seattle television station KING last spring, shows injured cattle being trampled. In one graphic scene, workers give a steer electric shocks by jamming a battery-powered prod into its mouth.

More than 20 workers signed affidavits alleging that the violations 16
shown on tape are commonplace and that supervisors are aware of them. The sworn statements and videos were prepared with help from the Humane Farming Association. Some workers had taken part in a

1999 strike over what they said were excessive plant production speeds. . . .

17   After the video surfaced, IBP increased worker training and installed cameras in the slaughter area. The company also questioned workers and offered a reward for information leading to identification of those responsible for the video. One worker said IBP pressured him to sign a statement denying that he had seen live cattle on the line. "I knew that what I wrote wasn't true," said the worker, who did not want to be identified for fear of losing his job. "Cows still go alive every day. When cows go alive, it's because they don't give me time to kill them."

18   Independent assessments of the workers' claims have been inconclusive. Washington state officials launched a probe in May that included an unannounced plant inspection. The investigators say they were detained outside the facility for an hour while their identities were checked. They saw no acts of animal cruelty once permitted inside. Grandin, the Colorado State professor, also inspected IBP's plant, at the company's request; that inspection was announced. Although she observed no live cattle being butchered, she concluded that the plant's older-style equipment was "overloaded." Grandin reviewed parts of the workers' videotape and said there was no mistaking what she saw. "There were fully alive beef on that rail," Grandin said.

Reflection and Discussion

1. How much more would you be willing to pay for a hamburger or steak in order to assure that the animal it came from was slaughtered humanely?

2. To what extent were you able to identify with the people working in these plants? Under what conditions could you imagine doing similar work?

Writing Matters

1. While Warrick focuses mainly on animal pain and suffering, workers in slaughterhouses are also at risk. Research safety conditions and accident rates in US meat-packing plants and slaughterhouses. How do they compare with figures in other job categories? Propose a plan for making slaughterhouses safer for workers. How will your plan impact company profits? What will be the effects on the price of meat and how can the American public be persuaded to accept your ideas?

2. When animal rights groups organized boycotts of McDonald's and Burger King, the companies responded by more closely auditing the slaughtering practices of their meat suppliers, suggesting that negative publicity is bad for business. Cite an example of negative publicity that

changed your perception of a company or product. What examples come to mind of companies spending large amounts of money to polish or alter their images? How difficult is it for businesses to rebound after their reputations have been tarnished? Provide examples.

Whistleblower or Troublemaker, Bunny Greenhouse Isn't Backing Down

Neely Tucker, *Washington Post*, October 19, 2005

The author is a staff writer for the Washington Post.

Whistleblower laws were created so that employees could expose fraud and wrongdoing in the workplace without losing their jobs. But employees who reveal violations can be punished in other ways. Under what circumstances would you consider being a whistle-blower at work?

Bunny Greenhouse was once the perfect bureaucrat, an insider, the top procurement official at the US Army Corps of Engineers. Then the 61-year-old Greenhouse lost her $137,000-a-year post after questioning the plump contracts awarded to Halliburton in the run-up to the war in Iraq. It has made her easy to love for some, easy to loathe for others, but it has not made her easy to know. In late August, she was demoted, her pay cut and her authority stripped. Her former bosses say it's because of a years-long bout of poor work habits; she and her lawyer say it's payback for her revelations about a politically connected company.

Now Bunnatine Hayes Greenhouse is becoming one of the most unusual things known in the upper echelons of government and industry—a top-shelf bureaucrat who is telling all she knows. For honesty's sake, she says. "It's not a process for the weak-hearted," says Jeffrey Wigand, the former tobacco company executive whose high-profile whistle-blowing inspired the film *The Insider.*

Greenhouse, whose case has also become a media event, unloaded more of her burn-the-house-down allegations on PBS's *Now* last week because, let her tell you, Bunny Greenhouse didn't grow up on the black side of the segregated tracks in Rayville, LA, to run from a fight—even if that includes the vice president of the United States. "[Expletive] yourself!" former Halliburton chief executive and current veep Dick Cheney snapped at a senator last year in an exchange related to Greenhouse's allegations. "If prison inmates don't like the warden

1

2

3

who keeps them from breaking out," Greenhouse says of her stewardship of Corps contracting, "do you replace the warden because the
inmates don't like him?" Ah. Metaphors equating the Corps of
Engineers with prison inmates. Expletives. Vice president. Throw in a
subtext of race, gender and war profits. You see the problem here.

4   In the dazzling eye of memory, she can see the wiry object twisting
there, perhaps in the lazy hours of a Sunday afternoon, when she
pulled it out to admire it once again. It was a bit of metal twisted in the
shape of an eye, a gift from her big sister. It was kept, in a childhood
pun, in a can: an Eye-Can. A reminder of can-do determination . . .

5   "My father always taught me to be strong and have dignity, to not
have to bow down or have anyone run over you," [her brother] once told
a Dallas newspaper, summing up the family creed. So it stands to reason
that Bunny was not only valedictorian of her high school class, not only
a magna cum laude graduate of Southern in three years (with a degree in
math), but she also went on to get three master's degrees over the
years—in business management from the University of Central Texas, in
engineering management from George Washington University and in
national resources strategy from the National Defense University at the
Industrial College of the Armed Forces. She married an Army man, Al
Greenhouse. She taught math and, during the lightning-rod year of local
integration, came back to teach at her hometown high school. She was
the first black teacher the white students had ever seen. . . .

6   She followed Al in his career as an Army procurement official, and
after 16 years as a teacher, entered government service. She started as
a mere GS-5, near the bottom of the scale, specialized in the minutiae
of contracting. She worked insane hours, attended endless job-
improvement seminars, raised three children and climbed the government ladder, working at the Pentagon and for the Army.

7   In 1997, it all came together—Lt. Gen. Joe Ballard hired her as one
of the top civilians in the Corps of Engineers. Her position was the
principal assistant responsible for contracting, or the PARC. She over-
saw the management of billions of dollars. The job elevated her into
the Senior Executive Service, the very top level of the federal government's 1.8-million-employee pyramid. Ballard hired her, he has said,
because she was "one of the most professional people I've ever met."
As the first black director of the Corps, he also wanted her to break up
the "good old boys'" network of informal contracting arrangements at
the Corps, he said, to professionalize the agency.

8   Greenhouse was an instant success. She handled the budgets, conducted workshops, gave speeches, produced a newsletter, developed
proposals for ways to save tens of millions of dollars, work records show.
"There wasn't another SES who could touch me sideways," she says.

Three years running, she was rated near or at the highest level possible in job reviews. Sample job review comments from those years: "Effective, enthusiastic, energetic, tenacious, selfless . . . ensured the epitome of fairness in Corps contracting . . . has ensured professionalism in the acquisition workforce second to none . . . made the tough decisions that reflect the highest degree of entrepreneurial and critical thought."

That should be the end of the story, shouldn't it? Isn't that the way 9 these up-from-poverty things go? In reality, there were fault lines developing in her job that would, during the Iraq war, blow up into national news. Ballard once witnessed a senior Corps attorney yelling at Greenhouse in a staff meeting with such vitriol that Ballard had to clear the room to lecture the man about civility, he wrote in a 2003 affidavit. He wrote in the same document that he had been told that staff officers routinely made racist comments about Greenhouse and that they were greatly resistant to the idea of more minorities working there. After he retired in 2000, he was told that the senior attorney in question had told a director of human resources that the attorney had pledged to fire her, and he used a vulgarity in describing the woman who prided herself on being refined.

It's impossible to survey the full story of what happened in subse- 10 quent years, because most records have not been made public, and the Corps declines all comment on personnel issues. But it is clear, looking at documents requested from and made available by Greenhouse's lawyer, veteran whistleblower attorney Michael Kohn, that her career hit an ugly wall shortly after Ballard left. Whether she failed at the larger aspects of her post or was undermined and removed under false pretenses is up for speculation.

Her new bosses said in an internal hearing that she was "hard- 11 headed." She says she was told that "nobody likes you." She was assigned a deputy who, her superior later acknowledged, had problems dealing with "a female boss." The man eventually left after bitter confrontations with Greenhouse, but the episode led her to file a complaint with the Equal Employment Opportunity Commission alleging race and gender discrimination (a complaint that has never been investigated, Kohn says).

Her annual job reviews went from the best possible to the worst 12 possible. Review panels twice instructed Corps officials to upgrade them, after concluding they were unwarranted. Sample remarks: "Needs to work harder to gain the respect of subordinates in her office . . . Interaction with headquarters staff and field commanders is poor . . . Attempts at counseling have been unproductive." Ballard reviewed those appraisals in retirement. He called them "absurd" in his affidavit. He wrote that the problem was that Greenhouse was insisting that the letter of the law be followed and that when she refused to back down, she was pushed aside. (He did not return five phone calls requesting comment for this article.)

13   Before the war in Iraq even started, Greenhouse and her superiors were quarreling almost daily. With the war looming, the agency wanted to award a no-bid "emergency" contract to Kellogg, Brown and Root (a Halliburton subsidiary) that was originally scheduled to last for two years—and up to five years—to provide a range of services in Iraq. A potential five-year emergency? Worth billions? On a no-bid contract? Greenhouse thought that was absurd. There were other companies who could do the work, she said, and they should be allowed to bid on it. She wrote that the original "emergency" contract should be limited to one year, with no options after that. She says when she got the final contract back, it was unchanged. So she wrote her reservations on it in ink.

14   Her notations became public through a media outlet's Freedom of Information Act request to see government war contracts. Given Halliburton's political connections, the issue eventually blew up into international news last fall, just before the elections. Greenhouse and Kohn gave interviews to national media. The FBI opened an investigation—still ongoing—into alleged price-gouging, overbilling and awarding of sole-source contracts to a politically connected company. Many of those questions still linger, and by no means do they all stem from Greenhouse, but from a range of sources. Greenhouse herself made several allegations of wrongdoing, but one of the most sensational charges, initially seeming to back up her concerns, was a Pentagon audit that found that KBR apparently overbilled the government $61 million for fuel in Iraq. The audit was quelled, however, when the Corps granted KBR a waiver from explaining the apparent discrepancy. The agency said KBR's pricing had been dictated by an Iraqi subcontractor.

15   As the chief contracting officer, Greenhouse was furious. She said her superiors made an end-run around her. They waited until she was out of the office, she said, then hurriedly approved the paperwork in a single day. She was never told about it until it hit the headlines. Halliburton spokeswoman Melissa Norcross wrote in an e-mail response to several questions that Greenhouse's claims of overcharges "are misinformed" and that the company "undertook substantial efforts—including two competitive procurement processes—to ensure that it was paying the lowest possible price." Norcross also noted that a Government Accountability Office report said the initial contract dealing with Iraq was "properly awarded."

The atmosphere in the office was getting worse than unpleasant— 16 the Corps was already trying to demote her—but Greenhouse was just getting a full head of steam. This past summer, when she prepared to testify before the Senate Democratic Policy Committee—the only congressional body that has expressed interest in her charges (though the committee has no oversight power)—Greenhouse's superiors told her it would not be in her "best interests" to do so. She thought about that over the weekend. She thought about the lessons her parents imparted to her, a half-century ago, in another time, another place. Then she testified: "I can unequivocally state that the abuse related to contracts awarded to KBR represents the most blatant and improper contract abuse I have witnessed during the course of my professional career."

It was stunning in its confrontational nature, its moral conviction, its 17 assurance—and, one might observe, in its full-blown career suicide. The Corps kicked her out of her job weeks later. In Greenhouse's dismissal letter, Lt. Gen. Carl A. Strock said her removal was "based on her performance and not in retaliation for any disclosures of alleged improprieties she may have made." She was moved to a lesser post in the civil works division. She says she was "totally" removed from contracting and was banished from the Senior Executive Service. She also says her yearly salary has been cut by $2,000. "They stuck me in a little cubicle down the hall, took my building pass," she said. "It's all about humiliation."

Her dismissal made national news, played out in editorials and 18 news stories as a whistleblower done wrong. "She was aware she was taking considerable risk," says Marty Linsky, author and professor at Harvard University's John F. Kennedy School of Government, who taught Greenhouse in a leadership seminar a few years ago. "She cared a lot about the values she believed in and was prepared to take risks that a lot people would not have." . . .

Alone in the house, Greenhouse sits at the table and considers the 19 fight of her life, and perhaps if she's lost it, or whether she should elevate it to federal court. "I learned very early that everything you did in life you did with every fiber of your being," she says, her voice a mix of pride and fury. "Why would I sit here now and let them tell me that I'm something I'm not? Why would I do that? I'm Bunny Greenhouse first, then I'm in a government position. I will not compromise who I am." In that sentence, in the expansive, quiet house, you hear the echoes of her parents talking to her and her siblings in that sleepy, cotton-picking delta town, a place where the world told you that you were second-rate, second-class, an afterthought of humanity. You wonder how this is all going to end up, here in another place and another time; you wonder if the lessons of youth can always hold sway over the lessons of the world.

Reflection and Discussion

1. How does Tucker show his feelings about Bunny Greenhouse? Point out specific word choices and examples. How has his attitude influenced your impressions of her?
2. What do you think of the way Bunny Greenhouse handled her objections to the Halliburton deal? What alternatives did she have?

Writing Matters

1. Bunny Greenhouse acted according to her rights under laws protecting whistleblowers. Research whistleblowing laws. When were they enacted and for what reasons? Are we better off now than we were before they came into being? Do these laws promote honesty? Do they foster tattle tales? How can they be abused? Cite examples and explain.
2. Despite laws protecting whistleblowers, employees have lost their jobs and suffered serious repercussions after exposing alleged abuses in their work environments. Using Bunny Greenhouse as an example, what factors should an employee weigh when considering a public disagreement with company policy? What are the personal and financial risks? When is "career suicide" worth it?

Weaving Your Community's Master Narrative

Jan Schaffer, excerpted from *The Local News Workbook for Civic Catalyst Newsletter,* Winter 2001

Jan Schaffer spent many years working as a reporter and editor at The Philadelphia Inquirer *where she won a Pulitzer Prize. She is Executive Director of the Pew Center for Civic Journalism, an organization which works closely with journalists and encourages citizens to become active participants in their communities.*

In your community, what important topics rarely get covered by mainstream news sources? Why?

1   Whenever I ask a group of journalists to name a subject that would make their readers squirm—not call to complain, but squirm—they readily nod their head and start volunteering responses: race relations, education, the haves vs. the have-nots, growth and sprawl. Then I ask if they are covering these issues—and how? There is an embarrassed silence. They know there are stories in their communities they are not covering well—and they want to cover them. But, often, they're not

sure how. Sometimes, the topics transcend traditional journalistic conventions. They don't easily fit into standard definitions of what makes "news." And the signposts crop up in so many different areas that no team or beat reporters have clear ownership.

Usually the issues are less about obvious external conflict between 2
two different stakeholders and more about figuring out subtler internal tensions that are manifesting themselves in a wide variety of ways in communities. Less about covering the noise in our communities—and more about covering the silences. Often the uncomfortable silences. These stories—many of us call them master narratives—are far more important to our readers than much of our coverage of incremental daily developments. And an increasing number of newsrooms are pioneering coverage models. The coverage goes by other names as well: franchise issues, common themes, trend stories.

"I prefer to think of such stories as 'evolving narratives,'" says 3
Jeannine Guttman, editor of the Portland (ME) *Press Herald*. Guttman's newspaper has developed narratives about a statewide alcoholism problem in its award-winning, "The Deadliest Drug" and on teenage life in its "On the Verge" coverage. "I understand the concept of a master narrative, but I think those words tend to limit our thinking and ultimately our reporting. The word master sounds like we have it all figured out. And I don't think we do."

Indeed, these narratives are not one-shot stories about a particular 4
trend. Not even a big enterprise or investigative piece. Rather they consist of an ongoing, overarching, all-pervasive narrative thread that underlies daily news developments. Put together, they are a body of work that pieces together and makes sense for readers the forces that are reshaping their world—the demographic, economic, social and cultural realities that would have been hard to imagine only 10 years ago. New demographics in San Francisco or new venture capital in Northern Virginia. An influx of Hispanics in Nebraska or senior citizens in Savannah. Growth and sprawl in Denver. Rural vs. urban tensions in Idaho. Newfound immigrants, failing education systems, rampant alcoholism, destructive domestic violence.

Think about master narrative coverage this way: You could cover 5
venture capitalists. Or you can cover venture capital. If you cover venture capitalists, you follow the money. But if you cover the master narrative of venture capital, you will find yourself following changing social norms, happy-hour hangouts, commercial real estate trends, even new tech language. In Silicon Valley, covering the master narrative of high technology is more than a story of software developers or dot-coms. It is also about the price of that prosperity, as KTVU television producer Roland DeWolk sees it: The loneliness of Indian

computer experts, the saga of the rich and homeless, the "hope disparity" between the haves and have-nots, the unparalleled new stream of
waste created by new riches.

6   "In most communities, there are a few (and only a few) vital underlying issues that will largely determine the community's future," says
Joe Smyth, board chair of Independent Newspapers Inc. and author of
Newsroom Guidelines for Independent Newspapers. "The outcome of those
issues will determine whether the community becomes a better or
worse place to live and work, whether it thrives or declines," he wrote
in a recent challenge to his editors. "Great community newspapers put
a lot of effort into meaningful coverage of those vital issues."

7   Identifying those issues then becomes one of the newsroom's most
important tasks. Newsrooms are using many strategies. At the former
San Francisco Examiner, an urban geographer at San Francisco State
took staff members on tours of the city's changing neighborhoods and
opened their eyes, their minds—and even their stomachs—to major
demographic narrative, a "New City" unfolding in its very backyard.
New people, new neighborhoods, new languages, new foods, new
music, even new sports. And the paper followed that thread through
20 major stories in 1998 alone.

8   At the Columbus (GA) *Ledger-Enquirer*, Editor Mike Burbach
embarked on a "small-r reorganization" by asking his staff: "What is
the master narrative of Columbus?" "It's a fascinating exercise," he
said. "Some people answer the question from 50,000 feet and some
from 5,000 feet, but there are definitely common themes. It's turned
out to be a very useful question. What I tend to find is that they want
to do journalism on the master narratives and they have thought
about it. But they are looking—not for the permission—but for the
mechanisms."

9   When a newsroom confronts hundreds of issues competing for
attention daily, how do we journalists identify and focus on the ones
that will really make a difference in our community? And, then, how
do we stay ahead of the story?

10   Here are some other strategies that newsrooms have used:

11 **Pay attention to micro news developments.** Sometimes, they may
be little more than a series of metro briefs. Maine's series on alcohol
addiction arose from the realization that alcohol was a common factor in a number of stories—car accidents, house fires, abused children, domestic violence—even suicides in the forest. Put together,
they told an overarching story that rang vividly true to readers. In
Savannah, an influx of retirees—often wealthy retirees—not only
changed the dominant age of the community, it also changed

housing patterns, medical care, recreational needs, philanthropic giving—and even politics. Many of these folks now had the time, and money, to run for office.

Listen to your beat reporters. When the St. Paul *Pioneer Press* began to chronicle the "New Face of Minnesota," senior editor Kate Parry noted, "As usual the first symptoms of population change came from the education team. They produced a story on how non-white students outnumbered white students in the Twin Cities public schools. Then they pitched a story on the 70 different foreign languages being spoken in the schools. Agriculture reporters told of turkey processing plants . . . where most of the workforce was Somali refugees." 12

Be counterintuitive. Admit you don't know much about a growing segment of your community. Abandon your preconceived notions, shelve your stereotypes and venture out to report. That's what reporters at the *New York Times* did in chronicling race relations in America. It's also what the *Portland Press Herald* did when editors realized they didn't know much about teen life and their own teen experiences were not that useful. 13

Get interactive. People don't simply want to hear the stories journalists have to tell. They want to tell their own stories as well. Create some space—civic space, cyberspace, op-ed space, news space—to let them do that. The process always generates more reporting opportunities for the newsroom. The *San Francisco Examiner*, for instance, published several "First Person" accounts as part of its "New City" narrative. For "On the Verge," the *Portland Press Herald*'s series on teen life, the paper handed out disposable cameras and asked teens to photograph what was important to them and mail the cameras back. The paper posted several photos online with captions the teens had written themselves. "The cameras helped me connect with the kids, who had great stories to tell," said reporter Barbara Walsh. "I would regularly go online to look at the photos and read the cutlines the teens had written." 14

Ask some different questions. When *The Sun News* in Myrtle Beach began grappling with growth in a "Boom Town," a few years ago, it distributed bright yellow postcards with a half dozen questions, including this one: "What really makes you mad right now?" "Tacky beachwear stores!" responded a significant batch of residents, to the surprise of the newsroom. This was not a subject that usually rises to a journalistic threshold, but nevertheless it was a clue about critical tensions in the community. 15

16 **Snowball some responses.** Start with a short, diverse list of people involved in your community and ask them all the same question, suggests INI's Smyth. "What are the three most critical local issues, the outcomes of which will make a real difference in how nice your community will be in the future?" Then ask what additional information they need on those issues and what other individuals or other communities might offer their expertise. Finally, suggests Smyth, "Go public with the process," and let your readers respond with a feedback coupon.

17 **Visit some "third places."** Stop and chat in these neighborhood gathering spots, places where people share information, and often you will see trends that you might have missed. "And suddenly it's very clear," says Kathy Spurlock, editor of *The News-Star* in Monroe, LA, who began to understand the frustration of neighborhoods that had no banks, no post offices.

18 **Knock down some newsroom walls.** Are new restaurants opening? Get your food writers involved. New businesses? Try your biz reporters. Likewise, if there are new sports or new music or a new arts scene in your community.

19 **Crunch some numbers.** Certainly new Census data will provide lots of new narrative clues. But then don't forget to look behind the numbers. When the *Baltimore Sun* saw that nearly 90 percent of the city's third graders couldn't read, it sought out more than the numbers. In its "Reading by 9" series, reporters delved into just how does a kid learn to read in the first place. All the while, you need to keep building that database of contacts and sources. Then, once you have done all of that, you need to take care to ensure that your narrative doesn't become an outdated myth, a story that is no longer true.

Reflection and Discussion

1. When you think of "news," what kinds of stories come to mind? How interested in them are you?
2. How important are newspapers, locally and nationally? If they were to disappear, who would the winners and losers be?

Writing Matters

1. Many of Schaffer's statements are based on assumptions about journalists, newsrooms and journalism as a profession. What are they? Isolate specific comments she makes and examine the logic behind them. For example,

when she asks, "how do we journalists identify and focus on the [issues] that will really make a difference in our community?" she assumes that critical issues are present in our communities and that journalists can make a difference by addressing them. Continue along these lines and comment on the validity of Schaffer's points using specifics and concrete examples.

2. Apply the concept of the master narrative to your college experience, your campus or your courses. How does the master narrative, as you see it, fit with the published description of your college or university? What about the syllabi of your courses? Where do your teachers fit in? Parents, employers and other authority figures also have definite impressions of what a college education means. What are they? How accurate or important are their opinions of the value of a college diploma?

Best Coverage Money Can Buy

Sharon Beder, *New Internationalist,* July 1999

Sharon Beder wrote Global Spin: The Corporate Assault on Environmentalism.

Who writes the news? What roles do researchers, reporters and editors play?

Press releases were invented by public-relations expert Ivy Lee in the 1 early years of the twentieth century in an effort to control media coverage of railway accidents for his client, Pennsylvania Railway. He decided that if the press was going to report the accidents it would be better to make sure they reported them from the company point of view. The strategy was so successful that by the late 1940s almost half the news was based on press releases from public-relations departments and firms.

Today there is a vast industry of public-relations specialists who 2 feed stories to journalists and set up "pseudo events" such as press conferences and tours, photo opportunities and pre-arranged interviews, all staged to provide reportable events for the media. This "source journalism" has largely replaced investigative reporting for harried journalists looking for easy stories. By initiating the story, PR people are better able to shape the angle it gets told from and determine which people get interviewed. The ultimate pre-packaged news is the video news release. This is sent to TV stations and often aired with little change or indication to the audience that what they are watching is not independent reporting. Most broadcasters, whether in Europe or the US, make use of these releases in putting together the news.

3   PR strategists also take advantage of the journalistic ideal of "balance." Take the case of global warming. Despite the overwhelming scientific consensus supporting the existence of global warming, the media often portray it as a controversial scientific debate. The handful of corporate-funded scientists who oppose this consensus is, in the interests of "balance" so widely quoted in the media that a distorted picture of scientific confusion is being propagated. According to Phil Lesly, author of a PR handbook: "People generally do not favor action on a non-alarming situation when arguments seem to be balanced on both sides and there is a clear doubt. Media organizations are owned by multinational, multi-billion-dollar corporations that are involved in a wide range of businesses. These owners influence the selection, shaping and framing of the news not only to protect their own diverse interests but to attract advertisers. For commercial television and radio stations ads are their life-blood. They do their best to create a media product that suits those advertisers and captures audiences."

4   Television soaps have their origins in advertisements by Procter & Gamble for their soap products. In the 1920s Procter & Gamble boosted soap sales by over 25 percent with a series of newspaper advertisements which featured a family that used Ivory soap and a villain that used colored and scented soaps. Following this success, Procter & Gamble tried radio shows which also featured stories that aimed to sell soap. These stories became known as "soap operas" or "washboard weepers." Today's soaps and television entertainment portray a high-consumption US lifestyle and are shipped out to over 100 countries, making up the bulk of what most local audiences watch.

5   Dioxin, once seen as one of the most toxic substances known to humanity, underwent a major PR facelift in the early 1990s with the help of the print media. The *New York Times* was one of the leading papers to downplay its dangers. One article, headlined "US Officials Say Dangers of Dioxin Were Exaggerated," stated: "Exposure to the chemical, once thought to be much more hazardous than chain-smoking, is now considered by some experts to be no more risky than spending a week sunbathing." Another called for relaxation of "the current strict and costly standards." No mention was made of the fact that the *New York Times* had major interests in four paper mills. At the time, one of these mills was the subject of a Canadian law suit claiming $900 million for polluting three rivers with dioxin.

6   The *Times* articles were reprinted in more than 20 other major US newspapers and the claims that dioxin was no longer dangerous were

repeated by dozens of other media outlets. The comparison with sun-bathing—which *Times* reporter Keith Schneider admitted he thought up himself—was repeated in many media outlets and variously attributed to "top federal scientists." New scientific studies indicating that the danger of dioxin was in fact worse than previously realized were hardly reported. Media coverage continued to suggest that the dangers of dioxin had all been exaggerated by emotional environmentalists.

Environmental reporting emphasizes individual action rather than underlying social forces and issues. A current-affairs TV show may expose Corporation X for spewing toxic waste into the local waterway, but it will seldom look at the way corporations have lobbied to weaken the legislation preventing such dumping; how under-funded regulators allow corporations to monitor their own discharges; or the lack of personal liability for corporate board members who would put profit first and damn the consequences. Journalists who try to expose these deeper societal maladies soon learn that it is the editor who decides which stories get aired or printed and how these are to be cut. Editors represent the owners in the news room. Journalists quickly learn which stories are likely to be run and internalize this message as a form of self-censorship—a helpful lesson in climbing the career ladder.

7

Reflection and Discussion

1. When the same large corporation owns many media sources—TV and radio stations, newspapers and magazines—how can this affect the information the public gets?
2. What can and should journalists do if they find important stories that run contrary to corporate interests?

Writing Matters

1. Beder faults the media for reporting on stories in isolation and for not revealing underlying, systemic problems. How accurate is her assessment? Why do most commercial television sources avoid "hard news"? When they do analysis, how deep do they go and when do they air these programs? Give examples. Where can you find honest, in-depth reporting?
2. A respected and popular TV journalist uncovers an incriminating secret about a business, which also happens to spend a lot of advertising money with the station where she works. The reporter knows several of the people involved and is good friends with her boss who will edit the story. What factors will come into play as she decides what to do with the story? What should her priorities be? How likely is the editor to run the story? In what form?

Secret Service: Against Privacy and Transparency

William J. Stuntz, *The New Republic,* April 17, 2006

William J. Stuntz teaches at Harvard Law School and is a frequent contributor to The New Republic.

Why does the government gather information about individuals? What advantages do individuals gain when they learn about what the government is keeping secret?

1   Politics in the age of information is often about secrets: who has them, who can keep them, who must tell them to whom. Can the NSA listen to my phone conversations? Can the police find out what books I buy or what movies I rent? Can I find out whether they know those things? As that set of questions suggests, secrets tend to pit individuals against the state. . . . Fifty years ago, legally protected privacy barely existed. In most places, police officers searched when, where, and whom they wished, without fear of legal consequence. To a degree that would astonish Americans today, individual lives were as open— as transparent—as the windows in Alfred Hitchcock's 1954 hit movie *Rear Window.* Jimmy Stewart played a photographer who solves a murder while sitting in his apartment nursing a broken leg and spying on the people in the building next door—all of whom live their private lives next to open windows. Only the killer kept the lights out and the blinds drawn. Today, no one would buy the story, because everyone's blinds would be drawn.

2   While individual lives were more transparent, government was much less so. Enlightened opinion favored secrecy, not openness. That is how Joe McCarthy was brought to heel: Dwight Eisenhower created a broad doctrine of executive privilege and used it to shut off McCarthy's information flow. Everyone but right-wing kooks thought Eisenhower got that one right. Robert Caro's book on Lyndon Johnson's Senate years describes '50s floor debates in which senators were actually trying to persuade one another, apparently without fear that the public was listening in—since it wasn't. Those scenes are unimaginable today. Floor debates are televised; anyone can hear them and anything interesting will prompt substantial news coverage. But no one says anything interesting. Funny coincidence, that.

3   Secret government snooping sounds Orwellian. But Orwell guessed wrong about some things. Today, the danger that American

democracy faces is not that rulers will know too much about those they rule, nor that too many decisions will be made without public scrutiny. Another danger looms larger: that effective, active government—government that innovates, that protects people who need protecting, that acts aggressively when action is needed—is dying. Privacy and transparency are the diseases. We need to find a vaccine, and soon. . . .

Conservatives embraced privacy and transparency because they 4 were inherently conservative ideas. The right to keep information private helps those who own the most information, and those who own information tend to own other things as well. Current Fourth Amendment law captures this point depressingly well. The law protects "reasonable"—meaning ordinary—privacy expectations. Poor people live less-than-ordinarily-private lives. The poor tend to live in apartments rather than detached houses, spend more of their lives in public spaces than in private ones (because their homes and workplaces tend to be small and unpleasant), and travel more by bus or subway than by car. By contrast, the lives of the wealthy are lived in spacious houses, offices, and cars. Like a tax code that charges the highest rates to those who make the least money, Fourth Amendment law protects houses more than apartments, private spaces more than public ones, and passengers in cars more than those who ride buses and subways.

Transparency also acts like a tax—a tax on activist government. 5 Anyone who has worked in a large institution understands why. For every good idea about how the institution might run better, employees generate ten bad ones. So the key to producing good ideas is encouraging ideas of all sorts. And the key means of encouragement is secrecy. Transparency, by contrast, is the ultimate status-quo rule: It punishes all suggested deviations from the norm. No wonder pro-business conservatives of the '40s liked it so much.

How did these conservative ideas come to be embraced by the polit- 6 ical left? With respect to transparency, the story is simple. Vietnam and Watergate made the left suspicious of government power generally and executive power in particular. When liberals looked for a way to make Richard Nixon's imperial presidency a little less imperial, they stumbled on weaponry that Taft's Republicans had used against Harry Truman: force the president to disclose as much as possible, as often as possible. It was an odd historical moment, a time when making government smaller and less active seemed a reasonable goal for the left. (A young Jerry Brown, then governor of California, made a name for himself by telling the world that "small is beautiful.") A quarter-century later, the world turned around again, as the right used the same weapon against Bill Clinton. In one sense, it backfired: Voters disliked the Lewinsky investigation and punished Republicans for it. But, while the right lost the battle, it won the war. Today and for the foreseeable future, presidents' personal relationships are open to press and public scrutiny. Which makes it harder for creative, energetic presidents to get things done.

7   Privacy, once the right's favorite right, became the left's friend thanks to the civil rights movement. In a time when J. Edgar Hoover was spying on Martin Luther King Jr. and Southern sheriffs were enforcing America's own version of apartheid, police snooping had a decidedly right-wing cast. When a liberal Supreme Court decided the time had come to rein in out-of-control cops, the justices used the legal tools that seemed best suited for that job: the Fourth Amendment's ban on unreasonable searches and the Fifth Amendment's prohibition of compelled self-incrimination. Constitutional texts designed by rich slaveholders in the late eighteenth century—texts used by rich corporations to protect laissez-faire economics in the late nineteenth century— became, in the late twentieth century, the chief means of protecting black suspects from abusive white cops. There was only one problem: It didn't work.

8   To see why, you need to think like a police chief deciding where to put your officers. For violent felonies and thefts, the decision is easy: Go where the crimes are. Drug crimes are different—there are no immediate victims, no 911 calls. The police must decide where to look for them. And, since drugs are omnipresent, where the police look determines whom they catch.

9   Fourth Amendment law makes it more expensive to look in middle- and upper-class neighborhoods. Upscale drug transactions take place indoors, with individually arranged meetings in different locations. Markets like that are hard for the police to penetrate. Privacy-based search and seizure rules like the Fourth Amendment's probable cause and warrant requirements make the job substantially harder. Open-air drug markets in poor neighborhoods are a piece of cake by comparison. Roll up, do the buy-and-bust, and go back to the station. No need to worry about privacy rules, since everything is out in the open. . . .

10   Transparency makes politics a running argument about decision-making, not about decisions. A few years back, Washington spent more time discussing which lobbyists were in the room when Dick Cheney crafted energy policy than actually debating energy policy. That perfectly captures the politics of transparency: The key questions are always who knew what and when, who was in the loop and who was left out. The merits disappear, drowned in a sea of procedural detail.

11   Nowhere is the focus on government process more destructive than in the work of counterterrorism. Law enforcement is a game of cat and mouse. The government makes its move, criminals respond, government adapts, and the game goes on. Thankfully, most criminals

are not too bright, so the game is easily won. Terrorists are different; the most dangerous ones are smart and well-motivated. Whatever information they have, they will use. There is something deeply crazy about publicly debating what law-enforcement tactics the government should use to catch people who are happily listening to the debate and planning their next moves.

A difficult governance problem lurks in the shadows here. On the 12 one hand, it is clear that free people will not remain so if government officials can do whatever they want—which is why someone, somewhere must place limits on what the government can do. But transparency throws out the baby with the bathwater. We avoid bad government ideas by punishing all ideas, and we tell our enemies exactly how they can best evade our efforts to catch them. There must be a better way. There is. Actually, there are several. The kinds of privacy people value most can be protected without disabling the government from gathering information. And, though transparency is a harder nut to crack, we can have a large measure of government secrecy without disabling key checks on the tendency of rulers to oppress those they rule.

Privacy first. Every year, tens of millions of Americans fill out their 13 tax returns, giving the IRS a tremendous amount of information about their finances. The affront to privacy mostly goes unnoticed. Why? Because anonymity matters more than privacy. Two key propositions follow. First, the more people whose lives the government invades, the better. When targets are few, anonymity disappears. If there were 100 tax forms filed instead of 100 million, the IRS might do more snooping than is healthy. The more phones are tapped, the less freedom is threatened. Second, the initial invasion of privacy isn't the problem; subsequent disclosure is. The true image of privacy intrusion is not some NSA bureaucrat listening in on phone calls, but rather Kenneth Starr's leaky grand jury investigation, which splashed a young woman's social life across America's newspapers and TV screens. That is the nightmare worth protecting against. The best way to stop the nightmare from happening is to limit not what information officials can gather, but what they can do with the information they find. Leaks and press conferences are much bigger risks to privacy than wiretaps and satellite feeds. I have mixed feelings about the Valerie Plame affair, but one aspect of Patrick Fitzgerald's investigation is salutary: It reinforces the idea that government officials are obliged not to trumpet secret information. That idea has more to do with genuine privacy protection than anything in Fourth Amendment law.

Another limit matters still more, and it is one we have lost over the 14 last generation or two. US criminal law once covered fairly serious crimes and not much else. There were, to be sure, busybody laws against minor vices and allegedly deviant sex acts. But, for the most part, the government couldn't send you to prison unless it proved you had done something that you clearly shouldn't have done. Not anymore. American criminal codes have metastasized. That may be why so many people find privacy rights so attractive: Giving the government information seems dangerous, since there are so many ways government can use information to punish ordinary citizens. But this gets causation backward. Legal codes are too broad in part because information is too hard to get. The courts make gathering evidence more difficult, so legislatures give police and prosecutors tougher laws to use against those they investigate—another kind of cat-and-mouse game. Better to end the game and make the following deal: The government can find out what it wants about me, but it can't call the local paper and turn over the juicy parts, and it can't prosecute me unless I've done something that was clearly wrong and harmful. I'd have more freedom under that deal than I enjoy now.

15   Transparency is a tougher problem. How can we restrain agencies like the NSA that make decisions and carry out investigations in secret? Two responses are key. First, require limited disclosure: say, to the key congressional committees and to any courts designed to supervise the relevant process. Second and more importantly, as decision-making procedure becomes less transparent, bottom lines should become more so. Today, the pros and cons of different surveillance plans are debated in the press. But, when the government arrests and prosecutes terrorists, it does so under the table, charging immigration fraud or some other small-potatoes crime and hiding the real reasons for punishment. Consequently, no one knows how many terrorists the government has caught or what has become of them.

16   Sometimes—campaign finance is a good example—transparent procedure is valuable. As the rise and fall of Jack Abramoff illustrates, money often passes invisibly from lobbyists to politicians, with adverse consequences for democracy. Corruption aside, though, voters are generally better at judging bottom lines than at assessing government procedures. Twenty-first-century US law and politics too often make bottom lines invisible, while leaving procedures open to public view. That may explain why our politics are both nastier and less productive than at any time in living memory.

17   Conservatives and liberals should be able to agree on these propositions. Getting privacy and transparency right is the key to making government work better. Conservatives should like that because, at least for now, they run the government. Liberals should want government to function better because they believe in it.

America's greatest triumphs—fighting and winning the Civil War, battling the Great Depression, defeating first fascism and then communism, winning civil rights for African Americans—all happened because government worked. Today, it usually doesn't. The reasons sound surprising, but they would have made sense to Americans of generations past: We have too much privacy, and those who govern us have too little.

Reflection and Discussion

1. Stuntz says that "the more phones are tapped, the less freedom is threatened." Explain his logic by providing the context for this remark. How much do you agree with him?
2. What is your trust or mistrust of the government based on?

Writing Matters

1. Stuntz claims that "the harder it is to tap our phones, the more government officials will seek out alternative means of getting information." Where do you stand on the surveillance of private citizens? What conditions might justify it? How threatened would you be to learn that the government was collecting information about your private activities? What confidence do you have that the government is acting in the best interests of the public when it eavesdrops on people? What protections and privacy safeguards do you feel Americans must maintain?
2. Take one or more of Stuntz's ideas and paint a picture of an America in which the government has vastly expanded its powers of surveillance. Who would be the beneficiaries? Who would suffer? What movies, TV dramas and works of fiction have dealt with government surveillance and what did they have to say about it? Comment on the likelihood of a more prying, more intrusive government succeeding in the US. On what do you base your opinions?

More Dirt

- A continent-sized area of ocean near the Hawaiian Islands—called the central Pacific gyre—has become the world's biggest floating garbage site. Scientists have found that whales, turtles, fish and birds are ingesting the plastic, mistaking it for food. Plastic isn't biodegradable. It deteriorates in sunlight into molecules of plastic that last forever.
  Source: Charles Moore, *Santa Barbara News-Press*, October 27, 2002

- The Radio Frequency Identification tags found in more and more consumer items help businesses locate and inventory goods, but they can also be used by identity thieves and others to collect private consumer information.
  Source: *Consumer Reports*, June 2006

- In 2003, Americans made over 3 million requests of government agencies under the Freedom of Information Act while the federal government made 14 million new documents secret, 60 percent more than in 2001.
  Source: OpenTheGovernment.org, 2004

- Check cashing companies are largely unregulated and may charge over 500 percent interest on a payday loan.
  Source: *The Economist*, June 5, 1999

MAKING CONNECTIONS

1. Research one of the dirty secrets in the chapter or another one you know about, making sure to get your information from reliable sources, confirming evidence of the claims. Why should people know about this secret? What has prevented the public from being more familiar with it? What type of action should people take, guided by this new knowledge?

2. Some argue that Americans don't take full advantage of the freedoms we have, especially freedom of the press. How well-informed are Americans compared to those living somewhere else? Select another country and compare its media freedoms to ours. Do the people living there have the choices we do? Is the information that goes out to the public balanced? Accurate? How might these differences inspire Americans to become more well informed?

3. A variety of awards recognize those who work in print and electronic media, among them the Pulitzer Prizes, Peabody Awards and the Radio-Television News Directors Association and Foundation Awards. Visit their websites and find out more about these organizations, paying special attention to the language they use to describe their prizes and prize winners. Look at the work of some of the prize winners to determine whether the awards are truly justified or just a reflection of popularity or commercial viability. Based on this review, write an essay defining the criteria for excellence in journalism common to all media.

4. News of broken promises, secrecy and lies can be discouraging. At the same time, all is not lost when people can get a view of the truth from those who work to keep us informed. Discuss your method for cultivating a sense of healthy skepticism, balancing a distrust of politicians, businesspeople or journalists with the belief that not everyone is a liar and the practical need for information. How has this personal philosophy developed over time?

5. Look at the website for Project Censored. How would you describe it and who does it seem aimed at? What points of view are being expressed? Read a story that interests you and follow related links or references. How valuable did you find the story and what were your impressions of its accuracy? How biased is the site and the story you focused on? What value, if any, do you find in a site like this?

FIGURE 9.2 Who is responsible for dealing with the dirt?

TAKING ACTION

Whistleblower protections apply primarily to present and former employees of businesses, agencies and organizations. They were designed to protect those who choose to expose waste or wrongdoing but may hesitate because of concerns over job security. In the short history of whistleblowing in the US, some would argue that these laws have fostered honesty and reduced fraud. In other cases, reputations and careers have been ruined; people have gone to jail.

With these considerations in mind, identify a law, rule, policy or regulation which you feel is not being enforced or has been enforced improperly. Then describe the situation carefully in writing. What is supposed to happen? What is actually taking place? What should be done? Show your findings and recommendations to others familiar with the situation for feedback and revision.

When you are satisfied that you have clearly identified the problem and explained what needs to be improved, decide on a course of action. Your findings and suggestions can be in the form of a letter or a detailed complaint.

Section

The Challenge of Change

Pollution, dwindling oil reserves, an exploding prison population are just a few of the issues that confront the nation today. In the face of such concerns, many feel powerless, unable to influence what is happening. As inaction means accepting whatever comes along, for many, conscious action makes more sense. Small movements have transformed even the habits of an entire culture; history teaches that individuals matter, whether defending tradition or changing society.

Chapter 10

Burning Issues—Energy and Cars

In an interdependent world where nations compete fiercely with one another for finite supplies of fuel, energy is a global problem of the highest order. And as America leads the world in per capita energy consumption, the spotlight is often on us: How will we respond to increasing energy demands and diminishing supplies? And what about other impacts—from escalating prices at the pump to changes in climate and weather aggravated by the burning of fossil fuels? Roads choked with automobiles have reopened debates on alternatives to the car at the same time that the cost of moving food across continents has created new markets for buying locally. If responsible environmental choices were once pleasant options for those who could afford them, we are now realizing that we all must think green.

BEFORE YOU READ

Although energy prices keep rising, petroleum products still cost far less in the US than they do in other parts of the world. What do you make of this? How long do you think the disparity will last? As a driver, how much would you be willing to pay for a gallon of gasoline before you explored other means of transportation? Overall, how important is energy conservation to you?

FIGURE 10.1
Stalled in a life of being
stuck in traffic?

America's Great Headache

The Economist, June 4, 2005

First published in the mid-nineteenth century, The Economist *is a British magazine focusing on news and commentary related to business, politics, economics and science. Circulation is approximately 1,000,000 copies per week, half of which are sold in the US.*

How much of an inconvenience is traffic in your life? What remedies should we pursue in order to improve traffic congestion?

What is the price of America's love affair with the car? According to a   1
recent "urban mobility study" from the Texas Transportation Institute, it adds up to $63.1 billion a year (plus another $1.7 billion if the latest petrol prices are included) in wasted time and fuel. Most drivers would add an emotional cost in frayed nerves. After all, who wants to spend

44% of their daily commute—the figure for the regions around Los Angeles and Washington, DC—in a crawl?

2   Most sufferers have no choice. As cities sprawl first into suburbs and then into car-dependent "exurbs," the daily commute becomes an ever more painful fact of life. According to the Census Bureau, Americans spend more than 100 hours a year commuting to work; and the annual delay for the typical rush-hour traveler in metropolitan areas of more than 3 million has grown, since 1982, from 16 hours to 47.

3   What, if anything, can be done about it? For an answer, look at California, home to 23 million licensed drivers and 33 million vehicles, and where "you are what you drive": Arnold Schwarzenegger has gas-guzzling Hummers, while immigrant Mexican gardeners have to make do with decrepit Chevrolet pickups. California's network of suburbs and "edge cities" has become the model for much of the growth around the rest of the country.

4   According to the Texas researchers, the average driver in L.A. spent 93 hours stuck in traffic in 2003. By contrast, a driver in New Orleans spent just 18. Whether it is the ghastly I-405 clogged up around Los Angeles airport, or the I-101 tailback from San Francisco's Bay Bridge, California boasts the worst traffic congestion in the country.

5   Some consider this a cause for celebration. "Long queues at restaurants or theatre box-offices are seen as signs of success," says Brian Taylor, director of the Institute of Transportation Studies at UCLA. He thinks congestion "is an inevitable by-product of vibrant, successful cities." The examples of Paris, London and New York all show he has a point.

6   His view is not shared by most Californians. Surveys consistently show that two-thirds of the residents of Los Angeles County regard traffic congestion as "a big problem." By contrast, only two-fifths cite crime. The non-partisan Legislative Analyst's Office reckons that congestion—defined as freeway traffic moving at less than 35 MPH at peak commuting times—costs Californians some $12.8 million a day in time and fuel in 2002. It also added 530 tons of foul emissions to the air.

7   Hence the search for remedies—each of which comes with its own problems. More public transport? Some of America's train and subway systems have been successful, notably San Francisco's BART. But they cost a fortune. Chi-Hsin Shao, a traffic consultant in San Francisco, reckons even light-rail systems cost at least $20 million a mile, while going underground can cost more than $200 million a mile. The still-puny subway system of Los Angeles has cost $4.5 billion, or some $258 million a mile; the city's light rail system has cost well over $35 million a mile.

Greens hope to get at least some of the long-distance passenger 8
traffic out of cars. But the fiasco of the Acela high-speed train system
between Washington, DC, and Boston is hardly likely to inspire confidence in a long-standing dream to build a 700-mile (1,100 km)
high-speed rail system from San Diego to San Francisco (a proposed
$9 billion bond issue is slated to go before the voters in November
next year).

Public transport works well when there is a central hub—like 9
Manhattan. But the Californian sprawl is "multimodal": it works on
the basis that everybody can go everywhere. Go to the Inland Empire
(the suburban sprawl covered by Riverside and San Bernardino coun-
ties), the fastest-growing bit of the state, and you find people commuting to Los Angeles, to Orange County, to Pasadena, to Ventura or to
any of the burgeoning edge cities within the Inland Empire itself. In
2000, 68% of Californians drove to work by themselves, but the figure
rose to 77% for the new neighborhoods, where half the new houses
were built in the 1990s. When the commute gets too long—40 minutes
is supposedly the cut-off point—people tend to move either their job or
their home.

Driving alone explains why car-pool lanes have a limited appeal. 10
High Occupancy Vehicle (HOV) lanes stretch for a mere 1,112 miles of
California's freeway system—and are often virtually empty. One idea
is Mr. Schwarzenegger's decision, still awaiting federal approval, to let
fuel-efficient hybrid cars use the HOV lanes whether they have passengers or not.

In the end, virtually all the solutions involve making drivers pay. 11
More realistic fuel prices would make a difference: a gallon of petrol
costs around $2.50 in California, compared with $5.90 in Britain. There
are some subsidies for greener fuels, but there is no enthusiasm for a
carbon tax, even though petrol taxes produce in real terms about one
third of the revenue per vehicle mile that they did in 1970.

Road-pricing has been a little more successful. California has a few 12
straightforward toll roads, such as state route 73, north of San Diego.
But most tax-paying drivers fiercely oppose them. An alternative is the
toll lane. High Occupancy Toll (HOT) lanes, such as those on state
route 91 in Orange County, allow single drivers to drive on them for an
extra fee—with the toll collected electronically and varying according
to the level of congestion.

Early criticism of SR-91 was that a HOT lane amounted to a "Lexus 13
lane," favoring the wealthy solo mogul over the blue-collar pick-up-
truck driver. In practice, it has worked out more democratically.
Mr. Taylor says 250,000 drivers have bought the transponders needed

for the electronic billing system, and they use them—rich and poor alike—when speed is important.

14   The paradox, say the skeptics, is that HOT-lanes, like HOV-lanes, may actually increase car use: by freeing up extra capacity on the freeways, they allow more cars to use them. Nonetheless, simply to get at least some people from A to B quickly, it would surely be sensible to make more HOT-lanes available.

15   Another scheme being mooted in San Francisco is to imitate London and impose a congestion charge on drivers who enter the central area of the city. Jake McGoldrick, chairman of the San Francisco County Transportation Authority, calls this "a home run": it would relieve congestion, lessen pollution and provide money for public transport. Unfortunately, there are relatively few other American cities with the public transport systems in place to follow the London example—and voter opposition would be a near-certainty.

Just Stop That

16   In some cases, fighting congestion does not mean Californians coming up with ingenious ways to prevent it, so much as stopping doing things that encourage it. Donald Shoup and Michael Manville, colleagues of Mr. Taylor at UCLA, point to the way that Los Angeles requires both office and residential buildings to provide parking spaces for their tenants. Whereas New York and San Francisco have strict limits on parking in their central business districts, Los Angeles "pursues a diametrically opposing path."

17   Thus, the Louise Davis Hall, home to the San Francisco symphony orchestra, was built without a parking garage; when concerts end, the audience streams out into local bars and restaurants. By contrast, L.A.'s Disney Hall has a six-level, 2,188-space underground garage that cost a hefty $110 million. Disney Hall now has to guarantee at least 128 concerts each winter in order to generate enough parking revenue to service the garage's debt. And, when concerts end, the audience drives away, leaving L.A.'s moribund downtown virtually untouched by their presence.

18   This reflects land-use laws. Under the current rules, for every single job in the central business district of Los Angeles there is 0.52 of a parking space; in San Francisco, there is 0.14 of a parking space for each job; in New York, just 0.06. Last week, a $1.8 billion project to revitalize L.A.'s downtown area around Grand Avenue was unveiled: it envisages offices, a 275-room hotel, up to 2,600 housing units—and as many as 5,500 new parking spaces. Land-use policies help explain why San Francisco County's licensed drivers have a mere 518,405 cars between them, while L.A. County's 5.9 million drivers have 5.9 million.

All true. But the main reason why both Disney Hall and the new 19
Grand Avenue developments have huge parking spaces is simple:
nobody would go there if they didn't. California is a car culture—as is
most of suburban America. Congestion is the inevitable result.
Politicians could reduce that congestion by charging motorists more
for the petrol they guzzle and the roads they use. But it will only be a
change at the margin. Californians have the traffic they deserve.

Reflection and Discussion

1. Consider the expression "you are what you drive." How is your car a
   reflection of your priorities and values? If you don't drive, what kind of car
   would you like and what does this choice say about you?
2. Which of the remedies for traffic congestion make the most sense to you
   and why?

Writing Matters

1. Some cities have imposed or are considering a "congestion charge" on
   drivers who enter downtown areas of cities during peak times. Argue for
   or against this proposal in a large metropolitan area you are familiar with.
   Research the effectiveness and costs of such a plan against other possible
   solutions for reducing traffic.
2. Governments have given breaks to drivers of hybrids, from tax advantages
   to privileges in carpool lanes. Discuss why hybrid owners do or do not
   deserve special treatment. What other incentives should be available to
   drivers of cars that reduce congestion and pollution? On the other side of
   the coin, should drivers of gas guzzlers be punished? If so, how?

The Autonomist Manifesto

John Tierney, *New York Times*, September 26, 2004

John Tierney writes a regular column on the Op-Ed page of the New York Times, *his
subjects ranging from politics and the environment to economics and technology. He
has written numerous articles in publications including* Rolling Stone, Newsweek,
Esquire, Playboy *and* Reader's Digest.

**What makes people love driving? On the other side, why would
someone hate cars?**

Americans still love their own cars, but they're sick of everyone else's.   1
The car is blamed for everything from global warming to the war in

Iraq to the transformation of America into a land of strip malls and soulless subdivisions filled with fat, lonely suburbanites. Al Gore called the automobile a "mortal threat" that is "more deadly than that of any military enemy." Cities across America, with encouragement from Washington, are adopting "smart growth" policies to discourage driving and promote mass transit. Three years ago, at a ribbon-cutting ceremony for a new freeway just outside Los Angeles, Gov. Gray Davis declared that it would be the last one built in the state. Standing at the cradle of car culture, he said it was time to find other ways to move people.

2   I sympathize with the critics, because I don't like even my own car. For most of my adult life I didn't even own one. I lived in Manhattan and pitied the suburbanites driving to the mall. When I moved to Washington and joined their ranks, I picked a home in smart-growth heaven, near a bike path and a subway station. Most days I skate or bike downtown, filled with righteous Schadenfreude as I roll past drivers stuck in traffic. The rest of the time I usually take the subway, and on the rare day I go by car, I hate the drive.

3   But I no longer believe that my tastes should be public policy. I've been converted by a renegade school of thinkers you might call the autonomists, because they extol the autonomy made possible by automobiles. Their school includes engineers and philosophers, political scientists like James Q. Wilson and number-crunching economists like Randal O'Toole, the author of the 540-page manifesto *The Vanishing Automobile and Other Urban Myths*. These thinkers acknowledge the social and environmental problems caused by the car but argue that these would not be solved—in fact, would be mostly made worse—by the proposals coming from the car's critics. They call smart growth a dumb idea, the result not of rational planning but of class snobbery and intellectual arrogance. They prefer to promote smart driving, which means more tolls, more roads and, yes, more cars.

4   Drawing on authorities ranging from Aristotle to Walt Whitman, the autonomists argue that the car is not merely a convenience but one of history's greatest forces for good, an invention that liberated the poor from slums and workers from company towns, challenged communism, powered the civil rights movement and freed women to work outside the home. Their arguments have given me new respect for my minivan. I still don't like driving it, but now when the sound system is blaring "Thunder Road"—These two lanes will take us aaanywhere—I think Bruce Springsteen got it right. There is redemption beneath that dirty hood.

Beautiful Sprawl

Suppose you have a choice between two similarly priced homes. One is 5 an urban town house within walking distance of stores and mass transit; the other is in the suburbs and requires driving everywhere. Which one would you pick?

If you chose the town house, you're in a distinct minority. Only 6 17 percent of Americans chose it in a national survey sponsored by the real-estate agents' and homebuilders' trade associations. The other 83 percent preferred the suburbs, which came as no surprise to the real-estate agents or others who spend time in subdivisions. For all the bad press that suburbs get in books like "The Geography of Nowhere"— whose author, James Kunstler, calls America a "national automobile slum"—polls repeatedly show that the vast majority of suburbanites are happy with their neighborhoods.

You could argue that Americans are deluded because they haven't 7 been given a reasonable alternative. Smart-growth advocates say that suburbs have flourished at the expense of cities because of government policies promoting cheap gasoline, Interstate highways and new-home construction. What if the government, instead of devastating urban neighborhoods by running expressways through them, instead lavished money on mass transit and imposed high gasoline taxes to discourage driving?

As it happens, that experiment has already been conducted in 8 Europe with surprisingly little effect. To American tourists who ride the subways in the carefully preserved old cities, the policies seem to have worked. But it turns out that the people who live there aren't so different from Americans. Even with $5-per-gallon gasoline, the number of cars per capita in Europe has been growing faster than in America in recent decades, while the percentage of commuters using mass transit has been falling. As the suburbs expand, Europe's cities have been losing people, too. Paris is a great place to visit, but in the past half-century it has lost one-quarter of its population.

"Cities are spreading virtually everywhere in the world despite all the 9 antisprawl measures," says Peter Gordon, a professor at the University of Southern California School of Policy, Planning and Development. "As soon as people have enough money, they want their car."

Of course, just because individuals crave cars doesn't mean that 10 cars are good for society. Jane Holtz Kay, the author of *Asphalt Nation: How the Automobile Took Over America and How We Can Take It Back*, sums up the popular anxiety about the social and environmental costs of cars when she writes, "A nation in gridlock from its auto-bred lifestyle, an environment choking from its auto exhausts, a landscape sacked by its highways has distressed Americans so much that even this go-for-it nation is posting 'No Growth' signs on development from shore to shore." But while Kay is right that Americans resist new development near their homes and fear the traffic it will bring, they might feel differently about sprawl if they understood it better.

11 Consider some of the prevailing beliefs:

12 Sprawl traps drivers in traffic hell. It's true that highways have gotten much more congested, but the worst traffic tends to be in densely populated urban areas that haven't been building new roads, like New York and Chicago—the kind of places hailed by smart-growth planners but now avoided by companies looking for convenient offices. During the 1990s, the number of suburban workers surpassed the number downtown. These commuters still encountered traffic jams, but by not driving downtown they could still get to work reasonably quickly. The length of the average commute, now about 25 minutes, rose just 40 seconds in the 1980s and about 2 minutes in the 1990s. Sprawl didn't trap drivers—it gave them an escape.

13 Suburban car culture traps women. Critics complain that mothers in the suburbs are sentenced to long hours chauffeuring children to malls and soccer games and piano lessons, which are tasks that do indeed require a car. But so do most of their jobs. In his book *Edge City*, the writer Joel Garreau traces the golden age of sprawl to the surge in women entering the work force in the 70s and 80s, when the number of cars in America doubled as developers rushed to build office parks and malls for women who didn't have time to take the bus downtown. The only way to juggle all their responsibilities was to buy a car and find a job close to the stores and schools and day-care centers near their homes.

14 Sprawl is scarring the American landscape. If by "landscape" you mean the pasture or forest near your home that has been paved, then sprawl does look like an abomination. Who wouldn't prefer to be surrounded by greenery, especially when you're not paying property taxes for it?

15 But if you look at the big picture, America is not paving paradise. More than 90 percent of the continental United States is still open space and farmland. The major change in land use in recent decades has been the gain of 70 million acres of wilderness—more than all the land currently occupied by cities, suburbs and exurbs, according to Peter Huber, author of *Hard Green: Saving the Environment From the Environmentalists*. Because agriculture has become so efficient, farmers have abandoned vast tracts of land that have reverted to nature, and

rural areas have lost population as young people migrate to cities. You may not like the new homes being built for them at the edge of your town, but if preserving large ecosystems and wildlife habitat is your priority, better to concentrate people in the suburbs and exurbs rather than scatter them in the remote countryside.

Mass transit is the cure for highway congestion. Commuter trains 16 and subways make sense in New York, Chicago and a few other cities, and there are other forms of transit, like express buses, that can make a difference elsewhere. (Vans offering door-to-door service are a boon to the elderly and people without cars.) But for most Americans, mass transit is impractical and irrelevant. Since 1970, transit systems have received more than $500 billion in subsidies (in today's dollars), but people have kept voting with their wheels. Transit has been losing market share to the car and now carries just 3 percent of urban commuters outside New York City. It's easy to see why from one statistic: the average commute by public transportation takes twice as long as the average commute by car. . . .

The T-Word

Drivers sitting in a traffic jam outside San Diego used to glance across 17 the median strip of I-15 at a maddening sight: car-pool lanes without any carpoolers. The lanes were so empty that engineers decided to let solo drivers share them for a price, which is displayed on electronic signs at the entrance to the lanes. A computer counts how many cars take the offer and then recalibrates the price every six minutes, raising the toll if too many cars accept, cutting it if not enough do.

The morning I watched, the computer set a price of $1.25 at 7:10, 18 raised it to $1.50 six minutes later, then jacked it up to $2.25 at 7:22 and added another quarter at 7:28. The $2.50 toll apparently scared off drivers, and the computer reacted by dropping the toll to $1.75, at which point traffic increased and the toll went back up to $2. As rush-hour traffic waned, the toll fell quickly, and by 8:20 the computer was willing to let drivers into the lanes for a dollar. Those who paid could drive into San Diego without slowing down even to pay the toll. It was collected by radio transmitters overhead that could read each car's FasTrak transponder (California's version of E-Z Pass) at speeds up to 120 miles per hour.

When this experiment began in 1996, some critics said it was 19 unfair to create these "Lexus lanes." But by now, even drivers who won't pay the toll have come to appreciate the lanes because they divert traffic from the regular highway. And while affluent drivers are more likely to pay the bill, surveys have found people of all incomes using the lanes. Most of the ones I interviewed were budget-conscious, middle-class commuters who used the free lanes when possible. But when the traffic got heavy, they considered the toll a bargain.

20   "Isn't it worth a couple of dollars to spend an extra half-hour with your family?" said T.J. Zane, a political consultant who drives a 1997 Volkswagen Jetta. "That's what I used to spend on a cup of coffee at Starbucks. Now I've started bringing my own coffee and using the money for the toll." . . .

21   It's hard to imagine traffic ever flowing freely in New York, but engineers say anything is possible for a price. Peter Samuel, the editor of Tollroadsnews, has proposed getting trucks off the streets by building them a tunnel from New Jersey to Brooklyn and turning some of Brooklyn's railroad tracks into truck roads. Samuel I. Schwartz, who coined the term "gridlock" when he was chief engineer for the city's Department of Transportation, envisions tunneling underneath streets and highways to create new lanes, and he wants to unclog Manhattan's streets by charging tolls, as London Mayor Ken Livingston did with his streets.

22   Some politicians still object to tolls as unfair to the poor, but the opposition seems to be dwindling. Democrats in Congress joined with Republicans in passing changes in the current highway bill to encourage new toll lanes. "If we want to expand road capacity to meet the growing population, we have to rely on tolls," says Robert Atkinson of the Progressive Policy Institute, the research arm of the centrist Democratic Leadership Council. He sees tolls as a progressive tax system: the more affluent drivers pay for new toll lanes while less affluent drivers get a free benefit because the existing roads become less congested, and bus riders get to use the new express lanes without paying for them. . . .

The Car-Culture War

"[They will] only encourage the common people to move about needlessly."

The Duke of Wellington, on early steam railroads . . .

23 "Our first order of business is to shape our cities and regions to provide viable alternatives to the car," said Peter Calthorpe, a "new urbanist" architect and a leader of the smart-growth movement. "Only then can you begin to use taxes to set up an incentive system that levels the playing field." Neha Bhatt, the coordinator of the Sierra Club's Challenge to Sprawl Campaign, doubted a gas tax would do much

good. "People will pay to keep driving," she said, "because the harsh reality in America today is that you need to transport yourself pretty long distances. We need a more holistic approach to planning."

But if people are willing to pay to keep driving, why are they and 24 their cars any more objectionable than the commoners who offended the Duke of Wellington with their desire to ride the railroad? Intellectuals' distaste for the car and suburbia, and their fondness for rail travel and cities, are an odd inverse of the old aristocratic attitudes. The suburbs were quite fashionable when only the upper classes could afford to live there. Nineteenth-century social workers dreamed of sending crowded urbanites out to healthy green spaces. But when middle-class workers made it out there, they were mocked first for their "little boxes made of ticky-tacky" and later for their McMansions. Land Rovers and sports cars were chic when they were driven to country estates, but they became antisocial gas-guzzlers once they appeared in subdivisions.

"Aristocratic attitudes toward mobility for the masses haven't 25 really changed from the Duke of Wellington to the Duchess of Huffington," says Sam Kazman of the Competitive Enterprise Institute, referring to Arianna Huffington, one of the wealthy Hollywood activists behind the Detroit Project, which has been running ads against gas-guzzlers. (She and a colleague in this campaign to save energy, Laurie David, the wife of the comedian Larry David, have inspired a new term: Gulfstream liberal, in honor of the jet their set uses. Critics like to point out that on a cross-country trip, it burns 10 times more fuel per passenger than an airliner, and twice as much as a Hummer.)

The autonomists have been losing the public-relations war, but 26 they're trying to fight back. O'Toole has founded the American Dream Coalition to do battle with what he calls the "congestion coalition," his term for opponents of new roads. The autonomists collect stories of smart-growth problems, especially from Portland, OR, which became planners' poster city by building light-rail lines, eschewing highways and severely restricting suburban development. But nearly 90 percent of its commuters still drive, and highway congestion increased in Portland more than any other American city in the 15 years after the first light-rail line opened. Meanwhile, housing prices rose sharply, making Portland one of the less-affordable cities for home buyers.

But the autonomists want to do more than play defense. They 27 want Americans to love the car again. They quote Walt Whitman from *Leaves of Grass*: "Lo, soul! seest thou not God's purpose from the first?/The earth to be spanned, connected by net-work." They cite historians like Macaulay, who observed in the 19th century that "every improvement of the means of locomotion benefits mankind morally and intellectually, as well as materially." They celebrate the car's role in the famous Montgomery bus boycott, when blacks shunning the segregated transit system relied on carpools and an informal taxi service. The police, aided by the laid-off bus workers, tried to stop them by enforcing minor traffic violations—Martin Luther King was arrested for going 30 miles per hour in a 25-mile-per-hour zone—but the drivers persisted and triumphed. The private car also became a popular symbol of liberation behind the Iron Curtain. When Communist leaders imported the movie "Grapes of Wrath" to illustrate the evils of capitalism, audiences took away a different revolutionary lesson. Watching the dispossessed farmers head for California, they were amazed that even unemployed Americans owned cars and could drive wherever they wanted to find work.

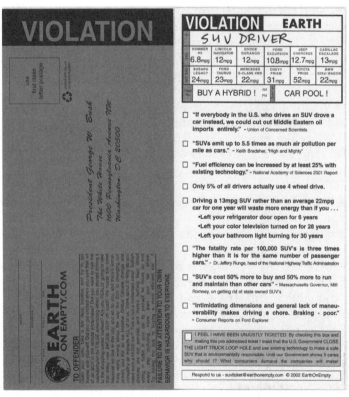

FIGURE 10.2 The environmental group Earth on Empty claims to have put tickets like these on over one million vehicles in 500 American cities. What is your reaction to the campaign? What message is the group sending? How would you react if you got a ticket like this on your SUV?

Reflection and Discussion

1. What feelings do you have about drivers paying more to use private toll lanes? In what ways are the costs different from what drivers pay to cross a bridge, for example?
2. Consider the quotes and historical references Tierney uses at the end of his article. How effective are they? When have you used similar citations and how well did they work?

Writing Matters

1. Tierney has used a variety of modes of transportation, from skates and a bicycle to cars and public transportation. Research places in the world where non-car transportation is particularly popular. In what American cities are bikes and other non-motorized means of transportation common? What conditions contribute to their success? Which ones could be adapted or expanded to work in your community?
2. In many articles about automobiles, we often read of their negative effects—from accidents and pollution to urban sprawl and traffic. Tierney, though, describes cars as "one of history's greatest forces for good." Argue either for or against this statement, using a variety of facts, examples and statistics. Consider also those likely to disagree with you and try, if not to win them over, to at least gain their respect.

Kicking the Petroleum Habit: Ending Auto-Domination

Jane Holtz Kay, *Green Guide,* Fall 2001

Jane Holtz Kay is the author of the books Asphalt Nation *and* Lost Boston. *She frequently writes for* The Nation *on topics related to architecture, energy and contemporary culture.*

What signs do you see that Americans may (or may not) be reevaluating purchases like oversized cars and houses?

As the globe simmers and ecosystems succumb, more and more   1
Americans unite in their disdain of the biggest of the big. Endorsing
small-is-beautiful and enough-is-enough, the green-minded set their
sights on the heavies of environmental gluttony. SUVs are up for
scorn, McMansions for maligning. Those who care about the last-
chance landscape wring their hands at Big Macs and humongous
Home Depot Expos. Americans are dismayed by the nation's behemoths

of consumption. Large enough to be singled out by an orbiting satellite camera, the Hummer hugging two lanes and the Wal-Mart wrapped with parking lots are the usual suspects.

2   And why shouldn't environmentally-minded consumers cast aspersions on the Big Box Store drawing 10,000 sprawl-breeding car trips a day, jamming first-growth-forest planks on its shelves and Amazon forest-razed cattle sitting as slabs of beef in superscale freezers. These spongers and soilers of land and water and energy are, indeed, our most destructive footprint. And, measuring and criticizing that massive imprint is, indeed, a first step to reducing it.

A New Take on "Small Is Beautiful"

3   And yet . . . and yet . . . for all the distaste these objects inspire in conservationists and careful consumers, there is a problem with focusing on the super big—and that is overlooking the fact that it is not simply these biggest consumers that are damaging the environment. It is not the biggest in the flood of products and by products that wreak havoc on our surroundings, not the oversized but the overdose of the little that, in the end, erodes the earth and pollutes the planet.

4   Now, as the pace of ecological destruction seems to multiply and global warming threatens, it seems to me that it is time to dust off the old "Small is Beautiful" ethos; that we should pause in our preoccupation with Big as Bad and recall Pogo's words of an older ethos: that "we have met the enemy and it is us," meaning the smaller practices that combined one by one, replicate the singularly more injurious habits of the nation. For all the deserved disdain for the looming intruders, the facts and figures tell us that it is not the SUV alone, not the megabuildings swallowing land, but the everyday expansion of the small that is doing the most harm. It is the automobile times 220 million of them rolling across the land. It is the home heating and energy use everywhere. It is the 953,000 homes constructed last year, sprawling at the end of the highway rather than in the compact urban communities that are so much more energy-efficient and gentler to the land.

5   One by one, as automobiles accumulate faster than drivers, it is that multitude that sends 30 percent of our CO_2 emissions skyward accelerating global warming. It is the mid-sized cars that swallow most of the nation's 7.7 million barrels of gasoline a day, roughly a third more than two decades ago. It is the production of 16,000,000 vehicles a year that consumes yet another one-third of their energy and resources in production: the tip of the (melting) iceberg.

6   Likewise, in our built environment, it is not simply the starter mansion but the sprawl bred by subdivision after subdivision of small

single homes on the fringes. Unplanned and uncontrolled by our communities, their construction consumes another third of our energy, covers 62,000 acres of wetlands and destroys 1.2 million acres of farmland a year, and now, consumes six times as much physical space per person as at the last census count.

Certainly, there is no question that in our many small exertions we 7
have become a deeper shade of green. We recycle more, we buy green, we turn out the lights and lower the thermostat. In harmony with these sustainable gestures, many focus on our own small and singular decisions that sidetrack environmental efforts; they tally the cost of putting the pedal to the metal instead of public transportation; they work on the political scale that produces good land use and planning, and think about sustainable mobility. But we need to see that focusing on consumer excesses doesn't lead to neglecting everyday consumer expansion.

Beyond Motown and MPG

It is not just the ordinary Janes or Joes who need to keep an eye trained 8
on the bigger picture. From his post along the Potomac, the Sierra Club's Dan Becker told Reuters that, "the single biggest step to curbing global warming is making cars go further on a gallon of gas." Becker, the head of the Club's global warming campaign, praised Ford Motor Company's announcement to cut gas consumption in new cars. "Ford is a big part of the problem," he noted. "They're trying to become part of the solution, and they deserve credit for that," he said barely a New York (or Detroit) minute before the company came out against better fuel efficiency for trucks. Becker's comments had some merit, but his focus was unfair to the organization which has focused on the real solution: controlling sprawl and creating better public transportation in local groups across the nation and looking at small, but cumulatively enriching acts of community.

Suppose, instead of signing on for 40- or 60-mile per gallon "clean 9
cars" now making automakers' back order lists swell, drivers shed a car and join a car-sharing club, help create safe routes to school so kids can walk and parents can cut trips to school. Get bike paths, get political. Study the deeper problems of auto-dependency—from the toxic chemicals to manufacture them, to the highways that hold them, to the runoff, the disruption of habitat, the erosion of urban spaces, and the harassed life of a car-based society—and it is clear that it will take more than good mileage to wean America from its oil-dependency.

To do so there are many ways—personal and political, local 10
and national—to shift a federal budget of $59.5 billion, which sends $31.6 billion to highways, $13 billion to aviation, a scant $6.6 billion for

transit, and invisible sums for bike paths or walkable sidewalks. And the fight goes on to get Amtrak a mere $12 billion for 10 years. Criticism of the biggest should be accompanied by positive action for the small and incremental for transportation alternatives: for support for rail transport, for transit-oriented development, for good land use planning and zoning at home.

11   Sweat the small stuff and you begin to see how 4 percent of the world's population can use up 24 percent of the world's energy and emit 25 percent of all greenhouse gases. For myself, I have begun to realize that it is time not just to be circumspect in my consumption—not just to "reuse, reduce, recycle" in my household habitat and work and play artifacts, but to consider one more word—"reject" not just in everyday taking, making, wasting of household goods but in the largest single energy and resource consumers: the car and the spatial gluttony of car-based communities. For myself, I sold my car and reexamined the world I live in.

12   Is that possible? "We can see," notes the *Consumer's Guide to Effective Environmental Choices*, put out by the Union of Concerned Scientists, "that individual consumer action works best when it does not require significant consumer sacrifice." CFCs were quickly removed from suntan oil, but CFC-carrying air conditioners in cars and trucks linger on, they observed. And they are right. Kicking the car addiction is not easy. But car-dependency is not only an addiction. It is also the result of economic and political decisions to construct a society dependent on a ton or two of wheel and steel to do the most mundane daily chores and chauffeuring.

13   By working to stop planning practices that permit sprawl, by fighting to get more than a paltry share of our local budgets for public transportation; by advocating good zoning, and moving developers to revive Main Street, we can traverse with a far smaller, human footprint.

Walking the Talk

14 Consider, for one statistic, that a third of the average American's mileage is spent on shopping, another third on chauffeuring (with only 8 percent for trips and 22 for the commute) and try for new choices to shrink hours behind the wheel. Bunch your trips. Do the math and calculate the cost of your first (or second) car at $8000 a year, according to Runzheimer International. That money might buy you cabs, senior citizen vans and other para-transit. No way to get groceries? Deliveries come easily in a denser place. Push for multi-family compact neighborhoods, for transit-oriented communities.

Live on the fringes? Then package your errands. Share services. 15
Make a personal commitment to reduce your 12,000 miles a year (that's
a pound of carbon dioxide heaved for each mile you drive). Pick your
percentage of the Kyoto Protocol to reduce greenhouse gases. Analyze
your lifestyle and do as Cities for Climate Protection does in communities from New York to Los Angeles: weatherize, support renewable
energy, buy green on the small scale that becomes big in the best way.
Don't buy at all.

Expand your green values to larger planning causes. Push for alter- 16
nate transportation. Work towards saving and filling in town and city
centers and x-ing out sprawl. Push zoning boards and master plans to
follow these principles. Get busy with your community. Get political.
Do your representatives take campaign funds from developers to build
bad buildings in bad places? Vote them out.

Fight highway departments stuck in the Dark Ages. Go to meet- 17
ings of Metropolitan Planning Councils (MPCs) or Councils of
Government (COGs) who the make decisions. Fight more widenings
and extensions, too. "If you build them, they (more cars) will come"
and with them a rush hour of even longer than the six hours a day
recently reported by the Texas Transportation Institute. Let "no more
roads to nowhere" and "lots more help to Main Street" be your guide.
"Yes" to infill building and reclaimed brownfields in older neighborhoods. "No" to subdivisions in exurban greenfields.

In short: it is time to battle for a positive agenda to begin the 18
process of weaning ourselves from the petroleum habit. Sure, we need
to fight not-so-green gigantism and super-scale consumption. But, an
army of one charging in the right direction, supporting personal and
political environmental advances, is truly the most beautiful of all.

Reflection and Discussion

1. How were you affected by Kay's statement that she had given up her car?
2. Why do you think Kay chose to use military terminology in her article?
   Explain which words do or don't work.

Writing Matters

1. Articles about the state of the environment can be depressing. Evaluate the
   balance of bad versus good news in Kay's piece. How well does she
   frighten readers compared with the positive solutions she offers? Which
   parts of her article did you find the most useful and why? Comment on her
   use of imperatives such as "expand," "work," and "push." How effective
   are they?

2. Research one of Kay's suggestions and explain how it could be put into effect in your community. Include incentives for encouraging people to use their cars more wisely and rely on them less. How could lawmakers and politicians get involved?

Fueling Our Transportation Future

John B. Heywood, *Scientific American,* September 2006

John B. Heywood is Professor of Mechanical Engineering at the Massachusetts Institute of Technology and has written extensively on matters related to science, technology, energy and transportation.

How much faith do you have in science and technology to solve the energy challenges of America and the world? What role can individuals play?

1   If we are honest, most of us in the world's richer countries would concede that we like our transportation systems. They allow us to travel when we want to, usually door-to-door, alone or with family and friends, and with our baggage. The mostly unseen freight distribution network delivers our goods and supports our lifestyle. So why worry about the future and especially about how the energy that drives our transportation might be affecting our environment?

2   The reason is the size of these systems and their seemingly inexorable growth. They use petroleum-based fuels (gasoline and diesel) on an unimaginable scale. The carbon in these fuels is oxidized to the greenhouse gas carbon dioxide during combustion, and their massive use means that the amount of carbon dioxide entering the atmosphere is likewise immense. Transportation accounts for 25 percent of worldwide greenhouse gas emissions. As the countries in the developing world rapidly motorize, the increasing global demand for fuel will pose one of the biggest challenges to controlling the concentration of greenhouse gases in the atmosphere. The US light-duty vehicle fleet (automobiles, pickup trucks, SUVs, vans and small trucks) currently consumes 150 billion gallons (550 billion liters) of gasoline a year, or 1.3 gallons of gasoline per person a day. If other nations burned gasoline at the same rate, world consumption would rise by a factor of almost 10.

3   As we look ahead, what possibilities do we have for making transportation much more sustainable, at an acceptable cost?

Our Options

Several options could make a substantial difference. We could improve 4
or change vehicle technology; we could change how we use our vehicles; we could reduce the size of our vehicles; we could use different fuels. We will most likely have to do all of these to drastically reduce energy consumption and greenhouse gas emissions.

In examining these alternatives, we have to keep in mind several 5
aspects of the existing transportation system. First, it is well suited to its primary context, the developed world. Over decades, it has had time to evolve so that it balances economic costs with users' needs and wants. Second, this vast optimized system relies completely on one convenient source of energy—petroleum. And it has evolved technologies—internal-combustion engines on land and jet engines (gas turbines) for air—that well match vehicle operation with this energy-dense liquid fuel. Finally, these vehicles last a long time. Thus, rapid change is doubly difficult. Constraining and then reducing the local and global impacts of transportation energy will take decades.

We also need to keep in mind that efficiency ratings can be mis- 6
leading; what counts is the fuel consumed in actual driving. Today's gasoline spark-ignition engine is about 20 percent efficient in urban driving and 35 percent efficient at its best operating point. But many short trips with a cold engine and transmission, amplified by cold weather and aggressive driving, significantly worsen fuel consumption, as do substantial time spent with the engine idling and losses in the transmission. These real-world driving phenomena reduce the engine's average efficiency so that only about 10 percent of the chemical energy stored in the fuel tank actually drives the wheels. Amory Lovins, a strong advocate for much lighter, more efficient vehicles, has stated it this way: with a 10 percent efficient vehicle and with the driver, a passenger and luggage—a payload of some 300 pounds, about 10 percent of the vehicle weight—"only one percent of the fuel's energy in the vehicle tank actually moves the payload."

We must include in our accounting what it takes to produce and 7
distribute the fuel, to drive the vehicle through its lifetime of 150,000 miles (240,000 kilometers) and to manufacture, maintain and dispose of the vehicle. These three phases of vehicle operation are often called well-to-tank (this phase accounts for about 15 percent of the total lifetime energy use and greenhouse gas emissions), tank-to-wheels (75 percent), and cradle-to-grave (10 percent). Surprisingly, the energy required to produce the fuel and the vehicle is not negligible. This total life-cycle accounting becomes especially important as we consider fuels that do not come from petroleum and new types of vehicle

technologies. It is what gets used and emitted in this total sense that matters.

8   Improving existing light-duty vehicle technology can do a lot. By investing more money in increasing the efficiency of the engine and transmission, decreasing weight, improving tires and reducing drag, we can bring down fuel consumption by about one third over the next 20 or so years—an annual 1 to 2 percent improvement, on average. (This reduction would cost between $500 and $1,000 per vehicle; at likely future fuel prices, this amount would not increase the lifetime cost of ownership.) These types of improvements have occurred steadily over the past 25 years, but we have bought larger, heavier, faster cars and light trucks and thus have effectively traded the benefits we could have realized for these other attributes. Though most obvious in the US, this shift to larger, more powerful vehicles has occurred elsewhere as well. We need to find ways to motivate buyers to use the potential for reducing fuel consumption and greenhouse gas emissions to actually save fuel and contain emissions.

9   In the near term, if vehicle weight and size can be reduced and if both buyers and manufacturers can step off the ever increasing horsepower/performance path, then in the developed world we may be able to slow the rate of petroleum demand, level it off in 15 to 20 years at about 20 percent above current demand, and start on a slow downward path. This projection may not seem nearly aggressive enough. It is, however, both challenging to achieve and very different from our current trajectory of steady growth in petroleum consumption at about 2 percent a year.

10   In the longer term, we have additional options. We could develop alternative fuels that would displace at least some petroleum. We could turn to new propulsion systems that use hydrogen or electricity. And we could go much further in designing and encouraging acceptance of smaller, lighter vehicles.

11   The alternative fuels option may be difficult to implement unless the alternatives are compatible with the existing distribution system. Also, our current fuels are liquids with a high-energy density: lower-density fuels will require larger fuel tanks or provide less range than today's roughly 400 miles. From this perspective, one alternative that stands out is nonconventional petroleum (oil or tar sands, heavy oil, oil shale, coal). Processing these sources to yield "oil," however, requires large amounts of other forms of energy, such as natural gas and electricity. Thus, the processes used emit substantial amounts of greenhouse gases and have other environmental impacts. Further, such processing calls for big capital investments. Nevertheless,

despite the broader environmental consequences, nonconventional petroleum sources are already starting to be exploited; they are expected to provide some 10 percent of transportation fuels within the next 20 years.

Biomass-based fuels such as ethanol and biodiesel, which are often considered to emit less carbon dioxide per unit of energy, are also already being produced. In Brazil ethanol made from sugarcane constitutes some 40 percent of transport fuel. In the US roughly 20 percent of the corn crop is being converted to ethanol. Much of this is blended with gasoline at the 10 percent level in so-called reformulated (cleaner-burning) gasolines. The recent US national energy policy act plans to double ethanol production from the current 2 percent of transportation fuel by 2012. But the fertilizer, water, and natural gas and electricity currently expended in ethanol production from corn will need to be substantially decreased. Production of ethanol from cellulosic biomass (residues and wastes from plants not generally used as a food source) promises to be more efficient and to lower greenhouse gas emissions. It is not yet a commercially viable process, although it may well become so. Biodiesel can be made from various crops (rapeseed, sunflower, soybean oils) and waste animal fats. The small amounts now being made are blended with standard diesel fuel. 12

It is likely that the use of biomass-based fuels will steadily grow. But given the uncertainty about the environmental impacts of large-scale conversion of biomass crops to fuel (on soil quality, water resources and overall greenhouse gas emissions), this source will contribute but is unlikely to dominate the future fuel supply anytime soon. 13

Use of natural gas in transportation varies around the world from less than 1 percent to 10 to 15 percent in a few countries where tax policies make it economical. In the 1990s natural gas made inroads into US municipal bus fleets to achieve lower emissions; diesels with effective exhaust cleanup are now proving a cheaper option. 14

What about new propulsion system technology? Likely innovations would include significantly improved gasoline engines (using a turbocharger with direct fuel injection, for example), more efficient transmissions, and low-emission diesels with catalysts and particulate traps in the exhaust, and perhaps new approaches to how the fuel is combusted might be included as well. Hybrids, which combine a small gasoline engine and a battery-powered electric motor, are already on the road, and production volumes are growing. These vehicles use significantly less gasoline in urban 15 driving, have lower benefits at highway speeds and cost a few thousand dollars extra to buy.

16 Researchers are exploring more radical propulsion systems and fuels, especially those that have the potential for low lifecycle carbon dioxide emissions. Several organizations are developing hydrogen-powered fuel cell vehicles in hybrid form with a battery and an electric motor. Such systems could increase vehicle efficiency by a factor of two, but much of that benefit is offset by the energy consumed and the emissions produced in making and distributing hydrogen. If the hydrogen can be produced through low-carbon-emitting processes and if a practical distribution system could be set up, it has low-greenhouse-emissions potential. But it would take technological breakthroughs and many decades before hydrogen-based transportation could become a reality and have widespread impact.

17 Hydrogen is, of course, an energy carrier rather than an energy source. Electricity is an alternative energy carrier with promise of producing energy without releasing carbon dioxide, and various research teams are looking at its use in transportation. The major challenge is coming up with a battery that can store enough energy for a reasonable driving range, at an acceptable cost. One technical barrier is the long battery recharging time. Those of us used to filling a 20-gallon tank in four minutes might have to wait for several hours to charge a battery. One way around the range limitation of electric vehicles is the plug-in hybrid, which has a small engine onboard to recharge the battery when needed. The energy used could thus be largely electricity and only part engine fuel. We do not yet know whether this plug-in hybrid technology will prove to be broadly attractive in the marketplace.

18 Beyond adopting improved propulsion systems, a switch to lighter-weight materials and different vehicle structures could reduce weight and improve fuel consumption without downsizing. Obviously, though, combining lighter materials and smaller vehicle size would produce an even greater effect. Maybe the way we use vehicles in the future will differ radically from our "general purpose vehicle" expectations of today. In the future, a car specifically designed for urban driving may make sense. Volkswagen, for example, has a small two-person concept car prototype that weighs 640 pounds (290 kilograms) and consumes one liter of gasoline per 100 kilometers (some 240 miles per gallon—existing average US light-duty vehicles use 10 liters per 100 kilometers, or just under 25 miles per gallon). Some argue that downsizing reduces safety, but these issues can be minimized.

Promoting Change

Better technology will undoubtedly improve fuel efficiency. In the 19 developed world, markets may even adopt enough of these improvements to offset the expected increases in the number of vehicles. And gasoline prices will almost certainly rise over the next decade and beyond, prompting changes in the way consumers purchase and use their vehicles. But market forces alone are unlikely to curb our ever growing appetite for petroleum.

A coordinated package of fiscal and regulatory policies will need to 20 come into play for fuel-reduction benefits to be realized from these future improvements. Effective policies would include a "feebate" scheme, in which customers pay an extra fee to buy big fuel-consumers but get a rebate if they buy small, fuel-efficient models. The feebate combines well with stricter Corporate Average Fuel Economy (CAFE) standards—in other words, with regulations that require automobile makers to produce products that consume less fuel. Adding higher fuel taxes to the package would further induce people to buy fuel-efficient

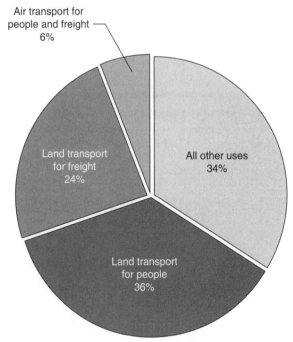

Millions of barrels per day

Air transport for people and freight 6%

Land transport for freight 24%

All other uses 34%

Land transport for people 36%

FIGURE 10.3 Daily Use of Petroleum Worldwide

models. And tax incentives could spur more rapid changes in the production facilities for new technologies. All these measures may be needed to keep us moving forward.

Reflection and Discussion

1. Heywood ends the first and third paragraphs with questions. How effective is this strategy? How often do you ask questions in your own writing? Do you ever find yourself doing it too often? What alternatives do you have?
2. Heywood mentions options for reducing the energy used in the vehicles we drive. Rank them from easiest to most difficult and be prepared to explain your choices.

Writing Matters

1. Explain your reactions to Heywood's "feebate" idea. What are its strongest and weakest features? How likely are American politicians to raise taxes on energy? What alternatives do you see? How much do Europeans, Japanese and others pay for the equivalent of a gallon of gas? How have gasoline prices influenced energy consumption in those countries and what are the implications for US consumers?
2. View the movie *Who Killed the Electric Car?* and explain what you believe was most responsible for the electric car's demise. What other political or practical influences were at work? What recommendations would you make for someone proposing a car that operates on an alternative form of energy?

The Long Emergency

James Howard Kunstler, *Rolling Stone,* March 23, 2005

James Howard Kunstler has written for a number of publications including the Atlantic Monthly *and the* New York Times Sunday Magazine. *In addition to writing novels, he wrote* The Geography of Nowhere, *which deals with urban architecture and how it has been transformed by the automobile.*

What value do you place on protecting the environment for future generations? What are you doing now to make it happen?

1 Carl Jung, one of the fathers of psychology, famously remarked that "people cannot stand too much reality." What you're about to read may challenge your assumptions about the kind of world we live in, and especially the kind of world into which events are propelling us. We are in for a rough ride through uncharted territory.

It has been very hard for Americans—lost in dark raptures of non- 2
stop infotainment, recreational shopping and compulsive motoring—
to make sense of the gathering forces that will fundamentally alter the
terms of everyday life in our technological society. Even after the terrorist attacks of 9/11, America is still sleepwalking into the future. I call
this coming time the Long Emergency.

Most immediately we face the end of the cheap-fossil-fuel era. It is 3
no exaggeration to state that reliable supplies of cheap oil and natural
gas underlie everything we identify as the necessities of modern life—
not to mention all of its comforts and luxuries: central heating, air
conditioning, cars, airplanes, electric lights, inexpensive clothing,
recorded music, movies, hip-replacement surgery, national defense—
you name it.

The few Americans who are even aware that there is a gathering 4
global-energy predicament usually misunderstand the core of the
argument. That argument states that we don't have to run out of oil to
start having severe problems with industrial civilization and its
dependent systems. We only have to slip over the all-time production
peak and begin a slide down the arc of steady depletion.

The term "global oil-production peak" means that a turning point 5
will come when the world produces the most oil it will ever produce in
a given year and, after that, yearly production will inexorably decline.
It is usually represented graphically in a bell curve. The peak is the top
of the curve, the halfway point of the world's all-time total endow-
ment, meaning half the world's oil will be left. That seems like a lot of
oil, and it is, but there's a big catch: It's the half that is much more difficult to extract, far more costly to get, of much poorer quality and
located mostly in places where the people hate us. A substantial
amount of it will never be extracted.

The United States passed its own oil peak—about 11 million bar- 6
rels a day—in 1970, and since then production has dropped steadily. In
2004 it ran just above 5 million barrels a day (we get a tad more from
natural-gas condensates). Yet we consume roughly 20 million barrels a
day now. That means we have to import about two-thirds of our oil,
and the ratio will continue to worsen.

The US peak in 1970 brought on a portentous change in geo- 7
economic power. Within a few years, foreign producers, chiefly OPEC,
were setting the price of oil, and this in turn led to the oil crises of the
1970s. In response, frantic development of non-OPEC oil, especially the
North Sea fields of England and Norway, essentially saved the West's
ass for about two decades. Since 1999, these fields have entered depletion. Meanwhile, worldwide discovery of new oil has steadily declined
to insignificant levels in 2003 and 2004.

8   Some "cornucopians" claim that the Earth has something like a creamy nougat center of "abiotic" oil that will naturally replenish the great oil fields of the world. The facts speak differently. There has been no replacement whatsoever of oil already extracted from the fields of America or any other place.

9   Now we are faced with the global oil-production peak. The best estimates of when this will actually happen have been somewhere between now and 2010. In 2004, however, after demand from burgeoning China and India shot up, and revelations that Shell Oil wildly misstated its reserves, and Saudi Arabia proved incapable of goosing up its production despite promises to do so, the most knowledgeable experts revised their predictions and now concur that 2005 is apt to be the year of all-time global peak production.

10   It will change everything about how we live.

11   To aggravate matters, American natural-gas production is also declining, at five percent a year, despite frenetic new drilling, and with the potential of much steeper declines ahead. Because of the oil crises of the 1970s, the nuclear-plant disasters at Three Mile Island and Chernobyl and the acid-rain problem, the US chose to make gas its first choice for electric-power generation. The result was that just about every power plant built after 1980 has to run on gas. Half the homes in America are heated with gas. To further complicate matters, gas isn't easy to import. Here in North America, it is distributed through a vast pipeline network. Gas imported from overseas would have to be compressed at minus-260 degrees Fahrenheit in pressurized tanker ships and unloaded (re-gasified) at special terminals, of which few exist in America. Moreover, the first attempts to site new terminals have met furious opposition because they are such ripe targets for terrorism.

12   Some other things about the global energy predicament are poorly understood by the public and even our leaders. This is going to be a permanent energy crisis, and these energy problems will synergize with the disruptions of climate change, epidemic disease and population overshoot to produce higher orders of trouble.

13   We will have to accommodate ourselves to fundamentally changed conditions. No combination of alternative fuels will allow us to run American life the way we have been used to running it, or even a substantial fraction of it. The wonders of steady technological progress achieved through the reign of cheap oil have lulled us into a kind of Jiminy Cricket syndrome, leading many Americans to believe that anything we wish for hard enough will come true. These days, even people who ought to know better are wishing ardently for a seamless transition from fossil fuels to their putative replacements.

The widely touted "hydrogen economy" is a particularly cruel 14
hoax. We are not going to replace the US automobile and truck fleet
with vehicles run on fuel cells. For one thing, the current generation of
fuel cells is largely designed to run on hydrogen obtained from natural
gas. The other way to get hydrogen in the quantities wished for would
be electrolysis of water using power from hundreds of nuclear plants.
Apart from the dim prospect of our building that many nuclear plants
soon enough, there are also numerous severe problems with hydrogen's nature as an element that present forbidding obstacles to its use
as a replacement for oil and gas, especially in storage and transport.

Wishful notions about rescuing our way of life with "renewables" 15
are also unrealistic. Solar-electric systems and wind turbines face not
only the enormous problem of scale but the fact that the components
require substantial amounts of energy to manufacture and the proba-
bility that they can't be manufactured at all without the underlying
support platform of a fossil-fuel economy. We will surely use solar and
wind technology to generate some electricity for a period ahead but
probably at a very local and small scale.

Virtually all "biomass" schemes for using plants to create liquid 16
fuels cannot be scaled up to even a fraction of the level at which things
are currently run. What's more, these schemes are predicated on using
oil and gas "inputs" (fertilizers, weed-killers) to grow the biomass
crops that would be converted into ethanol or bio-diesel fuels. This is a
net energy loser—you might as well just burn the inputs and not
bother with the biomass products. Proposals to distill trash and waste
into oil by means of thermal depolymerization depend on the huge
waste stream produced by a cheap oil and gas economy in the first
place.

Coal is far less versatile than oil and gas, extant in less abundant 17
supplies than many people assume and fraught with huge ecological
drawbacks—as a contributor to greenhouse "global warming" gases
and many health and toxicity issues ranging from widespread mercury
poisoning to acid rain. You can make synthetic oil from coal, but the
only time this was tried on a large scale was by the Nazis under
wartime conditions, using impressive amounts of slave labor.

If we wish to keep the lights on in America after 2020, we may 18
indeed have to resort to nuclear power, with all its practical problems
and eco-conundrums. Under optimal conditions, it could take ten
years to get a new generation of nuclear power plants into operation,
and the price may be beyond our means. Uranium is also a resource in
finite supply. We are no closer to the more difficult project of atomic
fusion, by the way, than we were in the 1970s.

19   The upshot of all this is that we are entering a historical period of potentially great instability, turbulence and hardship. Obviously, geopolitical maneuvering around the world's richest energy regions has already led to war and promises more international military conflict. Since the Middle East contains two-thirds of the world's remaining oil supplies, the US has attempted desperately to stabilize the region by, in effect, opening a big police station in Iraq. The intent was not just to secure Iraq's oil but to modify and influence the behavior of neighboring states around the Persian Gulf, especially Iran and Saudi Arabia. The results have been far from entirely positive, and our future prospects in that part of the world are not something we can feel altogether confident about.

20   And then there is the issue of China, which, in 2004, became the world's second-greatest consumer of oil, surpassing Japan. China's surging industrial growth has made it increasingly dependent on the imports we are counting on. If China wanted to, it could easily walk into some of these places—the Middle East, former Soviet republics in central Asia—and extend its hegemony by force. Is America prepared to contest for this oil in an Asian land war with the Chinese army? I doubt it. Nor can the US military occupy regions of the Eastern Hemisphere indefinitely, or hope to secure either the terrain or the oil infrastructure of one distant, unfriendly country after another. A likely scenario is that the US could exhaust and bankrupt itself trying to do this, and be forced to withdraw back into our own hemisphere, having lost access to most of the world's remaining oil in the process.

21   We know that our national leaders are hardly uninformed about this predicament. President George W. Bush has been briefed on the dangers of the oil-peak situation as long ago as before the 2000 election and repeatedly since then. In March, the Department of Energy released a report that officially acknowledges for the first time that peak oil is for real and states plainly that "the world has never faced a problem like this. Without massive mitigation more than a decade before the fact, the problem will be pervasive and will not be temporary."

22   Most of all, the Long Emergency will require us to make other arrangements for the way we live in the United States. America is in a special predicament due to a set of unfortunate choices we made as a society in the twentieth century. Perhaps the worst was to let our towns and cities rot away and to replace them with suburbia, which had the additional side effect of trashing a lot of the best farmland in America. Suburbia will come to be regarded as the greatest misallocation of resources in the history of the world. It has a tragic destiny. The psychology of previous investment suggests that we will defend our drive-in utopia long after it has become a terrible liability.

Before long, the suburbs will fail us in practical terms. We made the ongoing development of housing subdivisions, highway strips, fried-food shacks and shopping malls the basis of our economy, and when we have to stop making more of those things, the bottom will fall out. 23

The circumstances of the Long Emergency will require us to down-scale and re-scale virtually everything we do and how we do it, from the kind of communities we physically inhabit to the way we grow our food to the way we work and trade the products of our work. Our lives will become profoundly and intensely local. Daily life will be far less about mobility and much more about staying where you are. Anything organized on the large scale, whether it is government or a corporate business enterprise such as Wal-Mart, will wither as the cheap energy props that support bigness fall away. The turbulence of the Long Emergency will produce a lot of economic losers, and many of these will be members of an angry and aggrieved former middle class. 24

Food production is going to be an enormous problem in the Long Emergency. As industrial agriculture fails due to a scarcity of oil- and gas-based inputs, we will certainly have to grow more of our food closer to where we live, and do it on a smaller scale. The American 25

"We're not certain why they disappeared, but archeologists speculate that it may have had something to do with their size."

FIGURE 10.4 Will SUVs die or evolve? And what about us?
Source: © The New Yorker Collection 2000, Harry Bliss, from cartoonbank.com. All Rights Reserved.

economy of the mid-twenty-first century may actually center on agriculture, not information, not high tech, not "services" like real estate sales or hawking cheeseburgers to tourists. Farming. This is no doubt a startling, radical idea, and it raises extremely difficult questions about the reallocation of land and the nature of work. The relentless subdividing of land in the late twentieth century has destroyed the contiguity and integrity of the rural landscape in most places. The process of readjustment is apt to be disorderly and improvisational. Food production will necessarily be much more labor-intensive than it has been for decades. We can anticipate the re-formation of a native-born American farm-laboring class. It will be composed largely of the aforementioned economic losers who had to relinquish their grip on the American dream. These masses of disentitled people may enter into quasi-feudal social relations with those who own land in exchange for food and physical security. But their sense of grievance will remain fresh, and if mistreated they may simply seize that land. . . .

26   These are daunting and even dreadful prospects. The Long Emergency is going to be a tremendous trauma for the human race. We will not believe that this is happening to us, that 200 years of modernity can be brought to its knees by a world-wide power shortage. The survivors will have to cultivate a religion of hope—that is, a deep and comprehensive belief that humanity is worth carrying on. If there is any positive side to stark changes coming our way, it may be in the benefits of close communal relations, of having to really work intimately (and physically) with our neighbors, to be part of an enterprise that really matters and to be fully engaged in meaningful social enactments instead of being merely entertained to avoid boredom. Years from now, when we hear singing at all, we will hear ourselves, and we will sing with our whole hearts.

Reflection and Discussion

1. Many people think of petroleum use primarily in terms of what we use to operate our cars or heat and cool our homes. Comment on how effectively Kunstler was able to communicate a sense of the big picture—the relationship of energy to the price of food, clothes, national defense.

2. Kunstler uses dates and facts to reinforce his points but, unlike some other authors in this book, he doesn't say where he got his information. Why? Explain how this affects your response to his article.

Writing Matters

1. How would you characterize Kunstler's tone and which words in particular help establish it? How would you describe his attitude toward the average

American? Where in the article does he make this clear? Who is his audience? What influence can audience have on the words a writer chooses?

2. Write a response to "The Long Emergency" with a new title and a different tone. Describe a future in which humans have risen to the occasion and met the challenges mentioned in the piece. Include options that the author may have left out, making sure that your response is detailed and reasonable. Refer to writers, scientists or others whose vision of the future is different than Kunstler's and explain the foundations for their optimism.

Can America Go Green?

Elizabeth Kolbert, *New Statesman*, June 19, 2006

A former reporter for the New York Times, *Elizabeth Kolbert is on the staff of* The New Yorker. *She has written many articles on science and the environment and has had pieces published in* Vogue *and several other magazines. She is author of the book* Field Notes from a Catastrophe: Man, Nature and Climate Change.

What obligation does America have to set an example in energy conservation?

Certainly, there are few questions more urgent than how—and how quickly—the US will react to climate change. As is well known, Americans represent less than 5 percent of the world's population, and yet they produce roughly 25 percent of its carbon-dioxide emissions. The country is one of only two industrialized nations that has rejected the Kyoto Protocol and, with it, mandatory emissions cuts. (The other is Australia.) Even as European leaders are pushing for negotiations to begin on a post-Kyoto treaty, the US has refused to participate. And on and on. At this point, it is almost impossible to imagine how the world will avoid disastrous climate impacts without a fundamental, and prompt, change in US policy.

[Former Vice President Al] Gore's professed optimism that such a change is at hand, which is shared, at least for the purposes of public consumption, by many of the country's leading environmentalists, rests on what might be called the democratic (with a small "d") imperative. As Gore points out, accurately enough, companies such as ExxonMobil and General Motors, working in concert with right-wing think-tanks such as the George C. Marshall Institute, have spent millions of dollars trying systematically to obscure the facts. (Indeed, as if on cue, the Competitive Enterprise Institute greeted the première of Gore's movie with a pair of 60-second TV ads full of jumping gazelles and kids skipping rope, carrying the tag line: "Carbon dioxide: they call it pollution; we call it life.") Add to this an American press corps axiomatically devoted to the notion of "balance," and the result has been confusion. But as soon as Americans understand "the inconvenient truth" about climate change, Gore has asserted, they'll do the right thing.

3   Making generalizations about an entire nation is always a dubious enterprise, and this is especially true of the US. The modern environmental movement was born in America and enjoyed its first successes there. Even under George W. Bush—perhaps the most polluter-friendly president in the nation's history—the country still spends more money than any other on environmental science; as the president likes to boast, this year alone, the federal government will spend roughly $2 billion on climate research and monitoring. Britain's Met Office has the Hadley Centre: the US supports three climate modeling teams— one at NASA, the second at the National Oceanic and Atmospheric Administration (NOAA) and the third at the National Centre for Atmospheric Research (NCAR).

4   All around the country there are towns and cities and state governments that are actively working to reduce their emissions in spite of— or perhaps one should say because of—federal inaction. In February 2005 the mayor of Seattle, Greg Nickels, began to circulate the "US Mayors Climate Protection Agreement," which calls on cities to "strive to meet or beat the Kyoto Protocol targets in their own communities"; as of this month, 243 mayors, representing communities as diverse as Miami, Racine in Wisconsin and Charleston, South Carolina, had signed on. New York, New Jersey and several other northeastern states have pledged to freeze their power-plant emissions at current levels and, eventually, to begin to roll them back. Even Governor Arnold Schwarzenegger, the Hummer collector, has joined in the effort: an executive order he signed last year calls on California to reduce its greenhouse-gas emissions to 2000 levels by 2010 and to 1990 levels by 2020. "I say the debate is over," Schwarzenegger declared before signing the order. "We know the science. We see the threat. And we know the time for action is now." The California Public Utilities Commission recently launched a $2.9 billion rebate program aimed at installing solar-power arrays on one million rooftops.

Ballooning House Sizes

5   If you focus on efforts such as these, it's tempting to conclude that the US is ready to shift course and, indeed, to some extent is already doing so. Look elsewhere, however, and it's far less clear. Consider what has happened to the average new home built in the country. Even as

average household size has declined, the size of the average house has ballooned. It was 1,000 square feet in 1950 and is nearly 2,500 square feet today. New homes, meanwhile, now routinely feature a gamut of energy-intensive conveniences, such as outdoor kitchens, professional-sized appliances and heated towel racks.

Or consider what has happened to the American automobile. At 6 the same time Americans were being presented with ever more compelling evidence of global climate change, they were also, in ever greater numbers, purchasing cars like GM's Yukon Denali, which has a 335-horsepower engine, weighs 7,000 lbs., comes equipped with heated leather seats, and gets 13 miles to the gallon. On average, passenger vehicles purchased in the US last year got 21.0 miles to the gallon; this was a worse gas mileage than the average passenger vehicle got 20 years earlier. In many parts of the country George Bush's recalcitrance isn't representative, but in others his equivocations look positively progressive: Senator James Inhofe, Republican of Oklahoma, who chairs the Senate committee on environment and public works, has famously called global warming the "greatest hoax ever perpetrated on the American people." Every year Senator John McCain, the Republican Party's most vocal proponent of action on climate change, brings to the floor a bill that would impose federal limits on CO_2 emissions. Every year it's a foregone conclusion that the bill will be defeated. It is worth noting that all the way back in 1992, Gore published a book, *Earth in the Balance*, which eloquently laid out the dangers of global warming. The book became a bestseller. Gore became the vice-president. And still nothing happened.

Are such patterns really the result of disinformation? Do 7 Americans drive around in 7,000 lb. cars because somehow they missed the many thousands of news stories and scientific studies documenting record high temperatures, rising sea levels and shrinking ice caps? As an American, I'd like to believe this is so. But it's hard to.

Life in the United States, more than just about anywhere else save 8 perhaps some of the oil-producing Gulf states, depends on cheap and plentiful energy. This is a fact of American culture and also of the American economy. Really addressing the problem of climate change will require many small-scale adjustments (no more heated towel racks) and also a great many more substantial ones: changes in energy consumption, energy production, patterns of land use, transportation systems, international relations. Rather than assume that Americans haven't done anything about global warming because they are skeptical about the threat, one could just as plausibly argue that they are skeptical about the threat because they don't want to do anything.

9   Shortly after Gore was elected vice-president, he proposed a tax on energy—specifically on the energy content of fossil fuels. It was defeated ignominiously, even though the Democrats still controlled Congress. Gore never raised the prospect of an energy tax again. Four years later he flew to Japan to salvage the Kyoto Protocol when negotiations seemed on the verge of breaking down. The Clinton administration eventually signed the protocol but never presented it to the Senate for ratification. Though Gore knew that the very future of the planet was at stake, he apparently concluded that pressing for action was hopeless, or politically inexpedient, or both. Talk about an inconvenient truth. . . .

Beyond the Tipping Point

10   Such is the inexorable nature of global warming that, at some point or other, even the US will be forced to acknowledge the scale of the problem. As McCain has observed: "This is clearly an issue that we will win on over time because of the evidence." The tragedy is: we don't have more time. The earth's climate system is vast and hugely inertial, and so already we are much further along the path to catastrophe than it appears. The rapid melting of mountain glaciers, the accelerating flow off the Greenland ice sheet, the 2003 heat wave in Europe, the 2005 hurricane season in the US—these are just the first faint harbingers of changes that have, by now, already become inevitable.

11   If we continue on our present course, at a certain point, truly terrible climatic disasters—the disintegration of the Greenland or the West Antarctic ice sheet, for instance—will become similarly unavoidable. These disasters may take centuries to play out fully, but once the process begins, it will become self-reinforcing and therefore virtually impossible to stop. This "tipping point" could be reached 20 years from now, or ten years from now, or, if truth be told, it could have already been reached ten years ago. Of course the US can go green. The question is: will it do so before it is too late?

Reflection and Discussion

1. Kolbert begins by highlighting the urgency of acting to combat world climate change. How effective is this as a writing strategy?
2. Kolbert criticizes the American press' devotion to balance. Think of examples when this commitment serves the public well. When has it given undeserved credibility to untenable points of view?

Writing Matters

1. Kolbert writes, "Rather than assume that Americans haven't done anything about global warming because they are skeptical about the threat, one could just as plausibly argue that they are skeptical about the threat because they don't want to do anything." Explain which of these alternatives you find most reasonable and why. Ask several people how they feel about global warming and what, if anything, they do about it. Then add these findings to your original response to the alternatives above.

2. In many places in America, people are taking climate change seriously. Research specific cities and states that are addressing pollution and energy conservation. Provide details. Which of these efforts make the most sense and why? What grass roots organizations are working on green causes and what are they doing? What roles do voting and political action play? How can our eating and buying habits influence the environment?

MAKING CONNECTIONS

1. What will it take to get most nations to agree to follow effective environmental standards? Research the Kyoto Protocol, not only the documents that resulted from the meetings in Japan but the participants and the political forces at work. Identify the good that was done and the work left to do. What issues and interests prevent nations from agreeing? What do you suggest the United States do?

2. A popular slogan says: "Think globally. Act locally." Review the articles in this chapter which show this principle at work. What makes this slogan a popular way of promoting change? What are the challenges and limitations of this approach? Suggest, if you can, a better slogan for getting people to change for the good of all.

3. In America, the automobile is king, linked not only to freedom and mobility but to status and self-image. Compare American attitudes toward cars with those of people in another country by examining prominent car manufacturers' websites—Toyota, Ford, BMW, for example. (Go to a company's main site and click on individual countries.) How do the marketing strategies compare and what do they tell you about how Americans and people living elsewhere view their cars?

4. In certain contexts, "carless" can have negative connotations. Extol the virtues of the carless life. What financial advantages are possible? What aggravations are absent? What compromises must be made or challenges overcome in order to live well without a car? Cite examples of people who have lived without a car and explain how well their choices have worked.

5. Either alone or with classmates, develop a questionnaire about energy consumption. Include questions about home energy use, driving habits, recycling, shopping. Then survey the people in your immediate community,

preferably people you know well. With the results, create a composite picture of how you and they relate to the environment. Consider the most effective ways that your community could move toward wiser energy use and outline a program for effecting these changes.

TAKING ACTION

Create a report on the advantages and disadvantages of owning a hybrid vehicle. Include factual information like initial cost, safety, maintenance, comfort and money spent on gas over a period of several years. (As an alternative, you could choose an electric car or one powered by biodiesel fuel.) Include information about where the best cars in each class can be purchased. Find an Internet site where people recommend cars and post it there. Check back to see how people responded.

Chapter 11

America Behind Bars

With over 2,000,000 people behind bars and the numbers growing daily, many are saying that the American prison system is on the verge of collapse. Overcrowding, deteriorating health care and escalating violence have caused politicians, social and religious leaders to declare the prison situation a national emergency. Add the staggering costs that weigh heavily on local and state budgets and we can appreciate the enormity of the problem, for every dollar spent on prisons means less money for schools, health services and other vital needs. Just as troubling are the moral questions of what to do about lives ruined on both the criminals and victims' sides. If recognizing a problem is the first step in solving it, then we will need to examine carefully questions that need immediate attention.

BEFORE YOU READ

Consider all of what you know about American prisons, including what you've heard about, read or experienced. What is their fundamental purpose? What pictures come to mind? What is the prison population like? What level of care do we owe prisoners and what attention should we pay them?

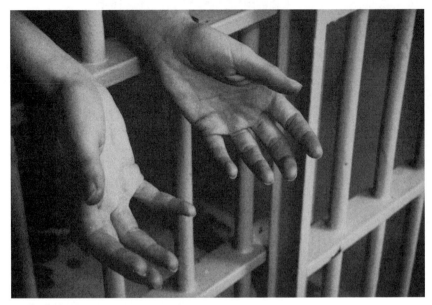

FIGURE 11.1 Should it be just punishment?

My So-Called Life

William Jelani Cobb, *Essence,* June 2004

William Jelani Cobb teaches at Spelman College in Atlanta where he is an assistant professor of history.

What do you know about the experiences of young people in prison?

1   The first thing you notice about 19-year-old Lexus Sirmans is his size. At six feet two inches tall and weighing 200 pounds, he has the imposing build of a heavyweight boxer, with long arms and broad shoulders and skin the color of obsidian. He would seem brooding were it not for his warm Georgia enunciation and a slightly embarrassed smile. He has old eyes too, which may be the most obvious mark of the two years he spent in prison, which included one year in Lee Arrendale State Prison, the adult correctional facility in Alto, Georgia.

2   In 2001 Lexus pleaded guilty to armed robbery. At age 16, he faced a minimum sentence of ten years in prison without parole, and although a plea agreement resulted in his sentence being reduced to five years, he would serve two years, not with other juveniles, but with adults.

Young men like Lexus—urban, angry, impoverished and unin- 3
cluded—find themselves at the center of a national debate on how to
address juvenile crime. "The trend has been to abandon the rehabilita-
tive model and embrace a more retributive form of punishment,"
explains the Reverend Roslyn Satchel, an attorney with the Southern
Center for Human Rights in Atlanta.

This often means trying juveniles such as Lexus as adults. Indeed, 4
under Georgia's 1994 Sentencing Reform Act, which sets the penalties
for trying juveniles, Lexus may actually have received more time than
an adult who had committed the same crimes because adults are routinely sentenced with the possibility of parole. Juveniles are not. In
Lexus's case, the conditions of his plea arrangement saved him from a
possible life sentence.

In February 2003 Lexus was released from prison after serving two 5
years and has gone about quietly and diligently making a good life for
himself on the outside. He found a job, went back to church immediately and began searching for a college to attend.

"He's trying really hard," says Peggy Lieurance, the founder of 6
Starfish Ministry, a correspondence-support ministry for incarcerated
youths, and Lexus's self-appointed mentor and staunch advocate.

Lieurance told me about Lexus, how she had come to care about 7
this teenager whose intelligence shone from the first conversation
they'd had shortly after he was arrested. "He's a wonderful young
man, despite all he has been through," she offered.

Every day, thousands of young Black men like Lexus leave correc- 8
tional institutions with no clear sense of what comes next. "There are
barriers everywhere when these young people reenter society," says
Satchel. "With a record, they often find it impossible to get jobs and
housing. Many of them have no home to return to." What, I wonder,
has made the difference for Lexus Sirmans? He faced the same challenges as other young men who had done time, yet he seemed to be
moving consistently forward. With all we hear about the crimes that
Black boys commit, we should also hear the story of one young man
who is trying to turn things around.

Man of the House

Following a phone introduction by Peggy Lieurance, Lexus and I met for 9
the first time a month after he was released. I wanted to know his story,
but I also hoped that I could share something with him that would spur
him on. It wasn't just the similarity of our impoverished, dangerous
inner-city childhoods; in fact, we looked as though we could be
brothers—two outsized Black men with broad features and reserved

demeanors. On the day of our first meeting, Lexus rolled into the parking lot of a fast-food joint just outside Atlanta. His car stereo thumped thick, drawling southern hip-hop. He had been free just over six weeks and was still delighting in things the rest of us take for granted, like being able to eat whenever he wanted to. Nevertheless, Lexus confesses, "The hardest thing about being out is having to make my own decisions. In prison they tell you when to eat, when to sleep, when to dress or see your family. You walk in a line. The only decision you get to make is whether or not you're going into the block," he says, referring to an isolation unit that some juveniles prefer to the more violent general-population cells.

10   As we talked that day, I learned Lexus was the first son in a family of four children. When he was 7 years old, his parents' marriage began to unravel. They divorced shortly after that. He seemed to be on the right track, excelling in school and sports until he hit adolescence and his easygoing manner began to give way to a simmering anger. His parents said little to him about the problems that had led to the divorce, but the issue became increasingly more important in his life as he grew older. He came to resent feeling that he was raising himself because his mother, Josephine Sirmans, worked such long hours as a nurse's aide. His father, Gary, contributed financially, but as Lexus recalls, needs often went unmet. For Lexus, his father's physical absence also left a void. As with the finances, Gary showed up when he could, but not necessarily when his children needed him most. When he did come around, conversations were brief, boiled down, the bare minimum. "I felt pressured to be the man of the house," Lexus tells me. "I was 14, the oldest male living there. It was just me and my little brother left in the house—the others had moved out. My mother wasn't making enough to take care of us, I didn't depend on my father back then."

11   For Lexus's mother, meeting the needs of her children was difficult and exhausting. She often worked double shifts at her job and was also studying to become a nurse practitioner so she could make a better life for her family. "He saw me struggling to work and go to school, and he would tell me that things would be OK and that one day he would buy me a house," she recalls. For Lexus, the breaking point came when he and his brother returned from school one day to find that there was nothing in the refrigerator. He tells me it was then and there that he decided something had to change.

Boy in the Hood

12   "I started cutting school and began to hustle," Lexus confesses. He and his best friend, Skip, hooked up with the neighborhood players and began selling weed. "I was sick of having nothing," Lexus says quietly.

"Sick of seeing my family with nothing." Sometimes Lexus still attended school, and he did well in his favorite classes. For a while he made the honor roll and even played linebacker on the football team, but by the time he was 15 he had become a full-time hustler.

"I went from being on the honor roll at school to just being about 13 money." With his drug earnings, Lexus bought clothes for himself and his brother, convincing his busy mother that the money came from odd neighborhood jobs.

His peers regularly indulged in drug use, "but I never even tried 14 any of it," he tells me. He was, even then, something of a loner, and not particularly concerned with impressing others. Instead, he embraced a Darwinist street ethic: "I felt that if I had to make things bad for some-one else because that was the only way to make things good for my family, then that was what was going to happen."

Screams in the Night

Viewed through the lens of music videos and the nightly news parade 15 of Black offenders that reduce our communities to thug habitats, the image of Black boys as predators-in-waiting has proliferated. Some experts cite this as a factor in the new, harsher juvenile-crime laws. But Nina Hickson, chief judge of the Fulton County Juvenile Court in Atlanta, is convinced that the harsher laws do nothing to deter crime. She's also troubled by the fact that they are most often applied to Black boys. "I don't buy the notion that you have more Black boys commit-ting serious acts," she says. "What you have is the issue of discretion. District attorneys decide which cases to pursue in adult court, and it's easier to prosecute an indigent child than a child of means." While youth crime has decreased, Hickson and a number of other advocates are quick to point out that it was declining even before the new laws were enacted.

In February 2001, Lexus and one of his crew were charged with 16 committing a car theft at gunpoint. They were apprehended shortly thereafter and tried separately. Lexus's trial ended in a hung jury, a sit-uation his attorney used to negotiate a plea bargain with a maximum sentence of five years. His friend was sentenced to a minimum of ten years in prison. While Lexus didn't get the severe mandatory sentence that so many of his peers did, he was ordered to serve his time in an adult facility.

By law, juvenile inmates in Georgia are to be separated by "sight 17 and sound" from the adult population. But a hearing held in January 2003 before the Georgia state legislature revealed widespread viola-tions of the age-segregation policy. In one particularly egregious incident at Alto, a group of minors (not including Lexus) was strip-searched in full view of the jeering adult population—an incident the Georgia Department of Corrections denies. But as Lexus commented, "You're not supposed to go across the yard to the adult facility until you're 18," he says, "but it didn't go down like that for me." Lexus spent every day of his sentence "across the yard."

18   Lexus was 17 years old with no prior criminal record when he entered the state prison at Alto. There he would see things that continue to haunt him. Almost inaudibly, he recounts the story of a friend of his—also a juvenile—who was invited to gamble with a set of older inmates. The young man quickly fell into debt, and the older men used this as an excuse to seize any of his belongings they desired. It didn't take long for the thefts to escalate into something much worse. The boy was raped one night, an incident Lexus overheard as he sat locked in his cell across the corridor. He tells me another story about a fight he witnessed between two adult inmates. "One guy kept getting stabbed so badly," Lexus says, his face turned away from mine.

19   What stays with him, echoing in his memory are the screams he used to hear in the Alto nights. "Sometimes, remembering those times still keeps me up at night," he whispers. Though his size may have played a role in protecting him from harm, Lexus believes he avoided trouble by keeping to himself, saying his prayers and "staying focused." He's big on this word focus. To hear him tell it, learning to focus is what got him through his time upstate. He focused on keeping busy—working out, reading and taking G.E.D. classes.

20   Josephine Sirmans spoke to her son after he was arrested, asking him how he would have felt if someone had robbed her at gunpoint. The question shook him. She urged her son to keep praying and to read his Bible every day. He explains that something clicked for him when he had sat on the witness stand talking about crimes he had committed. "I realized that being in jail wasn't me," he says simply. "There was too much out there in the world for me to do to be locked up. I started out wanting to help my family and keep my brother on the right path, but I couldn't do either one when I got arrested."

Father and Son

21 When Lexus was summoned to the visiting room one afternoon two months into his sentence, he thought his mother had left work early to take the long drive upstate for a surprise visit. He walked into the room to find his father, Gary, seated at a table waiting to speak to him. They hadn't seen each other in several months. Lexus's mother had called Gary shortly after her son was arrested. While Lexus's father

didn't attend the trial, or the hearing in which his son was sentenced, the more he thought about it, the more he blamed himself for his son's trouble. "I was never there for him like I should have been," Gary says. He came to Alto hoping to rebuild their relationship. "It was extremely painful seeing my boy locked away like that." He believes that his absence from the home had left Lexus with too much time on his hands and too few examples to counter "negative peer pressure." He took that first long drive upstate from Decatur to Alto, resolved to reconnect with his son. "I felt as if I had to let him know that I'm still his father and that I'd be there for him if he needed me," he says.

"I held a grudge against him at first," Lexus recalls. But during his father's biweekly visits, his resistance gradually dissolved. "We spent more time together when I was locked up than we ever did when I was on the street," Lexus says. The renewed relationship with his father, a heating and air-conditioning technician, helped Lexus let go of the anger he'd held inside for so long, the anger of a boy forced to be a man too soon. "I tried to keep his mind occupied on ways to make money other than selling drugs when he came home," Gary says. "I told him that I would have a job lined up for him when he got out." 22

Over the course of their conversations, a plan unfolded: Upon his release, Lexus would start out as an apprentice technician and enroll in night classes. When he had gained enough experience, the two would go into the refrigeration business together. Lexus soon resolved that when he came home, he would avoid the old crew, with the exception of his friend Skip, who had stopped dealing and returned to both the church and high school almost immediately after Lexus was arrested. "They call Alto 'the revolving door,'" Lexus reflects. "They told me that my chances of coming back to prison were eight out of ten. But I've never been one to fall for the same thing twice." 23

You Can Go Home Again

Still, returning home has been a challenge for him. "Coming home he found that he had changed, but nothing else had," says Peggy Lieurance. Many of the old crew were still around, floating from one dead-end hustle to the next. Lexus learned that he would have to remain focused on the outside as well. But by far the most difficult thing he had to confront was losing Skip: The week that Lexus was released, his boyhood friend was murdered, shot seven times on his eighteenth birthday during a dispute. "Before I even got a chance to say 'hey,' he was gone," Lexus says. 24

But as difficult as it was to come home, Lexus also had some sup- port. "Unlike many other young people, Lexus has a strong network," 25

Lieurance says. "He had a family who stuck by him all the way through this mess." And he has Lieurance. She has remained a presence in his life, calling regularly to check on his progress and to encourage him to keep working hard. She tells him he has much to offer the world if only he keeps believing in himself. Josephine Sirmans shifts uncomfortably in her chair when talking about her oldest boy and the page he is trying to turn. "He has worked very hard to make a life for himself," she says. "Thank God he's putting this behind him at an early age." The key has been prayer, she says. "This was something that God had to help him through."

26   Three weeks after Lexus was released, Gary Sirmans was able to get his son the job he had promised him as an apprentice repairman for a heating and air-conditioning company. The hours are long: He leaves home at 6:30 AM and often doesn't get back until 7 PM. But Lexus works in the same unit as his father and notes that the day goes by faster with good company. In the evenings, Lexus lifts weights on the porch or watches movies. Most nights, he's in bed by 11:30 PM. His rigid devotion to work is not really surprising considering his long-standing concern about being able to contribute financially to his family. But on another level, it seems that Lexus is trying to distill life on the outside down to its simplest polarities—work and rest—as a means of avoiding the gray areas that could lead to trouble. "I just want to work," he says.

College-Bound

27 Less than a month after his release, Lexus returned to the Regional Youth Detention Center to speak to young men who were being sent up to the adult facility. He talked with them about how to make the time serve them, rather than their serving the time. "As you get older, seeing young people incarcerated gets to be painful," he says, sounding aged beyond his years. "You know they're gonna wind up having bad memories." Going back inside may have been as useful for Lexus as it was for the young men he spoke to: It was an additional reminder that he didn't want to be one of the many who will find themselves back behind bars. Lexus advised his peers to "avoid troublemakers." Near the end of his talk, he told them to "stay focused."

28 Four months after our first meeting, Lexus calls, asking me to help him with his application to a local technical college. When I pick him up, we slap palms and run through the elaborate Brothers' Handshake before punctuating it with The One-Armed Hug. He whips out a picture

of his "lady friend," a young woman who's going away to college in a few weeks. We walk across Spelman's campus where I teach history. When I show him my office he marvels at the shelves of books I have. "I read this in prison," he says, holding a copy of *The Autobiography of Malcolm X*. I pull several of my favorite Walter Mosley novels off the shelf and give them to him. A few hours later, we mail off his application. As we part I tell him that he's out to do some big things. Lexus pauses, then cracks that slightly embarrassed smile.

Reflection and Discussion

1. Identify how Cobb makes this his story as well as the story of Lexus Sirmans. Why does he use this personal connection and how effective is it?

2. Under what conditions, if any, should juveniles be treated as adults in the criminal justice system? If they are tried and convicted as adults, what reasons could justify different punishment?

Writing Matters

1. Cobb mentions two models of prisoner treatment—rehabilitation and retribution. Research one of them, explaining the forces that shaped it. How does this model influence prison costs and recidivism rates? How likely is it to advance prison reform?

2. Talk to a cross-section of people, some of whom you consider successful and others who may need direction in their lives, and ask who have been major influences for them. Ask about the importance of mentors, relatives and friends. How did they find help when they needed it? Compare their experiences with yours. How might your findings apply to people who are at risk of going to jail?

Justice Statistics

- In 2001, 6.7 million Americans were either on probation, on parole or incarcerated.
- One in every 15 US residents born in 2001 (6.6 percent) will be incarcerated at some time.
- The lifetime chances of going to prison are 18.6 percent for African Americans, 10 percent for Latinos and 3.4 percent for Caucasians.
- African American prisoners in local jails outnumber Latinos 3 to 1 and Caucasians 5 to 1.

Source: Bureau of Justice Statistics as cited in *Human Rights: Journal of the Section of Individual Rights & Responsibilities*, Winter 2004

Hotel California: Prisons and Punishment

Staff, *The Economist,* February 26, 2005

This article was written by the staff at The Economist, *a British publication widely read in the US.*

TV, movies and songs describe prison life, but how would you expect the reality to be different?

1   You can check out, but you seldom leave.

2   "The purpose of prison is punishment," declares the mission statement at the entrance to the California State Prison, in Los Angeles County. The tattooed inmate known as K32096, some 11 years into a 13-year sentence for drug offences, has got the message: "There's no rehabilitation in prison. The CDC (California Department of Corrections) wants you to come back because it's their job security. And the medical treatment's bad: I've got hepatitis-C and I've been waiting five months to see a doctor." Other prisoners add their complaints while the guards patiently stand by.

3   Could it be otherwise, given the overcrowding of California's prisons? The Lancaster prison, in the high Mojave desert, opened 12 years ago to house 2,200 offenders; now it has 4,600. One gym has become a makeshift dormitory, with three-tiered bunks for 120 "special needs" prisoners (i.e., inmates who risk assault because they have reneged on drug debts, dropped out of the prison gangs or are serving time for child-molesting). The prison warden, one year into his job, finds it hard to recruit enough doctors and psychiatrists.

4   By California's ghastly standards, Lancaster is not particularly awful. There was a riot involving 300 inmates four years ago; last September one mentally disturbed prisoner killed his cellmate. All the same, one murderer describes it as "probably the calmest prison I've been in."

5   Just as Lancaster's woes—race-based gangs, drugs, rape, overcrowding—are fairly typical of California's penal system, so California's system is typical of America's. The state's imprisonment rate—455 out of every 100,000 people were inside in 2003—is a little below the national average and well behind Texas (702) and Louisiana (801); but it is still several times that of Britain or indeed any other developed country. California's jails now house 163,000 prisoners (each at an annual cost of $31,000); that is more than France, Germany and the Netherlands combined.

In an American context, California's prisons stand out for two   6
things: overcrowding and recidivism. The state has only 32 prisons,
which hold twice as many people as they were designed for. By contrast, New York state has 65,000 inmates in 70 prisons and Florida has
82,000 in 121 facilities. Worse, California's "correctional facilities" singularly fail to correct: three in four prisoners will be convicted of
another crime within three years—and three out of five will be back in
prison. (Nationally, a quarter are back in prison for new crimes and
another quarter are back in prison for parole violations.)

This marks a substantial reversal. Last year a committee headed by   7
George Deukmejian, a former Republican governor, pointed out that
from the 1940s through the 1970s the Californian correctional system
was seen as a national leader and "a model of efficiency." The
Deukmejian report is part of a flurry of prison-related activity under
Governor Arnold Schwarzenegger, who has made reforming the system a priority. On his very first day in office, in November 2003, he
appointed Roderick Hickman, a tough-talking former guard, to head
the state's Youth and Adult Correctional Agency (YACA), which oversees all the prisons. This week, he sent a reform plan to the legislature;
under Californian law the plan will automatically become law unless it
is voted down in the next 60 days.

But is the governor really confronting the problem? The debate   8
about why California's prisons became so terrible comes down to two
things: dramatically tougher sentencing policies and mismanagement.

Trends in sentencing account for the huge splurge in prisoners.   9
Back in 1970, the state housed 22,400 inmates; that figure had risen
nearly eightfold by the end of the century. The main spur—as it has
been everywhere in America—has been tougher mandatory sentencing, such as the state's infamous but extremely popular "three strikes"
law. More than 30,000 prisoners are now serving life terms.

Conservatives, including Mr. Schwarzenegger, insist that tough   10
sentences have helped reduce crime. The new laws have certainly
removed a large number of criminals from the streets; but each year
California has to set free some 100,000 people like K32096. And the link
between tough sentencing and crime rates is not absolute. California's
crime rate—3,944 crimes per 100,000 residents in 2002—is higher than
that in New York state (2,804), where the rate of imprisonment has
risen much more slowly.

Whatever the rights and wrongs of sentencing, mismanagement   11
has clearly made things much worse. Too few prisons have been built
to deal with the rush. No money has gone into rehabilitation. And the
whole system has been held to ransom by the politically powerful
prison-guards' union. The California Correctional Peace Officers

Association (CCPOA), which represents 31,000 guards, has been a generous donor to governors from both parties—and has been well looked after itself. The average guard's salary rose from $14,400 in 1980 to $54,000 in 2002, almost twice the national average for a prison officer.

12   One federal investigation reported last year that "rather than CDC staff correcting prisoners, some correctional officers acquire a prisoner's mentality: they form gangs, align with gangs, and spread the code of silence." In other words, no guard will "snitch" on his brother officers, even if they organize gladiatorial fights between inmates or negligently allow a prisoner to die (last year, an inmate who had pulled a dialysis shunt from his arm bled to death while the guards were watching the Superbowl on TV).

13   The problem is not just the guards. As the Deukmejian report notes, "each warden acts as a feudal baron, employing different standards and different operating procedures." The report pointed out that the YACA had "little or no power." It is very difficult for Mr. Hickman to remove bad wardens or indeed bad guards.

14   Mr. Schwarzenegger's plan has the YACA firmly in his sights. He wants to rename YACA the "Department of Corrections and Rehabilitation"; to make prison wardens directly responsible to Mr. Hickman; to put more emphasis again on education and rehabilitation; and, in order to break the infamous code of silence, to require prison guards to blow the whistle on any "misconduct, unethical or illegal behavior"—or face dismissal.

15   Mr. Schwarzenegger's reforms differ from the Deukmejian report in one important way: there is no independent civilian commission to oversee the correctional system. Mr. Hickman, pointing out that civilian overseers failed to rein in the Los Angeles Police Department, says civilian oversight would simply add an extra level of bureaucracy. However, Joe Gunn from the Deukmejian commission has argued that the culture of an organization cannot change "without having someone on the outside, free of politics, driving reform."

16   This is an indirect reference to the power of the prison guards. Mr. Schwarzenegger's supporters point out that he has refused to accept CCPOA donations; he has also tried to undo some of the huge wage increases promised by his Democratic predecessor, Gray Davis.

17   Yet the guards have still got a pretty good deal from the current governor, including better health-care benefits, pay rises well above inflation, and guarantees against lay-offs for two years. A federal judge has even accused Mr. Schwarzenegger of conceding too much power and threatened to appoint a receiver to run the prison system.

18   This matters, because for Mr. Schwarzenegger's reforms to stick, a lot depends on Mr. Hickman's determination to break the code of

silence. Ominously, the union, which was not involved in planning the reform, is being publicly skeptical, claiming that Mr. Hickman's vow to "blow up the boxes" (a Schwarzeneggerian metaphor) will be more like a shifting of the furniture.

The other, bigger problem with Mr. Schwarzenegger's plan is that 19 fundamental question about sentencing laws. For Mr. Schwarzenegger, these are non-negotiable: he is a strong supporter of the three-strikes law. Asked about the same law, Mr. Hickman replies: "If I can succeed at reducing the recidivism rate, the sentencing policy would be irrelevant." However, he envisages reducing the re-offending rate by only 2–3% a year.

As long as the courts continue to send huge numbers of people 20 (often for somewhat trivial offences) into an overburdened system with neither the resources nor the will to reform them, it is hard to see how the prisons will change much. And failure to consider sentencing as part of the problem gives some of Mr. Schwarzenegger's reforms an unreal aspect. Who, for example, could object to the goal of reducing the use of gyms as makeshift "bed space" by January 2006? But there are 9,000 prisoners crammed into such ugly beds at the moment—and more on the way.

Meanwhile, rehabilitation, according to the warden at Lancaster, 21 will take more staff—and therefore more money. No wonder the prisoners themselves are skeptical. As one Latino inmate, K84265, puts it: "If I go back to the streets, I can make $60,000 a week selling drugs. What's the Correction Department doing to give us jobs? Basically, this is a big warehouse for human beings who've done wrong."

Reflection and Discussion

1. How would you describe the mindset of the prisoners mentioned in the article? What factors are most responsible for this? How might their attitudes affect their behavior in prison and their preparedness to reintegrate into society?

2. What might explain why prison staff tends to adopt behavior that resembles the behavior of prisoners?

Writing Matters

1. When this article was written, each prisoner in California cost the state an average of $31,000 a year. Try to estimate how the money is spent. Then look up the current per-prisoner cost and check your approximations with a reliable source which breaks this number down. How close was your guess? What surprised you? What monetary decisions would you recommend and how would they affect prison conditions overall?

2. Most states have mandatory sentencing laws. Explain when and why they were enacted and identify the political forces that perpetuate them. Why have they been called "infamous"? How popular are they with the public? What about with politicians? How have they changed the landscape of American criminal justice?

Toxic Recycling

Elizabeth Grossman, *The Nation,* November 21, 2005

Elizabeth Grossman wrote Watershed: The Undamming of America *as well as other books and articles.*

What kinds of dangers are you willing to accept in the workplace?

1   About ten miles northwest of Merced, amid the dairy farms and orchards of California's San Joaquin Valley, sits the Atwater Federal Penitentiary, its tower and low-slung buildings the same mustard yellow as the dry fields that stretch out beyond the chain-link fence and concertina wire toward the Sierra Nevadas. Inside this maximum-security prison, inmates smash computer monitors with hammers, releasing dust that contains lead, cadmium, barium and other toxic substances. These inmates are employed by the electronics recycling division of Federal Prison Industries (better known as UNICOR). With sales that have nearly tripled since 2002, electronics recycling is UNICOR's fastest-growing business. But according to reports from prisons where this work is being done and interviews with former inmates employed by UNICOR, it's taking place under conditions that pose serious hazards to prison staff and inmates—and, ultimately, to the rest of America and the world.

2   In late 2004 Leroy Smith, Atwater's former safety manager, filed a formal complaint with the Occupational Safety and Health Administration. According to Smith, workers at Atwater's UNICOR facility are routinely exposed to dust from heavy metals. They were eating lunch in an area contaminated by lead, barium, beryllium and cadmium, he says, and using safety equipment that doesn't meet OSHA standards. Neither staff nor inmates were properly informed about the hazards, says Smith, who has more than a decade of experience with the Bureau of Prisons. After his superiors sent OSHA a report that downplayed and denied the problems, Smith sought whistle-blower protection. He's now on paid leave while his lawsuit works its way through the Justice Department.

With $10 million of revenue in 2004, seven prison facilities and about 3 1,000 inmate employees who last year processed nearly 44 million pounds of electronic equipment, UNICOR is one of the country's largest electronics recyclers. There are about 400 electronics recyclers in the United States—a burgeoning industry that is vital to solving one of the information age's peskiest problems. Americans own more than 2 billion pieces of high-tech consumer electronics. With some 5 to 7 million tons of this stuff becoming obsolete each year, e-waste is now the fastest-growing part of the US municipal waste stream. It's the most challenging mass-produced trash we've ever had to deal with.

The cathode ray tubes (CRTs) in computer and television monitors 4 contain lead, a neurotoxin, as do printed circuit boards. A typical desktop computer may contain up to eight pounds of lead. Mercury, another neurotoxin, is used in flat-panel display screens. Monitors contain cadmium, a known carcinogen. Circuit boards and exteriors use plastics containing flame retardants documented as disrupting thyroid hormone function and acting as neurotoxins in animals.

When high-tech equipment is intact, these substances are mostly 5 harmless. But when digital devices are physically damaged—almost inevitable during disposal—the toxins emerge. By 2001 an Environmental Protection Agency (EPA) report estimated that discarded electronics accounted for 70 percent of the heavy metals and 40 percent of the lead in US landfills. Synthetic chemicals used in electronics have been found in people, animals, food and household dust all around the world.

Given the hazards posed by landfilling and incinerating high-tech 6 electronics, the safest way to dispose of them is to separate their materials, which can then be reprocessed as feedstock for new products. But these materials are tightly packed, largely unlabeled and of variable design, making that separation process both expensive and labor intensive.

That's where UNICOR comes in. The United States—unlike the 7 European Union and several other countries, including Japan—has no national laws requiring electronics recycling. Yet over the past few years, individual states and local governments have begun enacting legislation to keep high-tech trash out of their landfills. At the same time, a growing number of businesses and organizations, concerned about the liabilities posed by dumping old computers, are opting to have equipment recycled. To save money many are sending equipment to UNICOR.

"UNICOR's program is labor intensive, so capital machinery and 8 equipment expenses are minimized; this helps keep prices low," says a company brochure. With a captive workforce UNICOR's electronics recycling program can afford to be labor intensive. Because it is run by the Bureau of Prisons, UNICOR does not have to pay minimum wages—recent wages were $0.23 to $1.15 an hour—or provide benefits. Though UNICOR is not taxpayer supported, its pay scale would not be possible without taxpayer support of the inmates.

9   The savings payoff for UNICOR: In 2004 UNICOR's Lewisburg, PA, prison facility won a contract from the Pennsylvania Department of Environmental Protection with a price one-quarter of that bid by private-sector recyclers. "I welcome the competition, but let's level the playing field," says Andy Niles of Scientific Recycling in Holmen, Wisconsin. Niles says he had to lay off about one-quarter of his staff after losing business to his state's prison industry.

10   "Busting up monitors exposes you to a lot more risk. But broken monitors saves on shipping costs," says Greg Sampson of Earth Protection Services, another private recycler. "Broken, you can fit about 100 into a carton, whereas only thirty-five or so will fit if they're intact. We don't break ours up." Neither do other private recyclers I contacted. "It's more expensive, but we pack them in lined boxes that are shipped with a manifest indicating hazardous material contents, and we use special machines to deactivate CRTs," explains Scott Sodenkamp, operations manager at the Noranda Recycling plant in Roseville, California. At Atwater, Leroy Smith told me, broken CRTs are packed in cardboard cartons and sealed with plastic wrap.

11   UNICOR doesn't just save money by busting up monitors and paying prison wages. Instead of investing in state-of-the-art disassembly equipment and durable safety gear, UNICOR reportedly distributed ball-peen hammers and cloth gloves to inmates working at Atwater. "The gloves ripped easily and there were lots of bad scratches and cuts," a former Atwater UNICOR worker told me. Staff and inmates who worked at UNICOR's Elkton, Ohio, and Texarkana, Texas, operations have similar accounts of broken glass, noxious dust and injuries resulting from inadequate tools.

12   UNICOR declined my request to visit the Atwater facility. But an OSHA inspector who toured it in late 2004 confirmed many of the inmates' complaints: "While conducting sampling, I observed, and numerous workers reported, the improper use of tools and techniques due to the lack of appropriate tools to more safely dismantle monitors."

13   "We were given light-particle dust masks and the stuff would get in behind them," the former Atwater inmate told me. "In the glass-breaking room, guys would be pulling junk out of their hair and eyebrows. We were coughing up and blowing out all sorts of nasty stuff, and open wounds weren't healing." The coveralls inmates wore on the job—kept on during breaks and meals—would come back from laundering with glass and metal dust in rolled cuffs, he says. Work boots were worn outside the factory, too, potentially contaminating other

areas of the prison—something OSHA regulations are designed to avoid. Prison staff, say Smith and others, wear regular uniforms and shoes in the factory, allowing contaminated dust to be transferred to their cars, homes and families.

In 2002, air samples taken at Atwater found lead levels twice OSHA's 14 permissible exposure level, and cadmium ten times the OSHA standard. Wipe samples found lead, cadmium and beryllium (which causes severe lung disease) on work surfaces and inmates' skin. Blood and urine testing found barium, cadmium and lead, some at elevated levels.

UNICOR's computer disassembly process releases so much lead, 15 in fact, that its dust qualifies as hazardous waste. Smith and former staff at UNICOR's Elkton, Ohio, facility say this waste has been improperly handled. "Prison staff were removing the filters that collect the dust from the glass-breaking without wearing respirators, and putting these filters in the general prison trash," says Smith, who showed me photographs of worktables covered with thick layers of pale gray dust.

Because UNICOR works behind bars, it has another advantage 16 over its competitors: It doesn't have to be prepared for unannounced OSHA inspections. And even though some factories opened in 1997, there were no OSHA inspections until 2004. The air tests in late 2004 found lead, barium and cadmium at Atwater—but below the levels at which OSHA requires the use of safety equipment. These test samples, however, were not taken around inmates "involved in the deliberate breaking of computer monitors," says the OSHA report. Even so, barium, beryllium, cadmium and lead were found on work surfaces; barium, cadmium and lead were found in the workers' dining area, creating the potential for accidental ingestion. But none of that violates OSHA standards. As the OSHA inspector noted, there are actually "no standards or regulatory levels for these metals on surfaces."

How toxic is the dust? Long-term exposure to low levels of cad- 17 mium damages kidneys and can lead to lung disease. Workers exposed to the levels of lead found in Atwater's air in 2002 would eventually have elevated blood lead levels—not enough to cause acute lead poisoning but plenty to cause kidney or neurological damage, according to leading environmental and occupational health scientists. "If a workplace has enough lead to fall near the OSHA standards, that would be enough to come home and pose a risk to children," says Howard Hu, a professor at the Harvard School of Public Health.

Inhalation exposure is the most dangerous in terms of getting lead 18 into the body, Hu says. OSHA standards—and those now set by the EPA—likely allow far higher exposure than is truly safe. In fact, says Dr. Bruce Lanphear, director of the Children's Environmental Health

Center at Cincinnati Children's Hospital Medical Center, "there is no safe level."

19   Despite the recent surge of concern about data security, most people know little about where discarded digital equipment ends up. Great quantities of e-waste sent to domestic recyclers end up overseas—in China, Africa, Southeast and South Asia, and other developing regions—where much of it is processed cheaply, under unsafe and environmentally unsound conditions. To avoid this, many recyclers and their clients demand rigorous documentation of the downstream flow of dismantled equipment.

20   "Environmental stewardship and social responsibility are critical issues for our clients," says Robert Houghton of Redemtech, which recycles electronics for Fortune 500 companies. Redemtech considered working with UNICOR, Houghton told me, but chose not to because UNICOR could not provide the downstream accountability Redemtech's customers required.

21   UNICOR says that no material it recycles will be landfilled or exported for dumping. UNICOR's no-export policy prohibits shipping electronic waste to any country barred by the US government from receiving US products. These countries, UNICOR told me, are Cuba, Iran, Iraq, North Korea, Libya, Sudan and Syria. But that leaves many countries to choose from, since US laws only prohibit exporting hazardous material destined for disposal—rather than recycling—or when it involves transfer of "sensitive" technology. "It's absolutely legal to send this stuff to Pakistan," says Houghton.

22   Much of what UNICOR recycles comes from the federal government, which buys about 7 percent of the world's computers and disposes of at least half a million each year. In 2002 the Defense Department sent some 17 million pounds of used electronics to UNICOR for recycling. UNICOR's website also lists several universities as clients. But some counted as customers no longer are—among them the University of Colorado, which wanted better documentation than UNICOR provided. Same with Johns Hopkins. "Using prison labor was not looked at very favorably," says a university employee who asked not to be named.

23   The United States is the only industrialized nation that uses prison labor for electronics recycling. "We can do without it, but are we willing to do without it?" asks Craig Lorch, whose company, Total Reclaim, is among the thirty or more that have pledged not to use prison labor. Until environmental and social benefits are given priority over the bottom line, UNICOR's low-cost option will continue to be used by the government and many others. But relying on workers who are not paid a living wage, and who work in unhealthy and environmentally unsound conditions, displaces rather than solves the e-waste problem.

The long-term environmental costs cannot even be calculated. As long as the United States does not require transparency and accountability from recyclers, it will be impossible to know how these toxic materials are treated, or where they go.

Reflection and Discussion

1. Why do you think American laws for recycling electronics equipment are more lax than those in Western Europe and Japan?
2. What obligation does UNICOR have to look out for the health and safety of its prison workers?

Writing Matters

1. How common do you think it is for prisoners to do this kind of dangerous work? Find out how many states require prisoners to work. What kinds of work do they do? How much are they paid? How do prisoners feel about working? How does the work they do affect other American companies and workers that compete with prison-made products and prison labor?
2. Grossman states that "most people know little about where discarded digital equipment ends up." Whose fault is that? Where should the burden be when potentially dangerous consumer goods need to be discarded? Should the owner be responsible for disposal costs? Should the government impose rules? Should manufacturers step in? Devise a workable program to address this issue.

Hundreds of Thousands of Inmates Mentally Ill

Fox Butterfield, *New York Times,* October 22, 2003

Fox Butterfield has written on a wide variety of subjects for major newspapers and is the author of All God's Children.

Once, people with serious mental handicaps were put in psychiatric hospitals. Where do you see them now?

As many as one in five of the 2.1 million Americans in jail and prison are 1
seriously mentally ill, far outnumbering the number of mentally ill who are in mental hospitals, according to a comprehensive study released Tuesday. The study, by Human Rights Watch, concludes that jails and

prisons have become the nation's default mental health system, as more state hospitals have closed and as the country's prison system has quadrupled over the past 30 years. There are now fewer than 80,000 people in mental hospitals, and the number is continuing to fall.

2   The report also found that the level of illness among the mentally ill being admitted to jail and prison has been growing more severe in the past few years. And it suggests that the percentage of female inmates who are mentally ill is considerably higher than that of male inmates. "I think elected officials have been all too willing to let the incarcerated population grow by leaps and bounds without paying much attention to who in fact is being incarcerated," said Jamie Fellner, an author of the report and director of United States programs at Human Rights Watch. But, Ms. Fellner said, she found "enormous, unusual agreement among police, prison officials, judges, prosecutors and human rights lawyers that something has gone painfully awry with the criminal justice system" as jails and prisons have turned into de facto mental health hospitals. "This is not something that any of them wanted." Reginald Wilkinson, director of the Ohio Department of Rehabilitation and Correction, said the "mere fact that this report exists is significant. Some people won't like it, and the picture it paints isn't pretty," Mr. Wilkinson said. "But getting these facts out there is progress."

3   Many of the statistics in the study have been published before by the Justice Department, the American Psychiatric Association or states. But the study brings them together and adds accounts of the experiences of dozens of people with mental illness who have been incarcerated. The study found that prison compounds the problems of the mentally ill, who may have trouble following the everyday discipline of prison life, like standing in line for a meal. "Some exhibit their illness through disruptive behavior, belligerence, aggression and violence," the report found. "Many will simply—sometimes without warning—refuse to follow straightforward routine orders."

4   Where statistics are available, mentally ill inmates have higher than average disciplinary rates, the study found. A study in Washington found that while mentally ill inmates constituted 18.7 [percent] of the state's prison population, they accounted for 41 percent of infractions. This leads to a further problem—mentally ill inmates who cannot control their behavior are often, and disproportionately, placed in solitary confinement, the study found. Solitary confinement is particularly difficult for mentally ill inmates because there is even more limited medical care there, and the isolation and idleness can be psychologically destructive, the report says. Medical care for mentally ill inmates is often almost nonexistent, the study says. In Wyoming, a Justice Department investigation found that the state penitentiary had a

psychiatrist on duty two days a month. In Iowa, there are three psychiatrists for more than 8,000 inmates.

There is no single accepted national estimate of the number of mentally ill inmates, in part because different states use different ways to measure mental illness. The American Psychiatric Association estimated in 2000 that one in five prisoners was seriously mentally ill, with up to 5 percent actively psychotic at any given moment. In 1999, the statistical arm of the Justice Department estimated that 16 percent of state and federal prisoners and inmates in jails were suffering from mental illness. These illnesses included schizophrenia, manic depression (or bipolar disorder) and major depression. The figures are higher for female inmates, the report says. The Justice Department study found that 29 percent of white female inmates, 22 percent of Hispanic female inmates and 20 percent of black female inmates were identified as mentally ill. One reason some experts have suggested for the higher numbers among female prisoners is that psychologists and psychiatrists working in prisons tend to be more sympathetic to women, finding

FIGURE 11.2 Would you let this happen to someone you loved?

them mentally ill, while they tend to evaluate male inmates as antisocial or bad. But Mr. Wilkinson said, "I think the differences are real; more female inmates are mentally ill." He suggested that prisons were seeing more severely mentally ill inmates now "only because the volume is greater," meaning that the number of people in prison has increased.

Reflection and Discussion

1. Butterfield provides evidence that jails and prisons are the wrong places for those with serious psychological problems. If virtually everyone in the criminal justice system believes this is wrong, why does it continue?
2. Butterfield says that mental health professionals working in prisons often tend to identify men as antisocial and women as mentally ill. Consider how men and women present their problems differently.

Writing Matters

1. Research to find out why so many psychiatric hospitals closed and how the mentally ill ended up in prisons. In what respect are the mentally ill at the lowest rung of the prison ladder? Who are their advocates? What priority should we afford them when it comes to health services and treatment? How can we "put a face" on this population? What will it take to improve their lot? Propose some practical solutions.
2. Human Rights Watch and Amnesty International are two groups that publicize cases of violence, torture and other human rights abuses across the world. How important are independent organizations like these? Visit their websites. What do they share in common with an organization like The Sentencing Project? How are they different?

Dying Well in Corrections: Why Should We Care?

Ira R. Byock, M.D, *Journal of Correctional Health Care, 2002*

Ira R. Byock is Research Professor of Philosophy at the University of Montana, Missoula.

How should prisoners be treated when they are dying?

Why Should We Care?

1 Dying in prison is what inmates dread most. They fear spending their last hours in agony, alone, separated from family outside and from friends within prison walls. Yet these worst dreams can come true for

over 2,500 prisoners a year who die manacled in hospitals or in prison infirmaries.

Why should we care where and how inmates die? This question is 2 implicit whenever prison hospice or compassionate release is discussed in the media and with politicians. Many people respond that we should care because prisoners are human beings, and humane treatment is the right thing to do. Others feel that convicted murderers, rapists, drug dealers, and the like deserve whatever they get. If they die suffering, in pain and alone, so be it.

But turning a blind eye is not an option. American courts have 3 forcefully distinguished punishment from brutality, and they have affirmed society's responsibility to provide care for prisoners (*Estelle v. Gamble*, 1976). Corrections has responded with guidelines and policies. Under scrutiny of prisoners and advocacy groups, institutions that fail to provide adequate care risk legal peril and fiscal liability, so that delivering medical care in corrections is aligned with society's (and taxpayers') best interests.

The Universality and Great Equalizer of Death and Dying

A more considered response to why we should care is that all of us, 4 even the well-to-do and law-abiding, are at risk of winding up in circumstances similar to prisoners as we approach life's end. There are striking similarities between a long prison sentence and the diagnosis of a terminal illness that forces confinement and restricts function and independence.

Terry Tempest Williams (1991) said of her mother's illness and 5 death:

> Tolstoy writes about a man, wrongly accused of a murder, who spends the rest of his life in a prison camp. Twenty-six years later, as a convict in Siberia, he meets the true murderer and has an opportunity to free himself, but chooses not to. His longing for home leaves him and he dies.
>
> Each of us must face our own Siberia. We must come to peace within our own isolation. No one can rescue us. "My cancer is my Siberia," said my mother.

All of us are at risk of entering that unfortunate group for whom 6 death is the "great equalizer"—along with its cousins: illness, dementia, physical debility, and advanced age. Dying prisoners are more similar to than different from others facing such unenviable conditions, all of whom are too frequently viewed as of no practical use to society and a drain on resources.

7   Jail is not the only imprisoner. Even one who has never broken a law but is seriously ill or physically dependent may feel defenseless in an uncaring environment. Most Americans would like to die at home, surrounded by their loved ones. Yet, fully 80% die in hospitals and nursing homes. A study of 104 terminal patients in an academic medical center and affiliated hospital found that 18% were in physical restraints within 48 hours of their deaths (Goodlin, Winzelberg, Teno, Whedon, & Lynn, 1998).

8   A posthumous article by a nursing home patient speaks poignantly of her last days:

> I tried once or twice to make my feelings known. I even shouted once. That gained me a reputation of being "crotchety." After I've asked for help more than a dozen times and received nothing more than condescending smiles and a "Yes, deary, I'm working on it," something begins to break. I only wanted to be taken to the bathroom.
>
> I'd love to go for a meal, to travel, to go to my church, to sing with my choir, to visit my friends.
>
> I've learned to accept loss of privacy. I'll close my door when my roommate (imagine having a roommate at my age) is in the TV room. I appreciate some time to myself, and I believe I have earned that courtesy. As I sit thinking or writing, one of the aides invariably opens the door unannounced and walks in as if I'm not there. Am I invisible? Have I lost my right to respect and dignity? I am still a human being, and I would like to be treated as one.
>
> The afternoons drag into evening. This used to be my favorite time of the day. Things would wind down. I would kick off my shoes and put my feet on the coffee table and open a bottle of Chablis and enjoy the fruits of my day's labor with my husband. He's gone. So is my health. This is my world. (Halgrim, 1994)

9   At the end of life, we are far more alike than different from one another. How we care for others may well determine how we are cared for ourselves.

Palliative Care and Hospice

10 Although "palliative care" and "hospice" are often used synonymously, as I define them, "palliative care" is a discipline of practice,

while "hospice" is a means of delivering that discipline to dying patients. Palliative care involves:

1. Respect for patient autonomy and the role of family and legal surrogates in making decisions when patients cannot
2. An interdisciplinary team approach
3. Caring for the dying individual *with* his or her family and close friends
4. Intensive symptom management for comfort and quality of life with no modality withheld
5. Understanding that dying is a time of life and part of the human cycle, in which a patient's *inner* life often comes to the fore as death comes near
6. Bereavement support for families and caregivers

(Last Acts Task Force, 1998; National Hospice Organization, 1997)

Although symptom management is often equated with palliative 11 care, it is but the first priority, which, if not under control, leaves patients unable to attend to anything else. Physical pain, for all our medical prowess, remains poorly treated, even in prestigious medical institutions (SUPPORT Principal Investigators, 1995). Undertreatment of pain in our nation's nursing homes and outpatient clinics may affect 50% of patients (Bernabei, et al., 1998; Breitbart, et al., 1996; Cleeland, et al., 1994).

Palliative care recognizes, however, that dying is more than a set of 12 medical problems to be solved. Dying is personal; it is experiential. Caring for people who are dying involves helping them to say and do the things that matter most *to them.*

The period of living we call "dying" holds important opportunities 13 for the patient to communicate, and to complete or reconcile strained relationships among family members and friends. There is a chance to tell one's stories, to review one's life, and to make a unique contribution to legacy. Those around the dying person can listen, receive, and reaffirm for the person departing the value of his or her being and explore the deeper questions of meaning and connection in the human condition (Byock, 1997, 1996).

Those who are "family" in this circumstance are not defined by 14 marriage or bloodline alone, but by the phrase "for whom it matters." Family members need to know that their loved ones are receiving the best possible care, that their wishes are honored, that they are treated with dignity, and that they had a chance to say and do the things that most matter to them. Families also need time to grieve together.

The Challenge of Palliative Care in Corrections

15 Although the challenges confronting correctional end-of-life care are more difficult, the obstacles are not fundamentally different from the pervasive barriers encountered providing health care for dying Americans. Several factors, however, complicate attempts to provide care and contribute to the suffering of dying inmates.

16   Prisons are rife with personality disorders, racism, and gangs. Isolation and anger abound, and hostility finds fertile ground. Seeds of compassion among personnel and inmates often find little soil in which to take root. Inmates are vulnerable in this environment, and their distrust causes tension with providers. Restrictions against diversion of medications may restrict access to narcotic analgesics on which hospice and palliative care rely. Continuity of care is not easy to achieve.

17   Formal standards and thoughtful research help claim the high ground. The American Correctional Association (1996) has called for the establishment of "hospice services for terminally ill offenders supported by a compassionate release program for those who qualify." The standards of the GRACE Project (2000) and the National Commission on Correctional Health Care (2003) both address end-of-life care. The Health Resources and Services Administration of the United States Department of Health and Human Services has issued a task force report on "Improving Palliative Care Practice in Jails and Prisons" (Dubler & Post, 2001). The Last Acts Task Force (1998) and the American Geriatrics Society (1997) offer guidelines for protocols and the education of clinicians, security and administrative personnel, legislators, and the public. The prospect of dying inmates actually receiving not only medically competent but genuinely compassionate care may seem implausible. Yet, 35 or more programs currently exist or are in development, most experiencing real success. Courageous, but also cautious, wardens and leaders in corrections departments have supported them without sacrificing the priorities of detention, safety, and security. Hospice leaders have reached out to correctional staff, sharing expertise and resources. Clinicians caring for inmates have shown true professionalism adapting palliative care and hospice to their environments.

18   Correctional administrators and managers will find hospice programs positive and cost-effective. By providing high quality care that measurably conforms to community standards, the correctional system also will earn some protection from legal allegations of deficient care.

The Use of Volunteers

Much of the credit for the success of hospice and palliative care in cor- 19
rections is attributable to volunteers, whose efforts and commitment
have been extraordinary. Visiting with prison hospice volunteers and
correctional staff has reminded me of William Golding's classic novel,
Lord of the Flies, which involved adolescents stranded on a remote
island without the usual constraints of civilized life. Cooperation gradually gave way to competition, conflict, and aggression. Penitentiaries
are islands within our society, yet prison hospices are the opposite of
Golding's chaotic island.

Inmate volunteers attest to the remarkable transformative effect of 20
hospice work:

> I have learned that life is precious and so is what I do
> with it. . . . Without the men who showed me death, I might
> never have learned to live. . . . I care more for people now.
> I volunteered for hospice because I saw it as an opportunity
> to do something positive for someone else, which in turn
> allows me to feel better about who I am. My motivation
> now comes from what I see in a patient's eyes as I enter the
> room. I know that if I'm of no value to anyone else, I am of
> value to him.

An inmate serving a life sentence at Oregon State Penitentiary has 21
written about his experience as a hospice volunteer for a fellow inmate
dying of cancer:

> I knew that Benito's death would be very painful for me if I
> allowed myself to get close to him. But keeping my distance
> or imposing boundaries on our relationship were never
> options for me. I wanted and needed to open my heart com-
> pletely, to be there for him unconditionally, no matter how
> painful it might be for me in the end.
>
> When Benito was overcome by fear of pain, I stayed
> through the night when I could. Sometimes we talked all
> night; sometimes I spent the night supporting his head with a
> pillow as he tried to nap in a wheelchair, the least painful
> position for him. Sometimes, I massaged knots out of tight
> pain-ravaged muscles, and sometimes I just sat quietly next to
> him so he wouldn't be alone.
>
> Benito's trust in me grew, and our bond deepened as
> we spent countless hours talking about the things that mat-
> tered most: family, love, memories, fears, regrets, spiritual

questions, pain, cancer, and death. He gave me a gift I will treasure until the day I die when he said, "A month ago I didn't know you existed, but now you are my family." A hospital vigil began for Benito when it was believed he was within 48 hours of death. His family was escorted to the infirmary where they joined Benito and me. We were with him around the clock, comforting him with cool washcloths and pillows, holding his hand, and doing anything else we thought might ease his suffering.

I attempted to stay in the background as the family shared their intimate stories, laughter, love, tears, and pain. But as the four of them were saying their good-byes, Benito called for me. Without hesitation, his family opened their hearts and allowed me to share in this profoundly intimate moment. We hugged and cried as each of us told Benito how special he was to us and how much we were going to miss him.

Gradually, he slipped into a coma-like state. We were all aware that he was about to die. Yet there was a deep sense of peace and resolve among us. We wanted him to know that we were all still with him. None of us wanted to leave his side. It was a rare moment that we all weren't touching him as Benito passed away. (M. Wilson, personal communication, 2000)

22   In contrast to the traditional image inmates hold of "dying inside," the process of dying, even "inside," can liberate people, creating a space of freedom *inside themselves* as they die. This is what success in hospice in corrections means.

Conclusion

23 Clinicians do not have to reconcile issues of legal or metaphysical guilt before caring for patients in corrections and their families and caregivers. These considerations are irrelevant to the task of caring. Genuine palliative care entails preserving the capacity of patients and families to grow through the end of life. Prison hospice workers observe personal qualities of openness, honesty, and tenderness in patients and volunteers—and sometimes real transformation. Sometimes, life's most profound lessons come from unexpected places. It is worth examining why, in prison hospices, inmates are choosing to work together, without recognition or material reward, to care for one another and to build a civil community. This compassion is evidence of goodness in the human condition where one might least expect to find it.

References

American Correctional Association. (1996). *Public policy on correctional health care.* Lanham, MD: Author.

American Geriatrics Society. (1997). Measuring quality of care at the end of life: A statement of principles. *Journal of the American Geriatrics Society, 45,* 526–527.

Bernabei, R., Gambassi, G., Lapane, K., Landi, F., Gatsonis, C., Dunlop, R., Lipsitz, L., Steel, K., & Mor, V. (1998). Management of pain in elderly patients with cancer. *Journal of the American Medical Association, 279*(23), 1877–1882.

Breitbart, W., Rosenfeld, B. D., Passik, S. D., McDonald, M. V., Thaler, H., & Portenoy, R. K. (1996). The undertreatment of pain in ambulatory AIDS patients. *Pain, 65,* 243–249.

Byock, I. R. (1996). The nature of suffering and the nature of opportunity at the end of life. *Clinics in Geriatric Medicine, 12*(2), 237–252.

Byock, I. R. (1997). *Dying well: The prospect for growth at the end of life.* New York: Putnam.

Cleeland, C. S., Gonin, R., Hatfield, A. K., Edmonson, J. H., Blum, R. H., Stewart, J. A., & Pandya, K. J. (1994). Pain and its treatment in outpatients with metastatic cancer. *New England Journal of Medicine, 303*(9), 592–596.

Dubler, N. N., & Post, L. F. (2001). *Improving palliative care practice in jails and prisons.* Rockville, MD: U.S. Department of Health and Human Services, Health Resources and Services Administration. Estelle v. Gamble, 429 U.S. 97 (1976).

Golding, W. (1999). *Lord of the flies.* New York: Penguin Books.

Goodlin, S., Winzelberg, G. S., Teno, J. M., Whedon, M., & Lynn, J. (1998). Death in the hospital. *Archives of Internal Medicine, 158,* 1570–1572.

GRACE Project. (2000). *Standards of practice for end-of-life care in correctional settings.* Alexandria, VA: Volunteers of America.

Halgrim, A. M. (1994, June 27). My turn. *Newsweek, 11.*

Last Acts Task Force. (1998). Precepts of palliative care. *Journal of Palliative Medicine, 1,* 109–112.

National Commission on Correctional Health Care. (2003). Care for the terminally ill. In *Standards for health services in prisons.* Chicago: Author.

National Commission on Correctional Health Care. (2003). End-of-life decision making. In *Standards for health services in prisons.* Chicago: Author.

National Hospice Organization. (1997). *A pathway for patients and families facing terminal illness.* Arlington, VA: Author.

SUPPORT Principal Investigators. (1995). A controlled trial to improve care for seriously ill hospitalized patients. *Journal of the American Medical Association, 274,* 1591–1598.

Williams, T. T. (1991). *Refuge: An unnatural history of family and place.* New York: Pantheon Books.

Reflection and Discussion

1. Byock believes that even murderers deserve to die with dignity. To what extent does this belief compete with the needs of the poor and homeless who have no guaranteed end-of-life care?

2. Which parts of the article are the most personal and how well does this human touch work? When have you done something similar in your writing?

Writing Matters

1. Argue for or against the release of terminally ill prisoners. Under what circumstances would your plan make the most sense? Should criminals who committed certain types of crimes be disqualified? Why?

2. Among the people you know, how many have been to jail or known someone who has? How have these associations affected them? Gather some of these experiences and relate them to one or more articles in this chapter. How do they confirm or conflict with what the articles have to say?

Changing the Lives of Prisoners: A New Agenda

Lawrence T. Jablecki, *The Humanist,* November/December 2005

Dr. Lawrence T. Jablecki has taught philosophy to prisoners in Rosharon, TX, and taught in the Department of Sociology at Rice University. He is also a contributor to The Humanist.

If you were asked to create a program to educate prisoners, what would you include?

1 Opinion polls of the last several years on crime and punishment in the United States demonstrate the consensus that two major consequences should occur in the lives of convicted criminals who are sentenced to prison. First, that the duration of their loss of freedom in society is for most of the sentence in real calendar time; and second, upon release they are "better" people. Increased prison capacity and the implementation of truth in sentencing are approximating the first demand. Presumably, a better person is understood to mean one whose thinking has been redirected or transformed during incarceration and who, following release, will be equipped to resist any temptation to return to a life of crime. There are no fairies to distribute magic wands to prison

administrators to wave over the heads of inmates immediately prior to their release that will sprinkle virtue dust on them and transform them into better people.

The research data of the same opinion polls inform us that the 2 "vast majority" of Americans believe that most prison inmates are capable of changing into law-abiding members of society and should during their incarceration be given a significant variety of opportunities for change. Therefore, a massive infusion of new funding into the annual budgets of the prison and parole components of all state and federal agencies is needed. Such prison program expenditures should be restricted to the following:

- The creation and expansion of general educational programs culminating in General Education Diplomas and high school diplomas and the creation and expansion of college and university programs in which inmates can earn undergraduate and graduate degrees.

- Though many, if not most, Americans have mixed feelings or are opposed to helping finance college or university degrees for prison inmates, the benefits of higher education for those who are capable is grounded in the research data of numerous evaluations, all of which verify that the recidivism rate of those who complete these programs is significantly less than for inmates who are released with lesser or no educational accomplishments. Of course, inmate opportunities shouldn't take anything away from any ordinary person who meets the eligibility criteria for educational grants and loans. In this connection, Congress should introduce legislation enabling prison inmates to receive Pell grants, which were previously discontinued when many in Congress were duped into believing that multitudes of needy and law-abiding citizens were being denied these grants because of awards to prison inmates.

- The creation and expansion of vocational programs, the completion of which would qualify inmates for good-paying employment in numerous blue-collar professions.

- The creation and expansion of counseling programs, staffed by well-qualified people, designed to meet the needs of those inmates with any substance abuse problem or psychological or psychiatric issue.

- The creation and expansion of visitation opportunities for families of inmates in order to strengthen and reestablish bonds of affection and support, which are of vital importance for successful reentry into communities.

3   Just doing these things will go a long way toward more effectively promoting the rehabilitation of inmates and a reduction in recidivism.

4   Then it's time to "think outside the box." With the aim of increasing the number of opportunities for all inmates eligible for release to participate in education programs capable of igniting the desire and strength of will to become a better person, a commitment should be made to Project Habilitation or Changing Lives through Literature.

5   Project Habilitation entails the abandonment of the "myth of rehabilitation" in favor of a much more accurate account of the thinking and behavioral habits of the majority of prison inmates. The universally accepted definition of rehabilitation is to restore a person to a former state of good health or a useful and constructive purpose. But most of the people in our prisons have never developed habits of thinking and conduct conducive to living a law-abiding life. Instead, they think and act as if they and their immediate desires are the center of the universe around which all human life revolves. It would therefore be a serious mistake to rehabilitate them. Habilitation, by contrast, is the civilizing, educational, and life-transforming experience caused by the power of knowledge to grab a human mind and redirect the course of a person's life. More specifically, habilitation is a "spiritual conversion" to thinking and acting in compliance with the cardinal requirement of an ethical life: namely, that our civil society is a moral community in which all members are entitled to certain human rights and are bound by the obligation to respect the rights of others.

6   Changing Lives through Literature is a bold experiment that can be used as a paradigm for creating similar programs in both state and federal prisons. It was designed in 1991 by Robert Waxler, a professor of English literature at the University of Massachusetts at Dartmouth, and Robert Kane, a district court judge in New Bedford, Massachusetts, to serve as a sentencing option for recalcitrant male probationers facing the prospect of a prison sentence. Waxler made the highly unconventional request that the court "send a group of eight to ten of those bad guys to me at the university and I will introduce them to the transformative power of some of the great works of literature." Kane embraced the challenge and "go to school and read books or go to jail" became a new choice for some probationers in New Bedford. In 1992, following a meeting with Waxler and Kane, Jean Trounstine, a professor of humanities at Middlesex Community College in Lowell, Massachusetts, with the enthusiastic support of District Court Judge Joseph Dever, instituted a similar program for female probationers.

7   The probationers selected for these programs aren't creamed from the group most likely to succeed but must demonstrate an eighth-grade reading level. The texts for the men's classes include *The Old Man*

and the Sea by Ernest Hemingway, *Of Mice and Men* by John Steinbeck, and *Animal Farm* by George Orwell. The texts for the women's classes include *The Bluest Eye* by Toni Morrison, *The House on Mango Street* by Sandra Cisneros, and *Their Eyes Were Watching God* by Zora Neale Hurston.

During its fourteen-year history this genuine revolution in crimi- 8 nal justice has spread to a significant number of other states, as well as to Canada and the United Kingdom. This is due largely to the indisputable findings of independent evaluations that numerous lives have been redirected in a crime-free path as a direct result of reading and discussing powerful presentations of the issues and questions endemic to the human condition. Qualified scholars in the humanities can assemble a long list of significant readings accessible to the mental abilities of most of the people incarcerated in our state and federal prisons.

The successful implementation of these new initiatives, however, 9 will require major changes in how we use some of our existing prison facilities, the criteria for the employment and retention of correctional officers, and the creation of new policies designed to reward inmates for good conduct and the completion of educational and vocational programs.

First, most prisons are extremely noisy places. Some of them, and 10 large sections of others, should be transformed into education units in which inmates are housed and can work, learn, and study in a quiet environment. Second, we must follow the lead of those who are working to transform the culture of correctional staff into a real profession, requiring some post high school education and entitlement to higher annual salaries. Third, it is totally unrealistic to expect masses of inmates to decide to become better people in the absence of a substantial incentive. This is where we have another opportunity to "think outside the box" by initiating a bold plan to satisfy legitimate grievances of parole-eligible inmates and maintain protection of the public interest.

Inmates are more likely to embrace educational and vocational 11 programs and behave with civility if the following information is given to them in written form and fully explained during their orientation and evaluation as incoming prisoners:

Every inmate, upon reaching eligibility for parole, is entitled to a 12 public hearing administered by a three-member panel of parole commissioners. This panel will allow oral and written testimony from all parties in favor of or against the granting of parole. This means that victims and prosecutors will appear in some cases to protest the release of a violent and dangerous person. It also means that witnesses for the inmate—for example, spouses, children, parents, clergy, and teachers—will be given time to state why they are urging the panel to grant parole. Inmates shall have the right to address the panel from the witness stand in order to explain their accomplishments and how they have changed subsequent to incarceration. Inmates shall have the right to retain counsel to prepare their case and to guide them through their testimony.

13   Any decision by the panel of parole commissioners would require two votes. Immediately following the admission of all testimony in a case, the members may vote and explain their judgment in the open hearing, or they may decide to take the matter under advisement for a period not to exceed thirty days. The hearing would then be reconvened, at which time each panel member would explain her or his vote to the inmate. This procedure is nearly equivalent to the inmate's trial at which evidence was presented, guilt was confessed or determined, and a sentence was imposed. In short, the critically important function of this procedure is that it steers clear of a nondiscretionary, mandatory release of inmates judged to be a continuing threat to society and encourages the decision makers to grant release to numerous inmates who, in the panel's judgment, have reached or are on their way to habilitation.

14   In this connection, state governors will need to resist the temptation to appoint their own cronies to these important positions in the administration of criminal justice. Parole commissioners should be assigned a caseload with a minimum-maximum range and this become the benchmark for determining the number of such positions in every state. The minimum qualifications for appointment should be a four-year degree from an accredited college or university, a documented knowledge of criminal justice, and a reputation for possessing the courage to express one's beliefs in a public forum. Appointments should be for a term of five years and eligibility restricted to two successive terms. These positions would be full time and earn an annual salary commensurate with responsibilities.

15   With these recommendations, however, the fact remains that some of the 600,000 people released annually from prisons are going to commit more crimes and spit defiantly in the face of any new policies and programs. There are no silver bullets armed with a guarantee to habilitate all of them. But we must not allow this grim and inevitable reality to derail our determination to stay the course. The inmates who complete counseling and vocational and education programs, and are nearing release, must be the focus of attention of the agencies charged with preparing them for reentry and with supervision following their release.

Of interest in this regard is the fact that Texas is the birthplace of a 16 paradigm that should be replicated and funded in every state and federal jurisdiction that supervises ex-offenders. It was in 1985 that a two-city experiment called Project RIO, the reintegration of offenders, was launched. The mission of this ambitious and optimistic state program was and is to provide job preparation services to prison inmates in order to give them a head start in the post-release search for employment. The project has been funded entirely by the state's general revenues and "represents an unusual collaboration between two state agencies . . . the Texas Workforce Commission (the state's employment agency) and the Texas Department of Criminal Justice (Institutional and Parole Divisions)." And from its small beginning to the present, Project RIO has established a track record of assisting and finding employment for thousands of ex-offenders, documented a significantly lower recidivism rate than comparable groups of non-participants, and saved the state millions of real tax dollars.

Given the publicly verified accomplishments of Project RIO and 17 the potential for nationwide replication, there should be a national commitment to fund and a sufficient number of professional and support staff to:

- provide a comprehensive job readiness orientation for all prison inmates within three to six months of their release
- recruit and train a legion of non-paid volunteers to serve as mentors to inmates prior to and after their release
- contact and recruit corporations, companies, and small business operations willing to hire ex-offenders
- support changes in federal and state legislation to increase tax credits for those who hire ex-offenders.

The lure of federal dollars, many tied to matching grants, should 18 be used to entice the majority of states to set in motion the guts of this new agenda.

Beyond the reintegration of the newly released comes the reintegra- 19 tion of the previously released. Toward this latter end, a governmental commission needs to be created—composed of some of the nation's most influential scholars in constitutional law, jurisprudence, criminal justice, and the humanities—with marching orders to make some realistic recommendations for eliminating most of the numerous barriers or collateral consequences preventing millions of former prison inmates from being eligible to receive assistance from a variety of state and federal programs. And they would also make recommendations regarding the timely restoration of the civil and political rights of the former prison inmates.

20   The goal of everything discussed here is simply to protect the lives and property of law-abiding citizens. This new agenda isn't based on the false belief that the majority of criminal offenders are victims of a sick society or some psychological illness and therefore actually deserve all the programs and services advocated. There is nothing here to throb a bleeding heart. There is no assumption that everyone, deep down inside, is basically a good person. Rather the motivation, plain and simple, is the public interest. This new agenda is purely practical. Thus it holds the promise of bipartisan support.

21   Compare this with the idealistic, unrealistic, impractical, and ideologically driven notion that sectarian faith is the answer. And understand that this new agenda requires no violation of or amendment to the US Constitution. Moreover, it is consistent with the proud tradition of "American know-how," "Yankee ingenuity," and that "can-do" spirit of rolling up one's sleeves to "get the job done."

Reflection and Discussion

1. Many Americans are against providing a college education for prisoners while they are in jail. How do you feel about the issue and why?
2. Jablecki draws a distinction between "rehabilitation" and "habilitation." How well does his explanation work?

Writing Matters

1. Jablecki calls for "a massive infusion of new funding into the annual budgets of the prison and parole components of all state and federal agencies." How likely is this to occur? Imagine a scenario in which it could. Where would the money come from? How could the program be promoted to the public? What kinds of sacrifices would be necessary? In what possible ways could prison reform pay for itself?
2. Jablecki proposes a course for inmates entitled Changing Lives Through Literature. How valuable is it compared to specific job training? In what ways can literature change a person? What books have you read that have changed you (or, at least, strongly influenced your ways of thinking and acting)? What do you think of his book list? What changes would you make?

MAKING CONNECTIONS

1. If you don't break the law, you might wonder why you should care about those behind bars. Argue either for or against getting involved in prison reform. Why should the average American bother about it? If prisons are

broken and getting worse, what difference can one person or one group make?

2. One could argue that the prison problem cannot be treated in isolation, that it is a symptom of a systemic problem. If that is true, what is wrong with the system? Untangle the web. Research how other conditions (attitudes, inequalities, injustices) contributed to the breakdown in our prisons. What do we as a society need to change in order to see positive effects in our prisons (or to see a reduction in the prison population)? You may wish to go into great detail on what you consider to be the one most important factor, or somewhat less detail on several factors, but limit your inquiry so that you can provide in-depth analysis.

3. How do media influence public response to the criminal justice system? Look at movies, books and TV programs that remind you of issues addressed in these readings and writers, artists and media personalities who have spoken out about prison conditions. What differences, if any, do you find between those who have been imprisoned themselves and those who haven't? To what extent do you support celebrities acting as experts on such issues?

4. Research the history of prisons. What role did religious beliefs play in how prisoners were regarded and treated? When have prisons been at their worst? Their best? What countries have been most successful in matters of crime and punishment and what can we learn from them?

TAKING ACTION

1. Many feel that the best way of ultimately addressing the prison problem—especially with respect to young people—is to go to the source, the individual. Change the individual, his or her thinking and behavior, and you change society. Efforts in this area are often directed at the population of at-risk youth. A wide range of organizations are involved in youth tutoring and/or mentoring, for example, the Big Brothers and Big Sisters Programs, the Kiwanis, Lions and Junior League. Others are Communities in Schools (CIS), SafeFutures and Children at Risk (CAR). Even VISTA and AmeriCorps volunteers provide this kind of help.

   Investigate the mentoring or literacy programs on your campus or in your community, especially those with experience helping delinquent or at-risk youth. Interview some of the volunteers as well as those being helped. Consider taking part yourself. Then compile your account of the lives affected in a portfolio of stories and experiences. Include an explanation of what you thought before you became involved and how you feel now.

2. Research to find the most effective tools for helping prisoners successfully reenter civilian life. Which of these are available in your community? Research should include studies as well as information about specific volunteer organizations. Summarize your findings in a letter to a local or state Department of Corrections official in order to get feedback or to learn who else to contact for advice.

Who Is a Patriot?

Among all symbols in American life, none is more familiar nor more powerful than the flag. Close your eyes and you can picture soldiers wearing it on their sleeves, children pledging allegiance to it, sports fans paying it respect, politicians displaying it in their campaigns and merchandisers in their ads. But when we ask ourselves what the flag means, the picture becomes less clear. During times of crisis, the flag has united the country and helped it heal. After the events of September 11, 2001, it was especially prominent, and, for many, the flag took on new meanings. While polls indicate that extremely high percentages of Americans call themselves patriotic, when we look more closely, we often find ourselves asking what the term means.

BEFORE YOU READ

How do you feel about the American flag? Does it have more positive associations for you in some contexts than others? What is the best way for people to oppose government policies they disagree with? How do you feel when someone steps on or burns the flag?

FIGURE 12.1 Where do flag images belong in our consumer culture? Where are they inappropriate?

Footprints on the Flag

Anchee Min, *The New Yorker*, October 15, 2001

The author was born in Shanghai and now lives in Los Angeles. She is known primarily as a writer, but she is also a musician, photographer and painter.

Were you raised to respect the flag? Have your attitudes toward it remained constant over time or have they changed?

I arrived in America on September 1, 1984, at the age of twenty-seven. Using the few English words I had memorized, I asked the immigration officer in Seattle for an opportunity to stay. "If I don't learn English in three months, I'll deport myself," I promised. After he stamped my passport, I flew to Chicago, where I had been accepted by the School of the Art Institute of Chicago, thanks to a friend who had helped me fill out the application. When the institute found out that I didn't speak English, I was sent to a language program at the University of Illinois. Over the next few months, I learned to speak English by watching "Sesame Street" and Oprah Winfrey, and I supported myself by working as a fabric painter—painting roses on women's underwear—and as a waitress in a Chinese restaurant.

2   My roommate, Alice, was a Black pre-med student from Mississippi. She didn't mind that I was quiet, because she loved to talk. One day, when I was reading an article about President Reagan in the local paper, she exclaimed, "Ronald Reagan is a dog! Do you understand?" I sprang up from my chair and looked over my shoulder. In China, you would be imprisoned for saying something like that about Mao.

3   I had grown up during Mao's Cultural Revolution and had been in the Red Guard since I was nine years old, when I had joined to avoid being beaten. I had been taught to write Mao's name before I learned to write my own, and had painted hundreds of portraits of him for parades. In the nineteen-seventies, I spent three years in a labor camp, following Mao's teaching, until I was discovered by the Shanghai Film Studio. Because of my "proletarian look"—weather-beaten face and a solid body—I was chosen to play leading roles in Madame Mao's propaganda films. After her downfall, I was denounced as "political debris" and was given a job at the film studio, working fourteen-hour days as a set hand. By the end of eight years, I had seriously considered committing suicide.

4   Eight months after coming to America, I started my studies at the Art Institute. I continued working at the restaurant, and got a job at the institute's student gallery. One of the exhibits was an American flag laid flat on the floor. About three feet above it, mounted on the wall, was a notebook-size diary. I noticed that viewers had to step on the flag in order to read the diary. Footprints had started growing on the flag like blotches of mold. I felt that I had neglected my duty. I quickly took off my jacket and used it to wipe the flag clean. When the next viewer came, I politely said, "Please be careful and do not step on the flag."

5   Two weeks later, the artist arrived to check on his work. When I told him that I had taken great pains to erase the footprints, he informed me, furiously, that he had intended to have people step on the flag. We argued. I said that I was grateful to America—if this country hadn't taken me in, I would not have survived. The artist replied that I had no idea of the terrible things the American flag symbolized. I needed to get my English straight, he said, so I could begin to understand what this country had done to its people and to the world.

6   I couldn't find the words in English that were filling my head in Chinese. I wanted to tell him that twenty years earlier I had done exactly what he was doing now. I had been taught to hate Americans,

and I had burned the American flag. We had watched films in which Americans poked out the eyes of pregnant Vietnamese women. When I was eleven, I had denounced my beloved teacher as an American spy. As a teenager, I had taken a wooden stick and attacked a body made of straw with a United States Army helmet on its head. We were preparing for a war should the Americans dare to set foot on the soil of China.

When the professor in my twentieth-century American art class 7 showed us Andy Warhol's Mao series, I thought, What's wrong with this country? I couldn't understand why a professor would project slides of Mao in an American classroom, when more than a billion Chinese were finally taking Mao buttons off their jackets, Mao portraits off their walls, and Mao quotations out of their speeches.

Most nights after class, I went to my waitressing job, where the 8 owner of the restaurant used to say, "The house is not on fire!" if I walked fast, and "I didn't hire you to be lazy!" when I slowed down. One evening, I said, "I quit."

FIGURE 12.2 Anchee Min writes of her experience with this art installation by Scott Tyler, entitled "What Is the Proper Way to Display a US Flag?" What message did the artist intend to communicate?

9　The awareness of myself as more than a screw in the Communist machine came slowly. This consciousness of the individual, I realized, was the essence of American art. Warhol's famous Mao series now seemed to say, "Who made Mao?" A year ago, I was described in a *Times Magazine* article as an "American writer." When I showed the story to my father, he smiled splendidly. To him, it meant that his daughter was finally free of fear. He said, "Anchee, now you are ready to write about China."

Reflection and Discussion

1. How has Min's story confirmed or made you reevaluate your opinions about the American flag?
2. When the author's roommate criticized President Reagan, Min's first reaction was fear. How comfortable do you feel speaking your mind about politics? Do Americans need to fear censorship or reprisals from our government?

Writing Matters

1. Min suggests that being called an "American writer" was something that she had to earn. Is her sense of being an American similar to or different than yours? How was her past in China a major influence on her thinking?
2. When the artist responsible for the flag exhibit took liberties with the flag, was this his right? Did he go too far? What point may he have been trying to make? What do you think of what he said to the author and how he said it?

Patriotism and Sacrifice

Todd Gitlin, excerpted from *The Intellectuals and the Flag,* 2006

Todd Gitlin is a professor of journalism and sociology at Columbia University. His books include Letters to a Young Activist *and* The Sixties: Years of Hope, Days of Rage.

Do you display the flag at home? Have you ever worn a flag symbol or put one on your car? Why do people do this?

1　Patriotism is almost always affirmed too easily. The ease devalues the real thing and disguises its weakness. The folklore of patriotism lends itself to symbolic displays wherein we show one another how patriotic we are without exerting ourselves. We sing songs, pledge allegiance, wave flags, display lapel pins, mount bumper stickers, attend (or tune in) memorial rites. We think we become patriotic by declaring that we are patriotic. This is activity but of a desiccated sort. It is striking how many of these touchstones we have now—how rituals of devotion are folded into ball games and concerts, how flags adorn the most commonplace of private activities. Their prevalence permits foreign observers to comment on how patriotic the simple-minded Americans are. But such displays are not so straightforwardly proofs of patriotism at all. They are at least equally substitutes. Schaar's stricture is apt here: patriotism "is more than a frame of mind. It is also activity guided by and directed toward the mission established in the founding covenant."[1] Patriotic activity starts with a sense of responsibility but does not discharge it with tributary rites of celebration and memory. Patriotism in this sense, genuine patriotism, is not enacted strictly by being expressed in fashion. It is with effort and sacrifice, not pride or praise that citizens honor the democratic covenant.

To put it this way is to erect an exalted standard. Yet to speak of the 2 burdens of patriotism points to something not so flattering about the patriotism that Americans so strenuously claim. Perhaps Americans celebrate patriotism so energetically at least in part because, when we get past the breast beating, our actual patriotic experience is thin on the ground. Perhaps Americans feel the need to tout Americanism and rout un-Americans precisely for this reason—not because we are such good patriots but for the opposite reason. In the United States we are not much for substantial patriotic activity. Ferreting out violations is the lazy person's substitute for a democratic life. If civic patriotism requires activity, not just symbolic display, Americans are not so patriotic after all.

The work of civic engagement is the living out of the democratic 3 commitment to govern ourselves. Actual patriotic experience in a democracy is more demanding—far more so—than the profession of sentiments; it is more easily advertised than lived up to. Democratic patriotism is also far more demanding than signifying loyalty to the regime. In a kingdom the patriot swears loyalty to the monarch. In a totalitarian society the patriot is obedient in a thousand ways—participating in mass rituals, informing on enemies, joining designated organizations, doing whatever the anointed leader requires. But democratic loyalty is something else, stringent in its own way. If the nation to which we adhere is a community of mutual aid, a mesh of social connections, then it takes work, engagement, time. It is likely to take money. It may take life. It is a matter, to borrow a phrase of 1776, of pledging "our lives, our fortunes, and our sacred honor." It may well require that we curb our individual freedoms—the indulgences that normally we count as the highest of values.

In a word, lived patriotism entails sacrifice. The citizen puts aside 4 private affairs in order to build up relationships with other citizens, with whom we come to share unanticipated events, risks, and outcomes.

These citizenly relationships are not ones we choose. To the contrary. When we serve on a jury or in Teach for America or ride in the subway, we do not choose our company. The community we partake of—like the whole of society—is a community of people whom we did not choose. (Thus the embarrassment to the individualistic ideal of self creation.) The crucial difference here is between a community, consisting of people crucially unlike ourselves, and a network, or "lifestyle enclave," made up of people like ourselves.[2] Many "communities" in the sense commonly overused today—"the business community," "the academic community"—are actually networks, a fact that the term disguises. Cosmopolitanism is also usually lived out as a network extension: it invites connections with people (usually professionals) like ourselves who happen to live in other countries.

5   Undemocratic societies require sacrifice, too, but unequally. There, what passes as patriotism is obeisance to the ruling elite. Democracy, on the other hand, demands a particular sort of sacrifice: citizenly participation in self-government. This is not the place to explore the difficult questions of where participation must stop and professional management must start. But the important principle is that the domain of popular involvement should be as large "as possible," the question of possibility itself deserving to be a contentious one. At the very least, at the local level the citizens should approve the agenda for governmental action. The result is twofold: not only policy that takes distinct points of view into account but a citizenry that takes pride in its identity as such. When the citizen enters the town meeting, the local assembly, or the jury, disparate qualifications hardly disappear, but they are tempered, counterbalanced by a common commitment to leave no voice unattended.

6   Decision making aside, democratic life also requires spheres of experience where citizens encounter each other with equal dignity. Put it another way. A democratic culture is one in which no one is exempted from common duties. Commonality and sacrifice are combined. This is the strong side of what has become known as communitarianism, which has also been called liberalism. As Mickey Kaus argued in *The End of Equality*, social equality requires bolstering three spheres: the armed forces and national service; public schools; and adult public domains (transportation, health, day care, public financing of elections). The operative word, of course, is public. It is in these sectors that the Republic's commonality lives, on the ground, in time and space. In the armed forces life is risked in common. In national service time is jointly invested in benefits that do not accrue to self-interest. When loopholes are closed, class mixing becomes integral to life. Privilege, however useful throughout the rest of life, can't buy you

everything. In public schools privilege doesn't buy superior opportunities. In amenities like public transportation, governments provide what private interests would not, and individuals experience themselves as sharing a common condition. If public spheres dwindle, sheer wealth and income grow in importance.[3]

We also need some common sacrifice of our self-indulgences—not 7 to test our Puritan mettle but to prevent ecological break-down. Having proven averse to eco-efficiency in production, consumption, and transportation, despite our robust achievements in global warming and air and water pollution, we have a particular responsibility to lean less heavily on the earth. Since oil dependency is a considerable factor behind some of the most egregious US foreign policies, true patriotism is fully compatible with, indeed intertwined with, ecological sanity that reduces fossil-fuel guzzling and promotes sustainable sources like solar and wind power. Yet Detroit automakers steadfastly resist hybrid gas-electric cars and increased fuel efficiency, and Washington permits them to get away with their profligacy. Patriots ought to endorse the environmentalist Bill McKibben's suggestion that "gas-sucking SUVs . . . should by all rights come with their own little Saudi flags to fly from the hood."[4]

Overall, egalitarian culture is patriotism's armature. No matter 8 how many commemorations Americans organize, no matter how many pledges we recite and anthems we stand for, the gestures are inessential. At times they build morale—most usefully when the suffering is fresh—but they do not repair or defend the country. For that, the quality of social relations is decisive. And the contrary follows, too: the more hierarchical and less equal the nation becomes, the less patriotic is its life. Not that the culture as a whole should be in the business of enforcing egalitarian norms—the ideal that populism defended and Stalinism made murderous. But there must be zones of social life, important ones, where the same social goods are at stake for everyone and individual distinction does not buy exemption. The most demanding, of course, is the military—and it is here where the stakes are highest and the precedents most grievous, that universality is most important. It must not be possible to buy substitutes, as the wealthy on both sides did in the Civil War. Many are the inequalities that are either morally legitimate or politically unbudgeable, but there must be equalities of sacrifice and encounter—not in order to strip the high and mighty of their individuality but purely and simply to treat everyone equally. Financial sacrifice on the part of the privileged is a proof that money cannot buy anything—it may not even be able to buy the most important thing, namely, personal safety. As long as equality prevails in one central zone of life—the most dangerous zone—the inequality of rewards in other zones does not become the be-all and the end-all of existence.

9   Many liberals demur. For whatever its merits conscription surely grates upon the ideal of self-control—that is precisely one of its purposes. Let's face it: most of us don't like to be told what to do. Moral preachments not only grate, they offend our sense that the only authority worth taking seriously is the authority of our own souls (or senses). Moral preachments about our duty sound to many Americans, left, right, and center, like the klaxon of a police state. To live our patriotism we would have to pick and choose, to overcome—selectively—some of the automatic revulsion we feel about laying aside some of our freedoms in the name of a higher duty. To be honest, it isn't clear to me how much of my own initiative I would gladly surrender for the common good. But "gladly" is not the point.

10   The principle of universal conscription is not only an abstract tribute to equality—worthy as that would be—but it undermines cavalier warfare. If the citizens asked to support a war are the ones who will have to fight it (or their relatives are), the hypocrisy factor weakens— the fervent endorsement of war in Iraq, for example, by Republican leaders whose children will not serve who, for that matter, thought the Vietnam War a "noble crusade" (Ronald Reagan's term) though somehow in their own persons somehow never found time for it. The principle that wars be popular with their soldiers is a good democratic requirement. Let it not be forgotten that Richard Nixon terminated the draft not to end the war—in fact, he continued the war from the air, killing at a pace that exceeded Lyndon Johnson's—but to insulate it from public exposure and dissent.

11   Other practical difficulties stand in the way of a draft. The principle of universality clashes with the limited need for troops. The military needs high-end recruits: what happens to universality, then? Should the brass be forced to make work for less-qualified conscripts? Should there be a universal draft for national service, with most draftees assigned to nonmilitary duties? Should there be some sort of lottery component? Legitimate questions not to be settled here. But the principle of some universal service should be the starting point.

12   Equal sacrifice of liberty in behalf of conscription ought to dovetail with equal civic opportunity of other sorts. We talk a lot about equality of opportunity, but as a nation we are ill prepared to amplify the principle—to enlarge it to the right to be healthy, to be cared for, to participate in government. As the elections of 2000 and 2004 demonstrated, we are not even terribly serious about guaranteeing the right to vote— and have one's vote counted. In a formula: Lived patriotism requires

social equality. It is in the actual relations of citizens, not symbolic displays, that civic patriotism thrives. In these palpable relations no one is elevated. Status does not count, nor wealth, nor poverty. One person, one vote. Absent these ideals in action, patriotism lapses into gestures—Pledges of Allegiance, not the allegiance itself.

Notes

1. John H. Schaar, "The Case for Patriotism," *American Review* 17 (1973):72
2. Robert N. Bellah et al., *Habits of the Heart: Individualism and Commitment in American Life* (New York: Harper and Row, 1985), p. 72, uses the term *lifestyle enclave*. The commonplace use of *network* came later.
3. Kaus argued in his 1992 book that liberals are mistaken to overemphasize economic inequality, and I do not follow him all the way to his bitter end. Surely, the appalling inequalities in the ratio between CEO and worker salaries, for example, of the order of 500 to 1, do not serve the entrepreneurial purposes that laissez-faire advocates rejoice in. That it would take confiscatory tax rates to eliminate this discrepancy does not mean that lesser reductions are pointless. Reducing the high-low income gap would work toward the principle of social equality.
4. Bill McKibben, "It's Easy Being Green," *Mother Jones*, July–August 2002, p. 36.

Reflection and Discussion

1. Gitlin says that most Americans don't practice patriotism. Provide some everyday examples to support or refute his opinion.
2. Gitlin distinguishes between communities and networks. Why does he find it necessary to make this distinction? How does it contribute to his definition of patriotism?

Writing Matters

1. Compared with a previous generation of Americans, have we as a people gone soft? Grown indulgent? Choose another time in our history and compare those who lived then with Americans of today. What did they do to show their love of country? What kinds of examples did they set? Is sacrifice the best way of showing patriotic sentiment? Can one be patriotic without it?
2. Argue for or against mandatory military (or civilian) service. Would it enhance or harm patriotic values in this country? How effectively does Gitlin defend conscription and on what grounds? In your argument, respond to his statement: "The principle that wars must be popular with their soldiers is a good democratic requirement."

And Our Flag Was Still There

Barbara Kingsolver, *San Francisco Chronicle,* September 25, 2001

Barbara Kingsolver is a novelist whose books include Animal Dreams *and* The Poisonwood Bible.

What is your opinion about the increase in the number of American flags displayed immediately after the events of September 11, 2001?

1   My daughter came home from kindergarten and announced, "Tomorrow we all have to wear red, white and blue." "Why?" I asked, trying not to sound wary. "For all the people that died when the airplanes hit the buildings." I fear the sound of saber-rattling, dread that not just my taxes but even my children are being dragged to the cause of death in the wake of death. I asked quietly, "Why not wear black, then? Why the colors of the flag, what does that mean?" "It means we're a country. Just all people together."

2   So we sent her to school in red, white and blue, because it felt to her like something she could do to help people who are hurting. And because my wise husband put a hand on my arm and said, "You can't let hateful people steal the flag from us." He didn't mean terrorists, he meant Americans. Like the man in a city near us who went on a rampage crying "I'm an American" as he shot at foreign-born neighbors, killing a gentle Sikh man in a turban and terrifying every brown-skinned person I know. Or the talk-radio hosts, who are viciously bullying a handful of members of Congress for airing sensible skepticism at a time when the White House was announcing preposterous things in apparent self-interest, such as the "revelation" that terrorists had aimed to hunt down Air Force One with a hijacked commercial plane. Rep. Barbara Lee cast the House's only vote against handing over virtually unlimited war powers to one man that a whole lot of us didn't vote for. As a consequence, so many red-blooded Americans have now threatened to kill her, she has to have additional bodyguards.

3   Patriotism seems to be falling to whoever claims it loudest, and we're left struggling to find a definition in a clamor of reaction. This is what I'm hearing: Patriotism opposes the lone representative of democracy who was brave enough to vote her conscience instead of following an angry mob. (Several others have confessed they wanted to vote the same way, but chickened out.) Patriotism threatens free speech with death. It is infuriated by thoughtful hesitation, constructive criticism of our leaders and pleas for peace. It despises people of

foreign birth who've spent years learning our culture and contributing their talents to our economy. It has specifically blamed homosexuals, feminists and the American Civil Liberties Union. In other words, the American flag stands for intimidation, censorship, violence, bigotry, sexism, homophobia, and shoving the Constitution through a paper shredder? Who are we calling terrorists here? Outsiders can destroy airplanes and buildings, but it is only we, the people, who have the power to demolish our own ideals.

It's a fact of our culture that the loudest mouths get the most air- 4 play, and the loudmouths are saying now that in times of crisis it is treasonous to question our leaders. Nonsense. That kind of thinking let fascism grow out of the international depression of the 1930s. In critical times, our leaders need most to be influenced by the moderating force of dissent. That is the basis of democracy, in sickness and in health, and especially when national choices are difficult, and bear grave conse- quences.

It occurs to me that my patriotic duty is to recapture my flag from 5 the men now waving it in the name of jingoism and censorship. This isn't easy for me. The last time I looked at a flag with unambiguous pride, I was 13. Right after that, Vietnam began teaching me lessons in ambiguity, and the lessons have kept coming. I've learned of things my government has done to the world that made me direly ashamed. I've been further alienated from my flag by people who waved it at me declaring I should love it or leave it. I search my soul and find I cannot love killing for any reason. When I look at the flag, I see it illuminated by the rocket's red glare.

This is why the warmongers so easily gain the upper hand in the 6 patriot game: Our nation was established with a fight for independ- ence, so our iconography grew out of war. Our national anthem cele- brates it; our language of patriotism is inseparable from a battle cry. Our every military campaign is still launched with phrases about men dying for the freedoms we hold dear, even when this is impossible to square with reality. In the Persian Gulf War we rushed to the aid of Kuwait, a monarchy in which women enjoyed approximately the same rights as a 19th century American slave. The values we fought for and won there are best understood, I think, by oil companies. Meanwhile, a country of civilians was devastated, and remains destroyed.

Stating these realities does not violate the principles of liberty, 7 equality, and freedom of speech; it exercises them, and by exercise we grow stronger. I would like to stand up for my flag and wave it over a few things I believe in, including but not limited to the protection of dissenting points of view. After 225 years, I vote to retire the rocket's red glare and the bullet wound as obsolete symbols of Old Glory. We desperately need a new iconography of patriotism. I propose we rip stripes of cloth from the uniforms of public servants who rescued the injured and panic-stricken, remaining at their post until it fell down on them. The red glare of candles held in vigils everywhere as peace-loving people pray for the bereaved, and plead for compassion and restraint. The blood donated to the Red Cross. The stars of film and theater and music who are using their influence to raise money for recovery. The small hands of schoolchildren collecting pennies, toothpaste, teddy bears, anything they think might help the kids who've lost their moms and dads.

8   My town, Tucson, AZ, has become famous for a simple gesture in which some 8,000 people wearing red, white or blue T-shirts assembled themselves in the shape of a flag on a baseball field and had their photograph taken from above. That picture has begun to turn up everywhere, but we saw it first on our newspaper's front page. Our family stood in silence for a minute looking at that photo of a human flag, trying to know what to make of it. Then my teenage daughter, who has a quick mind for numbers and a sensitive heart, did an interesting thing. She laid her hand over a quarter of the picture, leaving visible more or less 6,000 people, and said, "That many are dead." We stared at what that looked like—all those innocent souls, multi-colored and packed into a conjoined destiny—and shuddered at the one simple truth behind all the noise, which is that so many beloved people have suddenly gone from us. That is my flag, and that's what it means: We're all just people together.

Reflection and Discussion

1. Kingsolver was wary when her daughter's teacher asked students to wear red, white and blue to class. In what sense were her reservations justified? Exaggerated?

2. In your opinion, what points has the author left out of her article? Should it be more balanced?

Writing Matters

1. Kingsolver gives examples of violent reactions against innocent Americans after the attacks of September 11, 2001. How can we as a society do a better job of preventing incidents like these in the future? What can we learn from history about the importance of protecting minority opinions?

2. How practical is the author's call for "a new iconography of patriotism"? What problems do you see in trying to create a new symbol to represent our country? If you would change the American flag, what would you propose in its place?

FIGURE 12.3 During the playing of the National Anthem, Toni Smith stands with her back to the flag while holding hands with teammates. What does her posture suggest? What about the expression on her face?

Facing Away from the Flag

Gwen Knapp, *San Francisco Chronicle,* February 25, 2003

Gwen Knapp is a journalist whose main domain is sports and related social issues.

Do sports and politics mix? What prominent athletes have taken political stands?

I wonder how Toni Smith's critics feel about Muhammad Ali. They jeer   1
her at Manhattanville women's basketball games when the senior guard turns sideways, her face looking away from the American flag during the national anthem. Do they adore the Ali of today, and would they have hated him in the '60s, when he refused to serve in Vietnam? I doubt that Smith will ever be loved in the same way, that she will ever be cheered madly as she lights the torch at an Olympic Games. She isn't the Champ, one of the most charismatic athletes of her time. She plays basketball almost anonymously in suburban Purchase, NY.

2   Her protest, of course, won't cost as much as Ali's did. Smith won't lose the heavyweight boxing crown, and she won't have a five-year prison sentence hanging over her until the Supreme Court strikes down a criminal conviction. She simply has to endure relentlessly hostile chants from fans, a nasty confrontation with an opposing player whose brother serves in the military and the kind of media attention rarely bestowed on NCAA Division III athletes. The Manhattanville president has asked that Smith be treated with respect, that she not be harassed for expressing her opinion. His statement currently appears at the top of the school's Web site.

3   He is right that she shouldn't be physically accosted. The man who recently ran onto the court to confront Smith, saying that he was a Vietnam veteran offended by her stance, deserved to be removed from the arena. But the other kinds of heat that Smith faces—the verbal challenges and the miniature flags distributed at one game in protest of her protest—are all vital parts of her statement. If it were easy or fashionable to do what she is doing, the gesture would be hollow, like a team winning an uncontested game.

4   When I first heard about Smith's decision to turn her back on the flag, I assumed she was a grandstanding kid, trying to be provocative in the hope that a talk-show gig would be waiting for her at graduation. But it turns out she has been quietly shunning the flag all season, and her protests went largely unnoticed until two weeks ago.

5   Manhattanville traveled to the US Merchant Marine Academy, and newspaper accounts of the game say that at least 300 midshipmen turned out to wave flags at her, chanting "USA" and "Leave the Country." At halftime, 50 freshmen—known as plebes at the academy—positioned themselves across from the Manhatt-anville bench, each holding a flag. They stood there for the entire second half. That, more than anything, should have shaken her up. The plebes' display reflected real resolve. Smith's other critics have been variations on the rabid sports fan. At another game, one woman reportedly taunted Smith while wearing a halter top

Changing Definitions of "Patriot"
- Among many early American colonists, a patriot opposed tyranny and favored liberty and autonomy.
- In the 18th century, patriots opposed the unrestricted powers of the federal government.
- By the 19th century, patriots supported their government's authority and power.
- Around the time of the Civil War, many patriots demanded that the country remain true to the principles that inspired the Declaration of Independence.

Source: Janny Scott, "The Changing Face of Patriotism," *New York Times*, July 6, 2003

made of Stars & Stripes material. (Does anybody remember when it was considered desecration to wear the flag as if it were a team's colors?)

But even after the visit to the Merchant Marine, Smith kept up her silent protest. She finally issued a brief statement explaining her position last week, apparently to clarify that she is not simply opposing a war against Iraq. "The government's priorities," she wrote, "are not on bettering the quality of life for all of its people, but rather on expanding its own power." So far, she hasn't said anything else. According to Manhattanville coach Shawn Lincoln, the team has diverse opinions on the issue. He has declined to elaborate. One teammate held Smith's hand during the national anthem at Mount St. Mary last week. 6

It's been a while since sports and world politics had any serious interaction, unless you count athletes popping off à la John Rocker. They're certainly exercising their First Amendment rights, but with all the care and forethought of someone binging at a breakfast buffet. Rocker had no idea that buffoonery would damage his baseball career. When Ali defied the draft, and when Tommie Smith and John Carlos raised their fists in Mexico City, they knew they would pay. Just a generation after they were reviled, they are revered. The world came around. 7

Someday, Toni Smith may be vindicated, too, as brave rather than childish, as someone who cares more about her country than the people who refuse to challenge it. But her critics shouldn't be silenced any more than she should be. If her protest is easy, it doesn't really count. 8

Reflection and Discussion

1. How does Knapp feel about Toni Smith's protest? In the article, what clues indicate this?

2. Why does Knapp compare Smith to Muhammad Ali? Is the comparison appropriate?

Writing Matters

1. Explain your feelings about Smith's protest. Is she being disrespectful of the flag? If so, how? Is she exhibiting courage or trying to draw attention to herself? How would you react in the face of a protest like hers?

2. Discuss the response Smith's protest provoked among those who witnessed it. To what extent were their actions understandable? Why did the Manhattanville president ask people to respect Smith and avoid harassing her?

Representative Thune Introduces Flag Protection Amendment

US Federal News, April 14, 2005

John Thune is the junior Senator from South Dakota, first elected on November 2, 2004.

Should people who burn or show blatant disrespect for the American flag be punished?

1 The office of Sen. John Thune, R-SD, issued the following press release:

2   Sen. John Thune today introduced a constitutional amendment to protect the American flag, seeking to protect a universal symbol of freedom and a reminder of what veterans have sacrificed to defend it.

3   "When brave Americans risk life and limb defending our flag abroad, they should know the flag is safe at home," Thune said. "The American flag is a symbol of freedom and a constant reminder of those who died defending it. Out of respect for our men and women in uniform and our veterans, the flag should be protected."

4   Thune co-sponsored the amendment with a bipartisan group of senators, including Senators Hatch, Feinstein, Talent, and 47 other senators. Thune said the strong bipartisan endorsement behind the amendment and overwhelming public support would be critical to passing the amendment.

5   "Given the strong bipartisan support for this issue in Congress and throughout the nation, I am hopeful we can enact this important Amendment," Thune said. "The American people overwhelmingly believe the American flag should be protected. I am introducing this Amendment so those who have bravely defended our nation in the past—and those defending it today—can have the flag protected."

6   Members of Congress have worked since 1989 to protect the American flag, after the United States Supreme Court, in Texas v. Johnson, found a right within the Constitution that never before existed—the right to desecrate the American flag. A Constitutional Amendment with 41 Senate co-sponsors was introduced in the 108th US Congress, but was not acted upon by the full Senate.

Floor Statement of Senator John Thune, April 14, 2005

7 Thank you Mr. President. Today, it is my distinct honor and privilege to rise and speak on behalf of Senator Hatch, Senator Feinstein, Senator Talent, myself and 47 other Senators, as we introduce bi-partisan

legislation we believe to be long overdue. It is not reform legislation. It does not authorize new government programs, create new sources of tax revenue or provide incentives to stimulate our economy. It is none of those things. But it is a matter of great importance . . . the events of 9/11 have reminded us all of that. It is, instead, legislation that speaks to the core of our beliefs and hopes as a nation, and as a people. It is about a national treasure and a symbol of our country that the vast majority of Americans—and the majority of this great body, I might add—believe is worth special status and worthy of protection. It is about the American flag.

Mr. President, our American flag is more than mere cloth and ink. 8 It is a symbol of the liberty and freedom that we enjoy today thanks to the immeasurable sacrifices of generations of Americans who came before us. It represents the fiber and strength of our values and it has been sanctified by the blood of those who died defending it.

I rise today, Mr. President, to call upon all members of this body to 9 support a constitutional amendment that would give Congress the power to prohibit the physical desecration of the American flag. It would simply authorize, but not require, Congress to pass a law protecting the American flag. This amendment does not affect anyone's right to express their political beliefs. It would only allow Congress to prevent our flag from being used as a prop—to be desecrated in some ways simply not appropriate to even mention in these halls.

This resolution and similar legislation have been the subject of 10 debate before this body before. There is, in fact, a quite lengthy legislative history regarding efforts to protect the American flag from desecration. In 1989, the Supreme Court declared essentially that burning the American flag is "free speech." I think that is a decision the American people should make, particularly when this country finds itself fighting for democracy and expending American lives for that cause, on battlefields overseas.

South Dakota veterans and members of the armed forces from my 11 state know exactly what I'm talking about, as I'm sure they do from every state. In recent months, units of the 147th field artillery and 153rd engineer battalions of the South Dakota National Guard returned home after spending a difficult year in Iraq. Likewise, the 452nd ordinance company of the United States Army Reserve is preparing to depart for Iraq in September. My father, like many other veterans of World War II, understands the importance of taking this step. Veterans from across South Dakota have asked me to step up and defend the flag of this great nation and today I am answering that call.

Today, members of both political parties will introduce a proposed 12 constitutional amendment that would give back to the American people the power to prevent the desecration of the American flag. We know the gravity of this legislation. There is nothing complex about this amendment, nor are there any hidden consequences. This amendment provides Congress with the power to outlaw desecration of the American flag, a right that was widely recognized by Madison, Jefferson, and Supreme Court Justice Hugo Black, one of the foremost advocates of First Amendment freedoms. Most states officially advocate Congress passing legislation to protect the flag. Frankly, I do not see this as a First Amendment issue. It is an attempt to restore the traditional protections to the symbol cherished so dearly by our government and the people of the United States. Some acts are not accepted as "free speech" even in societies like ours where we consider free speech a cherished right. For example, an attempt to burn down this capital building as a political statement would never be viewed as someone's right of free speech. Our laws would not tolerate the causing of harm to others' property or life as an act of "free speech." Well, this flag happens to be the property of the American people in my opinion, and I believe this question should be put before the states and their people to decide how and if to protect it. I think the answer will come back as a resounding "yes."

13   There is little doubt that the debate over state ratification will trigger a tremendous discussion over our values, beliefs and whether we will ultimately bestow a lasting honor on our traditions. Importantly, it will be an indication of how we recognize our servicemen and women who are sacrificing—right now—in Iraq and Afghanistan, to protect those traditions and values for us. Will we honor them, and all the veterans who served and died in wars for this country and our flag over the last 200 years? That's not a question which a court should hold the final answer. I believe the time has finally come. I believe our country wants this debate. The majority of this Senate, I believe, wants this amendment. We begin it here, and we begin it now. Mr. President, let the debate begin. Thank you, and I yield the floor.

Reflection and Discussion

1. A majority of senators—Democrats and Republicans—are in favor of amending the Constitution in order to protect the flag. How do you explain this overwhelming support?

2. What constitutes a flag? Do we need a stricter definition of what a flag is?

Writing Matters

1. Rep. Thune says that "the vast majority of Americans" support his flag protection amendment. Do you? Is popular support sufficient reason to

amend the Constitution? What dangers, if any, do you see in changing a document that has existed for over two hundred years?

2. A 1989 US Supreme Court decision declared that flag burning was "free speech." Do you agree? When the courts and the American people disagree over vital matters, whose decision should prevail and why?

Desecration

William Safire, *New York Times,* July 31, 2005

William Safire is a lexicographer, historian and syndicated columnist. He was also a speechwriter in the administration of President Richard M. Nixon.

In your writing, how careful are you about choosing the precise word to express your meaning? How critical are you about word choices in the writing of others?

The House of Representatives, by more than the required two-thirds 1 majority, recently approved a proposed amendment to the Constitution that reads, "The Congress shall have the power to prohibit the physical desecration of the flag of the United States."

This was the House's thumb in the eye to the Supreme Court, 2 which by a 5–4 vote in 1989 ruled that laws against flag-burning by demonstrators were an unconstitutional restraint on free speech. Now the bill goes to the Senate, which will most likely take up the issue after its August recess. If two-thirds of the Senate approves, the proposal will go to the 50 states for ratification. If 38 agree, the Constitution will be amended, the Supreme Court overruled—and a great semantic mistake will have been made.

Set aside the roiling debate between those possessed with patriotic 3 fervor and those demonstrators eager to infuriate the vast majority of Americans. Consider only the meaning of the key word in the proposed change in our nation's basic law. Desecration is a noun steeped in the violation of religious belief. It is rooted in the Latin *sacrare* or *secrare*, source of "sacred" and "sacrifice," dealing through the millenniums with worship of a deity. To desecrate is to profane what is holy; *Merriam Webster* defines it as "to violate the sanctity of," *American Heritage* as "to violate the sacredness of" and the *Oxford English Dictionary* as "to take away its consecrated or sacred character." Houses of God and gravestones can be desecrated by people bent on reviling religion or embracing evil.

But national flags are not religious objects or symbols. Some lexi- 4 cographers report a secondary sense of mere "disrespect," but that is aberrant usage, not common usage. If strong words retain their meaning—with their "first" sense signifying widespread public understanding—then desecrate and its opposite, consecrate, are plainly understood to denote profoundly sacred themes and religious practices. Take the most famous use of consecrate. Lincoln at Gettysburg, dedicating a national cemetery: "We can not consecrate—we can not hallow this ground. The brave men, living and dead, who struggled here, have consecrated it. . . ." Lincoln's meaning was unmistakably spiritual: consecrate and hallow are synonyms meaning "to make holy."

5   It's unlikely that the proposers of this amendment, or those representatives who voted for it, intended to treat the nation's flag as a religious symbol. But that is what that word desecration does. Although I stand with Justice Antonin Scalia in upholding the right of professional infuriators to mock or even destroy the symbols of our nationhood, my political opinion has no place in a language column. Here, I defend only the words we use from having their meanings confused.

6   If two-thirds of the Senate is determined to go ahead with this, it should change the physical desecration of to something like "the ostentatious destruction or mockery of" or "the outrageous disrespect for." Then get the House to agree to change its bill to correct the error. And here's why:

The Ineradicable Typo

7   A typo (the 1878 shortening of "typographical error") exists in the amendments to our Constitution, and no matter how often the nation's fundamental document is reprinted, that typo cannot be removed. We are not talking about a seeming mistake by the framers, who spelled or capitalized words differently then, and also had to work behind closed doors through a blazing summer in Philadelphia without air-conditioning. Rather, we examine today an ineradicable error in the 25th Amendment to the Constitution, ratified as recently as 1967. This necessary addition to our basic law provided for the removal and replacement of a disabled or captured president, but its maddeningly permanent typo demonstrates how important it is to weigh every word of these amendments.

8   Section 4 of the 25th Amendment reads, "Whenever the Vice President and a majority of . . . the principal officers of the executive departments"—note the plural "departments," meaning members of the cabinet—declare in writing to Congress that the president cannot discharge his duties, the vice president becomes acting president. But in the next paragraph, arranging for the ousted president to seek to reclaim his office, Congress's power to block his return can be triggered by "a majority of the principal officers of the executive department"—with no s

after "department." Why the difference? Does the second usage mean "executive branch" or what? Did somebody goof by making "department" singular, and did a legion of proofreaders miss it—and if so, why has that embarrassment been left unfixed?

Former Senator Birch Bayh of Indiana, primary sponsor of the 9 25th Amendment (and father of the current senator, Evan Bayh), informs me: "In the hundreds of times I've read this thing, that's the first time I noticed that. Sounds to me like it should be the same in both places."

The writer of the definitive book about the amendment, and one of 10 the 25th's main authors, is John D. Feerick, a Fordham law professor and former dean of the law school. Reached recently, Professor Feerick recalls: "The conference committees of both houses met to iron out their differences. I remember getting a copy of their work a day or two later . . . and seeing the error in the draft. . . . I was chagrined and pointed it out, but it was too late; it had already gone to the states to be ratified. If you dig back through the drafts, you'll see 'executive departments' all the way back, except at the very end. Where it got in and how, I probably knew at some point, but now I don't. The meaning is still clear. . . ."

About fixing it, Birch Bayh notes ruefully: "It would have to go to 11 technical corrections, and even then you'd have to weigh whether you want to open the issue to debate. Presidential power is something we have to be very careful about." Which is why the Senate should take a hard look at the misused word desecration before it's too late.

Reflection and Discussion

1. Do you agree that "desecrate" is the wrong word to use when referring to a flag? If so, what term would you choose? Does it have the same power? Is your choice clearer?
2. Poll your friends or classmates to get a sense of how they were taught to treat the flag.

Writing Matters

1. All of us are acquainted with typos or proofreading mistakes in our writing. How much more serious is it when a document like the US Constitution is involved? Safire suggests that it is imperative to get the wording right the first time. What might happen if the term *desecrate* is accepted in an amendment to the Constitution?
2. Are linguists as well as language and writing teachers too strict about "proper usage"? Should rules and standards of "correct" language usage be upheld or relaxed? Explain your feelings about how standards of correctness are enforced at the elementary, secondary and college levels.

MAKING CONNECTIONS

1. Write an essay expressing your feelings about the American flag. Review the readings and address the major issues, promoting positions you agree with and refuting those you oppose. How should the flag be displayed and treated?

2. What does being patriotic mean to you? Make your definition come to life by providing examples of what a patriotic person looks and acts like. For example, do actions speak louder than words? How do you express your feelings toward your country? What words or actions would you consider unpatriotic? What differences do you see between the United States as a country and the United States government? In your opinion, how should citizens best express both approval and disapproval of government policies?

3. Research the distinction between patriotism and nationalism. When were these terms first used and how have their denotations and connotations changed over time? How important is it for us to understand the differences between them? Identify historical events or periods that best illustrate each term. What political climates tend to emphasize one or the other? When and where should lessons about patriotism and nationalism be taught?

4. Trace the history of the Pledge of Allegiance to gain insight into the current controversy. How did the early pledge differ from the one we know today? What words or concepts in it have inspired the most debate? What were your experiences with the pledge in school? What are the advantages and disadvantages of the Pledge of Allegiance being optional in schools? Who should decide whether or not it is used?

5. What is the role of dissent in a democracy? What often happens when matters of conscience conflict with established law? What forms of dissent do you admire most and which have proven to be most effective?

TAKING ACTION

Form a group of students in your class and create a questionnaire on the subject of flag desecration. On your own, ask 20 or 30 individuals the questions and record their answers. Then write a letter to your US congressional representative explaining the results of your survey. Express as clearly as possible how you and your respondents feel about flag desecration. Raise any questions or concerns you may have about a constitutional amendment that would make flag desecration a criminal offense.

Appendix

I

Writing with Sources

Writers do not compose in a vacuum; we read other authors, getting emotionally and intellectually engaged, and then write in response. We call on the research and ideas of others to support our ideas. Whether we use authors' exact words or paraphrase their ideas, we need to acknowledge the original writers, to give credit where credit is due and to let our readers track down the original source if they are interested. Failure to do so is plagiarism, a form of intellectual theft. At the most basic level, we name the originator of an idea because none of us would want someone else to take credit for something that we ourselves had written. But we also gain credibility for our own writing when we reference sources, letting our readers know that our ideas are backed up by research and theory. Newspapers and popular periodicals have their own styles of crediting sources, but academics use a number of more rigorous conventions. Your professor will tell you which citation system you should use for this class and recommend a handbook with the technical details for giving credit. This section will guide you in using the source information effectively in your own writing. The examples follow MLA format, but the principles are the same for whatever citation style you use.

INTEGRATING THE MATERIAL TO FIT YOUR PURPOSE

We refer to source material in different ways depending on our purpose. Sometimes we write essays to explain what an authority has to say; other times, we use these authorities to support what we want to say. Note the different ways materials are used in the examples below (based on the skateboarding article used in Figure 1 of the Introduction).

1. S.K. Andres describes the current deregulated state of skate board safety, noting that "26,000 skaters are treated in emergency rooms each year" (1). While this may be true, Andres ignores how many skate every day without injury and the fact that many are attracted to this sport precisely because of the risk involved.

2. With 26,000 skateboarders injured badly enough to be sent to the hospital each year, some even dying (Andres 1), we need to mandate and regulate safety gear for skaters as we do for motorcycle and bike riders.

3. Andres reports that 26,000 skateboarders are hospitalized each year (1). This means that on average, every week 500 are injured that badly.

In the first example, the student is highlighting and evaluating the main points of the article. The second student uses the key facts to justify his own point, while the third student just lays out the statistic and restates it, neither evaluating the source nor advancing her own position, forcing the reader to figure out how the information fits in the essay.

Carefully choose the words that introduce your citations. Communication verbs ("Smith states/says/writes") are neutral. "Reports" suggests that your source is sharing the result of a study or observation, while "claims" indicates the author is making an assertion. "Smith *mentions*" tells your reader that you are citing a minor aspect of an article, perhaps an afterthought.

Sometimes you'll cite facts that speak for themselves, but other times you will need to add your analysis to the reference. While you'll want to avoid the mechanical "this means," you'll find that phrases like "which suggests that . . . " or "indicating that . . . " will help you make a smooth transition from the citation to your own thoughts.

QUOTATIONS, PARAPHRASE OR SUMMARY?

Since you are writing the essay, most of the language should be your own. If too much of your essay is taken up by unedited, unanalyzed quotations and paraphrases, your audience may wonder why they aren't just reading the original article. Summarize articles to give your audience the benefit of your careful reading. Paraphrase the source when you are citing details that would get lost in a summary, using quotations only when the author's original phrasing needs to be preserved:

- The original text says it better than you can.
- Rephrasing would lose some of the meaning.

But you need only quote the part that is relevant to your essay or necessary to preserve the meaning of the passage. The skateboarding article includes the following quotation from an interview:

> "But the parks closed . . . [and] skate punks can't be bothered with helmets, [and] think you're trying to rip them off if you recommend helmets."

The ellipses (" . . . ") indicate that the writer has dropped an unimportant section. The bracketed "and" substitutes for a connecting phrase in the dropped section.

The Research Paper

A research paper can be either a source of pain and suffering or an instrument of discovery, an opportunity to explore in depth a subject that interests you. Which of these outcomes you experience can depend on how well you manage the particular challenges of the research paper—its size, the time needed to complete it, matters related to the topic. What you should remember, though, is that you will be using many of the skills you used on shorter assignments. Although research papers require more reading, more information gathering and better planning, if you can handle a four-page assignment, you should be able to manage one that is four or five times as long. By incorporating additional strategies into the ones you already have, you can tackle the increased scope and complexity of your project.

PURPOSE AND AUDIENCE

As with shorter assignments, the audience for longer papers will be your teacher and class members unless the prompt specifically indicates other readers. However, because your audience may be unfamiliar with your research topic and related details, you will have to work carefully on these elements.

Fortunately, most college students have already done research, but while high school research projects often asked you to inform an audience about an issue, college research assignments more often ask you to discuss, analyze or argue a position. If your teacher has assigned you a topic, study the prompt closely to get clues about the purpose of the paper and how to proceed. If you are writing a persuasive paper on a controversial topic, you'll still need to include background information, but only as much as your audience needs. For example, if your essay was inspired by a particular event on your campus, you'd only need to provide a brief summary of what happened if you were writing to your teacher and classmates, but you'd need to go into much more detail if your audience were unfamiliar with your school.

TIME MANAGEMENT

With a research paper, one of the biggest challenges is how best to use your time. If you wait too long to get started or have to rush key stages, you could compromise your entire project. Whether your paper is eight pages or eighteen, learn to think of it in parts, each of which you can work on separately. A fifteen-page paper with a one-page introduction and a one-page conclusion boils down to thirteen pages in the body. That might mean three, four or five smaller parts, depending on your topic and material. As you research, write and refine your thinking, the arrangement and size of the parts can change, but by dividing your paper into sections, you can work on each one independently.

Many teachers help students by imposing due dates for separate parts of the paper. For example, if students are allowed to choose a topic, a tentative choice will be due by a certain date; reading, research, and note-taking will fall on another, while plans, drafts and final products will have separate delivery times. Fixed dates like these are especially helpful for students who have trouble keeping their own deadlines, and they allow time for ideas to mature. Also, when the whole class is at the same stage in the research paper process, students can share advice about how best to master the task at hand.

Teachers who allow their students to establish their own deadlines still often provide suggested dates for completing topic selection, research and so on. Whatever deadline situation you find yourself in, do your best not to rush, but instead, create your own mini-deadlines: if your teacher gives you a week to submit an organizing plan, you might commit to identifying the major sections by Monday and then prepare the outline for the first section on Tuesday, the second on Wednesday, and so on. Good ideas bubble to the surface slowly. Allow your whole project time to evolve so that you can tinker with your topic, test out new ideas, reconfigure your plan and revise parts that need special attention. Research papers that don't grow are likely to become mechanical exercises yielding little of interest to readers or writers. On the other hand, a project that has developed through trial and error and matured with the input of others can be an experience that will stay with you for years.

Topic Selection

Faced with choosing topics of their own, some students rejoice while others panic. If you find yourself in the latter group, rest assured that controversies suitable for research papers are everywhere. Surfing the Internet (especially special interest websites), browsing in book stores, leafing through magazines and watching TV documentaries can yield issues ripe for exploration. Conversations with other students or people at work can also be fruitful. Many students find topics simply by gravitating toward what already interests them. Remember, though, that if you get stuck, your teacher will be one of the best resources for getting you going again.

Whatever your first choice, try to honestly gauge your enthusiasm for the topic. Is your interest sufficient to last over the whole span of your project? Are your readers likely to be drawn in? Think in terms of a provisional topic, one that you can submit to your teacher or classmates for consideration. You may have to experiment or do some adapting before feeling satisfied with it, which is why you will need sufficient time at this stage.

Check your topic to make sure it is neither too broad nor too narrow. At the broad end, you can find yourself flailing in a sea of information; at the other, you will be more like a thirsty traveler in an arid land. Although a topic like alternative energy sources sounds too general for a ten-page research paper, attempts at popularizing the electric car in the US might be more realistic. If you still find yourself with too much information, you could further restrict your topic to the experiments at General Motors with the EV1 automobile. Imagine during your initial research stage, you learn that GM spent millions on research and development, and then ended up abandoning the car. Curious to know why, you have discovered a research question for your paper—something which will give your topic an even more specific direction. A research question can narrow your topic to fit the dimensions of the assignment, helping to spark the curiosity of your audience and giving them a reason to read.

You'll feel more confident with your work if you ask for feedback from your teacher, tutors or friends you respect as you develop it. Their comments will also help you gauge what emotional reactions your topic is getting, which may help you reframe or refine it. Remember also that topics need to be rooted in more than personal belief. A research paper on who is currently the best actor in Hollywood may inspire a lot of opinion, but you'll find it difficult to come up with hard evidence to support your point of view.

EVIDENCE

To an increasing number of students, research means going immediately to the Internet. Without a doubt, your computer will be an enormous help as you conduct your research, but the trick is to employ it judiciously. College writing handbooks and reference guides provide detailed suggestions about finding reliable information on the Internet. In general, explore a variety of sites—government organizations, discussion forums, news sites, archives—for information that is as trustworthy as possible. Familiarize yourself with databases like ProQuest and LexisNexis. Use the Internet to its full advantage without depending on it exclusively.

Take advantage of your college library and ask questions of librarians and assistants who can direct you to print indexes where you can find books related to your topic and other material that predates the Internet. They may be able to offer advice about how best to search your library's book catalog or direct you to visual or audio material related to your topic. If your library doesn't have what you are looking for, a librarian may be able to help you access it from another college or university. So don't be afraid to ask.

If you allow yourself ample time at the reading and information-gathering stage and keep in touch with what others in your class are doing, you'll increase both your confidence and efficiency as a researcher. In your area of interest, certain names, book titles and publications will turn up repeatedly, perhaps a sign that these sources are essential reading. Writers who refer to other authors as experts or authorities might indicate that you should become familiar with their work. The more time you spend in the research phase, the better you will get at knowing who is respected in the field.

Although accumulating evidence can be fascinating—if for no other reason than you are learning so much—you will need to be selective. Remember that your teacher is interested in what your thoughts and opinions are, so don't let your research overwhelm your paper. Integrate your findings with ideas of your own and don't list facts or quote long passage after long passage. Comment on what you discover and weigh its value rather than letting readers come to their own conclusions.

In the final analysis, your research paper is an act of creation involving you and your sources. While you will be shooting for an "A" or solid "B," the real value of your efforts should extend well beyond whatever letter grade you receive.

CREDITS

TEXT

Altbach, Philip G., Student Power [box]: Altbach, Philip G. "Student Political Activism," *Youth Activism: An International Encyclopedia*. Greenwood. 2005.

Assad, Matt, From University Class President to Bank Robber: Assad, Matt. "How online gambling toppled Greg Hogan's world: Addiction led Lehigh U. class president, accomplished musician to rob a bank, halting his march to success." Greg Hogan Jr. to be sentenced today. *Morning Call*, Allentown, PA. August 17, 2006. Copyright 2006 by McClatchy-Tribune Regional News. Reproduced with permission of McClatchy-Tribune Regional News in the format Textbook via Copyright Clearance.

Bagnato, Kristin, Learning, Virtually: Bagnato, Kristin. (2004, May 10). "Learning, Virtually," *Community College Week*, 6–8.

Bauman, M. Garrett, Heroes I Have Taught—and Who Have Taught Me: Bauman, M. Garrett. (2003, December 12). "Heroes I have taught and who have taught me." *Chronicle of Higher Education, 50*(16).

Beder, Sharon, Best Coverage Money Can Buy: Beder, Sharon. "Best Coverage Money Can Buy," *New Internationalist*, July 1999.

Bennett, Drake, Doing Disservice: The Benefits and Limits of Volunteerism: Reprinted with permission from Drake Bennett, "Doing Disservice: The Benefits and Limits of Volunteerism," *The American Prospect*, Vol. 14, No. 9: September 30, 2003. The American Prospect, 2000 L Street, NW, Suite 717, Washington, DC 20036. All rights reserved.

Birkerts, Sven Reflections of a Non-Political Man: Birkerts, Sven. "Reflections of a Nonpolitical Man," *Readings*. GrayWolf Press, 1999, pp. 74–81.

Butterfield, Fox, Hundreds of Thousands of Inmates Mentally Ill: Butterfield, Fox. "Hundreds of Thousands of Inmates Mentally Ill," *The New York Times*, October 22, 2003.

Byock, Ira R, M.D., Dying Well in Corrections: Why Should We Care?: Byock, Ira R., M.D. "Dying Well in Corrections: Why Should We Care?" *Journal of Correctional Health Care*, 2002. Retrieved May 31, 2006, from http://www.correctionalhealth.org/resources/journal/9-2/Byock.pdf.

Center for Information & Research on Civic Learning & Engagement, The, Why Young People Are Volunteering in Record Numbers: The Center for Information & Research on Civic Learning & Engagement, "Why Young People Are Volunteering In Record Numbers," *Around the CIRCLE: Research & Practice*, November 2005.

Clark, Kim, Econ 101: College Is the Time to Budget: Clark, Kim, "Econ 101: College is the Time to Budget." *U.S. News & World Report*, December 12, 2005, Vol. 139, Issue 22.

Clark, Nancy, Mirror, Mirror on the Wall . . . Are Muscular Men the Best of All?: Clark, Nancy. "Mirror, Mirror on the Wall . . . Are Muscular Men The Best Of All? The Hidden Turmoil of Muscle Dysmorphia," *American Fitness*, January/February 2004, pp. 52–54.

Cobb, William Jelani, My So-Called Life: Cobb, William Jelani. "My So-Called Life," *Essence*, June 2004, pp. 184–92.

Consumer Reports, More Dirt [box]: 2006 *Consumer Reports*, June 2006.

Draut, Tamara, Generation Debt: The Dirty Business of Deregulated Credit: From *Strapped: Why America's 20- and 30- Somethings Can't Get Ahead* by Tamara Draut, copyright © 2005 by Tamara Draut. Used permission of Doubleday, a division of Random House, Inc.

Dunnewind, Stephanie, Internet Creates New Opportunities for Cheating, But Also Learning: Dunnewind, Stephanie. "Internet Creates New Opportunities for Cheating, But Also Learning," *Seattle Times*, C1, August 27, 2005.

eSchool News, Multi-tasking Hinders Learning [box]: "Multi-tasking Hinders Learning," (2006, July 26). *eSchool News*, http://www.eschoolnews.com/news/showStory.cfm?ArticleID=6453.

Foster, Andrea L., A Congressman Questions the Quality and Rigor of Online Education: Foster, Andrea L. (2006, March 31). "A Congressman Questions the Quality and Rigor of Online Education," *Chronicle of Higher Education*, 52(30).

Gibbon, Peter H., What is a Hero?: Gibbon, Peter H. (2002). *What is a Hero? From A Call to Heroism: Renewing America's Vision of Greatness*. Used by permission of Grove/Atlantic.

Gitlin, Todd, Patriotism and Sacrifice: Gitlin, Todd. "Patriotism and Sacrifice," excerpted from *The Intellectuals and the Flag*, New York: Columbia University Press. 2007, pp. 138–45.

Glater, Jonathan D., To: Professor@University.edu Subject: Why It's All About Me: Glater, Jonathan D. (2006, February 21). "To: Professor@University.edu Subject: Why It's All About Me," *New York Times*, A1.

Glover, Karen, Don't Discredit My Online Degree: Glover, Karen. (2005, October 15). "Don't Discredit My Online Degree," *Library Journal*, 39. Copyright 2005 by Reed Business Information. Reproduced with permission of Reed Business Information in the format Textbook via Copyright Clearance Center.

Goldberg, Stanley J., Fixing? Helping? Or Serving?: Goldberg, Stanley J. (2004). *Fixing? Helping? Or Serving? Templeton Power of Purpose Awards.* Retrieved May 30, 2005 from http://www.templeton.org/ powerofpurpose/essays/Fixing_Helping_Or _Serving-GOLDBERG.pdf. Used with permission from The Power of Purpose Awards, sponsored by John Templeton Foundation.

Gordon, Larry, and Louis Sahagun, Gen Y's Ego Trip: Gordon, Larry, and Sahagun, Louis, *Los Angeles Times,* February 27, 2007, Pg. B1.

Grossman, Elizabeth, Toxic Recycling: Grossman, Elizabeth. "Toxic Recycling," *The Nation,* November 21, 2005.

Hearn, Alison, Image Slaves: Everybody Wants to Be on Television: Hearn, Alison. "Image Slaves: Everybody Wants to be on Television" (original title "Image Slaves"). *Bad Subjects.* http://bad .eserver.org/issues/2004/69/hearn.html.

Henig, Robin Marantz, The Price of Perfection: Henig, Robin Marantz, "The Price of Perfection," *Civilization,* May/June 1996, pp. 56–62.

Herr, N., Television by the Numbers [box]: Herr, N. (2001). "Television and Health: The Sourcebook for Teaching Science." Retrieved May 30, 2006 from http://www.csun.edu/~vceed002/health/docs/ tv&health.html.

Heywood, John B., Fueling Our Transportation Future: Heywood, John B. "Fueling Our Transportation Future," *Scientific American,* September 2006. Vol. 295, Issue 3. pp. 60–3.

Human Rights: Justice Statistics [box]: A Statistical Look at Criminal Justice and Injustice. (2004). *Human Rights: Journal of the Section of Individual Rights & Responsibilities; 31*(1), p. 2.

Jablecki, Lawrence T., Changing the Lives of Prisoners: A New Agenda: Jablecki, Lawrence T., "Changing the Lives of Prisoners: A New Agenda," *The Humanist,* November/December 2005.

Jayson, Sharon, Shaped by 911, Millennials Are Socially Conscious: Jayson, Sharon. "Generation Y Gets Involved; Shaped by 9/11, Millenials Are Socially Conscious, If Not Radical," *USA Today,* October 24, 2006. Pg. 1D.

Johnson, Steven, Watching TV Makes You Smarter: Johnson, Steven. "Watching TV Makes You Smarter," excerpted from *New York Times Magazine,* April 24, 2005, Copyright 2005 The New York Times Company.

Kay, Jane Holtz, Kicking the Petroleum Habit: Ending Auto-Domination: Kay, Jane Holtz. "Kicking the Petroleum Habit: Ending Auto-Domination," *The Green Guide,* Fall 2001. http://www.janeholtzkay .com/Articles/kicking.html

Keeter, Scott, Cliff Zukin, Molly Andolina, and Krista Jenkins, Young Adults as Volunteers [box]: Keeter, Scott; Zukin, Cliff; Andolina, Molly; Jenkins, Krista. "The Civic and Political Health of the Nation: A Generational Portrait," September 19, 2002. Retrieved May 30, 2006, from http://www.civicyouth.org/ research/products/Civic_Political_Health.pdf.

Kershaw, Sarah, Hooked on the Web: Help Is on the Way: Kershaw, Sarah. *New York Times.* New York, N.Y.: Dec 1, 2005. pg. G.1

Kimmel, Michael, Chapter 8 "Making Connections": Kimmel, Michael. *Manhood in America: A Cultural History.* The Free Press: New York, 1996.

Kingsolver, Barbara, And Our Flag Was Still There: Kingsolver, Barbara. "And Our Flag Was Still There," *San Francisco Chronicle,* September 25, 2001.

Knapp, Gwen, Facing Away From the Flag: Knapp, Gwen. "Player's Protest Draws Anger: Facing away from the Flag," *San Francisco Chronicle,* February 25, 2003, p. C 1.

Kolbert, Elizabeth, Can America Go Green?: Kolbert, Elizabeth. "Can America Go Green?" *New Statesman,* June 19, 2006.

Kunstler, James Howard, The Long Emergency: "The Long Emergency" by James Howard Kunstler from RollingStone.com. March 23, 2005. © Rolling Stone LLC. 2005. All rights reserved. Reprinted by permission.

Lee, Ellen, Just Too Much: Young Folks Burn Out On Online Sharing: Lee, Ellen. "Just Too Much: Young Folks Burn Out On Online Sharing" (original title: "Social sites becoming too much of a good thing: Many young folks burning out on online sharing"), *San Francisco Chronicle,* November 2, 2006, p. A1.

Life Style Extra, Do We Really Need Skinny Models? [box]: "Research Backs 'Normal Size' Models in Ads," *Life Style Extra,* August 31, 2005, retrieved from http://www.lse.co.uk/ShowStory.asp?story= ZX3017071R&news_headline=research_backs_normal_ size_models_in_ads

Marcus, Jon, Fury Over Student Loan Kickback Allegation: Marcus, Jon. "Fury Over Student Loan Kickback Allegation" (original title "Fury Over Kickback Allegation"). *The Times Higher Education Magazine,* London, England, May 11, 2007. Reproduced by permission of Times Higher Education.

MCabe, Donald, Academic Integrity [box]: McCabe, D. (2005, Summer-Fall). "It Takes a Village: Academic Dishonesty." *Liberal Education,* 26–31. Retrieved May 3, 2006 from EBSCO Academic Elite.

McCain, John, Putting the "National" in National Service: Reprinted with permission from *The Washington Monthly.* Copyright © by Washington Monthly Publishing, LLC, 1319 F Street NW, Suite 710, Washington, DC 20004 (202-393-5155). Web site: www.washingtonmonthly.com.

Mehta, Julie, and Polly Sparling, Pretty Unreal: Mehta, Julie, and Sparling, Polly. "Pretty Unreal," *Current Health 2,* January 2005, pp. 15–19.

Min, Anchee, Footprints on the Flag: Min, Anchee, "Footprints on the Flag," *The New Yorker,* October 15, 2001, p. 181. Reprinted by permission of Sandra Dijkstra Literary Agency.

Morrow, Carol Ann, Jesuit Greg Boyle, Gang Priest: Morrow, Carol Ann. (1999, August). "Jesuit Greg Boyle, Gang Priest." *St. Anthony Messenger.*

Nellie Mae, Students as Credit Card Customers [box]: Nellie Mae, "Undergraduate Students and Credit Cards in 2004."

Nobel Foundation, Nobel Peace Prize [box]: Nobel Foundation (2006). "The Nobel Peace Prize— Laureates." Retrieved from http://nobelprize.org/ peace/laureates/index.html

Nobel, Alfred, Nobel Peace Prize [box]: Nobel, A. (1895). "Last will and testament." Retrieved from: http://nobelprize.org/nobel/alfred-nobel/biographical/will/index.html

Norris, Pippa, Does Television Erode Social Capital?: Norris, Pippa. "Does Television Erode Social Capital?" excerpted from *Political Science and Politics*, September 1996, pp. 474–480.

OpenTheGovernment.org, More Dirt [box]: OpenTheGovernment.org, retrieved from www.openthegovernment.org.

Perl, Sondra, Understanding Composing: Perl, Sondra. "Understanding Composing," *College Composition and Communication*, December 1980, Vol. 31, No. 4. pp. 363–9.

Pope, Carl, Whitewash at Ground Zero: Pope, Carl. "Whitewash at Ground Zero," *Sierra Magazine*, January/February 2004. Appears with permission of *Sierra*, the magazine of the Sierra Club.

Psychology Today, Who Carefully Studies the Shapes of Models? [box]: "The 1997 Body Image Survey," *Psychology Today*, February 1997, p. 42

Putnam, Robert,Tuning In, Tuning Out: Putnam, Robert. "Tuning In, Tuning Out: The Strange Disappearance of Social Capital in America," excerpted from *Political Science and Politics*, 280–4, December 1995, pp. 664–83.

Rey, Jay, "Alternative" Spring Breaks: Helping Poor and Homeless: Rey, Jay. (2006, March 11). "Alternative" Spring Breaks: Helping Poor and Homeless," *Buffalo News*, A1. Copyright 2006 by McClatchy-Tribune Regional News. Reproduced with permission of McClatchy-Tribune Regional News in the format Textbook via Copyright Clearance Center.

Roane, Kit R., and Dan Morrison, The CSI Effect: Roane, Kit R., and Morrison, Dan. "The CSI Effect," excerpted from *U.S. News & World Report*, May 2, 2005.

Rudman, Gary, The Techno-Flux Effect: Rudman, Gary. "The Techno-Flux Effect," *Brandweek*, 4/3/2006, Vol. 47, Issue 14. Copyright 2006 by Nielsen Business Media. Reproduced with permission of Nielsen Business Media in the format Textbook via Copyright Clearance Center.

Safire, William, Desecration: Safire, William. "Desecration." Copyright © 2005 The Corbett Corporation. Originally published in *The New York Times*. Reprinted by permission of the author.

Samuels, Alana,"Thinspiration": Online Websites Promote Eating Disorders: Semuels, Alana. "'Thinspiration': Online Websites Promote Eating Disorders," (original title "Thin Girls: Online Websites That Advocate Eating Disorders or Even Recovering From Them Have Health Experts Worried"), *Pittsburgh Post-Gazette*, June 22, 2005.

Schaffer, Jan, Weaving Your Community's Master Narrative: Schaffer, Jan. "Weaving Your Community's Master Narrative" excerpted from *The Local News Workbook* for *Civic Catalyst Newsletter*, Winter 2001, http://www.pewcenter.org/doingcj/civiccat/displayCivcat.php?id=274.

Scorza, Jason A., The Ambivalence of Political Courage: Scorza, Jason A. (2001). "The ambivalence of political courage." *A Review of Politics*, 63(4), 637–661.

Scott, Janny, Changing Definitions of "Patriot" [box]: Scott, Janny. "The Changing Face of Patriotism," *The New York Times*, July 06, 2003.

Seligman, Dan, The Ugliness Problem: Seligman, Dan. "The Ugliness Problem," *Forbes*, August 15, 2005, p. 96. Reprinted by permission of Forbes Magazine © 2009 Forbes LLC.

Sennett, Richard, Voluntary Work and the Needs of Strangers: Sennett, R. "Voluntary Work and the Needs of Strangers" (original title "Voluntary Work Creates an Impediment to Perceiving and Taking Seriously the Needs Of Strangers"), *New Statesman*, January 23, 2003, pp. 27–30.

Šiklová, Jiřina, Chapter 6 introduction: Šiklová, Jiřina. "Courage, Heroism, and the Postmodern Paradox." *Social Research*, 71(1), 145.

Singer, Maxine F., Heroines and Role Models: Singer, Maxine F. (2001). "Heroines and Role Models." *Science*, 253 (5017), 249. Reprinted with permission AAAS.

Singer, Natasha, For You, My Lovely, A Facelift: Singer, Natasha. "For You, My Lovely, A Facelift," *New York Times*, December 29, 2005, p. G1.

Singletary, Michelle, An Alert to the Dangers of Student Debt: Singletary, Michelle, "An Alert to the Dangers of Student Debt: The Student Debt Initiative" (original title: "An Alert to the Dangers of Student Debt"), *Washington Post*, November 17, 2005, p. D02.

Small, Cathy, writing as Rebekah Nathan, My Freshman Year: What a Professor Learned to Becoming a Student: Nathan, Rebekah. *My Freshman Year: What a Professor Learned by Becoming a Student*. New York: Penguin, 2005.

Smith, Frank, from "Reading without Nonsense": Smith, Frank. 2005. *Reading without Nonsense*. 4th Edition. New York: Teachers College Press.

Stuntz, William J., Secret Service: Against Privacy and Transparency: Stuntz, William J. "Secret Service: Against Privacy and Transparency," *The New Republic*, April 17, 2006.

Teixeira, Ruy, Generation We and the 2008 Election: Teixeira, Ruy, futuremajority.com, November 17, 2008. Retrieved April 2, 2009, from the World Wide Web: http://futuremajority.com/files/Generation%20We%20and%202008.pdf

The Economist, America's Great Headache: "America's Great Headache," *The Economist*, June 4, 2005. Vol. 375, Issue 8429.

The Economist, Hotel California: Prisons and Punishment: "Hotel California: Prisons and Punishment," *The Economist*, February 26, 2005.

The Economist, More Dirt [box]: *The Economist*, June 5, 1999.

Thompson, Clive, Meet the Life Hackers: Thompson, Clive. "Meet the Life Hackers," *New York Times Magazine*, October 16, 2005, p. 40.

Thune, John, Rep., Rep. Thune Introduces Flat Protection Amendment: "Rep. Thune Introduces Flag Protection Amendment," April 14, 2005.

Tierney, John, The Autonomist Manifesto: Tierney, John. "The Autonomist Manifesto," *The New York Times*, September 26, 2004.

Tucker, Neely, Whistleblower or Troublemaker, Bunny Greenhouse Isn't Backing Down: Tucker, Neely, "Whistleblower or Troublemaker, Bunny

Greenhouse Isn't Backing Down," (original title "Web of Truth: Whistleblower or Troublemaker, Bunny Greenhouse Isn't Backing Down), *Washington Post*, October 19, 2005, B1.

Veciana-Suarez, Ann, Take a Break From TV—Yeah, Right: Veciana-Suarez, Ana, "Take a Break from TV—Yeah, Right," *The Houston Chronicle*, April 19, 2006. Star Section, p. 5.

Wallis, Claudia, The Multitasking Generation: Wallis, Claudia. "The Multitasking Generation," *Time*. New York: March 27, 2006. Vol. 167, Issue 13, p. 48 (8 pgs).

Warrick, Joby, They Die Piece by Piece: Warrick, Joby, "They Die Piece by Piece," *Washington Post*, April 10, 2001.

Weinstein, J.W., and C.E. Dobkin, Academic Integrity [box]: Weinstein, J.W., & Dobkin, C.E. (2002). "Plagiarism in U.S. higher education: Estimating Internet plagiarism rates and testing a means of deterrence." Retrieved May 3, 2006, from the World Wide Web: http://webdisk.berkeley.edu/~Weinstein/Weinstein-JobMarketPaper.PDF

White, Emily, School Away From School: White, Emily. (2003, December 7). "School Away From School," *New York Times Magazine*. 34.

Williams, Dilafruz, Political Engagement and Serving Learning, a Gandhian Perspective: Williams, Dilafruz. "Political Engagement and Service Learning, a Gandhian Perspective," *ENCOUNTER: Education for Meaning and Social Justice*, Vol. 15, Number 2, Summer 2002, 6–13.

Williams, Jeffrey J., Debt Education Bad for the Young, Bad for America: Williams, Jeffrey J. *Dissent*. New York: Summer 2006. Vol. 53, Iss. 3; p. 53. Reprinted by permission.

Winston, Robert, Biology and Heroism: Winston, Robert. "Biology and Heroism," *Manchester Guardian*, October 24, 2002, p. 6.

Woods, Richard, The Next Step in Brain Evolution: Woods, Richard. "The Next Step in Brain Evolution," *Sunday Times*, London, July 9, 2006.

IMAGES

Index of Authors and Titles